STUDY GUIDE FOR USE WITH
MICROECONOMICS

Ninth Canadian Edition

McCONNELL • BRUE • BARBIERO

PREPARED BY

TORBEN ANDERSEN
Red Deer College

WILLIAM B. WALSTAD
University of Nebraska, Lincoln

ROBERT C. BINGHAM

 **McGraw-Hill**
Ryerson

Toronto Montréal Boston Burr Ridge, IL Dubuque, IA Madison, WI New York San Francisco
St. Louis Bangkok Bogotá Caracas Kuala Lumpur Lisbon London Madrid
Mexico City Milan New Delhi Santiago Seoul Singapore Sydney Taipei

McGraw-Hill
Ryerson Limited
A Subsidiary of The **McGraw·Hill** Companies

Study Guide for use with
Microeconomics
Ninth Canadian Edition

ISBN: 0-07-088670-9

1 2 3 4 5 6 7 8 9 0 CP 0 9 8 7 6 5 4 3 2 1

Printed and bound in Canada.

Care has been taken to trace ownership of copyright material contained in this text. The publishers will gladly take any information that will enable them to rectify any reference or credit in subsequent editions.

Senior Sponsoring Editor: Lynn Fisher
Economics Editor: Ron Doleman
Developmental Editor: Maria Chu
Marketing Manager: Kelly Smyth
Production Coordinator: Jennifer Wilkie
Printer: Canadian Printco, Ltd.

CONTENTS

CHAPTER 1

The Nature and Method of Economics

Chapter 1 introduces you to economics — the social science concerned with the efficient use of scarce resources to achieve maximum satisfaction of wants. You are given a sense of the kinds of topics economists study, how economists analyze these topics, and why economics is useful and important. You also learn about eight widely accepted economic goals that are important to our society.

At the heart of economics is the idea of scarcity: the fact that our limited resources are insufficient to produce all the goods and services we want. Accordingly, we must make choices about how to allocate our resources, and in these choices we face tradeoffs. When we choose to allocate resources to producing one thing we sacrifice the production of something else. This sacrifice is known as an opportunity cost.

Economic explanations of human behaviour are based on the assumption of "rational self-interest" and on "marginal analysis." People make rational decisions to maximize satisfaction of their personal goals. These goals differ between individuals and are not limited to material goals or to selfish goals. When people make decisions they weigh the marginal benefits and marginal costs of different courses of action. It is rational to do more of an activity if the marginal benefit exceeds the marginal cost.

The discipline of economics uses the scientific method. Based on observations of facts and data, we formulate hypotheses that are possible explanations of the causes and effects of economic phenomena. While these explanations may be somewhat abstract and simplified representations, they must be based on facts in the real world. Therefore, we test the predictions of our hypotheses to see whether they are supported by the data. Those explanations that produce predictions that are highly consistent with the data become accepted theories; those that have passed the test over and over are referred to as laws or principles. Policy economics entails the application of theories and data to formulate policies to solve economic problems or achieve certain economic goals.

In Canada we have eight economic goals for our society: economic growth, full employment, economic efficiency, price-level stability, economic freedom, equitable distribution of income, economic security, and a balance in foreign trade. Policy questions often centre on how these goals should be interpreted, and on the relative importance of different goals when there are tradeoffs between goals. Such questions move us from economic theory and positive economics, which investigates *what is*, to normative economics, which incorporates subjective or value-laden views of *what ought to be*.

Economics is divided into two broad categories: microeconomics and macroeconomics. Microeconomics studies the behaviour of individual or specific economic units. Macroeconomics studies economy-wide aggregates. Though they focus on different sorts of questions, both microeconomics and macroeconomics use the scientific method and are based on the scarcity principle.

Clear thinking about economic questions requires that we avoid many common pitfalls. Errors in thinking can occur from bias, loaded terminology, imprecise definitions, fallacies of composition, and causation fallacies. Awareness of these pitfalls will help you think more objectively about economic issues.

■ **CHAPTER LEARNING OBJECTIVES**

In this chapter you will learn:
☐ The Ten Key Concepts to retain a lifetime.

☐ The definition of economics.
☐ About the economic way of thinking.
☐ How economists construct theories.
☐ The distinction between microeconomics and macroeconomics.
☐ The pitfalls to objective thinking.

■ **CHAPTER OUTLINE**

1. Economics is the social science concerned with the efficient use of scarce resources to achieve maximum satisfaction of human wants.

2. The economic perspective on human behaviour is described in three interrelated ideas:
  (a) Scarcity of resources forces people to make choices and incur opportunity costs.
  (b) People make rational decisions based on their own self-interest.
  (c) People make choices by comparing marginal costs and marginal benefits.

3. Economists develop economic principles (also called theories, laws or models) to help us to understand the economy and formulate policies that will solve economic problems.
  (a) The object of economic theorizing is to systematically arrange and analyze facts so that we may discover regularities or trends. Without bringing such order to facts we could not discover the relationships between facts.
  (b) Economic theories are generalizations which are expressed as tendencies or trends. These tendencies need not hold true in every single case in order for theories to be useful.
  (c) Economic theories are abstractions from reality because they are simplifications designed to omit irrelevant facts.
  (d) An explanation that has not yet been tested is often called an hypothesis; one that has been tested and supported by the data is often called a theory; one that has been tested many times, and is regularly supported by the data, is often called an economic law or principle.
  (e) As an analytical tool, economists use the assumption of *ceteris paribus*, or "other things equal," in order to focus on only the variables of main interest.

4. Economic policy involves the application of economic principles to reach specific goals. The three steps in policy design are stating the goals, determining the policy options for achieving the chosen goals, and implementing and evaluating the effects of the selected policy.

5. At least eight major economic goals are widely accepted in Canada: economic growth, full employment, economic efficiency, price-level stability, economic freedom, equitable distribution of income, economic security, and balance of trade. Economic goals may be complementary or conflicting. When goals conflict, the tradeoffs must be assessed and value judgments made about how to balance them.

6. Economists derive principles of economic behaviour at the macroeconomic and the microeconomic level. Macroeconomics deals with the economy as a whole by examining aggregate measures (such as employment at the national level). Microeconomics looks at specific economic units (such as the real estate market in a particular city).

7. Economists deal with both positive economics and normative economics. Positive economics concerns the study of facts to determine *what is*, whereas normative economics involves value judgments to determine *what ought to be*. Sound economic policy decisions involve both because solutions cannot be implemented before the current situation is understood and value judgments are made about the desired situation.

8. Common pitfalls to avoid in order to think clearly and logically using the economic perspective include:
  (a) bias or preconceptions not warranted by facts
  (b) loaded terminology that appeals to emotions
  (c) careless use of terms that have precise technical definitions
  (d) the fallacy of composition, or the assumption that what is true for one is necessarily true for the group
  (e) the *post hoc* fallacy, or the mistaken belief that if event A precedes event B, A is the cause of B
  (f) confusion of correlation with causation

■ **TERMS AND CONCEPTS**

economics	tradeoffs
economic perspective	macroeconomics
marginal analysis	aggregate

scientific method
principles
generalizations
"other-things-equal"
  assumption
policy economics

microeconomics
positive economics
normative economics
fallacy of composition
"after this, therefore
  because of this" fallacy

(a) _____
(b) _____
(c) _____

5. Eight economic goals that are widely accepted in Canada include:
(a) _____
(b) _____
(c) _____
(d) _____
(e) _____
(f) _____
(g) _____
(h) _____

■ HINTS AND TIPS

1. You may have difficulty accepting the claim that economics is a science, especially because its theories are inexact. Economics is a science by virtue of its methodology. That economic generalizations are inexact does not disqualify economics from being a science, nor does it negate the value of these generalizations. Think of generalizations from cancer research, or from meteorology. Scientists have proven a link between smoking and lung cancer, even though their knowledge is not exact enough to identify which specific smokers will get cancer. Meteorologists' weather forecasts are not always correct, but we often follow these forecasts because they are generally better than the forecasts we could generate ourselves without the benefit of the inexact science of meteorology.

2. A way to remember the pitfalls to objective thinking in economics is to associate each with a specific example. Choose examples that are funny, or that have personal application. For example: "The day I ate ice cream at the lake it was really hot, so next time it gets too cool I will eat some ice cream." Which fallacy is this an illustration of?

■ FILL-IN QUESTIONS

1. Economics is concerned with the _____ use of _____ resources to attain the _____ satisfaction of human wants.

2. Deriving principles or theories is called _____ economics, whereas applying economic principles to solve problems is called _____ economics.

3. Studying the economy in aggregate is called (microeconomics, macroeconomics) _____, whereas studying a specific business or market is called _____.

4. The three steps involved in the formulation of economic policy are:

6. Two different types of statements can be made about economic topics. A (positive, normative) _____ statement explains *what is* by offering a scientific proposition about economic behaviour that is based on theory and facts. A _____ statement includes a value judgment that suggests *what ought to be.* Many of the reported disagreements among economists usually involve _____ statements.

7. The economic perspective has three interrelated features: (1) It recognizes that scarcity requires _____; (2) that people make decisions in a _____ manner based on their _____; and (3) that weighing the costs and benefits of a decision is based on _____ analysis.

■ PROBLEMS AND PROJECTS

1. Use the idea of opportunity cost to provide some possible explanations for these observations:
(a) Ashley's parents offered her a free trip to California but she declined because the trip was the week before her midterms.
(b) Dennis decided to use a realtor to sell his house, even though he could have avoided the realtor's fee by selling it himself.
(c) The St. Amand family buys a dishwasher from Sears because they didn't know that the same model was available at a lower price at a discount warehouse store.

2. Below are five statements, each containing an example of a common pitfall in thinking about economics. Indicate, in the space following each statement, the type of pitfall involved.

(a) The Second World War resulted in forty-five years of economic expansion in Canada. _____

(b) "An unemployed worker can find a job if he or she looks diligently and conscientiously for employment; therefore, all unemployed workers can find employment if they search diligently and conscientiously." _____

(c) "Just tell me when rain will be needed and I will schedule my vacation for that week." _____ _____

(d) "The players, not the team owners, deserve to benefit from the recent explosion in revenues experienced by the National Basketball Association; after all, it is the players that fans pay to see." _____

(e) "The North American Free Trade Agreement is making Canadian workers pawns of the powerful corporations who can move their sweat shops to Mexico." _____

3. Indicate in the space beside each statement whether it is positive (P) or normative (N).

(a) Tuition fee increases are causing university enrolments to decrease. _____

(b) Agricultural subsidies in Europe are killing small towns in Saskatchewan. _____

(c) Higher income tax rates reduce the number of people willing to be employed. _____

(d) The Employment Insurance program is too generous because it gives people the incentive to quit their jobs. _____

(e) Free trade can improve the standard of living of a country. _____

(f) The federal government should do more to eliminate regional disparity in Canada. ____

4. Match the following terms on the left-hand list with the descriptions on the right-hand list.

(a) hypothesis   (i) explanation supported by data
(b) law   (ii) proposed explanation
(c) theory   (iii) explanation supported by data many times

■ **TRUE-FALSE**

Circle T if the statement is true, F if it is false.

1. Economics deals with the activities by which people earn their living and try to improve their standard of living.   **T F**

2. The "other things equal" or *ceteris paribus* assumption is made in order to simplify the reasoning process.   **T F**

3. Abstraction in economic theory is useful because it eliminates unnecessary complexity and irrelevant facts.   **T F**

4. A common reason that individuals disagree on what economic policy should be chosen is that they disagree on the goal or desired result. **T F**

5. Making value judgments as to preferred goals of an economy is known as positive economic analysis. **T F**

6. The statement: "Increased patent protection for the Canadian pharmaceutical industry will result in increased research and development activity in Canada" is a positive statement.   **T F**

7. Rational self-interest is the same thing as being selfish.   **T F**

8. If two variables are correlated with one another, changes in one must be causing changes in the other.   **T F**

9. Microeconomic analysis is concerned with the behaviour of individual households and business firms.   **T F**

10. Scarcity is caused by the fact that people make choices.   **T F**

11. In economics the word "marginal" means additional, or extra.   **T F**

■ **MULTIPLE-CHOICE**

Circle the letter that corresponds to the best answer.

1. Which statement is the best one to complete a short definition of economics? "Economics is the study of:

(a) how businesses maximize profits."

(b) the triumph of the capitalistic system over communism."

(c) monetary transactions."

(d) the efficient use of scarce resources."

2. The statement that "there is no free lunch" refers to what economic concept?

(a) correlation does not imply causality
(b) everything has an opportunity cost
(c) nothing is free because government taxes everything
(d) individuals have different tastes and preferences

3. One economic principle states that, *ceteris paribus*, the lower the price of a commodity the greater will be the quantity of the commodity consumers will wish to purchase. On the basis of this principle alone, it can be concluded that:
(a) if the price of mink coats falls, consumers will purchase more mink coats
(b) if the price of mink coats falls, there must have been a decrease in the demand for clothes made of fur
(c) if the price of mink coats falls and there are no important changes in the other factors affecting their demand, consumers will purchase more mink coats
(d) if more mink coats are purchased this month than last month, it is because the price of mink coats has fallen

4. An economic model is *not*:
(a) an ideal type of economy or economic policy that we should strive to achieve
(b) a tool economists employ to enable them to predict
(c) an abstract representation of the economy or some part of the economy
(d) an explanation of how the economy or a part of the economy functions in its essential details

5. Which of the following is *not* among the dangers encountered when constructing or applying an economic model?
(a) it may contain irrelevant facts and be more complex than necessary
(b) it may come to be accepted as "what ought to be" rather than as "what is"
(c) it may be overly simplified and so be a very poor approximation of the reality it explains
(d) it may result in a conclusion that is unacceptable to people

6. A theory in economics:
(a) is useless if simplifying assumptions are used
(b) is of little use if it is abstract

(c) is useful if the predictions of the theory usually correspond to actual economic occurrences
(d) is useless if its predictions are not always correct

7. Which of the following would not be contained in an economic theory?
(a) predictions that follow from that theory
(b) definitions that clearly set out the variables included in the model
(c) statements of the relationships among the variables in the model
(d) normative statements about the most preferred outcomes

8. During World War II, Canada used price controls to prevent inflation; some people called this "a fascist and arbitrary restriction of economic freedom" and others called it "a necessary and democratic means of preventing ruinous inflation." Both labels are examples of:
(a) economic bias
(b) the fallacy of composition
(c) misuse of common-sense definitions
(d) loaded terminology

9. If one individual decides to consume less beef, there will be little or no effect on beef prices. To argue, therefore, that if all individuals consume less beef there will be little or no effect on beef prices is an example of:
(a) the *post hoc, ergo propter hoc* fallacy
(b) the fallacy of composition
(c) an oversimplified generalization
(d) using loaded terminology

10. The Great Depression that began in 1929 was preceded by a stock market crash. To conclude that the Depression was therefore caused by the crash in the stock market is an example of:
(a) the *post hoc, ergo propter hoc* fallacy
(b) the fallacy of composition
(c) the *ceteris paribus* assumption
(d) using loaded terminology

11. Which of the following is not a widely accepted economic goal?
(a) price-level stability
(b) zero taxation
(c) economic efficiency
(d) economic freedom

12. Which of the following would be studied in microeconomics?

   (a) the output of the entire economy
   (b) the national unemployment rate
   (c) the effect of money supply changes on the Consumer Price Index
   (d) the price and output of apples

13. If economic growth tends to produce a more equitable distribution of income among people in a nation, then the goals of growth and equitable income distribution seem to be:

   (a) deductive
   (b) conflicting
   (c) complementary
   (d) mutually exclusive

14. To say that two economic goals are conflicting means that:

   (a) there is a tradeoff in the achievement of the goals
   (b) some people do not agree with these goals
   (c) the achievement of one goal results in achievement of the other goal
   (d) it is impossible to quantify both goals

15. Which of the following is a macroeconomic topic?

   (a) the effect of cigarette tax reductions on cigarette consumption
   (b) the effect of government set stumpage fees on the amount of lumber being exported to the United States.
   (c) the effect of the cod fishery closure on the unemployment rate in Halifax
   (d) the effect of the falling Canadian dollar on Canada's exports and imports

■ **DISCUSSION QUESTIONS**

1. What are some issues that you face in your personal or work life for which a knowledge of economics could provide you with useful skills?

2. What is a "laboratory experiment under controlled conditions?" Why are such experiments not normally possible in economics? What does economics have instead of a laboratory?

3. What is the relationship between facts and theory?

4. Why are economic principles and models necessarily generalizations and abstractions?

5. Sketch a map showing me how to get from your home to the nearest grocery store. In what ways is your map realistic, and in what ways is it unrealistic (abstract)? Would your map necessarily be more helpful to me in finding the store if it was more realistic? Would it be worth making it more realistic? How do these issues concerning your map relate to issues concerning economic theories?

6. Explain each of the following:

   (a) fallacy of composition
   (b) loaded terminology
   (c) the *post hoc, ergo propter hoc* fallacy

7. Explain briefly the difference between:

   (a) macroeconomics and microeconomics
   (b) correlation and causation

■ **ANSWERS**

FILL-IN QUESTIONS
1. efficient, scarce, maximum
2. theoretical, policy
3. macroeconomics, microeconomics
4. (a) stating goals; (b) analyzing policy options; (c) evaluating policy effectiveness
5. full employment; economic growth; price-level stability; balance of trade; equitable distribution of income; economic efficiency; economic security; economic freedom
6. positive, normative, normative
7. choices; rational; self-interest; marginal

PROBLEMS AND PROJECTS
1. Each of these decisions was presumably made because the opportunity cost was too high: (a) by going to Disneyland, Ashley would lose study time and her exam results would suffer; (b) selling his own house would have cost Dennis some time, and perhaps some money if he couldn't get as high a price as a professional realtor; (c) shopping at every store to find the absolute lowest price is not usually worth the cost for time and travel.
2. (a) *post hoc ergo propter hoc* fallacy; (b) the fallacy of composition; (c) confusing correlation and causation; (d) bias; (e) loaded terminology
3. P; (b) P; (c) P; (d) N; (e) P; (f) N
4. (a)-(ii); (b)-(iii); (c)-(i)

TRUE-FALSE
1. T
2. T
3. T
4. T
5. F   Value judgments imply normative economics
6. T   The statement is positive, whether true or false
7. F   Generosity may be in one's self-interest
8. F   Don't confuse correlation with causation

9. T
10. F   The other way around
11. T

MULTIPLE-CHOICE
1. (d) This is the most comprehensive one
2. (b) Everything has a cost in some form
3. (c) *Ceteris paribus* means "other things remaining constant"
4. (a) An economic model explains how the world is, not how we want it to be
5. (d) Perhaps the conclusion will be unacceptable to some people, but this should not affect the theory
6. (c) Good theories always involve assumptions and abstractions, and may not predict correctly in *every* case.
7. (d) Theories are limited to positive aspects
8. (d) Loaded terminology appeals to emotions
9. (b) What is true for one need not be true for all
10. (a) Because B happened *after* A does not prove that B *caused* A
11. (b) Zero taxation is the only one not on the list of eight goals
12. (d) Only this topic deals with a single market
13. (c) Complementary because they can be achieved together, without tradeoff
14. (a) To move towards one goal entails moving away from the other
15. (d) All of the others deal with specific markets

APPENDIX TO CHAPTER 1
Graphs and Their Meaning

The old saying that "a picture is worth a thousand words" is true in economics because economists use graphs to "picture" relationships between economic variables. A graph can display a lot of information in a manner that is precise yet quick to comprehend. Because we rely so much on these "pictures," you need to be skilled in constructing and interpreting graphs. Even if you are already familiar with the fundamentals of graphing, perhaps from previous classes in math and sciences, you should review this appendix. If none of this material seems familiar, relax: all of the basics that you need are explained in this appendix.

The appendix shows how to construct a graph from a table of data on two variables (using the example of income and consumption). Each variable is represented on one of the two axes, so each axis should be labelled with the variable name, its units of measurement, and marked off with a consistent measurement scale. Once the data points are plotted and a line drawn to connect the plotted points, one can determine whether there is a direct or inverse relationship between the variables.

Economists usually, but not always, measure the independent variable on the horizontal axis and the dependent variable on the vertical axis of a graph. The curve plotted to illustrate the relationship between the two variables is drawn based on the *ceteris paribus* condition. If any other variable that influences the dependent variable happens to change, then we must plot a whole new curve through a different set of points. This is called a shift in the curve.

A relationship that is linear (a straight line on the graph) can be defined by two simple elements: the slope and the vertical intercept of the line. The slope is the ratio of the vertical change (rise) to the horizontal change (run). The slope often has economic meaning, because slopes measure effects of mar-

ginal changes. As discussed in Chapter 1, marginal analysis is key in economics.

For a nonlinear curve the slope is not constant; it varies as one moves along the curve. The slope at a particular point can be estimated by determining the slope of a straight line drawn tangent to the curve at that point. The vertical intercept of a line is the value on the vertical axis when the value of the horizontal axis variable is zero. A linear relationship is easily expressed in equation form once the slope and the vertical intercept are found from a graph or table of data.

■ APPENDIX LEARNING OBJECTIVES

When you have studied this appendix, you should be able to:
□ Understand why economists use graphs.
□ Construct a graph of two variables using numerical data from a table.
□ Construct a table with two variables from an algebraic function or from data on a graph.
□ Determine whether a graph shows a direct or an inverse relationship between two variables.
□ Identify dependent and independent variables in economic examples and graphs.
□ Determine the slope of a straight line.
□ Determine the vertical intercept of a line.
□ Write and interpret a linear equation using the slope and the vertical intercept.
□ Estimate the slope of a nonlinear curve at a point using a line tangent to the curve at that point.

■ APPENDIX OUTLINE

1. A graph is a visual representation of the relationship between variables and is helpful in describing economic theories and models.

2. To construct a simple graph, plot numerical data about two variables from a table. Sometimes the tabular data must be found first by using an equation relating the two variables.

   (a)   Each graph has a horizontal and a vertical axis that is labelled for each variable and then scaled for the range of the data points that will be measured on the axis. Along a given axis a certain increment of distance represents a consistent increment in the variable.

   (b)   Data points are plotted on the graph by drawing perpendiculars from the scaled points on the two axes to the place on the graph where the perpendiculars intersect.

   (c)   A line or curve can then be drawn to connect the points plotted on the graph. If the line is straight the relationship is "linear."

3. The slope of the line on a graph indicates the relationship between the two variables.

   (a)   A line that is upsloping to the right indicates a positive or direct relationship between the two variables: an increase (a decrease) in one is associated with an increase (a decrease) in the other.

   (b)   A line that is downsloping to the right indicates a negative or inverse relationship between the two variables because the variables are changing in opposite directions: an increase (a decrease) in one is associated with a decrease (an increase) in the other.

4. Economists are concerned with determining cause and effect in economic events.

   (a)   An independent variable is the variable that changes first, and causes another variable to change.

   (b)   A dependent variable is one that changes as a result of a change in another variable.

   (c)   Economists do not always follow the convention used in mathematics whereby an independent variable is placed on the horizontal axis and a dependent variable on the vertical axis.

5. A two-variable graph is a simplified representation of an economic relationship. In such a graph there is an implicit assumption that all other factors are being held constant. This "other things equal" or *ceteris paribus* assumption is a simplification that helps us focus on the two variables of interest. If another variable that influences the dependent variable does change, then the curve on the graph will shift to a new position.

6. A slope and vertical intercept can be calculated for a linear relationship (straight line graph). These values also define the equation of the line.

   (a)   The slope of a straight line is the ratio of the vertical change to the horizontal change between two points.

   (b)   The slope measures the marginal effect on one variable of a small change in the other.

   (c)   A positive (negative) slope indicates a direct (inverse) relationship between the two variables.

   (d)   The vertical intercept is the value where the line intersects the vertical axis of the graph.

   (e)   A linear equation is written as $y = a + bx$. If the values for the intercept a and the slope b are known, then given any value of variable x, the value of variable y can be determined.

7. A straight line has a constant slope, but a nonlinear curve has a continually changing slope. To estimate the slope of a nonlinear curve at a point, calculate the slope of a line tangent to the curve at that point.

■   **APPENDIX TERMS AND CONCEPTS**

horizontal axis	**independent variable**
vertical axis	**dependent variable**
direct relationship	**slope of a straight line**
inverse relationship	**vertical intercept**

■   **HINTS AND TIPS**

1.   Some students are comfortable with economic graphs right away, but others initially have an aversion to graphs. If you are in the first group, you are fortunate because economics will come more easily to you. If you are in the second group, do not run because you cannot hide! It is incredibly important that you quickly develop basic skills with graphing. If you find this appendix very difficult you should seek extra help with these tools.

2.   The text includes a number of graphs of real world data showing relationships between two variables. These graphs often take the form of a "scatter diagram" with a "best-fitting line." That is, the data points may be somewhat scattered, rather than lying exactly on a curve. In many of these graphs no precise relationship is evident in the data, but there is a discernible tendency or pattern in the data, indicating that the variables are related. A "best-fitting line" through the data points indicates this pattern. If

you take a statistics course you will learn the proper techniques for determining such best-fitting lines, and for judging when you can be confident that the points in a scatter diagram do indicate some relationship. To understand this textbook you need only have a rough idea of a "best-fitting line."

3.   All graphs in this appendix have actual numerical values marked on the axes. Later in the text you will see graphs without any numbers on the axes. In such cases the specific numbers are not necessary for the explanation, but you should recognize that there are numbers implicit on the axes. If at first you have difficulty comprehending such abstract graphs, you could pencil in arbitrary values on the axes until you get used to such graphs.

■   **FILL-IN QUESTIONS**

1. The relationship between two economic variables can be visualized with a two-dimensional graph.
   (a)   The (dependent, independent) _____ variable is said to change because of a change in the _____ variable.
   (b)   The vertical and horizontal (scales, ranges) _____ on the graph are calibrated to reflect the _____ of values in a table of data points on which the graph is based.

2. The graph of a straight line that slopes downward to the right indicates that there is (a direct, an inverse) _____ relationship between the two variables. A graph of a straight line that slopes upward to the right tells us that the relationship is (direct, inverse) _____. When the value of one variable increases and the value of the other variable increases, then the relationship is _____; when the value of one increases, and the other decreases, the relationship is _____.

3. The slope of a straight line between two points is defined as the ratio of the (vertical, horizontal) _____ change over the _____ change. The point at which the line meets the vertical axis is called the _____.

4. We can express the graph of a straight line with a linear equation that can be written as $y = a + bx$.
   (a) a is the (slope, intercept) _____ and b is the _____.
   (b)   If a was 2, b was 4, and x was 5, then y would be _____.

5. The slope of a (straight line, nonlinear curve) _____ is constant throughout; the slope of a _____ varies from point to point. The slope of a nonlinear curve at a point can be estimated by calculating the slope of a straight line that is _____ to the point on the curve.

■   **PROBLEMS AND PROJECTS**

1. The data below represent the relationship between the mortgage interest rate and the number of new houses built.

Mortgage Rate (% per year)	Housing Starts (thousands per year)
12	70,000
10	90,000
8	110,000
6	130,000
4	150,000

(a)   Which variable is dependent? _____ Which is independent? _____
(b)   On the axes of the graph below, set up the scales to best suit these data. Label each axis of the graph (including the units of measurement).
(c)   Plot the five data points given in the table.

(d)   The curve is (up-, down-) _____ sloping, meaning that the relationship between the mortgage interest rate and housing starts is (direct, inverse) _____.

2. (a) Based on the relationship found in question 1, if the mortgage rate increases by 1%, *ceteris paribus*, then housing starts will (decrease, increase) _____ by _____ thousands per year.

(b) If household incomes rise, new homes would become more affordable, so there would be more new housing starts at the same interest rate as before. On the graph, this would cause a (leftward, rightward) _____ shift of the curve in question 1.

(c) If lumber prices increase, new homes would become less affordable, so there would be fewer new housing starts at the same interest rate as before. On the graph, this would cause a (leftward, rightward) _____ shift of the initial curve.

3. The Hammerheads, a very mediocre club band, have just released a CD. They will immediately sell 10 copies to their parents and friends. Thereafter, they can sell 4 copies for each performance they give in a club.

(a) Based on this information, complete the table below.

Performances	CD Sales
0	_____
5	_____
10	_____
15	_____
20	_____

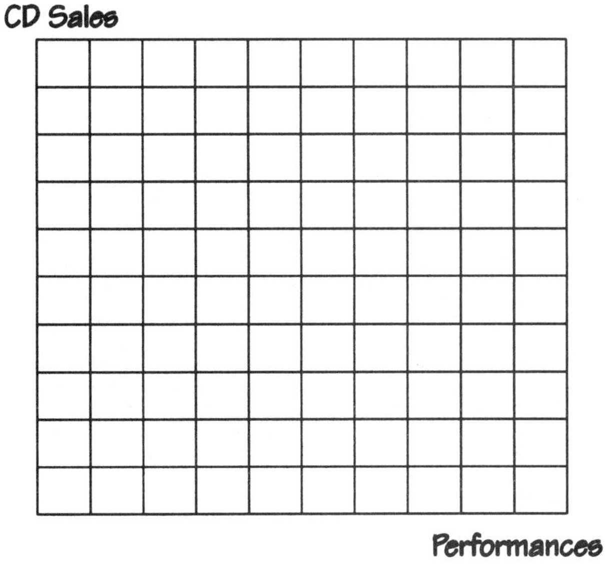

CD Sales

Performances

(b) Which variable is dependent? _____ Which is independent? _____
(c) Plot the data on the graph below.
(d) The vertical intercept value is _____.
(e) The slope value is _____.
(f) Write the equation for this relationship:
_____.

4. This question is based on the graph below.
(a) The function has a negative slope between the X values of _____ and _____. Over this range the relationship between X and Y is (direct, inverse) _____.
(b) Find the slope of the curve at the following points:
A: _____, B: _____, C: _____

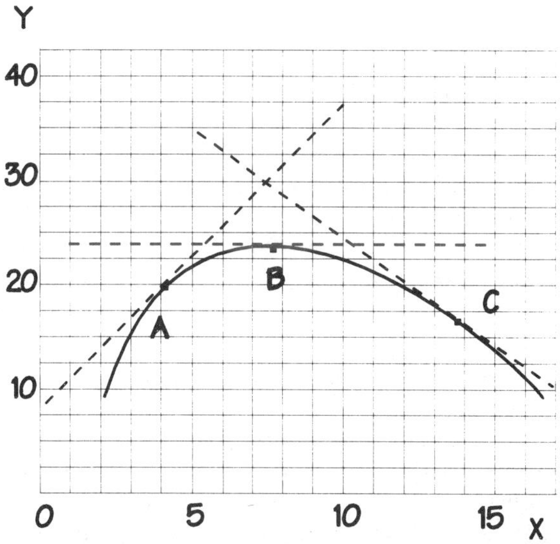

5. An economist is hired to determine the relationship between real estate value and proximity to the waterfront in a Manitoba lakeshore resort community. The table below gives recent selling prices for undeveloped building lots.

(a) On the graph provided, create a "scatter diagram" with lot prices on the vertical axis and distance to shore on the horizontal axis.
(b) The scatter diagram suggests that lot prices are (directly, inversely, not) _____ related to their proximity to the waterfront.
(c) With a ruler, draw in what appears to be the "best-fitting" line through these data points.
(d) The value of the vertical intercept is _____. This value indicates price for a lot that is _____.

(e) The value of the slope is _____. This value indicates that price (falls, rises) _____ by $_____ for each metre from the waterfront.
(f) The expression for the equation of this line is: _____.

Lot	Distance to Shore (m)	Price ($)
A	200	9,000
B	0	18,000
C	50	16,000
D	100	15,000
E	50	17,000
F	150	10,000
G	200	7,000
H	125	12,000

Price (thousand $)

Distance to shore (m)

■ **TRUE-FALSE**

Circle T if the statement is true; F if it is false.

1. Graphs provide a visual representation of the relationship between two variables. **T F**

2. If the straight line on a two-variable graph is upward sloping to the right, then there is a positive relationship between the two variables. **T F**

3. A variable that changes as a consequence of a change in another variable is considered to be a dependent variable. **T F**

4. *Ceteris paribus* means that the value of all other variables is set equal to zero. **T F**

5. In the ratio for the calculation of the slope of a straight line, the horizontal change is divided by the vertical change. **T F**

6. If the slope of the linear relationship between consumption (on the vertical axis) and income (on the horizontal axis) is 0.90, then it tells us that for every $1 increase in income there will be a $0.90 increase in consumption. **T F**

7. The slope of a straight line is 0. **T F**

8. If a linear equation is $y = 10 + 5x$, the vertical intercept is 10. **T F**

9. A function with a constant slope becomes steeper as the independent variable increases. **T F**

10. If the slope of a straight line on a two-variable (x, y) graph is 2 and the vertical intercept is 6, then if the value for x is 10, the value for y is 22. **T F**

11. A slope of 4 for a straight line in a two-variable graph indicates the two variables are inversely related. **T F**

12. If there is an inverse relation between price and quantity demanded, the graph of this function will be downward-sloping. **T F**

13. In the relationship between snowfall and demand for snowblowers, snowfall is the dependent variable. **T F**

14. If the line tangent to a nonlinear curve is upsloping, this indicates that the slope of the curve is positive at that point. **T F**

15. If two points described by the (x, y) combinations of (13, 10) and (8, 20) lie on a straight line, then the slope is 2. **T F**

16. On a graph relating the number of visitors to Canada's national parks to the price of admission to the parks, an increase in levels of rainfall would likely shift the curve to the left. **T F**

■ MULTIPLE-CHOICE

Circle the letter that corresponds to the best answer.

1. If an increase in variable *A* is associated with a decrease in variable *B*, then we can conclude that *A* and *B* are:
 (a) nonlinear
 (b) directly related
 (c) inversely related
 (d) positively related

2. Economists:
 (a) always put the independent variable on the vertical axis
 (b) always put the independent variable on the horizontal axis
 (c) sometimes put the dependent variable on the horizontal axis
 (d) use only linear functions

3. If the curve in a two-variable graph shifts, what does this indicate?
 (a) the two variables are positively related
 (b) the two variables are negatively related
 (c) the relationship between the two variables must be nonlinear
 (d) some third variable must have changed

4. If *y* is plotted on the vertical axis and *x* is on the horizontal axis, which of the following is a false statement regarding the equation $y = 100 + 0.4x$?
 (a) the vertical intercept is 100
 (b) the slope is 0.4
 (c) when *x* is 20, *y* is 108
 (d) the graph is nonlinear

5. If a straight line drawn tangent to a nonlinear curve has a slope of zero, then at the point of tangency the curve is:
 (a) vertical
 (b) horizontal
 (c) upsloping
 (d) downsloping

6. Consider a graph relating gasoline consumption (on the vertical axis) to population (on the horizontal axis). All of the following will affect gasoline consumption, but which one will **not** shift the curve?
 (a) increased consumer incomes
 (b) increased availability of public transit
 (c) increased population

 (d) more efficient gasoline engines

Answer questions 7 through 10 on the basis of the following diagram.

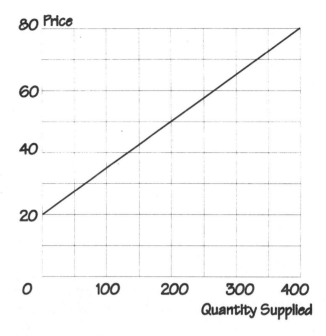

7. The graph indicates that price and quantity supplied are:
 (a) positively related
 (b) negatively related
 (c) indirectly related
 (d) nonlinear

8. The slope of the line is:
 (a) 0.15
 (b) 0.20
 (c) 1.50
 (d) 6.67

9. The vertical intercept is:
 (a) 0
 (b) 10
 (c) 20
 (d) 80

10. The linear equation for the function is:
 (a) $p = 20 + 0.15q$
 (b) $q = 20 + 6.67p$
 (c) $p = 20 + 6.67q$
 (d) $q = 20 + 0.15p$

11. Which of the following statements is true?
 (a) a vertical line has a slope of zero
 (b) a horizontal line has a slope of infinity

(c) a nonlinear curve has different slopes at different points

(d) an upsloping line has a negative slope

■ DISCUSSION QUESTIONS

1. Why do economists use graphs?

2. If the vertical intercept increases in value but the slope of a straight line stays the same, what happens to the graph of the line? If the vertical intercept decreases, what will happen to the line?

3. If you know that variables X and Y are inversely related, what does this tell you about the slope of a line showing the relationship between these two variables? What do you know about the slope when X and Y are positively related?

4. Identify the dependent and independent variables in the following economic statement: "A decrease in business taxes gave a big boost to investment spending." How does one tell the difference between a dependent and independent variable when examining economic relationships?

5. Why is an assumption made that all other variables are held constant when we construct a two-variable graph of the price and quantity of a product?

6. If you were to plot a two-variable graph of the price of gasoline versus per capita use of gasoline, using the data for various nations, what sort of graph would you expect, and what sort of relationship would this represent? The data points would probably be somewhat scattered, rather than consistently located along a precise line or curve. Give some reasons why the data points might be somewhat scattered.

■ ANSWERS

FILL-IN QUESTIONS

1. (a) dependent, independent; (b) scales, ranges

2. an inverse; direct; direct, inverse

3. vertical, horizontal; vertical intercept

4. (a) intercept, slope; (b) 22

5. straight line; nonlinear curve; tangent

PROBLEMS AND PROJECTS

1. (a) housing starts; mortgage interest rates; (d) down; inverse; (b) and (c):

2. (a) decrease, 10; (b) rightward; (c) leftward

3. (a) 10, 30, 50, 70, 90; (b) CD sales; performances; (d) 10; (e) 4; (f) CD Sales = 10 + 4 Performances; (c) see graph

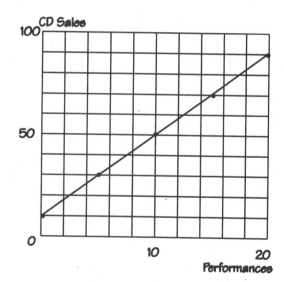

4. (a) 8; 17; inverse; (b) 3.0; 0; -2.1.

5. (a) see graph; (b) inversely; (c) see graph; (d) about $19,000; on the waterfront; (e) vertical change/horizontal difference is approximately = (8,000-19,000)/(200-0) = -11,000/200 = about −55; falls; about $55. (f) Price = 19,000 − 55 Distance.

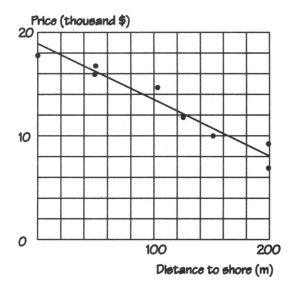

7. (a) The curve is upsloping
8. (a) (80-20)/(400-0) = 0.15
9. (c)
10. (a) See the answers to questions 8 and 9
11. (c)

TRUE-FALSE

1. T
2. T
3. T
4. F   It means "other things equal"
5. F   Vertical change divided by horizontal change
6. T
7. F   A slope of zero indicates a horizontal line
8. T   Yes, the vertical intercept is the simple constant term in the equation
9. F   A constant slope means constant steepness
10. F   The equation is $y = 6 + 2x$; at $x = 10$, $y = 26$
11. F   The slope would be negative for an inverse relationship
12. T
13. F   The amount of snowfall does not depend on how many snowblowers are purchased
14. T   An upsloping curve
15. F   (20-10)/(8-13) = -2
16. T   Rainfall would likely be one of the variables held constant on the original graph, so if rainfall changes the curve will shift

MULTIPLE-CHOICE

1. (c) Variables changing in opposite directions are inversely or negatively related
2. (c) There is no consistent convention
3. (d) The original curve assumed "other things equal"
4. (d) Because the slope is a fixed number, the graph is a straight line
5. (b)
6. (c) Population change is reflected in a movement along the original curve

CHAPTER 2

The Economic Problem: Scarcity, Wants, and Choices

The field of economics is based on two fundamental facts: our wants are unlimited or insatiable, and the resources available for satisfying these wants are limited, or scarce. Consequently, we face the economic problem, or the need to make choices about how to allocate our scarce resources. The main categories of these resources are land, capital, labour, and entrepreneurial ability. Given scarcity, all resources must be fully employed and used efficiently in order to satisfy wants to the fullest possible extent. Efficiency has two elements: productive efficiency is achieved if resources are used in the least cost manner, and allocative efficiency is achieved if resources are used to produce those goods society wants most.

The production possibilities table and the production possibilities curve are useful for illustrating many concepts in this chapter: scarcity, choice, the law of increasing opportunity cost, allocative and productive efficiency, unemployment, and economic growth. The production possibilities model is both very basic and very important.

Every society uses some sort of economic system to address the problem of scarcity. No two economies use exactly the same system, but there are two general types: the market system and the command system. In a market system most resources are owned privately and economic activity is coordinated spontaneously, with little government interference. In a command system government owns most of the property resources and economic activity is centrally planned. Canada's economy is mainly a market system, but with some elements of a command system.

The circular flow model illustrates how businesses and households interact in a market system. These economic agents interact in resource markets (where households sell and businesses buy),

and in product markets (where households buy and businesses sell).

■ CHAPTER LEARNING OBJECTIVES

In this chapter you will learn:
- ☐ The foundation of economics.
- ☐ The nature of economic efficiency.
- ☐ How to achieve economic growth.
- ☐ The two general types of economic systems society can choose to coordinate production and consumption decisions.
- ☐ What the circular flow model is.

■ CHAPTER OUTLINE

1. The study of economics rests on two facts:
   (a) Society's wants are essentially unlimited and insatiable.
   (b) The resources for producing goods and services to satisfy these wants are limited or scarce.

2. The four categories of resources are land, capital, labour, and entrepreneurial ability. The payments received by those who provide resources are, respectively: rental income, interest income, wages, and profits.

3. Economics is the social science concerned with the problem of using scarce resources to attain the maximum fulfillment of society's unlimited wants. To achieve this goal society must use its resources efficiently, achieving both full employment and full production.
   (a) Full employment occurs when all available resources are being used.

(b) Full production occurs when the resources are being used as efficiently as possible. Two kinds of efficiency must be achieved:

(i) productive efficiency — where any particular mix of goods and services is produced in the least costly way.

(ii) allocative efficiency — where the resources are used to produce that particular mix of goods and services most wanted by society.

4. The production possibilities table, or a production possibilities curve, indicates the alternative combinations of goods and services an economy can produce when it has achieved full employment and productive efficiency.

5. Four assumptions are made when constructing a production possibilities table or curve:

(a) full employment and productive efficiency
(b) fixed resources
(c) fixed technology
(d) two goods are being produced

6. Any point on the production possibilities curve is attainable, but society must choose one point (one particular combination of goods). If the chosen combination provides the greatest satisfaction, the economy is said to be allocatively efficient.

7. Points outside the curve are unattainable, so the production possibilities curve illustrates the condition of scarcity.

8. Given full employment and full production, society can produce more of one good only by producing less of the other good. This foregone output is termed the opportunity cost and arises because resources must be shifted from producing one good to producing the other.

9. The marginal opportunity cost of producing additional units of a product usually increases as more of that product is produced. This generalization is the law of increasing opportunity costs.

(a) Opportunity costs are increasing because resources are not perfectly adaptable from one production use to another.

(b) Increasing opportunity costs cause the production possibilities curve to be concave (bowed out from the origin).

10. The amount of resources allocated to the production of a good is optimal where the marginal benefit received from the last unit produced equals its marginal cost. This marginal cost is the opportunity cost in terms of other goods that could have been produced with the same resources.

(a) The optimal production level corresponds to the point of allocative efficiency.

(b) Marginal benefit falls as more is produced.

(c) Marginal cost rises as more is produced.

11. Dropping the assumptions underlying the production possibilities model gives some additional results.

(a) An economy experiencing unemployment and productive inefficiency is operating at a point inside its production possibilities curve, and is therefore failing to meet its productive potential.

(b) Economic growth occurs through improvements in technology or expansions in resource supplies, causing the production possibilities curve to expand, or shift outward.

(c) Resource allocation decisions made today help to determine production possibilities in the future; the more capital or future goods that we produce today, the more the production possibilities curve will expand in the future.

(d) If a nation specializes and trades with other nations, then the nation is not limited to points inside the production possibilities curve.

12. Many current and historical events and problems can be analyzed with the production possibilities model. These include: recessions, discrimination, land-use controversies, priorities for government spending, and technological change.

13. Different societies use different economic systems for addressing the fundamental economic problem of scarcity. Systems differ mainly in the ownership of resources, and in the method used to coordinate and direct economic activity.

(a) At one extreme is the market system, or capitalism, which relies upon private ownership of resources, the profit motive, and coordination through the use of prices and markets. The type of capitalism used in Canada also relies on government having a significant role in the economy.

(b) At the other extreme, the command economy uses public ownership of resources and decisions are made by central planning. In recent years a number of command economies have incorporated elements of the market system.

14. The circular flow model illustrates the interaction between businesses and households in resource markets and product markets. In exchange for resources that households supply to firms, firms pay incomes that households in turn use to demand goods and services produced by firms.

■ **TERMS AND CONCEPTS**

economic problem
utility
resources
land
capital
investment
labour
entrepreneurial ability
factors of production
full employment
full production
productive efficiency
allocative efficiency
consumer goods
capital goods

production
  possibilities table
production
  possibilities curve
opportunity cost
law of increasing
  opportunity cost
economic growth
economic system
capitalism
market system
command system
resource market
product market
circular flow model

■ **HINTS AND TIPS**

1. The production possibilities curve is the first instance where graphing skills are needed. If you have serious difficulty mastering the graphical analysis you may have a general weakness in graphing that you should address immediately. Graphs are used constantly in the chapters that follow. Spend extra time on the graphical questions in this study guide, the relevant sections of the chapter, and with Appendix 1A of this study guide. Your instructor may also have additional resources or advice for you.

2. A movement from one point on the production possibilities curve to another point on the same curve indicates a change in what combination of products society *chooses*. In contrast, a shift of the whole production possibilities curve indicates a change in the *set of choices* available to society.

3. Many students initially confuse the coordinates of a point on the production possibilities curve with the intercepts of the curve. The intercepts indicate the *maximum*, or *potential*, production for each good (if all resources are dedicated to producing that

good), whereas the coordinates of the production point show *actual* production for each good.

■ **FILL-IN QUESTIONS**

1. The two fundamental facts that provide the foundation of economics are:
  (a) Society's wants are _____.
  (b) Society's resources are _____.

2. Consumer goods satisfy human wants (directly, indirectly) _____ and capital goods satisfy these wants _____.

3. Economic efficiency requires that there be both full _____ of resources and full _____.

4. Below is a production possibilities curve for tractors and suits of clothing.

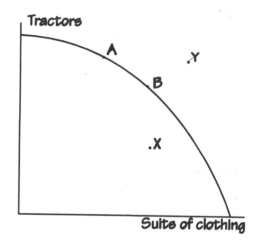

  (a) If the economy moves from point *A* to point *B*, it will produce (more, fewer) _____ tractors and (more, fewer) _____ suits.
  (b) If the economy is producing at point *X*, some of the resources of the economy are either _____ or _____.
  (c) If the economy is to produce at point *Y*, it must either expand its supply of _____ or improve its _____.

5. The quantity of other goods and services an economy must go without in order to produce more low-cost housing is the _____ of producing the additional low-cost housing.

6. If Canada attempts to expand her apple industry, the opportunity cost per apple produced will tend to increase because resources are not completely

_____ to different uses. This is an example of the generalization known as the law of _____.

7. For each situation below, indicate whether there is overallocation, underallocation, or optimal allocation of resources to the production of the good in question.

(a) marginal benefit is greater than marginal cost at the current output level _____

(b) marginal benefit equals marginal cost at the current output level _____

(c) marginal benefit is less than marginal cost at the current output level _____

8. If some available resources are unemployed, productive efficiency (is, is not) _____ met, and the economy is (inside, outside, on) _____ its production possibilities curve.

9. Productive efficiency means that the _____ production techniques are used in the production of wanted goods and services.

10. Production is allocatively efficient when, given the distribution of resources, the economy produces that combination of goods _____ by society.

11. All points on the production possibilities curve are _____ efficient but some points are not _____ efficient.

12. Full production implies that both _____ efficiency and _____ efficiency are achieved.

13. Improvements in oil drilling technology would shift Canada's production possibilities curve to the (right, left) _____. Depletion of forest resources would shift our production possibilities curve to the _____.

14. In pure capitalism property resources are (publicly, privately) _____ owned; in a command economy resources are _____ owned.

■ **PROBLEMS AND PROJECTS**

1. Match the resources on the left with the corresponding resource payments on the right.

labour	rental income
capital	profits
land	wages
entrepreneurial ability	interest income

2. Below is a list of resources. Indicate in the space to the right of each whether the resource is land (Ld), capital (K), labour (L), or entrepreneurial ability (EA).

(a) fishing grounds in the North Atlantic _____

(b) a farmer's inventory of wheat _____

(c) Maple Leaf Gardens in Toronto _____

(d) the work performed by the late Henry Ford _____

(e) Cavendish beach in Prince Edward Island _____

(f) Stelco's steel plant in Hamilton, Ontario ___

(g) the tasks accomplished in making the Apple Computer a commercial success _____

(h) the work done by a welder on an assembly line _____

3. An economy produces two products, timber (T) and fish (F), according to the production possibilities table below. The usual assumptions apply.

(a) Plot the data from the production possibilities table on the graph provided. Place T on the vertical axis and F on the horizontal axis.

(b) Can the economy produce 4 of F and 22 of T? _____ If not, why? _____ What is the maximum amount of T that can be produced in combination with 4 of F?_____

Combination	Timber	Fish
a	0	6
b	7	5
c	13	4
d	18	3
e	22	2
f	25	1
g	27	0

(c)   If the economy is producing 2F and 15T, what problem is being experienced? _____
(d)   Assuming that the economy is productively efficient, what is the opportunity cost of producing 1F instead of none? _____ What is the opportunity cost of the second unit of F? _____ And the third F? _____
(e)   As more units of F are produced, what is the trend in the number of units of T that must be given up to get the extra F? _____. Due to this trend, the shape of the production possibilities curve is _____ to the origin.

4. For each case below you are given an initial production possibilities curve between timber and fish. Sketch a new curve to show the result of the events given.
(a)   The nation's supplies of labour and capital expand.

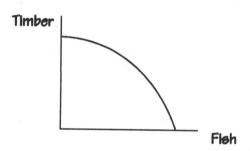

(b)   New tree-planting techniques improve the success of reforestation operations.

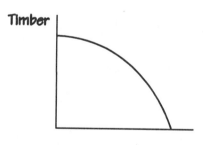

(c)   An ecological disaster wipes out a large part of the fish stocks.

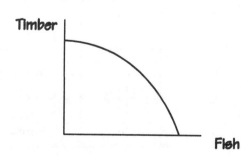

5. An economy is achieving full production, producing a combination of automobiles and food. Now a technological advance occurs which enables this economy to produce automobiles with fewer resources than previously. How is it possible for the society to consume more automobiles *and* more food as a result? Illustrate below using the production possibilities diagram.

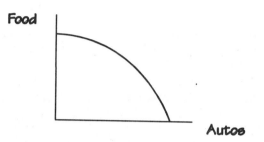

6.   Below is a list of economic goods. Indicate in the space beside each whether the good is a consumer good (C), a capital good (K), or that it depends (D) upon who is using it and for what purpose.
(a)   a dairy cow   ____
(b)   a tractor   ____
(c)   a shopping mall parking lot   ____
(d)   a telephone pole   ____
(e)   a telephone   ____
(f)   your refrigerator   ____
(g)   a refrigerator in a restaurant   ____

7.   A department store is installing video cameras to reduce shoplifting. The marginal costs and marginal benefits of additional cameras are:

Camera	MB ($/month)	MC ($/month)
1	300	100
2	250	125
3	160	150
4	50	175

(a)   If the store must choose one of the numbers shown in the table, the optimal number of cameras is _____.
(b)   How much better off is the store with the optimal number than with one camera fewer? $____
(c)   How much better off is the store with the optimal number than with one camera more? $____

■ TRUE-FALSE

Circle T if the statement is true, F if it is false.

1. If you must stand in line for six hours to get into a free concert by the Tragically Hip, there is no opportunity cost to you for seeing the concert. **T F**

2. Money is a resource and is classified as "capital." **T F**

3. A Canada Savings Bond is classified as a capital good. **T F**

4. Profit is the reward paid to those who provide the economy with capital. **T F**

5. If the main opportunity cost of going to college is the foregone earnings, college enrolment should increase during periods of high unemployment, other factors remaining constant. **T F**

6. The opportunity cost of producing wheat tends to increase as more wheat is produced because land less suited to its production must be reallocated from other uses. **T F**

7. A production possibilities curve that is concave to the origin reflects the law of increasing opportunity costs. **T F**

8. The problem of scarcity is likely to be solved someday by technological progress. **T F**

9. An economy that is employing the least cost productive methods has achieved allocative efficiency. **T F**

10. Given full employment and full production, it is impossible for an economy that can produce only two goods to increase production of both. **T F**

11. Economic growth can be represented by a shift of the production possibilities curve to the right. **T F**

12. The more capital goods an economy produces today, the greater will be its ability to produce all goods in the future, *ceteris paribus*. **T F**

13. Most nations use economic systems somewhere between the extremes of pure capitalism and command economy. **T F**

14. In a command economy most resources are privately owned and are allocated by the market system. **T F**

15. In the circular flow model, households act on the demand side of resource and product markets. **T F**

■ MULTIPLE-CHOICE

Circle the letter that corresponds to the best answer.

1. In her role as an "innovator" an entrepreneur:
   (a) makes policy decisions in a business firm
   (b) combines factors of production to produce a good or service
   (c) invents a new production process
   (d) takes risks in the market place

2. An economy is efficient when it has achieved:
   (a) full employment
   (b) full production
   (c) either full employment or full production
   (d) both full employment and full production

3. When a production possibilities curve is drawn, four assumptions are made. Which is **not** one of those assumptions?
   (a) only two goods are produced
   (b) wants are unlimited
   (c) the economy has both full employment and full production
   (d) the quantities of all resources available to the economy are fixed

Answer the next four questions on the basis of the following diagram.

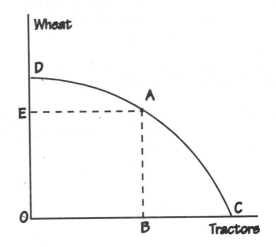

4. At point *A* on the production possibilities curve:
   (a) less wheat than tractors is being produced
   (b) fewer tractors than wheat are being produced
   (c) the economy is employing all its resources
   (d) the economy is not employing all its resources

5. The opportunity cost of producing 0*B* of tractors is:
   (a) 0*D* of wheat
   (b) 0*E* of wheat
   (c) *ED* of wheat
   (d) 0*C* of tractors

6. If there occurred a technological improvement in the production of tractors but not wheat:
   (a) point *D* would remain fixed and point *C* shift to the left
   (b) point *C* would remain fixed and point *D* shift upward
   (c) point *D* would remain fixed and point *C* shift to the right
   (d) point *C* would remain fixed and point *D* shift inward

7. From one point to another along the same production possibilities curve:
   (a) resources remain fixed but are reallocated between the production of the two goods
   (b) resources are increased and are reallocated between the two goods
   (c) resources are increased and production of both goods increased
   (d) idle resources are put to work to increase the production of one good

8. If opportunity costs are constant, instead of increasing, the production possibilities curve will be:
   (a) concave to the origin
   (b) convex to the origin
   (c) a downward sloping straight line
   (d) parallel to the horizontal axis

9. Which of the following would cause a nation's production possibilities curve to shift inward toward the origin?
   (a) more people in the labour force
   (b) increased international trade
   (c) rising unemployment of workers
   (d) not replacing capital equipment as it wears out

10. Which of the following will slow down the rate at which Canada's production possibilities curve shifts rightward?
    (a) increasing rate of technological change
    (b) increased immigration
    (c) depletion of Canada's oil and gas deposits
    (d) freer trade between Canada's provinces

11. The opportunity cost of providing a governmentally financed stadium for a city's baseball team is:
    (a) the interest on the money borrowed to finance the stadium
    (b) the future tax increase the public will be forced to bear to pay for the stadium
    (c) the other goods and services that must be sacrificed so that resources can be used for stadium construction
    (d) there is no opportunity cost since Ottawa will finance the stadium under a regional development program

12. Private ownership of property resources, use of the market system to direct and coordinate economic activity, and the presence of the profit motive are characteristic of:
    (a) pure capitalism
    (b) the command economy
    (c) market socialism
    (d) communism

13. Central planning is associated with which economic system?
    (a) pure capitalism
    (b) laissez-faire capitalism
    (c) market economy
    (d) command economy

14. Productive efficiency is attained when:
    (a) resources are all employed
    (b) output is produced at least possible cost
    (c) there is no government involvement in the economy
    (d) the production possibilities curve is concave

15. The term "laissez-faire" refers to:
    (a) the absence of government intervention in markets
    (b) the absence of monopoly
    (c) the absence of competition in markets
    (d) efficient use of employed resources

■ DISCUSSION QUESTIONS

1. Explain what is meant by the "economic problem." Why are resources scarce?

2. When is a society economically efficient? What is meant by "full production," and how does it differ from "full employment"?

3. What four assumptions are made in drawing a production possibilities curve? How do technological progress and an increased supply of resources in the economy affect the curve?

4. Why cannot an economist determine which combination in the production possibilities table is "best"? What determines the optimum product-mix?

5. What is opportunity cost? What is the law of increasing opportunity costs? Why do opportunity costs increase?

6. Would the economic problem disappear if the affluent countries, including Canada, offered to pay more for the products of the Third World countries? Explain.

7. During the Cold War, Russia seemed to be quite competitive with the United States in terms of military strength even though Russia's overall production capabilities were much lower than America's. Use the production possibility curve model to resolve this paradox.

8. If resources in an economy are fully employed, what would be the effect on living standards if the government decided to increase the output of goods for the future? Explain using the production possibilities curve.

9. Explain why you agree or disagree with the statement: "The opportunity cost of allocating large numbers of people to clean up Ontario's lakes during a recession is different from the opportunity cost during a period of full employment."

10. Explain the difference between productive and allocative efficiency.

11. What are the roles of households and of businesses in the resource market and the product market?

■ ANSWERS

FILL-IN QUESTIONS

1.   (a) unlimited; (b) scarce (or limited)

2.   directly; indirectly

3.   employment, production

4.   (a) fewer, more; (b) unemployed, underemployed; (c) resources, technology

5.   opportunity cost

6.   adaptable; increasing opportunity costs

7.   (a) underallocation; (b) optimal allocation; (c) over-allocation

8.   is not; inside

9.   least costly

10.   most wanted

11.   productively, allocatively

12.   productive, allocative

13.   right; left

14.   privately, publicly

PROBLEMS AND PROJECTS

1.   labour: wages; capital: interest income; land: rental income; entrepreneurial ability: profits

2.   (a) Ld; (b) K; (c) K; (d) EA; (e) Ld; (f) K; (g) EA; (h) L

3.   (b) No; this combination lies outside the production possibilities curve; 13 T; (c) productive inefficiency (unemployment or underemployment); (d) 2T = 27T − 25T, 3T, 4T; (e) increasing, concave

4.   (a) Both T and F intercepts shift out; (b) T intercept shifts out, F intercept is unchanged; (c) F intercept shifts in, T intercept is unchanged

5.   More automobiles can now be produced with a given amount of resources, so the automobiles intercept shifts out. By moving some resources from autos to food, the

society can produce more food and more automobiles. Show this on your diagram by shifting the production possibilities curve, then showing a movement to a new point that is northeast of the original point.

6.   (a) K, (b) K, (c) K, (d) K, (e) D, (f) C, (g) K

7.   (a) 3 cameras, because for each of the first three, the MB > MC; (b) $10/month is the net benefit for the 3rd camera ($160-150); (c) $125/month is the net loss for the 4th camera ($50-175)

TRUE-FALSE

1. F   Your time has value
2. F   Money is not an economic resource
3. F   CSB's are financial assets, not real capital
4. F   Profit goes to entrepreneurs; capitalists earn interest income
5. T   High unemployment means more people would not lose wages by choosing to go to college
6. T
7. T
8. F   Even as we become able to produce more our wants will continue to expand
9. F   Allocative efficiency is not achieved unless the most wanted combination of goods is being produced
10. T
11. T
12. T
13. T
14. F   The statement describes capitalism or market system
15. F   Households are suppliers, not demanders, in resource markets

MULTIPLE-CHOICE

1. (c) The others are roles of entrepreneurs, but not the innovator role
2. (d) Both forms are necessary conditions
3. (b) Demands for goods are not relevent to production possibilities
4. (c) Because point A is on the curve
5. (c) Wheat production falls from point D to point E
6. (c) Maximum tractor output increases; maximum wheat does not change
7. (a) Increased resources would imply a shift; if resources were previously idle the economy was not on the curve
8. (c) Such a line would have a constant slope, or trade-off ratio between the two goods
9. (d) The capital stock would shrink, meaning a reduction in the supply of resources
10. (c) Reduction in our supply of resources
11. (c) Ultimately the opportunity cost must be measured in other goods given up
12. (a) All are critical to a capitalist or market economy

13. (d) Including socialism and communism
14. (b) Using resources in the most productive way, and minimizing cost of production go hand in hand
15. (a) "Let it be" is government's attitude toward the economy in a "laissez faire" system

CHAPTER 3

Individual Markets: Demand and Supply

This chapter presents the most important tool of economic analysis: the demand and supply model. We use this model to analyze how various events affect the price and quantities of goods and services traded in highly competitive markets where there are many buyers and sellers trading a standardized product.

The law of demand asserts an inverse relationship between price and quantity demanded, *ceteris paribus*. The law of supply states a positive relationship between price and quantity supplied, *ceteris paribus*. The demand and supply relationships can be expressed in several ways: as algebraic equations, schedules in tables, or graphs. Given the demand and the supply in a market, there is only one price at which the quantity demanded by consumers exactly equals the quantity supplied by sellers. This is the equilibrium or market-clearing price. The equilibrium quantity is the quantity demanded and supplied at the equilibrium price.

Starting from an equilibrium, a change in any demand or supply determinant will shift the demand or supply curve, and throw the market out of equilibrium — creating either a shortage or a surplus. To eliminate the shortage (or surplus) the price must rise (or fall) to restore the balance between how much consumers are willing and able to buy and producers are willing and able to sell.

The first step in analyzing how an event affects the market equilibrium is to determine which curve is directly affected by the event: supply or demand. The second step is to decide whether that curve increases or decreases. From there it is a simple matter to decide the direction of change for the equilibrium price and quantity.

To master the supply and demand model one must clearly understand the definitions of demand and supply, and the key distinctions between "de-mand" and "quantity demanded" and between "supply" and "quantity supplied." Practice with the graphical model of demand and supply will greatly help clarify these concepts.

■ CHAPTER LEARNING OBJECTIVES

In this chapter you will learn:
□ What markets are.
□ What demand is and what factors affect it.
□ What supply is and what factors affect it.
□ How demand and supply together determine market equilibrium.

■ CHAPTER OUTLINE

1. A market is any institution or mechanism that brings together the buyers and sellers of a particular good or service. In this chapter we assume that markets are highly competitive.

2. Demand is the relationship between the price of a product and the amount of the product that the consumer is willing and able to purchase in a specific time period. The relationship can be expressed in a table, graph, or equation.

3. The law of demand states that, other things being equal, as price falls, the quantity demanded rises. That is, there is an inverse relationship between price and quantity demanded.

4. Along with plenty of strong evidence for the law of demand, there are also three analytical reasons:
(a) If consumers experience *diminishing marginal utility* then they will be willing to buy additional units of a good only if price is reduced.

(b)   When price falls there is an *income effect*: the consumer's overall buying power increases so the consumer buys more of the good.

(c)   When price falls there is a *substitution effect*: the consumer is motivated to buy more of the good that is now relatively less expensive instead of other goods for which it is a substitute.

5. The demand curve is a graphic representation of the law of demand.

(a)   The graph has price on the vertical axis, and quantity demanded on the horizontal axis.

(b)   A change in price leads to a movement along the demand curve. This is called a change in quantity demanded.

6. The market demand is derived by "adding up" the individual consumer demands at each possible price. The law of demand applies to both individual and market demand curves.

7. The price determines the quantity demanded of a good, but factors other than price determine the location of the whole demand curve. These factors are known as the demand determinants:

(a)   tastes (or preferences) of buyers;
(b)   number of buyers in the market;
(c)   incomes of consumers;
(d)   prices of related goods (substitutes and complements);
(e)   expectations.

8. A change in a demand determinant will shift demand to the left (a decrease) or the right (an increase), creating an entirely new demand curve. This is called a change in demand.

(a)   If tastes shift in favour of a good, its demand will increase.

(b)   If the number of buyers of a good increases, its demand will increase.

(c)   If consumer incomes increase, demand will increase if the good is normal, and demand will decrease if the good is inferior.

(d)   If an increase in the price of one good causes the demand for another good to decrease, the two goods are complements; if the price increase causes demand for the other good to increase, the two goods are substitutes.

(e)   If consumers expect prices or incomes to rise in the future they may increase their demand now.

9. A change in demand and a change in the quantity demanded are not the same thing. This is obvious on the graph where a change in the price of the good causes a change in the quantity demanded, or movement along the curve, whereas a change in demand shifts the entire curve to a new location.

10. Supply is the relationship between the price of a product and the amount of the product that suppliers will offer to sell in a specific time period. The law of supply states that, other things being equal, as price rises, the quantity supplied rises. That is, there is a positive relationship between price and quantity supplied. The quantity supplied rises with price because the supplier can profitably produce more output at a higher price.

11. The supply curve is a graphic representation of supply and the law of supply.

(a)   The graph has price on the vertical axis, and quantity supplied on the horizontal axis.

(b)   A change in price leads to a movement along the supply curve. This is called a change in quantity supplied.

12. The determinants of supply are:

(a)   resource prices;
(b)   technology;
(c)   taxes and subsidies;
(d)   prices of other goods;
(e)   price expectations;
(f)   number of sellers in the market.

13. A change in any of the determinants will shift supply to the left (a decrease) or the right (an increase), creating an entirely new supply curve. This is called a change in supply.

(a)   If prices of production resources fall, supply will increase.

(b)   A technological change will improve the efficiency of production and increase the supply.

(c)   A new tax will raise the producer's costs and reduce the supply; a new subsidy will increase the supply.

(d)   Producers may reallocate their resources if the price of a related good changes. Depending on the case, supply could increase or decrease.

(e)   It is also difficult to generalize about how a change in expectations about the future price will change today's supply.

(f)   An increase in the number of sellers will increase the supply.

14. A change in supply and a change in the quantity supplied are not the same thing. The difference is most obvious on a graph. A change in the price of the good causes a change in the quantity supplied, which on the graph is a movement to a different point on the same supply curve, whereas a change in supply involves a shift to a whole new supply curve.

15. The market-clearing or equilibrium price of a good is that price at which quantity demanded and quantity supplied are equal; the equilibrium quantity is equal to the quantity demanded and supplied at the equilibrium price.

(a) If price is above the equilibrium, quantity demanded is less than quantity supplied, so there is a surplus. This will cause price to fall.

(b) If price is below the equilibrium, quantity demanded is greater than quantity supplied, so there is a shortage. This will cause price to rise.

(c) The only sustainable price is the equilibrium price.

(d) The rationing function of price is to create consistency between the decisions of sellers and of buyers, so as to eliminate any shortages or surpluses from a market.

16. Any change in a determinant of demand or supply will cause the curve to shift, and result in a new equilibrium price and quantity.

(a) Most changes shift only one of the two curves.

(b) When demand changes, and supply is unchanged, equilibrium price and quantity change in the same direction as the change in demand.

(c) When supply changes, and demand is unchanged, quantity moves in the same direction as the supply change, but equilibrium price moves in the opposite direction.

(d) In complex cases where both supply and demand change, both curves will shift; either the direction of price change or quantity change will be predictable, the other will be indeterminate.

17. It is always important to keep in mind that specific demand and supply curves show relationships between prices and quantities demanded or supplied, holding all other determinants equal.

■ TERMS AND CONCEPTS

market	change in quantity
demand	demanded

demand schedule
law of demand
diminishing marginal utility
income effect
substitution effect
demand curve
determinants of demand
normal goods
inferior goods
substitute good
complementary good
change in demand

supply
supply schedule
law of supply
supply curve
determinants of supply
change in supply
change in quantity supplied
surplus
shortage
equilibrium price
equilibrium quantity
rationing function of price

■ HINTS AND TIPS

1. This chapter is the most important one in the book. Be sure to spend extra time on it, and to return to it to review the fundamentals if you run into difficulties in later chapters.

2. You have not mastered the chapter until you can clearly distinguish between a change in demand and a change in quantity demanded; the same for supply vs. quantity supplied. You should be able to articulate the difference verbally, and graphically.

3. Perhaps more than any other chapter, this chapter requires active practice. Pick up your pencil and draw graphs. Begin by plotting demand and supply schedules onto graphs. Study carefully the examples in the text and study guide to learn the appropriate labels for such graphs. Once you are confident of working with graphs with concrete numbers, go to the next step of drawing abstract graphs where numbers are implied on the axes, but not explicitly given.

4. If algebraic work with demand and supply is relevant in the economics course you are studying, please look at the Appendix to Chapter 3.

■ FILL-IN QUESTIONS

1. A market is the institution or mechanism that brings together the _____ and the _____ of a particular good or service.

2. The demand schedule reflects a (positive, negative) _____ relationship between price and quantity demanded. The supply schedule reflects a _____ relationship between price and quantity supplied.

3. Factors that shift the demand curve when they change are called demand _____ .

4. The Latin phrase meaning "all other things being equal" is _____ .

5. When demand or supply is graphed, price is placed on the _____ axis and quantity on the _____ axis.

6. The graph of the demand schedule is called the demand _____ and according to the law of demand is _____ sloping.

7. A change in price causes a change in (demand, quantity demanded) _____ , and results in a (movement along, shift in) _____ the demand curve. A change in consumer incomes causes a change in (demand, quantity demanded) _____ , and results in a (movement along, shift in) _____ the demand curve.

8. Marianne tends to buy more books when the price of books falls because:
   (a) her purchasing power is increased, so she can afford to buy more books and other goods; this is called the _____ effect.
   (b) books become less expensive relative to magazines, so Marianne tends to buy more books and fewer magazines; and this is called the _____ effect.

9. Don likes to have spare drill bits for various projects around the house. He is willing to pay less for each successive drill bit because he is successively less likely to actually need each extra one he buys. This is an example of the principle known as diminishing _____ .

10. A change in price causes a change in (supply, quantity supplied) _____ , and results in a (movement along, shift in) _____ the supply curve. A change in resource costs causes a change in (supply, quantity supplied) _____ , and results in a (movement along, shift in) _____ the supply curve.

11. An increase in supply is shown by a shift of the entire supply curve to the (left, right) _____ . A

decrease in supply is shown by a shift of the entire supply curve to the _____ .

12. If quantity demanded exceeds quantity supplied, price is (above, below) _____ the equilibrium price. This creates a (shortage, surplus) _____ that will cause the price to (rise, fall) _____ .

■ **PROBLEMS AND PROJECTS**

1. (a) Plot the demand and supply schedules below on the graph provided. Indicate on the graph the equilibrium price and quantity by drawing lines from the intersection of the demand and supply curves to the price and quantity axes, and labelling the values P* and Q*.

Price per Unit	Quantity Demanded	Quantity Supplied	Shortage (-) or Surplus (+)
$13	18	54	_____
12	21	48	_____
11	24	42	_____
10	27	36	_____
9	30	30	_____
8	33	24	_____
7	36	18	_____
6	39	12	_____

(b) At equilibrium, P* = _____, and Q* = _____ .
(c) Fill in the last column of the table showing the amount of shortage or surplus that would exist at each price shown.

2. (a) Three individuals' demand schedules for bread are shown below. Assuming these are the only buyers, fill in the market demand schedule for bread.

Price (per loaf)	Quantity Demanded (loaves per month)			
	Doug	Leslie	Chong	Total
$1.20	10	6	8	_____
1.10	12	8	10	_____
1.00	15	11	12	_____
0.90	19	15	14	_____
0.80	24	18	16	_____

(b) If the market supply of bread is fixed at 48 loaves per month, what will be the equilibrium price, and how many loaves will each consumer buy at this price?

Price = $_____ per loaf

Doug: _____ loaves; Leslie: _____ loaves; Chong: _____ loaves

3. Below are some events that affect the market for wine. In each space, indicate whether the event shifts demand (D) or supply (S), and whether it is an increase (+) or decrease (-) in the curve.

(a) Increase in the price of grapes _____
(b) Increase in population of consumers _____
(c) Increase in the price of cheese _____
(d) Improvement in production technology _____
(e) New subsidies for wine production _____
(f) Increase in the price of beer _____
(g) Consumers expect a new tax on wine _____

4. Suppose that the demand and supply model is applicable to the Canadian beef market. For each of the following events, sketch a demand and supply graph showing the effect on the equilibrium price and quantity of beef in Canada.

(a) A popular singer remarks that red meat in the diet may be a contributing factor in heart and circulatory diseases.
(b) The East Coast cod fishery is closed due to depleted fish stocks.
(c) Hoof and mouth disease in Europe leads to destruction of much of the supply of beef imported from Europe.
(d) The price of livestock feed grains falls sharply due to a record harvest.
(e) Agriculture Canada discovers a new growth hormone that will increase the weight of beef cattle by 20% with the same feed intake.

(f) Numerous hamburger restaurants go out of business as a result of sharp increases in the minimum wage rate.

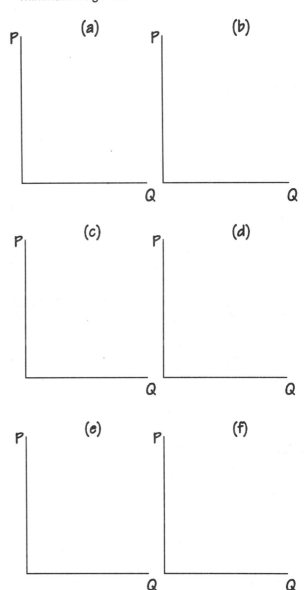

5. The table on the next page shows a number of different cases of a change in demand and/or supply. In the columns for price change and quantity change, fill in the direction in which the equilibrium will change: increase (+), decrease (-), or indeterminate (?).

Case	Demand	Supply	Price change	Quantity change
a	increases	constant	_____	_____
b	constant	increases	_____	_____
c	decreases	constant	_____	_____
d	constant	decreases	_____	_____
e	increases	increases	_____	_____
f	increases	decreases	_____	_____
g	decreases	decreases	_____	_____
h	decreases	increases	_____	_____

6. In the 1990s, most golf courses in Canada raised their green fees (the price of playing golf), but also had more golfers coming to play at their courses. This case (is, is not) _____ a violation of the law of demand. Three possible reasons for the observed behaviour are:

(a) _____
(b) _____
(c) _____

7. The graph below shows the demand and supply for daily parking spots in the downtown core of a Canadian city.

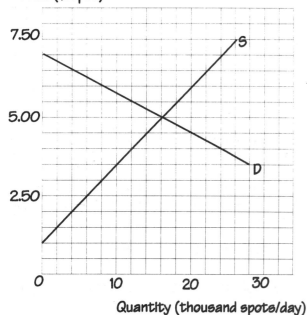

Price ($/spot)

(a)   The current equilibrium price is _____ per spot, and _____ spots are rented each day.
(b)   Suppose that city council levies a new tax on parking lot operators in order to raise revenue to pay for a rapid transit system. The tax is set at $1.50 per spot rented. If the consumer pays

$6.00, the supplier keeps $6.00-$1.50=$4.50. If the consumer pays $5.00, the supplier keeps _____ .

(c)   Show the new supply curve reflecting the tax. (The supply curve will shift upward by the amount of the tax because suppliers require this much extra in order to be willing to maintain the same supply as before.)
(d)   The new equilibrium price is _____ per spot, and _____ spots are rented each day. Accordingly, the price consumers pay for one spot has (fallen, risen) _____ by $_____ , and the price that suppliers keep has _____ by $_____. Therefore, the consumers' burden of the tax is _____ percent, and the suppliers' burden is _____ percent.

8. The table below shows the demand and supply schedules for firewood in two small towns, Eastwick and Westwood. At first each town is a separate competitive market because there is no passage across the river separating the towns.

Price	Eastwick Qd	Eastwick Qs	Westwood Qd	Westwood Qs	Total Qd	Total Qs
$225	80	100	45	105	___	___
200	90	90	55	95	___	___
175	100	80	65	85	___	___
150	110	70	75	75	___	___
125	120	60	85	65	___	___

(a)   In Eastwick the equilibrium price is _____ per cord, and the equilibrium quantity is _____ cords per year.
(b)   In Westwood the equilibrium price is _____ per cord, and the equilibrium quantity is _____ cords per year.

Now a bridge is built across the river, turning Eastwick and Westwood into one combined market.
(c)   Fill in the market demand and supply schedules in the blank columns.
(d)   The new equilibrium price is _____ per cord. This represents an increase in (Westwood, Eastwick) _____ and a decrease in _____.
(e)   In Westwood quantity demanded is now _____ cords per year, and quantity supplied is now _____ cords per year. In Eastwick quantity demanded is now _____ cords per year, and quantity supplied is now _____ cords per year. Therefore, the town of _____ must import

_____ cords per year from the town of
_____.

9. How would a lengthy strike by transit drivers in a major city affect the market for gasoline in that market? Work this out by considering the relationships between buses and cars, and between cars and gasoline.

■ TRUE-FALSE

Circle T if the statement is true, F if it is false.

1. The classified ads section of a student newspaper could be considered a market.   **T F**

2. The law of demand states that as price increases, the demand for the product decreases, *ceteris paribus*.   **T F**

3. In graphing supply and demand schedules, supply is put on the horizontal axis and demand on the vertical axis.   **T F**

4. A fall in the price of snowboards will cause the demand for skis to decrease.   **T F**

5. If two goods are complements, an increase in the price of one will cause the demand for the other to decrease.   **T F**

6. An increase in income increases the demand for normal goods.   **T F**

7. If Wimpy experiences diminishing marginal utility, then the additional satisfaction he gets from eating his sixth hamburger of the day is less than the satisfaction from the fifth hamburger.   **T F**

8. Since the amount purchased must equal the amount sold, demand and supply must always equal each other.   **T F**

Questions 9-11 are based on the accompanying graph.

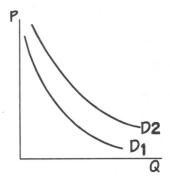

9. If the demand curve moves from D_1 to D_2 demand has increased.   **T F**

10. The shift of the demand curve from D_1 to D_2 could be caused by a decrease in the price of complements.   **T F**

11. The shift of the demand curve from D_1 to D_2 could be caused by a decrease in supply.   **T F**

12. A decrease in quantity supplied can be caused by an increase in production costs.   **T F**

13. If the supply curve for green lipstick shifts to the right, the supply of green lipstick has decreased.   **T F**

14. When quantity supplied exceeds quantity demanded, the market price will tend to fall.   **T F**

15. The equilibrium price is also referred to as the market-clearing price.   **T F**

16. The rationing function of prices is the elimination of shortages and surpluses.   **T F**

17. There is an inverse relationship between a change in supply and the resulting change in equilibrium price.   **T F**

■ MULTIPLE-CHOICE

Circle the letter that corresponds to the best answer.

1. An increase in the quantity demanded of oranges can be caused by:
  (a) a shift to the left of the supply curve of oranges
  (b) a shift to the right of the supply curve of oranges

(c) a decline in the demand for orange juice
(d) a rise in the demand for orange juice

2. A decrease in the quantity demanded:
(a) shifts the demand curve to the left
(b) shifts the demand curve to the right
(c) is a movement down along the demand curve
(d) is a movement up along the demand curve

3. If skiing at Banff and skiing at Whistler are substitutes, an increase in the price of skiing at Banff will:
(a) decrease the demand for skiing at Whistler
(b) increase the demand for skiing at Whistler
(c) decrease the quantity demanded of skiing at Whistler
(d) increase the quantity demanded of skiing at Whistler

4. Which pair of goods would most consumers regard as complementary goods?
(a) coffee and tea
(b) hockey sticks and skates
(c) hamburger meat and bus rides
(d) books and televisions

5. Which of the following is **not** among the determinants of demand?
(a) consumer incomes
(b) consumer expectations of future prices
(c) prices of substitute goods
(d) cost of resources

6. If an increase in income causes the demand for a particular good to decrease, then that good is:
(a) normal
(b) inferior
(c) substitute
(d) complement

7. According to the law of supply:
(a) equilibrium quantity will increase when equilibrium price increases
(b) equilibrium quantity will decrease when equilibrium price increases
(c) the supply curve has a negative slope
(d) if other things remain the same, the quantity supplied increases whenever price increases

8. A supply curve indicates:
(a) the profit-maximizing quantities sellers place on the market at alternative prices

(b) the minimum quantities sellers place on the market at alternative prices
(c) the maximum quantities sellers will place on the market at different prices for inputs
(d) the quantities sellers place on the market in order to meet consumer demand at that price

9. The supply curve of the firm slopes upward in the short run because:
(a) the increased production requires the use of inferior inputs
(b) hiring more inputs for the extra production requires the payment of higher input prices
(c) the increased technology to produce more output is expensive
(d) productive efficiency declines because certain productive resources cannot be expanded quickly

10. A movement along a supply curve for a good would be caused by:
(a) an improvement in the technology of production
(b) an increase in the price of the good
(c) an increase in the number of suppliers of the good
(d) a change in expectations

11. Which of the following would increase the supply of books?
(a) an increase in the demand for books
(b) an increase in the price of books
(c) an increase in the cost of paper
(d) a decrease in the wages paid to printers

12. A market is in equilibrium when:
(a) inventories of the good are not rising
(b) suppliers can sell all of the good they decide to produce at the prevailing price
(c) quantity demanded equals quantity supplied
(d) demanders can purchase all of the good they want at the prevailing price

13. When the price of toothpaste falls, what will happen?
(a) quantity demanded decreases
(b) demand increases
(c) supply decreases
(d) quantity supplied decreases

Questions 14 to 17 are based on the following diagram.

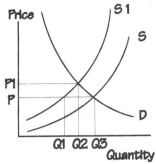

14. Given the original demand and supply curves are *D* and *S:*
   (a) the equilibrium price and quantity were P and Q_1
   (b) the equilibrium price and quantity were P and P_1
   (c) the equilibrium price and quantity were P_1 and Q_1
   (d) the equilibrium price and quantity were P and Q_3

15. The shift of the supply curve from *S* to S_1 is termed:
   (a) an increase in supply
   (b) an increase in quantity supplied
   (c) a decrease in supply
   (d) a decrease in quantity supplied

16. The shift in the supply curve from *S* to S_1 could be caused by:
   (a) an increase in the price of the good
   (b) a technological improvement in the production of the good
   (c) a decrease in demand
   (d) an increase in the cost of the resources used in the production of the good

17. If the price were prevented from adjusting when the supply shifted from *S* to S_1 the result would be:
   (a) a surplus of Q_3 - Q_1
   (b) a shortage of Q_2 - Q_1
   (c) a shortage of Q_3 - Q_1
   (d) a surplus of Q_3 - Q_2

18. Which of the following events would likely cause a furniture manufacturer to increase his supply of oak tables:
   (a) an increase in the price of oak tables
   (b) an increase in the cost of oak lumber
   (c) a decrease in the demand for pine tables
   (d) an increase in wages paid to staff

19. An increase in supply and an increase in demand will:
   (a) increase price and increase the quantity exchanged
   (b) decrease price and increase the quantity exchanged
   (c) affect price in an indeterminate way and decrease the quantity exchanged
   (d) affect price in an indeterminate way and increase the quantity exchanged

20. If scalping NHL playoff game tickets is profitable, this is a sign that the initial price at which the tickets were issued was:
   (a) below the equilibrium price
   (b) equal to the equilibrium price
   (c) above the equilibrium price
   (d) unreasonably high

21. A shortage of paper would cause the price of paper to go up. This would in turn alleviate the shortage by:
   (a) giving buyers incentives to use less paper
   (b) giving producers incentives to find ways to supply more paper
   (c) increasing the amount of paper being recycled
   (d) all of the above

22. In 2001 fewer tents are sold, and the price of tents is higher, as compared to 2000. Which one of the following might have caused the change?
   (a) demand for tents was greater in 2001
   (b) demand for tents was less in 2001
   (c) supply of tents was greater in 2001
   (d) supply of tents was less in 2001

23. Which of the following could raise the price of movie rentals in Saskatoon?
   (a) a drop in the number of movie rental stores
   (b) an increase in the price of VCRs
   (c) a decrease in the population of Saskatoon
   (d) a decrease in the price of admission to movie theatres

24. If new reserves of natural gas were discovered and brought into production, and population were to grow at the same time:
   (a) the price of natural gas would rise
   (b) the price of natural gas would fall
   (c) the price of natural gas would not change
   (d) the price of natural gas might rise or fall

■ DISCUSSION QUESTIONS

1. What is a market? For what kinds of goods does a laundromat bulletin board, or classified pages in a student newspaper, often serve as a market?

2. Carefully state the law of demand and explain the three reasons presented in this chapter to justify downward sloping demand curves.

3. The last time OPEC succeeded in sharply increasing the price of oil, drivers reacted by significantly reducing their gasoline consumption. Explain this in terms of the income effect and substitution effect.

4. Explain the difference between an increase in demand and an increase in quantity demanded. What factors cause a change in demand?

5. Define supply and explain why supply curves are upward sloping.

6. Explain the differences between a change in supply and a change in quantity supplied. What are the factors that cause a change in supply?

7. Neither demand nor supply remains constant for long. Economic circumstances are always changing so the actual prices we see are often not equilibrium prices. Why then do economists spend so much time trying to determine the equilibrium price and quantity if these magnitudes change so frequently?

8. How are normal, inferior, substitute, complementary, and independent goods defined? During a recession (when consumer incomes are falling), who would fare better, firms that sell normal goods, or firms that sell inferior goods?

9. Analyze the following quotation and explain the fallacies contained in it. "An increase in demand will cause price to rise; with a rise in price, supply will increase and the increase in supply will push price down. Therefore, an increase in demand may or may not result in a price increase."

10. To reduce emissions of greenhouse gases, Canada wants to reduce the burning of fossil fuels. Explain why a new tax on automobiles or a subsidy for bicycles would help the pursuit of this goal.

11. From the supply and demand perspective, what would you say has happened in the market for cell phones in the last decade? Are the falling prices and increased numbers of cell phones in use consistent with our economic theory?

■ ANSWERS

FILL-IN QUESTIONS

1. buyers, sellers (either order)

2. negative, positive

3. determinants

4. *ceteris paribus*

5. vertical, horizontal

6. curve, downward (negative)

7. quantity demanded, movement along; demand, shift in

8. (a) income; (b) substitution

9. marginal utility

10. quantity supplied, movement along; supply, shift in

11. right, left

12. below; shortage, rise

PROBLEMS AND PROJECTS

1. (b) $9, 30; (c) from top to bottom: +36, +27, +18, +9, 0, -9, -18, -27.

2. (a) 24, 30, 38, 48, 58; (b) $0.90 (where Qd = Qs). Doug: 19; Leslie: 15; Chong: 14.

3. (a) S-; (b) D+; (c) D- (complements); (d) S+; (e) S+; (f) D+ (substitutes); (g) D+ (buy more now before price rises).

4. (a) D shifts left: P -, Q -; (b) Fish and beef are complements for consumers, so as fish prices rise, then in the beef market D shifts right: P +, Q +; (c) S shifts left: P +, Q -; (d) Resource prices fall, so S shifts right: P -, Q +; (e) Improved production technology causes S to shift right; P -, Q +; (f) Less buyers of beef, so D shifts left: P -, Q -.

5. (a) +, +; (b) -,+; (c) -,-; (d) +,-; (e) ?,+; (f) +,?; (g) ?,-; (h) -,?

6. is not; (a) population growth, (b) increased incomes, (c) increased preferences for golf, or increased prices for substitute recreation activities, etc.

7. (a) $5.00, 16,000; (b) $3.50; (c) the new S curve is parallel to the original and $1.50 above it; (d) about 5.50, 12,000, risen, 0.50, fallen, 1.00; 33, 67.

8. (a) $200, 90; (b) $150, 75; (c) Qd = 125, 145, 165, 185, 205; Qs = 205, 185, 165, 145, 125; (d) $175, Westwood, Eastwick; (e) 65, 85; 100, 80; Eastwick, 20, Westwood.

9. Cars and buses are substitutes, so when buses are not available more people will drive cars. Cars and gasoline are complements, so more gasoline will be used. The demand for gasoline shifts to right. Equilibrium price and quantity both increase.

TRUE-FALSE

1. T
2. F   The change is in quantity demanded, not demand
3. F   Quantities of supply and demand are both on the horizontal axis and price is on the vertical
4. T   Assuming skis and snowboards are substitutes
5. T
6. T
7. T
8. F   They are necessarily equal only at the equilibrium price
9. T
10. T
11. F
12. F   The decrease is in supply, not quantity supplied
13. F   The supply has increased
14. T
15. T
16. T
17. T   As supply increases, price decreases

MULTIPLE-CHOICE

1. (b) There is a movement along the demand curve when the supply shifts, changing the equilibrium price
2. (d) This is caused by a rise in price
3. (b) Some skiers choose Whistler instead of Banff
4. (b) Complementary goods are used together
5. (d) Cost of resources affects supply, not demand
6. (b) For example, generic macaroni and cheese
7. (d) This law states a positive relationship between quantity supplied and price
8. (a) Sellers try to maximize profits
9. (d) For example, a restaurant cannot quickly expand its kitchen facilities

10. (b) All of the others shift the supply curve
11. (d) Lower wages means lower production costs and an increase in supply
12. (c) The other choices are only partially correct
13. (d) A movement down along the supply curve
14. (d) Where S and D intersect
15. (c) Less is supplied at every possible price
16. (d) S to S1 is a decrease in supply
17. (c) At the moment after supply shifts, Qd is still at Q3, but Qs is now at Q1
18. (c) The supply of oak tables could shift right if producers move their resources away from making pine tables and more into making oak tables
19. (d) Depending on which shifts more, demand or supply, price could rise or fall
20. (a) Scalpers depend on there being a shortage at the price at which tickets are first issued
21. (d) These are all aspects of the rationing function of prices
22. (d) Of the possibilities given, only the supply decrease affects both price and quantity as specified
23. (a) Fewer stores would mean a decrease in supply
24. (d) Both supply and demand shift to the right, so the price change depends on the relative extent of the two shifts

APPENDIX TO CHAPTER 3

The Mathematics of Market Equilibrium

This appendix shows how the demand and supply model can be represented mathematically. The demand curve and the supply curve can be expressed in equation form as functions of price. Only at the equilibrium price do both functions generate the same value for quantity. Therefore, given the equations for demand and supply, we can set the two equal to solve for equilibrium price and quantity.

This appendix deals with only straight-line demand and supply curves, so their equations can be represented as simple linear equations. Demand is given by $P = a - bQd$, and supply is given by $P = c + dQs$. Each parameter in the equations has an economic meaning. If the price reaches a or higher, the amount demanded will be zero. If the price reaches c or lower, the amount supplied will be zero. The value b indicates the amount by which price would have to rise to reduce quantity demanded by one unit. The value d indicates the amount by which price would have to increase to increase quantity supplied by one unit.

Normally the values for a, b, c, and d are known. With these parameters known, P and Qd are unknown in the demand equation, and P and Qs are unknown in the supply equation. There appear to be three unknowns (P, Qd, and Qs), but at the equilibrium price, Qd and Qs are equal. Therefore the only unknowns are equilibrium price and quantity, which can be represented as Q^* and P^*.

■ APPENDIX LEARNING OBJECTIVES

When you have studied this appendix, you should be able to:
☐ Understand how demand and supply curves can be represented in equations.
☐ Solve supply and demand equations to find equilibrium price and quantity.

■ APPENDIX OUTLINE

1. A market equilibrium can be expressed as a price and quantity pair (Q^*, P^*) and occurs where quantity demanded equals quantity supplied $(Qd = Qs)$.

2. The market equilibrium results from the negotiating process that brings together the sellers' behaviour and the buyers' behaviour.

3. The buyers' behaviour is represented in the equation: $P = a - bQd$. Buyers will buy only at prices below a, and b reflects how quantity demanded and price are related.

4. The sellers' behaviour is represented in the equation: $P = c + dQs$. Sellers will sell only at prices above c, and d reflects how quantity supplied and price are related.

5. The equilibrium values are solved from the parameter values as follows:
$$P^* = (ad + bc)/(a + d)$$
$$Q^* = (a - c)/(b + d)$$

■ HINTS AND TIPS

1. Solving for the equilibrium price at which the demand and supply equations are equal is no different from locating the intersection on a demand and supply graph to find the equilibrium price. There is only one value for price at which the two equations, or the two curves, have the same value for quantity.

2. If price is not at the equilibrium value there will be a shortage or a surplus, which can also be de-

termined from the equations by substituting the given price into both equations and then comparing the resulting values for quantity demanded and quantity supplied.

■ FILL-IN QUESTIONS

1. The maximum price that buyers are willing to pay for a product is given by the (slope, intercept) _____ term in the (demand, supply) _____ equation.

2. The extent to which the producers are willing to supply more when price increases is reflected in the (slope, intercept) _____ term in the (demand, supply) _____ equation.

3. If demand is given by $P = a - bQd$, an increase in the value of parameter a indicates that the demand curve shifts to the (left, right) _____, and equilibrium price will (decrease, increase) _____.

4. If supply is given by $P = c + dQs$, a decrease in the value of parameter c indicates that the supply curve shifts to the (left, right) _____, and equilibrium price will (decrease, increase) _____.

■ PROBLEMS AND PROJECTS

1. The demand and supply in the market for jeans are given by the following equations:
$P = 100 - 0.1\ Qd$ $P = 50 + 0.4\ Qs$
(a) Rewrite the demand equation as a function of Qd: _____
(b) Rewrite the supply equation as a function of Qs: _____
(c) Using these new equations, fill in. the table.
(d) Solve for the equilibrium price: _____

Price ($/pair)	Qd (pairs/yr)	Qs (pairs/yr)
100	____	____
90	____	____
80	____	____
70	____	____
60	____	____
50	____	____

2. Suppose that the market for lemons can be characterized by the following equations:

$P = 4 - 0.01\ Qd$
$P = 1 + 0.02\ Qs$
(a) Solve for the equilibrium quantity: _____
(b) Solve for the equilibrium price: _____
(c) If price was fixed by government policy at $P = 2$, would there be a shortage or a surplus, and what would the amount be?
(d) If price was fixed by government policy at $P = 3.5$, would there be a shortage or a surplus, and in what amount?

3. The data below represents the market for computer printers.

Price ($/printer)	Qd (printers/yr)	Qs (printers/yr)
100	4000	0
200	3000	0
300	2000	1000
400	1000	2000
500	0	3000

(a) Based on the demand schedule, what is the demand equation? _____
(b) Based on the supply schedule, what is the supply equation? _____
(c) Use the supply and demand equations to solve for equilibrium: $P^* =$ _____, $Q^* =$ _____

■ TRUE-FALSE

Circle T if the statement is true, F if it is false.

1. If the demand curve is given by $P = 12 - 2\ Qd$, then quantity demanded will be 3 if price is 6.   T F

2. If the supply curve is given by $P = 5 + 4\ Qs$, then price will be 7 if quantity supplied is 2.   T F

3. A change in either of the parameters in the demand equation will change the market equilibrium price.   T F

4. A change in either of the parameters in the supply equation will change the market equilibrium price.   T F

5. A change in either of the parameters in the demand equation will change the parameters in the supply equation.   T F

■ MULTIPLE-CHOICE

Circle the letter that corresponds to the best answer.

Answer questions 1 through 6 on the basis of the following demand and supply equations:
$P = 100 - 2\ Qd$
$P = 40 + 4\ Qs$

1. The equilibrium price, P^*, will be:
   (a) 50
   (b) 60
   (c) 70
   (d) 80

2. The equilibrium quantity, Q^*, will be:
   (a) 10
   (b) 20
   (c) 30
   (d) 40

3. The lowest price at which producers are willing to begin selling output is:
   (a) 10
   (b) 20
   (c) 30
   (d) 40

4. Quantity demanded would become zero if the price rises above what level?
   (a) 70
   (b) 80
   (c) 90
   (d) 100

5. If price were 60, what would the situation be in this market?
   (a) a surplus of 15
   (b) a shortage of 15
   (c) a surplus of 20
   (d) a shortage of 20

6. The demand equation given could also be re-written as:
   (a) $Qd = 100 - 2\ P$
   (b) $P = 50 - Qd$
   (c) $Qd = 100 - 0.5\ Qd$
   (d) $Qd = 50 - 0.5\ P$

■ DISCUSSION QUESTIONS

1. What aspect of a demand equation shows that the equation is consistent with the law of demand? What aspect of the supply equation ensures that there is a positive relation between price and quantity supplied?

2. Sketch a hypothetical straight-line demand curve. How would the position of this curve change if there were an increase in the parameter *a*? What if there were an increase in *b*?

3. Sketch a hypothetical straight-line supply curve. How would the position of this curve change if there were an increase in the parameter *c*? What if there were an increase in *d*?

■ ANSWERS

FILL-IN QUESTIONS

1. intercept, demand
2. slope, supply
3. right, increase
4. right, decrease

PROBLEMS AND PROJECTS

1. (a) $Qd = 1000 - 10\ P$; (b) $Qs = 125 + 2.5\ P$: (c) from top to bottom: Qd: 0, 100, 200, 300, 400, 500; Qs: 375, 350, 325, 300, 275, 250: (d) by setting the two equations equal, or by reading the table, we see that $P^* = 70$, where $Qd = Qs = 300$.

2. (a) 100; (b) 3; (c) $Qd = 200$, $Qs = 50$, so a shortage of 150; (d) surplus of 75

3. (a) $P = 500 - 0.1\ Qd$; (b) $P = 200 + 0.1\ Qs$; (c) $P^* = 350$, $Q^* = 1500$

TRUE-FALSE

1. T Substitute in 6 for P and solve for Qd
2. F Substitute in 2 for Qs and $P = 13$
3. T If *a* or *b* changes the demand curve will shift
4. T If *c* or *d* changes the supply curve will shift
5. F The parameters for one curve have no effect on the parameters for the other curve

MULTIPLE-CHOICE

1. (d) Set $Qd = Qs$ and solve for P^*
2. (a) Substitute $P^* = 80$ into either the Qd or the Qs equation
3. (d) Set $Qs = 0$
4. (d) Set $Qd = 0$
5. (b) Find that $Qd = 20$ and $Qs = 5$ at this P
6. (d)

CHAPTER 4

An Overview of the Market System and the Canadian Economy

Chapter 3 explained how prices and quantities are determined in individual markets. This chapter widens the focus to consider the nature of the market system as a whole, with emphasis on describing the Canadian economy in particular.

The market system or capitalism has six defining characteristics: the institution of private property; freedom of choice for consumers and freedom of enterprise for suppliers; the pursuit of self-interest; competition among economic units; coordination through markets and prices; and an active, but limited, role for government. Households make choices about supplying the resources that they own, and about spending the incomes from these resources on those goods and services that will best satisfy their wants. Firms employ resources to produce goods that seem to them likely to yield the greatest profit. The profits depend on producing goods that consumers are willing to pay for, and on producing these goods using the most efficient techniques. These demand and supply decisions determine market prices; these in turn provide incentives and signals to consumers and producers, thereby providing a coordinating mechanism for allocating society's resources.

Consumers and producers have the freedom to follow their self-interest as they exchange their property. Where these interactions occur in competitive markets with large numbers of independent buyers and sellers, and where there is easy entry and exit, no individual will have significant power or control in the market. The discipline of competition ensures that self-interested choices made by individual consumers or producers are also in the interests of society — as though individuals are guided by an "invisible hand" to serve the public interest. Accordingly, the role of government is quite limited.

Modern industrial economies have three other characteristics that increase dramatically the amount of goods and services that can be produced: (1) extensive use of advanced technology and capital goods; (2) specialization in production; and (3) use of money. Specialization stimulates the creation of new technology and capital goods, and creates the need for a monetary system that can facilitate exchanges and eliminate the reliance on barter.

The challenge for any market economy can be summarized in four fundamental questions: (1) what goods and services will be produced; (2) how will the goods and services be produced; (3) who will get the goods and services; and (4) how will the system accommodate change?

The market system features three key virtues: efficiency, incentives, and freedom. However, in some cases the market fails to produce an efficient allocation of resources. When spillover effects occur, some of the costs or benefits of production or consumption of a good affect someone other than the immediate producer or consumer. Since these "spillover" costs or benefits are ignored by those choosing the levels of production or consumption, the levels will end up being too high or too low. Goods that everyone can benefit from collectively, and which non-payers cannot be excluded from enjoying, are called public goods. Users' incentives to "free-ride" rather than pay may make it impossible for private firms to supply such goods. Such inefficiencies can be corrected by government intervention.

The chapter closes with a thumbnail sketch of the structure of the Canadian economy and its evolution. In recent decades the tertiary (service) sector has grown as a share of Canada's employment and output while the primary sector (e.g., agriculture, forestry, mining) and secondary (manufacturing) sector have declined. High levels of foreign ownership are prevalent in many sectors.

■ CHAPTER LEARNING OBJECTIVES

In this chapter you will learn:
□ The basic institutions required for a market economy.
□ The Four Fundamental Questions any economy faces.
□ How the "invisible hand" helps to close the gap between private and public interests.
□ The role of government in the market economy.
□ About the structure of the Canadian economy.

■ CHAPTER OUTLINE

1. The market system, or capitalism, is an economic system with six defining characteristics: private property, freedom of enterprise and choice, self-interest, competition, self-regulating markets, and an active, but limited role for government.
   (a) Resources are the private property of households and firms who are free to obtain, control, employ, and dispose of their property as they see fit.
   (b) Freedom of enterprise means that firms are free to make business decisions about what to produce, where to sell, etc. Freedom of choice means that consumers can spend their incomes on whatever goods they want, and resource owners can supply their land, labour, etc. as they see fit.
   (c) Self-interest is the motivating force behind decisions: consumers try to maximize their satisfaction, and entrepreneurs try to maximize their profits.
   (d) Because each market has many independent buyers and sellers, each of whom are free to enter or exit the market, competition is pervasive and no individual buyer or seller has much economic power.
   (e) In the market system signals and incentives are conveyed through prices. Because buyers and sellers respond spontaneously to price changes, resource allocation is coordinated in a decentralized and spontaneous fashion, as if by an "invisible hand."
   (f) Markets create a sufficiently self-regulating, self-adjusting, and efficient allocation of resources that the government plays a limited, though active, role in the economy.

2. All modern industrial economies have three other main characteristics:
   (a) There is extensive use of new technologies and the use of roundabout production whereby complex capital goods (e.g., tools, machinery, and computers) are produced in order to raise the efficiency of producing final goods for consumers.
   (b) Specialization prevails at all levels. Division of labour among workers means that each person produces only a very narrow range of goods, and relies on the existence of markets and prices to be able to trade for goods that others have specialized in producing. The same is true of regions and nations. Specialization creates efficiencies by making use of ability differences, by allowing learning by doing, and by saving time.
   (c) In order to overcome the inconvenience and transactions costs of bartering, some system of money emerges in every modern society. It is impossible to sustain a highly specialized economy without some form of money to facilitate exchanges. Anything that is generally accepted by sellers in exchange for goods and services is considered money.

3. The competitive market system functions with two primary groups of decision makers: households (consumers) and firms (businesses). Households are the ultimate suppliers of resources, and firms are the suppliers of goods purchased by consumers with the incomes from their resources. The market system communicates the decisions of millions of individual households and firms, and coordinates these decisions in a coherent allocation of resources.

4. Faced with unlimited wants and scarce resources, every economy must find answers for the Four Fundamental Questions: what goods and services will be produced; how will the goods and services be produced; who will get the goods and services; how will the system accommodate change.

5. The market system, or price mechanism, is a communication and coordination system that provides answers to the Four Fundamental Questions.

(a) Consumer demands for products and firms' desires for profits determine the types and amounts of goods to be produced, and at what price. Goods that can be produced at a profit will be produced, and those whose production would lead to loss will not be produced.

(b) The desires of businesses to maximize profits motivate them to use production methods that economize on resources, especially those resources that are relatively expensive.

(c) Goods are distributed to consumers on the basis of their willingness and ability to pay the existing market prices for these goods. Consumers' incomes are determined by the quantities and prices of the labour, property, and other resources they supply in resource markets. The market system does not guarantee an equitable distribution of income and consumer goods.

(d) Changes in consumer tastes, technology, and resource supplies are signalled by price changes that give households and firms incentives to adjust their choices; thus the economy spontaneously accommodates changes.

6. Competition in the economy compels firms and households acting in their own self-interest to promote (as though led by an "invisible hand") the interests of society as a whole, though this is not their intention. Adam Smith first noted this concept in his 1776 book, *The Wealth of Nations*.

7. The market system has several merits. The two economic virtues of the system are the efficient allocation of resources and the incentives for using resources productively. The personal freedom allowed in a market economy is its major noneconomic virtue.

8. Market failure occurs when the competitive market system results in the "wrong" production level for some goods, or fails to produce any of certain goods. Spillover effects and public goods are two main kinds of market failure. Both can be corrected by government action.

9. Government can be added to the circular flow model. Government buys goods and services from the product market, employs labour, capital, etc. from resource markets, and finances its expenditures from net tax revenues collected from businesses and households.

10. Any economy can be divided into three major sectors: primary, secondary, and tertiary. The tertiary (service) sector has become a much bigger part of the Canadian economy. Employment in agriculture and manufacturing have been shrinking, particularly due to tremendous amounts of technological change that have decreased the amount of labour needed in these sectors.

11. Canada's economy has high levels of foreign ownership and control: particularly by American companies and investors.

■ **TERMS AND CONCEPTS**

private property	consumer sovereignty
freedom of enterprise	dollar votes
freedom of choice	derived demand
self-interest	guiding function of
competition	prices
roundabout production	creative destruction
specialization	"invisible hand"
division of labour	spillover costs
medium of exchange	spillover benefits
barter	exclusion principle
money	public goods
Four Fundamental Questions	free-rider problem
	quasipublic goods

■ **HINTS AND TIPS**

1. The crux of the market system is the dual role played by prices: to provide both signals and incentives. An increase in the price of a product signals that for some reason scarcity of this product has increased. The price increase gives consumers the incentive to reduce their consumption (as they ration their limited incomes) and gives producers the incentive to produce more (in order to maximize profits).

2. Think about what an amazing thing it is that a market system works at all! How can millions of independent decisions by consumers and producers possibly add up to a coherent allocation of resources that virtually guarantees that your neighbourhood store will have milk and bread every time you come to buy them? The system coordinates resource allocation in a spontaneous and decen-

tralized manner. Nobody is in control of the whole economy; nobody has the responsibility to coordinate the allocation of resources. Yet, as if guided by an "invisible hand," the economy is coordinated.

■ FILL-IN QUESTIONS

1. The ownership of resources by private individuals and organizations is the institution of _private property_

2. In a market system private businesses have freedom of _enterprise_ and consumers have freedom of _choice_.

3. In a market system, an increase in the scarcity of a product is signaled by a(n) (increase, decrease) _increase_ in the _demand_ of the product. This change gives consumers and producers the incentive to revise their choices in furthering their own _self-interest_.

4. List the six characteristics of the market system.
   (a) _private property_
   (b) _freedom of enterprise + choice_
   (c) _self-interest_
   (d) _competition_
   (e) _self regulating markets_
   (f) _active but limited govt. role_

5. If Robinson Crusoe spends time building a canoe to help him to catch more fish, he is engaging in _roundabout_ production.

6. Economic units seeking to further their own self-interest and operating within the capitalistic system will simultaneously, as though directed by an _invisible hand_ promote the _societies_ interest.

7. List the Four Fundamental Questions to which every society must respond.
   (a) _What goods + services will be produced_
   (b) _How much will be produced_
   (c) _Who will get the goods + services_
   (d) _How will the system accomodate change_

8. Three ways in which division of labour enhances a society's output are:
   (a) _making use of ability differences_
   (b) _allowing learning by doing_
   (c) _saving time_

9. In an economy where specialization of labour is extensive, individuals are extremely (independent, interdependent) _interdependent_, and in order to benefit from the specialization these individuals must _trade_ with each other.

10. An economy based on specialization and trade cannot operate efficiently without a system of _money_.

11. International specialization and exchange requires a system of exchanging _currencies_

12. Exchange by barter requires a _coincidence_ of wants.

13. Government frequently reallocates resources when it finds instances of _market_ failure. The two major cases of such failure of the competitive market involve _spillover_ effects and _public_ goods.

14. Spillovers occur when benefits or costs associated with the production or consumption of a good are incurred by a _third_ party. Spillovers are also called _externalities_

15. Governments can resolve the problem of spillover costs through the use of _specific taxes_ or _regulation_.

16. If spillover benefits accompany the production of a good, then resources will be _underallocated_ to the production of that good by the market economy.

17. Governments can resolve the problem of spillover benefits through _____ paid to the _____ or the _____ of the good.

18. Public goods are not subject to the _____ principle. Once a public good is produced, the benefits from the good cannot be confined to the purchaser. This results in a _____ effect.

19. A _____ good is a good that could be made exclusive, but is commonly provided by government because it has substantial spillover benefits.

20. In the expanded circular flow model, the net tax flow is obtained by subtracting all government _____ to business firms and _____ to households from the taxes paid by firms and households.

■ PROBLEMS AND PROJECTS

1. Consider a college with fewer parking spots than students who want to drive to school. At present the college offers free parking on a first-come-first-served basis. They are considering charging for parking, setting the fee high enough that there would always be a few spots open.

(a) Why would the system of charging for parking change the allocation of parking spots?

(b) Why would some students be in favour of the change while others would not?

(c) What socially beneficial incentives would be created by the proposed parking fee?

2. Suppose that a firm can produce 100 units of product X by combining labour, land, capital, and entrepreneurial ability in three different ways as shown in the table below. It can hire labour at $2 per unit, land at $3 per unit, capital at $5 per unit, and entrepreneurial ability at $10 per unit.

	Method		
Resource	A	B	C
Labour	4 8 16	13 26	10 20 30
Land	4 12	3 9	3 9
Capital	4 20	2 10	4 20
Entrepreneurial ability	1 10	1 10	1 10

46 56   55 68   59 69

(a) Which is the least cost method of producing 100 units of X? *B at 55*

(b) If the wage for labour rises from $2 to $3 per unit, which is the least cost method to produce 100 units of X? *A*

(c) If the firm produces 100 X, the increase in the wage rate gives the firm the incentive to (increase, ~~decrease~~) its use of labour from *13* units to *8* units.

3. In 2001 electric power prices increased sharply in Alberta.

(a) What did the price increase signal? *decrease in supply*

(b) What incentives for consumers and producers of electric power were created by the price increase?

(c) If households and businesses responded to these incentives, how would this be socially beneficial?

(d) What is the primary motivation for consumers and producers to make choices that are socially beneficial?

4. The circular flow diagram below includes business firms, households, and government (the public sector). Product and resource markets are also shown.

(a) Identify the sector that corresponds to each box:

a. _____

b. _____

c. _____

d. _____

e. _____

(b) Supply a label or an explanation for each of the twelve flows in the model:

1: _____

2: _____

3: _____

4: _____

5. _____

6: _____

7: _____

8: _____

9: _____

10: _____

11: _____

12: _____

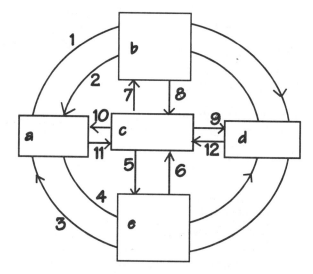

(c) If government wished to increase the production of public goods and decrease the production of private goods in the economy, which flows could it increase? _____, _____, _____.

5. The grade that you earn in your economics course this term will be the product of your work, and you probably consider this grade your private property.

(a) How would your incentives to study change if you did not have the right to communicate your grade to potential employers or other colleges or universities?

(b) How would your incentives change if you had to share your "output" on exams with your classmates (i.e., everybody is awarded the class average grade)?

(c) Are there any reasons for restricting your property rights in your grade? For example, should you be able to sell or give your grade to another student?

6. Match each example on the right with the type of situation on the left:

(a) spillover cost   (1) a radio broadcast
(b) spillover benefit   (2) a noisy house party
(c) public good   (3) vaccinations

■ **TRUE-FALSE**

Circle T if the statement is true, F if it is false.

1. Self-interest means the same as selfishness. **T F**

2. In the real world there are usually legal limits placed on the rights of private property. **T F**

3. In a competitive market every seller has significant influence over the market price. **T F**

4. In the market system most prices are set by a government agency. **T F**

5. If property rights did not exist for intellectual property, individuals would have less incentive to create music, books, and computer programs. **T F**

6. In the market system prices serve as signals for the allocation of resources. **T F**

7. Because the market system is efficient in resource use, it follows that every person is better off under this form of economic organization than any alternative. **T F**

8. The distribution of output in the market economy depends upon the distribution of resources. **T F**

9. In a market system competition serves to regulate self-interest for the benefit of society. **T F**

10. The employment of capital to produce goods and services implies that there will be roundabout production. **T F**

11. Specialization allows for a more efficient use of resources. **T F**

12. Money is a device for facilitating the exchange of goods and services. **T F**

13. "Coincidence of wants" means that two persons desire to acquire the same good or service. **T F**

14. The market system ensures that all households will receive an equitable share of the economy's output of goods and services. **T F**

15. The "invisible hand" refers to government intervention in the market. **T F**

16. Pollution is a cause of market failure because the price of the polluting product does not reflect all the resource costs used in its production. **T F**

17. A spillover or externality is a cost or benefit that is imposed upon an individual or group external to the market transaction. **T F**

18. A specific tax imposed on producer that create pollution will lower the marginal cost of production and increase supply. **T F**

19. A public good is any good or service that is provided free by the government. **T F**

20. For public goods the free-rider problem occurs when people can receive benefits without contributing to the cost of providing the good. **T F**

■ **MULTIPLE-CHOICE**

Choose the letter that corresponds to the best answer.

1. Which of the following is not one of the six characteristics of the market system?
(a) competition
(b) freedom of enterprise and choice
(c) self-interest
(d) central economic planning

2. The "invisible hand" is used to explain how in the market system:

(a) property rights are defined
(b) taxes and subsidies are determined
(c) the self-interest of individuals is harnessed for the benefit of society
(d) spillover effects occur

3. In the market system a decrease in the demand for a good should result in all but:
(a) an increase in the price of the resources producing the good
(b) a decrease in the profitability of producing the good
(c) a movement of resources out of the production of the good
(d) a decrease in the price of the good

4. Roundabout production refers to:
(a) the use of resources by government
(b) the use of resources to produce consumer goods directly
(c) the use of resources to produce services
(d) the use of resources to produce capital goods that in turn are used to produce other goods

5. Which of the following is **not** an example of a capital good?
(a) money
(b) a warehouse
(c) a forklift
(d) a computer

6. Which of the following is **not** a condition for a market to be highly competitive:
(a) the presence of a large number of buyers
(b) the freedom to enter or leave a particular market
(c) the presence of a large number of sellers
(d) a fair price determined by a public agency

7. Which of the following is a reason that specialization in production increases efficiency?
(a) trade is rendered unnecessary
(b) barter transactions are rendered unnecessary
(c) individuals usually possess very similar resources and talents
(d) experience or "learning-by-doing" results in increased output

8. Barter:
(a) is the main method of trading in a market economy

(b) is the action of haggling over the price of a good
(c) is the exchange of a good for money
(d) is the exchange of a good for a good

9. Which of the following is **not** a necessary consequence of specialization?
(a) people will barter
(b) people will engage in trade
(c) people will be dependent upon each other
(d) people will produce more of one thing than they would produce in the absence of specialization

10. Which of the following is **not** a virtue of the market system?
(a) allocative efficiency
(b) productive efficiency
(c) equitable distribution of income
(d) ability to adapt to changes in tastes, technologies, and resource supplies

11. The term "division of labour" means the same as:
(a) specialization
(b) barter
(c) economies of scale
(d) coincidence of wants

12. All modern economies have the following characteristics except for:
(a) specialization
(b) limited government interference
(c) use of money
(d) roundabout means of production

13. The economist who first wrote about the "invisible hand" was:
(a) John Maynard Keynes
(b) Karl Marx
(c) David Ricardo
(d) Adam Smith

14. If external benefits accompany the production of a good:
(a) too much of the good will be produced by a competitive market
(b) too little of the good will be produced in a competitive market
(c) a tax on the production of the good will result in the optimum production of the good
(d) the good is exported to foreign countries

15. In the case where producing a good creates spillover costs, government could promote the optimal output by:

   (a) banning production of the good
   (b) taxing the producers of the good
   (c) subsidizing consumers of the good
   (d) subsidizing producers of the good

16. Which of the following is a good example of a good or service providing spillover benefits?

   (a) a video game
   (b) landscaping
   (c) a sofa
   (d) an oil change for a car

17. Suppose that in order to relieve traffic congestion, user charges are imposed on drivers using urban expressways. This would be a response to what economic problem?

   (a) spillover benefits
   (b) spillover costs
   (c) the free-rider problem
   (d) inequitable income distribution

18. Public goods differ from private goods in that public goods are:

   (a) divisible
   (b) subject to the exclusion principle
   (c) not subject to the free-rider problem
   (d) *not* divisible and *not* subject to the exclusion principle

19. Quasi-public goods are goods and services:

   (a) to which the exclusion principle could be applied
   (b) that have large spillover benefits
   (c) that private producers would overproduce
   (d) that have large spillover benefits, and to which the exclusion principle could be applied

20. If the market system tends to overallocate resources to the production of good X:

   (a) good X could be a public good
   (b) good X could involve spillover benefits
   (c) good X could involve spillover costs
   (d) good X could be prone to the free-rider problem

21. Government expenditures, taxes, and transfer payments in the circular flow affect:

   (a) the distribution of income
   (b) the allocation of resources
   (c) the level of economic activity

   (d) all of the above

22. What is an important reason for the decrease in the percentage of Canadian workers employed in agriculture?

   (a) Canada's demand for food has decreased because we get food from other countries
   (b) fewer Canadians want to be in farming
   (c) technological improvements have reduced the need for labour in agriculture
   (d) all of the above

■ **DISCUSSION QUESTIONS**

1. List the Four Fundamental Questions that all economies must answer. Which of these questions does the market system answer, and how so?

2. What property rights does the owner of a motor vehicle have? What restrictions or limits are there on those rights, and why do these restrictions exist? Do these restrictions increase or decrease the value of owning a vehicle?

3. How does the pursuit of self-interest by all economic units in the market system model ultimately benefit society? Give an example of a choice you make that is in your self-interest, but not selfish.

4. At one time the world price of oil was expected to hit $100 a barrel by the 1990s. If so, the Canadian economy would presumably have allocated more resources to oil production. How would market forces have produced such a result? How would market forces have changed the gasoline consumption habits of Canadian households?

5. What are the advantages of "indirect" or "roundabout" production?

6. In order for a market to be competitive, why must there be many buyers and many sellers? What might be some consequences if there are few buyers or few sellers?

7. How does an economy benefit from specialization and division of labour?

8. What are the disadvantages of barter, and how does money overcome these disadvantages?

9. What is "market failure" and what are the two major kinds of such failures?

10. If the person living down the hall from you plays her music very loudly, is there a spillover cost or spillover benefit? If a homeowner builds an extra high fence between his house and his neighbours', is there a spillover cost or spillover benefit?

11. Based on ideas from this chapter, what is the case for government supporting needle exchange programs for intravenous drug users?

12. Discuss how the concepts of spillover effects and public goods might apply to the Internet?

13. How are private goods different from public goods? Why does there tend to be underallocation of resources to public goods in the absence of government intervention?

14. What basic method does government employ in Canada to reallocate resources away from the production of private goods and toward the production of public goods?

■ **ANSWERS**

FILL-IN QUESTIONS

1. private property

2. enterprise, choice

3. increase, price; self-interest

4. private property; freedom of enterprise and choice; self-interest; markets and prices; competition; limited, but active government

5. roundabout

6. "invisible hand," social (or public)

7. what goods and services will be produced?; how will the goods and services be produced?; who will get the goods and service?; how will the system accommodate change?

8. making use of differences in ability, fostering learning by doing, saving time

9. interdependent, trade

10. money

11. currencies

12. coincidence

13. market; spillover, public

14. third; externalities

15. specific taxes, regulations

16. underallocated

17. subsidies, consumers, producers

18. exclusion; free-rider

19. quasipublic

20. subsidies, transfer payments

PROBLEMS AND PROJECTS

1. (a) Some students currently willing and able to arrive early or to spend time hunting for a spot may be unwilling to pay for a spot, whereas others may be willing and able to pay; (b) differences in availability of money and time; (c) students who place a low value on parking would have incentive to walk, bus, carpool; firms seeking profit would have more incentive to provide near campus parking for a fee.

2. (a) B at $55; (b) A at $66; (c) decrease, 13, 8.

3. (a) increased scarcity of electricity; (b) to consume less, for instance by economizing on energy use or switching to alternate sources; and to produce more; (c) there would be electric power available, and the available amount would be allocated to highest valued uses, thus minimizing the effects of increased scarcity.

4. (a) If you could not use a good grade to help you get jobs, scholarships, etc. you may have less incentive to study; (b) If you get a better mark on an exam, your share of that improved mark would be very small, so you would have less incentive to study; (c) Restricted property rights in grades are probably justified because if students could sell their grades to other people then good grades would no longer indicate what they are supposed to, and would therefore no longer be meaningful or valuable.

5. (a) a: business firms, b: resource markets, c: government, d: households, e: product markets; (b) 1: businesses pay costs for resources that become money income for households, 2: households provide resources to businesses, 3: household expenditures become receipts for businesses, 4: businesses provide goods and services to households, 5: government spends money in product market, 6: government receives goods and services from product market, 7: government spends money in resource market, 8: government receives resources from resource market, 9: government provides goods and services to households, 10: government provides goods and services to businesses, 11: businesses pay net taxes to government, 12: households pay net taxes to government; (c) (1) 9, 10, 11.

6. (a) 2: neighbours suffer cost; (b) 3: one person being vaccinated reduces the risk of disease for other people, too; (c) 1: everybody can listen to a radio broadcast.

TRUE-FALSE

1. F You might consider it in your self-interest to help other people, or donate to charities
2. F For example, there are limits on how you can operate your vehicle, or on what you can build on your land
3. F No seller has significant influence
4. F Most prices are set mainly by market forces
5. T The prospect of earning royalties is an incentive to produce
6. T
7. F Some individuals fare poorly under a market system, particularly those who have few resources
8. T Those with more resources can earn higher incomes and have more spending power
9. T Adam Smith had this insight
10. T For example, when machine is built and used in a factory
11. T
12. T
13. F Person A must want to acquire what person B is offering to trade, and B must want to acquire what A has to offer
14. F The market offers no guarantees of equitability
15. F The "invisible hand" refers to market forces
16. T
17. T
18. F Such a tax would raise the marginal cost of production and decrease supply
19. F Many goods provided by government free of charge are not public goods
20. T Because the exclusion principle does not apply

MULTIPLE-CHOICE

1. (d) There is no central planning in the market system
2. (c) Socially beneficial results stem from self-interested behaviour, without any central control
3. (a) Less demand for the good means less demand and lower price for resources used in producing the good
4. (d)
5. (a) All of the others are human-made resources designed to help produce other things
6. (d) There is no assumption that government or any public agency would be involved
7. (d) We become more experienced, and therefore more efficient, at doing those tasks in which we specialize
8. (d) Price haggling is "bargaining"
9. (a) When we specialize we must trade, but it need not be by the inefficient barter system
10. (c) The market system often produces extreme discrepancies in incomes that do not seem equitable
11. (a)
12. (b) Many modern economies have a great deal of government interference
13. (d) In his book *The Wealth of Nations*
14. (b) Too little is produced because the producer will not take into account some of the benefits of the good
15. (b) Banning the product would reduce output to zero; this would often be below the optimal amount
16. (b) Landscaping provides benefits not only for the owner of the garden, but also for neighbours and passersby
17. (b) Each driver adds to the highway congestion, thereby slowing down other drivers and imposing time costs on them
18. (d) They cannot be divided into small units and sold to individuals, and individuals who do not pay cannot be excluded from using them
19. (d) Both aspects of this description are necessary
20. (c) All of the others are prone to underproduction
21. (d) Check the circular flow diagram
22. (c) Many Canadians who would prefer to farm have moved to other sectors because technological change has reduced the demand for labour in agriculture

CHAPTER 5

Canada in the Global Economy

As members of the global economy, Canadian consumers depend on many goods produced in other nations, and many Canadian workers and businesses depend on selling goods in foreign markets. In addition to these flows of goods and services, resources, information, technology, and financial capital flow back and forth across international borders. Why does international trade occur, and how does trade benefit us? These are fundamental questions of this chapter.

Canada's imports and exports have mushroomed in recent years. Today our exports and imports each total nearly 40% of our economic activity. We trade many different products, and many of our major exports are also our major imports (e.g., automotive products, machinery and equipment, and industrial goods and materials). The United States is our most important trading partner, and we trade mainly with industrialized countries. World trade has increased because of improved technologies for transportation and communications, and because of reductions in tariffs and other trade barriers. The number of important players in world trade has increased, especially among the newly industrializing Asian nations, including China.

The circular flow model is easily amended to add the "rest of the world" sector to the product market. Export flows are paid for by foreign expenditures, and import flows are paid for by expenditures from the domestic economy. From this diagram it is easy to understand how instability in foreign economies can introduce instability into the Canadian economy, and vice versa.

The principle of comparative advantage shows the reason that nations trade. In the simplest scenario, there are two nations, each producing two goods at constant opportunity cost ratios. If the opportunity costs differ between the two nations, each should specialize in producing that good for which their domestic opportunity cost is below the other nation's. If both nations follow this rule, both goods will be produced and traded, and both nations can end up with more output than they could produce if they remained self-sufficient. Perhaps surprisingly, all nations can reap these benefits from trade, even nations that are absolutely less productive than their trading partners.

In reality, nations usually do not barter goods with one another, as represented in the simplified scenario of the comparative advantage model. Instead, international trade is conducted through monetary transactions between households and firms in different countries acting as buyers and sellers. Such transactions require a foreign exchange market where currencies may be traded. The exchange rate, or equilibrium price of one currency in terms of another, is determined by the supply and the demand for the currency. The basic principles of supply and demand that you studied in Chapter 3 apply to foreign exchange markets also. Shifts in the supply or demand for a currency will change its price. If the currency's price rises (falls) in terms of another currency it has appreciated (depreciated) relative to the other currency.

In spite of important benefits from specialization and international trade, many nations try to limit trade. The major barriers to world trade are: (1) protective tariffs, (2) import quotas, (3) non-tariff barriers, and (4) export subsidies. So why do governments seek to reduce imports and/or increase exports? One reason may be the mistaken yet common belief that exports are beneficial because they create jobs, whereas imports are harmful because they destroy jobs at home. Another explanation is found by examining who gains and who loses from policies that limit trade. Domestic firms facing tough competition from imports often lobby governments to impose tariffs or quotas. Governments sometimes give in to such demands because the consumers who are hurt by higher prices resulting from the tariff bear costs that are relatively obscure and dispersed. Therefore, government may enjoy more political success by imposing tariffs and quotas than by supporting free trade.

Protectionist measures taken by one nation may lead other nations that lose exports to retaliate with protectionist measures of their own. In order to prevent such conflicts and to reduce existing trade barriers, various multilateral trade agreements and free trade zones have evolved. The most important agreements are the General Agreement on Tariffs and Trade (GATT), and its successor, the World Trade Organization (WTO). Important free trade zones include the European Union (EU) and the North American Free Trade Agreement (NAFTA). These agreements enable member nations to enjoy freer trade with other member nations, but critics are concerned that free trade policies may undermine national sovereignty, for instance by enabling corporations to circumvent national labour and environmental laws. Most critics and proponents do agree that freer trade increases competition and brings pressure to restructure the economy to better compete on the basis of comparative advantage.

■ CHAPTER LEARNING OBJECTIVES

In this chapter you will learn:

☐ That trade is crucial to Canada's economic well-being.
☐ The importance of specialization and comparative advantage in international trade.
☐ How the value of a currency is established on foreign exchange markets.
☐ The economic cost of trade barriers.
☐ Multilateral trade agreements and free trade zones.

■ CHAPTER OUTLINE

1. The volume of international trade is now so large, and national economies so interdependent, that the world can be thought of as a "global economy."

2. Compared to most other nations, Canada relies relatively heavily on trade.
   (a) The market in Canada is too limited to allow for efficient production of the full range of goods and services, so we import many goods, and export others to pay for the imports.
   (b) Exports and imports are nearly 40% of our national output.
   (c) The bulk of Canada's trade is with other industrialized nations, including over 80% with the United States.
   (d) In 1997, Canada's three major exports, in order, were automotive products, machinery and equipment, and industrial goods and materials. Our three major imports, in order, were the same.

3. Several factors have facilitated rapid growth of world trade since World War II:
   (a) improvements in transportation technology,
   (b) improvements in communications technology,
   (c) general decline in tariffs

4. In sheer volume of trade, the world's major players are the United States, Japan, and Western Europe. Despite recent problems, a number of Asian nations are becoming more important in world trade: Hong Kong, Singapore, South Korea, Taiwan, and China. Eastern European countries are also building trading relationships.

5. The circular flow model reflects the international trade dimension once we add the "rest of the world" box. This box is connected to the Canadian product market through flows of imports and exports, and the Canadian and foreign expenditures on these goods.

6. Specialization and trade among economic units (individuals, firms, provinces, regions, or nations) are based on the principle of comparative advantage. Specialization and trade increase productivity and output. Adam Smith wrote about this in 1776, and the idea was fully explained by David Ricardo in the early 1800s.

7. The basic principle of comparative advantage is shown with an example of two individuals able to do two jobs, or with an example of two nations producing two goods.
   (a) A chartered accountant (CA) needing her house painted can paint it herself, or can hire a house painter. The CA will try to minimize her opportunity cost. By comparative advantage, even if the CA can do the job in less time than the painter can, if the CA incurs a lower opportunity cost by hiring the painter, the CA will specialize in

accounting. Likewise, the painter will specialize in painting, and hire a CA to prepare his tax return, if this minimizes his opportunity costs.

(b) Mexico and Canada both can produce corn and soybeans. Assuming each nation has a constant opportunity cost ratio, then each nation has the lower opportunity cost — and therefore comparative advantage — in producing one of the two goods. By specializing in producing one good, each nation can trade for the other nation's good. The terms of trade, or ratio at which one good is traded for another, lies between the cost ratios for the two nations.

(c) When two nations specialize and trade according to their comparative advantage, both nations can consume more of both goods than their domestic production possibilities curves would permit. This reduces the scarcity problem.

8. National currencies are traded in highly competitive foreign exchange markets. Such markets establish the exchange rates — the rates at which various national currencies are traded for one another. Exchange rates link all domestic prices with all foreign prices.

9. Supply and demand for a currency determine its exchange rate. Shifts in the supply and demand cause exchange rate appreciation or depreciation.

(a) Increased demand or decreased supply for a currency will cause it to appreciate, or rise in price as measured in other currencies.

(b) Decreased demand or increased supply for a currency will cause it to depreciate, or fall in price as measured in other currencies.

10. Governments implement protectionist policies, that is, policies to restrict trade between nations:

(a) Such policies include protective tariffs, import quotas, non-tariff barriers, and export subsidies.

(b) Trade restrictions may be imposed because of misunderstanding the gains from trade, or because governments have strong political incentives to protect domestic businesses from international competition.

(c) Regardless of the government's motives, restrictive trade policies usually impose costs that outweigh the benefits. Consumers pay higher prices, exporters have less access to foreign markets, and the nation makes less efficient use of its resources.

11. To fight protectionism and promote trade, Canada and many other nations have signed arrangements to reduce tariffs, and to create free trade zones.

12. Begun in 1947, the General Agreement on Tariffs and Trade (GATT) has been the most comprehensive forum for reducing tariffs on a multilateral basis. The GATT now has 128 member nations, and has been the vehicle for eight rounds of negotiations to reduce trade barriers. Through the Uruguay Round, major changes are being phased in between 1995 and 2005: reductions in thousands of tariffs and quotas, inclusion of services, reductions in farm subsidies, and protection of intellectual property.

13. The Uruguay Round agreement also established the World Trade Organization (WTO) as a body to oversee trade agreements among member nations and rule on disputes among them.

14. The European Union (EU) is a regional free-trade zone, or trade bloc that has:

(a) abolished tariffs between EU countries, enabled free movement of labour and capital within the EU, and developed some common economic policies.

(b) increased trade and efficiency of production for nations in the bloc, but has also created frictions with nonmember nations.

(c) established a common currency – the euro.

15. In 1989 Canada and the United States signed the Free Trade Agreement (FTA). In 1993 the bloc formed by the FTA was extended to include Mexico under the North American Free Trade Agreement (NAFTA). Fears that Canadian jobs would be lost to Mexico where wages are low and the workplace is less regulated seem to have been too pessimistic. Employment in Canada has grown significantly since the passage of NAFTA.

16. Globalization of trade intensifies competition for Canadian producers. Many succeed by keeping costs low, using new technology, etc. to retain market shares in Canada and to capture new markets abroad. Other firms are unable to compete and have gone out of business. Many of the unsuccessful firms previously enjoyed long periods of protection from imports (via tariffs or quotas). Note also that the increased competition tends to benefit consumers by leading to lower prices.

■ TERMS AND CONCEPTS

multinational corpora-
tions
comparative advantage
terms of trade
foreign exchange mar-
ket
exchange rate
depreciation (of the
dollar)
appreciation (of the
dollar)
protective tariff
import quota
non-tariff barrier

export subsidies
**General Agreement
on Trade and Tar-
iffs (GATT)
World Trade Organi-
zation (WTO)
European Union (EU)
trade bloc
euro
North American Free
Trade Agreement
(NAFTA)**

■ HINTS AND TIPS

1. Finding which producer of a good has the comparative advantage depends on being able to compare opportunity costs across producers. If the data on production possibilities reflect constant costs, opportunity costs can be found easily by dividing a producer's maximum outputs of each of the two goods. For example, suppose Norway's maximum outputs are 100 fish or 20 tables. What is the cost of 1 table? Divide the number of tables into the number of fish: 100 fish/20 tables = 5 fish per table. What is the cost of 1 fish? Divide the number of fish into the number of tables: 20 tables/100 fish = 1/5 table per fish.

2. Foreign exchange rates are confusing because they can be expressed in two ways. Is Canada's exchange rate the amount of foreign currency that one Canadian dollar can buy, or the amount in Canadian dollars needed to buy one unit of foreign currency? Surprisingly, either form is correct, as long as you specify which one you are using. For example, our exchange rate with Mexico could be 5 pesos for $1, or $0.20 for 1 peso. These are reciprocal expressions of exactly the same rate! Always be clear on which form of the exchange rate you are using.

■ FILL-IN QUESTIONS

1. A nation is more likely to rely on international trade the more (diversified, limited) _____ its resource base is and the (larger, smaller) _____ its domestic market is.

2. In recent decades Canada's trade has (increased, decreased) _____ in absolute terms, and _____ as a percentage of our national income. Canada trades mainly with (developing, developed) _____ nations. Our major trading partner is _____.

3. Factors that have facilitated growth in trade since World War II include improvements in _____ and _____ technology, and a general decline in _____.

4. In the circular flow model, imports and exports are added as flows to the _____ market. Canadian expenditures pay for (exports, imports) _____, and foreign expenditures pay for _____.

5. If Nigeria can produce 10 kg of coffee at a cost of 1 barrel of oil, and Kenya can produce 25 kg of coffee at a cost of 1 barrel of oil, then _____ has the lower cost for producing oil, and _____ has the lower cost of producing coffee. The comparative advantage for oil lies with _____ and for coffee lies with _____.

6. The amount of one product that a nation must export in order to import one unit of another product is the _____.

7. When the dollar price of foreign currency increases, the dollar has (appreciated, depreciated) _____, while foreign currency has _____.

8. In the market for Japanese yen, an increase in the (demand for, supply of) _____ yen will decrease the dollar price of yen, while an increase in the _____ yen will increase the dollar price of yen. If the dollar price of yen increases, then Japanese goods imported into Canada will be (more, less) _____ expensive to Canadians, while Canadian goods exported to Japan will be _____ expensive for Japanese.

9. The major government policies that restrict trade include protective _____, import _____, _____ barriers, and _____ subsidies.

10. Governments may mistakenly intervene in trade with other nations because they mistakenly think of

(exports, imports) _____ as helpful, and _____ as harmful for their own economy.

11. Tariffs and quotas (benefit, cost) _____ domestic firms and their employees in the protected industries but _____ domestic consumers of their products in the form of (lower, higher) _____ prices than would exist if there were free trade.

12. The three cardinal principles established in the GATT are:
   (a) _____, _____ treatment for all member nations;
   (b) reduction of _____ by multilateral negotiations; and
   (c) the elimination of import _____.

13. The trade bloc first formed as the Common Market in 1958 is now known as the _____. The specific aims of the Common Market were to abolish tariffs and quotas among (member, non-member) _____ nations, to establish common tariffs on goods imported from _____ nations, to permit free movement of capital and _____ within the Common Market nations, and to adopt other common policies.

14. The FTA joined Canada in a trade bloc with _____ in the year _____. Under the name NAFTA, the FTA was extended in the year _____, when _____ joined the bloc.

- **PROBLEMS AND PROJECTS**

1. Julius and Murray are tailors. Their production possibilities tables for trousers and jackets are given below. Initially they work independently, with Julius choosing production alternative D, and Murray choosing E from his alternatives.

JULIUS: Production Possibilities Table

Product	Production Alternative					
	A	B	C	D	E	F
Trousers	75	60	45	30	15	0
Jackets	0	10	20	30	40	50

MURRAY: Production Possibilities Table

Product	Production Alternative						
	A	B	C	D	E	F	G
Trousers	60	50	40	30	20	10	0
Jackets	0	5	10	15	20	25	30

(a) For Julius 1 pair of trousers costs _____ jackets, and 1 jacket costs _____ pairs of trousers.
(b) For Murray 1 pair of trousers costs _____ jackets, and 1 jacket costs _____ pairs of trousers.
(c) The comparative advantage in making trousers lies with _____ because his opportunity cost is (lower, higher) _____. The comparative advantage in making jackets lies with _____ because his opportunity cost is (lower, higher) _____.
(d) If Julius and Murray form a partnership, Julius should specialize in making _____, and Murray should specialize in _____.
(e) Working independently Julius and Murray would produce a total of 50 pairs of trousers and 50 jackets. If each specializes fully, their combined output will be _____ pairs of trousers, and _____ jackets. Thus, the gain from specialization is _____ pairs of trousers and _____ jackets.

2. Venezuela and Costa Rica have the production possibilities tables shown below.
(a) Find the opportunity costs:
   Venezuela: 1 apple costs _____
        1 banana costs _____
   Costa Rica: 1 apple costs _____
        1 banana costs _____
(b) Determine which country has the comparative advantage in each good:
   Apples: _____ Bananas: _____

VENEZUELA: Production Possibilities Table

Product	Production Alternative					
	A	B	C	D	E	F
Apples	40	32	24	16	8	0
Bananas	0	4	8	12	16	20

COSTA RICA: Production Possibilities Table

Product	Production Alternative					
	A	B	C	D	E	F
Apples	75	60	45	30	15	0
Bananas	0	5	10	15	20	25

(c) From the information given we cannot determine specifically what the terms of trade will be. However, the terms of trade must be greater than _____ apples per banana, and less than _____ apples per banana.
(d) Suppose that each nation would choose production alternative C if specialization and trade were impossible. The combined production

in the two countries would be _____ apples and _____ bananas.

(e) If each nation specializes completely according to comparative advantage, their combined production will be _____ apples and _____ bananas.

(f) Their combined gains from specialization will be _____ apples and _____ bananas.

(g) Suppose that the nations specialize and then agree to trade 25 apples for 10 bananas. This trade will leave Venezuela consuming _____ apples and _____ bananas. Costa Rica will consume _____ apples and _____ bananas.

(h) Compared to production alternative C, this leaves Venezuela with a gain of _____ apples and _____ bananas. Compared to production alternative C, this leaves Costa Rica with a gain of _____ apples and _____ bananas.

3. The table below shows four different currencies and how much of each can be purchased with 1 Canadian dollar.

(a) In the blanks indicate whether the Canadian dollar appreciated (A) or depreciated (D) against these currencies from Year 1 to Year 2.

Currency per Canadian $				
Country	Currency	Year 1	Year 2	A or D
France	Franc	4.7	4.6	_____
Germany	Mark	1.40	1.44	_____
China	Renminbi	5.2	5.3	_____
Japan	Yen	80	82	_____

(b) Compute the amount of Canadian currency one would have to exchange to get 100 units of each of the four foreign currencies. Use Year 1 exchange rates.

100 Francs = $ _____

100 Marks = $ _____

100 Renminbi = $ _____

100 Yen = $ _____

■ **TRUE-FALSE**

Circle T if the statement is true, F if it is false.

1. Canada is completely dependent on other nations for many products that we do not produce domestically. **T F**

2. No nation in the world has a higher percentage of GDP represented by exports and imports than Canada does. **T F**

3. The first economists to explain the principle of comparative advantage were Adam Smith and David Ricardo. **T F**

4. The principle of comparative advantage applies just as well to individuals or regions as it does to nations. **T F**

5. If two nations produce only coal and lumber, one of the nations could have the comparative advantage over the other in both coal and lumber. **T F**

6. If two nations have identical cost conditions for producing two goods, neither nation will have a comparative advantage. **T F**

7. A nation that has resources that are more productive in every good than another nation's resources will be unable to gain by trading with the less productive nation. **T F**

8. Specialization and trade according to comparative advantage will enable a nation to have combinations of goods that lie outside the nation's production possibility curve. **T F**

9. In the foreign exchange market graph, if the British pound price of Japanese yen is plotted on the vertical axis, on the horizontal axis must be the quantity of British pounds. **T F**

10. An increase in incomes of Canadian households would tend to increase the supply of Canadian dollars in the exchange market. **T F**

11. If the supply of Canadian dollars in the foreign exchange market increases, the Canadian dollar will appreciate relative to foreign currencies, *ceteris paribus*. **T F**

12. If the U.S. dollar price of the Canadian dollar is $0.70, then the Canadian dollar price of the U.S. dollar must be $1.30. **T F**

13. An appreciation of the Canadian dollar will make our imports less expensive to Canadian consumers, and our exports more expensive to foreign consumers. **T F**

14. Export subsidies are government payments to domestic producers to encourage them to export more. **T F**

15. The formation of a trade bloc encourages efficiency in production because access to larger markets enables producers to benefit from large-scale production. **T F**

16. The NAFTA has benefited some Canadian firms and has harmed others. **T F**

17. The NAFTA includes Canada, the United States, Mexico, and some Central American nations. **T F**

18. The EU's plans call for the euro to be the only currency to be accepted for payment by July 1, 2002. **T F**

■ **MULTIPLE-CHOICE**

Circle the letter that corresponds to the best answer.

1. Imports and exports amounted to roughly what fraction of Canada's GDP?
- **(a)** 10%
- **(b)** 15%
- **(c)** 25%
- **(d)** 40%

2. Based on the data in the text, which sector represents the largest percentage of Canadian exports?
- **(a)** agricultural products
- **(b)** automotive products
- **(c)** energy products
- **(d)** forest products

3. Based on recent data in the text, which sector represents the largest percentage of Canadian imports?
- **(a)** agricultural products
- **(b)** automotive products
- **(c)** consumer products
- **(d)** machinery and equipment

Questions 4 through 7 are based on the data in the table that shows maximum production levels for the regions of Heath and Cliff, both of which have constant costs of production, and are able to trade with one another.

Heath		Cliff	
Wool	Peat	Wool	Peat
100	20	120	40

4. In Heath, the domestic opportunity cost of:
- **(a)** 1 wool is 5 peat
- **(b)** 1 wool is 1/5 peat
- **(c)** 1 wool is 1.2 wool
- **(d)** 1 peat is 1/5 wool

5. In Cliff, the domestic opportunity cost of:
- **(a)** 1 peat is 3 wool
- **(b)** 1 peat is 2 peat
- **(c)** 1 wool is 3 peat
- **(d)** 1 peat is 1/3 wool

6. Which of the following statements is **not** true?
- **(a)** Heath has the comparative advantage in wool
- **(b)** Cliff should specialize in peat
- **(c)** Heath and Cliff could both gain from trading with one another
- **(d)** Heath has the comparative advantage in both wool and peat

7. The terms of trade will be:
- **(a)** more than 3 wool for 1 peat
- **(b)** fewer than 5 wool for 1 peat
- **(c)** between 3 and 5 wool for 1 peat
- **(d)** not between 3 and 5 wool for 1 peat

8. If Canada can produce 1 bottle of syrup at a cost of 2 cigars, and Cuba can produce 1 bottle of syrup at a cost of 6 cigars, what would be a mutually beneficial term of trade:
- **(a)** 2 cigars per 1 syrup
- **(b)** 3 cigars per 1 syrup
- **(c)** 6 cigars per 1 syrup
- **(d)** 8 cigars per 1 syrup

9. The foreign exchange market is a market for:
- **(a)** imports and exports
- **(b)** shares in multinational corporations
- **(c)** bonds sold by foreign government
- **(d)** currencies

10. If the equilibrium exchange rate changes so that the dollar price of Japanese yen increases:
- **(a)** the dollar has appreciated
- **(b)** the yen has depreciated

(c) Canadians can now buy more Japanese goods
(d) Japanese can now buy more Canadian goods

11. If the United States begins to demand more Mexican goods:
(a) the demand for the peso will increase, causing the peso to appreciate
(b) the demand for the peso will increase, causing the peso to depreciate
(c) the supply of U.S. dollars will decrease, causing the dollar to appreciate
(d) the supply of U.S. dollars will decrease, causing the dollar to depreciate

12. Which of the following is designed to restrict trade?
(a) export subsidies
(b) NAFTA
(c) GATT
(d) import quotas

13. If Canada imposes more stringent product packaging standards on imported food than on domestically produced food, this could be an example of:
(a) an import tariff
(b) a non-tariff barrier
(c) an import quota
(d) an export subsidy

14. Why do governments often restrict international trade?
(a) to expand their nation's production possibilities
(b) to protect domestic industries from foreign competition
(c) to encourage efficiency in production
(d) to benefit consumers

15. One important outcome of the Uruguay Round of the GATT was:
(a) elimination of services from the agreement
(b) greater restrictions on patents and copyrights
(c) increasing tariffs on manufactured products
(d) reductions in agricultural subsidies

16. The European Common Market:
(a) helped to abolish tariffs and import quotas among its members

(b) aimed for the eventual free movement of capital and labour within the member nations
(c) imposed common tariffs on products imported from countries outside the Common Market
(d) did all of the above

17. One potential problem with the European Union is that:
(a) a free flow of labour and capital within the EU is likely to create mass unemployment
(b) economies of large-scale production will result in higher consumer prices
(c) trade with nonmember nations may diminish
(d) all of the above

18. A trade bloc is the same thing as a:
(a) non-tariff barrier
(b) import quota
(c) free-trade zone
(d) trade restriction

19. For Canada, one advantage of NAFTA is:
(a) higher prices for consumer goods
(b) access for Canadian producers to larger markets
(c) the opportunity to reduce our reliance on imports
(d) more low-wage job opportunities for Canadians

20. Which Canadian firms are best able to compete effectively under a system of freer world trade?
(a) firms that were previously protected by tariffs and quotas
(b) firms in industries where Canada has a comparative advantage
(c) firms that had monopoly power in the Canadian market
(d) very few Canadian firms will be able to compete

■ **DISCUSSION QUESTIONS**

1. What are Canada's principal exports and imports? Why does Canada trade so much with the United States? Why is international trade more important to the Canadian economy than to the U.S. economy?

2. What are some factors contributing to the growth in international trade since World War II?

3. Sketch how the international trade component can be built into the circular flow model.

4. Explain how comparative costs determine which producer has the comparative advantage. What determines the terms of trade? What is the gain that results from specialization and trade according to comparative advantage?

5. Suppose that Dr. Ocula is an outstanding eye surgeon with good enough hand-eye coordination that he keyboards faster than anyone else in town. Use the principle of comparative advantage to explain why he hires someone else to do the word-processing in his office, even though he could do it faster himself.

6. How might an appreciation of the value of the Canadian dollar relative to the American dollar depress the Canadian economy? Which Canadians would be harmed, and which would benefit?

7. What are the major types of trade barriers, and how do they work to restrict international trade?

8. Hypothetically, suppose that Canada has a 20% import tariff on shoelaces. Also suppose that there are only about twenty manufacturers of shoelaces in Canada. If the tariff raises shoelace prices in Canada by about 25 cents a pair, how much would this tariff cost you each year? Estimate the annual benefit of the tariff to each Canadian manufacturer. Do you know whether in fact there is a shoelace tariff? Do you think that Canadian shoelace manufacturers know? How do you explain the difference in the knowledge, and how does this help explain why the government might have implemented this tariff?

9. What does Canada gain from participating in GATT? Which kinds of Canadian industries would be most likely to support the GATT initiatives? And which would be most likely to oppose them?

10. Is it possible that Canada, the United States, and Mexico can all gain from the NAFTA? If so, how?

11. How will the adoption of the euro as a common currency in the EU help member countries? Can you see any problems that the adoption of the euro might create?

12. "Canadian firms cannot compete in the global economy because wages are too high in Canada." Discuss this claim.

■ ANSWERS

FILL-IN QUESTIONS

1. limited, smaller

2. increased, increased; developed; United States

3. transportation, communications, tariffs (trade barriers),

4. product; imports, exports

5. Nigeria, Kenya; Nigeria, Kenya

6. terms of trade

7. depreciated, appreciated

8. supply of, demand for; more, less

9. tariffs, quotas, non-tariff, export

10. exports, imports

11. benefit, cost, higher

12. equal or non-discriminatory; tariffs; quotas

13. European Union; member, nonmember, labour

14. United States, 1989; 1993, Mexico

PROBLEMS AND PROJECTS

1. (a) 2/3, 1 1/2; (b) 1/2, 2; (c) Murray, lower, Julius, lower; (d) jackets, trousers; (e) 60, 50; 10, 0

2. (a) 1/2 banana, 2 apples, 1/3 banana, 3 apples; (b) Costa Rica, Venezuela; (c) 2, 3; (d) 69, 18; (e) 75, 20; (f) 6, 2; (g) 25, 10, 50, 10; (h) 1, 2, 5, 0

3. (a) D, A, A, A; (b) 21.28, 71.43, 1.25

TRUE-FALSE

1. T   for many goods we import all we consume
2. F   the Netherlands has a higher percentage
3. T
4. T   opportunity cost ratios can differ between individuals or regions
5. F   if there is comparative advantage, each nation will have the advantage in one of the two goods

6. T   so there is no gain to specialization and trade
7. F   no nation has a lower opportunity cost ratio for all goods
8. T   because imported goods can be acquired for an opportunity cost lower than the domestic production cost
9. F   quantity of yen should be on the horizontal
10. T   Canadians increase their imports
11. F   the Canadian dollar will depreciate
12. F   the reciprocal of .70 is 1.43
13. T
14. T
15. T   costs per unit are lower when more units can be sold
16. T   some gained market share and profits while others lost
17. F   only Canada, the U.S., and Mexico
18. T

MULTIPLE-CHOICE

1. (d)
2. (b)
3. (b)
4. (b)   100W = 20P, therefore 1W = 0.2P
5. (a)   120W = 40P, therefore 3W = 1P
6. (d)   Heath's opportunity cost is lower than Cliff's for peat, but not for wool
7. (c)   only this range is between the opportunity cost ratios in both regions
8. (b)   any of the other choices benefit only one of the two nations
9. (d)
10. (d)   a given number of yen can now buy more dollars, and therefore more goods in Canada
11. (a)   higher demand for pesos means a higher price (appreciation) for the peso
12. (d)   the others are meant to promote trade
13. (b)   by raising costs for importers to get goods into Canada
14. (b)   production, efficiency, and benefits to consumers all suffer
15. (d)
16. (d)
17. (c)   unemployment and prices are likely to fall
18. (c)   the EU is an example
19. (b)   larger markets enable producers to lower their per unit production costs
20. (b)   this is the central lesson of the principle of comparative advantage

CHAPTER 6

Supply and Demand: Elasticities and Government-Set Prices

This chapter extends some of the basic tools of demand and supply from Chapter 3, and applies the tools to the analysis of some important real world situations. If you feel less than confident with the material from Chapter 3, you should review that chapter now.

The law of demand states that when price rises, quantity demanded will fall, *ceteris paribus*, but it does not tell us by how much it will fall. The concept of price elasticity of demand is a numerical measure of the degree of responsiveness of quantity demanded to price changes. You must understand: (1) what elasticity measures; (2) how the price elasticity formula works; (3) how to interpret elasticity coefficient values; (4) how total revenue varies according to elasticity; (5) the determinants of this elasticity; and (6) how to apply the concept to economic questions.

Four applications show the practical significance of price elasticity of demand. First, because demand for farm products is highly inelastic, total farm incomes tend to be lower when there are bumper crops. Second, we find that in order to maximize their revenues governments usually put taxes on commodities with inelastic demand (such as cigarettes and gasoline). Third, we learn that the effects of decriminalizing illegal drugs would depend on the elasticity of demand; if demand is inelastic the price would drop sharply, usage would not increase very much. On the other hand, if the demand is elastic, there could be sharp increases in usage, in street crime, and many associated problems. Fourth, we find that the impact of the minimum wage law on those workers who are affected depends crucially on the price elasticity of demand for their labour.

The next section deals with other elasticities. Price elasticity of supply measures responsiveness of quantity supplied to price changes. Here again it is important to distinguish between elastic and inelastic, and to understand the role of time in determining the elasticity. Next, the responsiveness of quantity demanded to changes in income is termed income elasticity of demand. The sign of this elasticity value indicates whether the good is normal or inferior. Finally, the responsiveness of quantity demanded to a change in the price of *another* good is called cross elasticity of demand. The sign of this value shows whether the two goods are substitutes or complements.

The chapter closes with some key supply and demand applications that utilize elasticity concepts. First is an analysis of the incidence of a tax levied on producers. The burden of the tax is shared by producers (who receive a lower net price) and by consumers (who pay a higher net price). The incidence, or sharing of the burden, depends on the price elasticity of the demand and of the supply.

The second application deals with price controls that prevent the market forces from establishing the equilibrium price, and therefore create a rationing problem. Price ceilings create shortages, and price floors create surpluses. Both create a host of unintended side effects, including black market transactions, as disappointed or frustrated market participants try to get around the intended effects of the price controls.

■ CHAPTER LEARNING OBJECTIVES

In this chapter you will learn:

☐ The concept of the price elasticity of demand and how to calculate it.

☐ The factors that determine the price elasticity of demand.

☐ The concept of the elasticity of supply and how to calculate it.

☐ The cross and income elasticity of demand and how to calculate them.

☐ To apply the concept of elasticity to various real-world situations.

■ **CHAPTER OUTLINE**

1. Price elasticity of demand is a measure of the responsiveness, or sensitivity, of the quantity demanded to changes in the price of the product. Elasticity is measured as a number that can be computed from data on two points on the same demand curve (or schedule).

(a)   The formula for the price elasticity of demand coefficient is:

E_d = % change in quantity demanded
        % change in price

(b)   The changes are measured in percentages so that the elasticity coefficient is not affected by the choice of units used to measure price and quantity. Use of percentages also facilitates comparisons between different goods.

(c)   From the law of demand, price and quantity demanded are inversely related, so the price elasticity of demand coefficient is technically a negative number. For convenience, we ignore the minus sign and refer simply to the absolute value of the coefficient.

(d)   Say the elasticity coefficient is 3. Then at this particular point on the demand curve a 1 percent change in price will cause a 3 percent change in quantity demanded. Because price and quantity demanded are inversely related, the price and quantity will change in opposite directions.

(e)   The elasticity coefficient can range in (absolute) value from 0 to infinity. A perfectly inelastic demand has a coefficient of 0, while a perfectly elastic demand has a coefficient of infinity. Demand is termed elastic (inelastic, unit elastic) when the elasticity coefficient is greater than (less than, equal to) 1.

(f)   To calculate the percentage changes in quantity and in price between two price-quantity combinations, use the average of the two quantities and the average of the two prices as the reference points. Using this "midpoints formula" avoids annoying ambiguity in the exact value of the elasticity coefficient.

(g)   Elasticity is not the same as slope. This can be shown with a straight-line demand that has the same slope at each point but a different elasticity at each point.

2. Suppliers' total revenue is the price per unit multiplied by the number of units sold. Whether total revenue rises or falls when price changes depends on the product's price elasticity of demand.

(a)   With an elastic (inelastic) demand the change in price and the change in total revenue go in opposite (the same) directions.

(b)   Where elasticity is one, total revenue is maximized. A small price change will lead to no change in revenue because quantity demanded changes by the same percentage as price. The price and quantity changes have exactly offsetting effects on total revenue.

3. There are four key determinants of price elasticity of demand. Demand for a product is more price elastic the more good substitutes the product has, the greater the proportion of the consumer's budget is spent on the good, if the good is a luxury good rather than a necessity, and (usually) the longer the period of time under consideration.

4. Price elasticity of demand is important in many public policy issues and in the setting of prices by the individual business firm.

(a)   Because demand for agricultural products is inelastic, bumper crops lead to huge price decreases and lower total revenues for producers.

(b)   Governments seeking increased revenues through sales taxes will tend to tax commodities with inelastic demands.

(c)   Whether legalizing drugs would be advisable depends in part on the elasticity of demand for heroin and crack cocaine, for example. If demand is inelastic, then lower prices caused by legalization will lead to little extra drug use, and likely a drop in crime, as addicts need less money to purchase drugs. On the other hand, if demand is elastic then there will be much more drug use and associated crime.

(d)   A minimum wage law increases wage rates, but also reduces the number of workers demanded, particularly teenage workers. However, research suggests that the demand for teenage workers is inelastic, so the total income earned by teenagers will rise because the gain in the hourly wage will be proportionally larger than the loss in jobs or hours worked.

5. Price elasticity of supply measures the sensitivity of quantity supplied to changes in the price of the product.
   (a) E_s = % change in quantity supplied / % change in price
   (b)   The elasticity of supply is greater the more time sellers have to adjust to a price change. Therefore we distinguish between elasticities in the market period, short run, and long run.
   (c)   The market period is the time immediately after a price change during which producers cannot respond by adjusting quantity supplied. If such a time exists for a particular seller, then elasticity of supply is zero.
   (d)   The short run is a period over which the plant capacity of individual producers and the industry is fixed. Because there is time to adjust the production by adjusting some resources, the supply curve has some elasticity.
   (e)   The long run is a period where producers have enough time to make all desired resource adjustments, and there is enough time for the number of producers to change. The elasticity of supply is greatest in the long run.

6. Cross elasticity of demand measures the sensitivity of quantity demanded for one product to changes in the price of another product.
   (a) xy % change in quantity demanded of good X / % change in price of good Y
   (b)   The sign of the cross elasticity determines the relationship between the two goods: if positive, the two goods are substitute goods; if negative, the two goods are complementary goods; if zero, the two goods are independent.

7. Income elasticity of demand measures the sensitivity of quantity demanded to changes in income.
   (a) E_i = % change in quantity demanded / % change in income
   (b)   A positive income elasticity designates a normal (or superior) good, whereas a negative income elasticity designates an inferior good.
   (c)   When incomes are growing across the economy, industries that produce normal goods with high income elasticities will tend to be growing faster than other industries.

8. A sales tax shifts the supply curve up by the amount of the tax, creating a new equilibrium at a higher price. The price increase is the consumer's tax burden. The after-tax price received by the producers is lower than the pre-tax price. The drop is the producer's burden.
   (a)   Given the supply, the more inelastic the demand, the larger the portion of the tax shifted to consumers.
   (b)   Given the demand, the more inelastic the supply, the larger the portion of the tax borne by producers.

9. Sometimes governments impose price ceilings when prices seem unfairly high to buyers, or impose price floors when prices seem unfairly low to sellers. Such controls prevent market forces from performing the rationing function.
   (a)   A price ceiling is a maximum legal price. It results in a shortage of the commodity; may bring about formal rationing by the government and a black market; and causes a misallocation of resources.
   (b)   A price floor is a minimum legal price. It results in a surplus of the commodity; may induce government to take measures to restrict the supply, increase demand, or purchase the surplus; and causes a misallocation of resources.
   (c)   Examples of price ceilings are: rent controls on apartments, proposed controls on gasoline prices, and proposed usury laws to limit credit card interest rates. Examples of price floors are agricultural price supports and minimum wage laws.
   (d)   Price controls invariably involve controversial tradeoffs because any benefits provided by the controls entail costs for some parties, and come at the expense of various unintended, undesirable side effects.

■   TERMS AND CONCEPTS

price elasticity of demand	price elasticity of supply
elastic demand	market period
inelastic demand	short run
unit elasticity	long run
perfectly inelastic demand	cross-elasticity
perfectly elastic demand	income elasticity of demand
total revenue	price ceiling
total-revenue test	black market
	price floor

■ HINTS AND TIPS

1. Most of the chapter deals with price elasticity of demand. Once you are fully comfortable with this elasticity you will have little trouble understanding the other elasticities. Any elasticity is a measure of responsiveness of some dependent variable to changes in an independent variable. The percentage change in the dependent variable is in the numerator, and the percentage change in the independent variable is in the denominator.

2. Do *not* judge elasticity from the slope of the demand curve (except for horizontal and vertical demand curves). Remember that even a constant slope demand curve has a different elasticity at each point. It is also useful to know that on a straight line demand curve the price elasticity equals one at the midpoint.

3. Master the total-revenue test for assessing price elasticity of demand. If you need only determine whether demand is elastic or inelastic, determining the direction of total revenue change can be easier than computing price elasticity. Also be aware that if you know whether elasticity is greater or less than one that you infer the direction of change in total revenue for a given price change.

■ FILL-IN QUESTIONS

1. Elasticity of demand is a measure of the responsiveness of quantity demanded to changes in the price of the good and can be computed from the formula: E_d = percentage change in __quantity__ / percentage change in __price__.

2. Suppose that when Duffers' Paradise Golf Club raises their green fees from $23 to $27 that the number of golfers falls from 105 per day to 95 per day. The change in quantity demanded is __10__ golfers. The average of the two quantities is __100__ golfers. Therefore the percentage change in quantity is (__10__ / __100__) x 100% = __10__%. The change in price is $ __4__ . The average of the two prices is $ __25__ . Therefore the percentage change in price is (__4__ / __25__) x 100% = __16__%. The elasticity coefficient is (__10__ %/ __16__ %) = __0.63__ .

3. If a relatively large rise in price results in a relatively small drop in quantity demanded, demand is __inelastic__ ; if a relatively small rise in price results in a relatively large drop in quantity demanded, demand is __elastic__ .

4. The price elasticity formula uses __percentage__ changes rather than __absolute__ changes in order to avoid the problem of an arbitrary choice of units, and in order to facilitate comparisons between different __goods__ .

5. To avoid ambiguous results when computing elasticity of demand, one uses the __average__ of the two quantities and the __average__ of the two prices when calculating the percentage change in these two values.

6. Complete the summary table.

If demand is:	The elasticity coefficient is	If P rises, TR will	If P falls, TR will
Elastic	>1	decrease	increase
Inelastic	<1	increase	decrease
Unit elastic	1	not change	not change

7. If a change in price causes no change in quantity demanded, demand is perfectly (elastic, inelastic) __inelastic__ and the demand curve is (horizontal, vertical) __vertical__ . The elasticity coefficient at any point on this demand curve is __zero__ . If an extremely small change in price results in an extremely large change in quantity demanded, demand is perfectly __elastic__ and the demand curve is nearly __horizontal__ . The elasticity coefficient at any point on this demand curve is nearly __infinity__ .

8. If the price of a commodity declines:
(a) when demand is inelastic, the loss of revenue due to the lower price is (greater than, less than, equal to) __greater than__ the gain in revenue due to the greater quantity demanded;
(b) when demand is elastic, the loss of revenue due to the lower price is __less than__ the gain in revenue due to the greater quantity demanded;
(c) when demand is of unitary elasticity, the loss of revenue due to the lower price is __equal to__ the gain in revenue due to the greater quantity demanded.

9. For all straight-line demand curves, demand tends to be more __elastic__ in the upper-left portion than in the lower-right portion.

10. List four determinants of price elasticity of demand.

    (a) _good substitutes available_

    (b) _proportion of income spent on the good_

    (c) _luxury vs necessity_

    (d) _time_

11. Legislatures that want to maximize tax revenue from the imposition of excise taxes will place the taxes on products with (elastic, inelastic) _inelastic_ demands.

12. If the supply curve is vertical then supply is infinitely _inelastic_. In this case a change in price causes _no_ change in the quantity supplied.

13. The main factor affecting the price elasticity of supply is _time_. In the _market_ period producers are unable to adjust to demand changes. This is reflected in a _vertical_ supply curve. In the _short_ run firms have enough time to use existing plants more intensively. This is reflected in an _up-sloping_ supply curve. In the _long_ run there is time for existing firms to _increase_ their plant capacities, and for the number of firms to _increase_. This is reflected in a supply curve that is _more_ elastic than the short run supply curve.

14. A given increase in demand will result in a larger increase in the equilibrium price the more _inelastic_ the supply curve.

15. An income elasticity of 0.5 indicates that a 10% increase in _income_ would result in a _5_ % increase in _quantity demanded_

16. Substitute goods have a (positive, negative) _____ cross elasticity of demand. Complementary goods have a _____ cross elasticity.

17. Because cigarettes have few good substitutes, their demand is _inelastic_. If government increases the excise tax on cigarettes by $1.00 per package, the _supply_ curve will shift _upward_ by the amount of the tax. If the equilibrium price increases by $0.75, the producers' tax burden is _25¢_.

18. In order to be effective, a ceiling price must be set (above, below) _below_ the equilibrium price, whereas a floor price must be set _above_ the equilibrium.

19. A price ceiling prevents the market mechanism from performing its _rationing_ function. Some other means must be found for allocating the available supply. Transactions that occur illegally are called _black_ market transactions.

■ **PROBLEMS AND PROJECTS**

  1. Fill in the table below by computing total revenue at the seven price levels, the six price elasticity coefficients between these prices, and indicating whether the character of demand is elastic, inelastic, or unit elasticity between each pair of prices. (Each elasticity coefficient is entered between two prices because it is an "average" over that price interval.)

P	Qd	Total Revenue	Elasticity coefficient	Character of demand
10	300	3000		
			2.71	elastic
9	400	3600		
			1.89	elastic
8	500	4000		
			1.36	elastic
7	600	4200		
			1	unit elastic
6	700	4200		
			.73	inelastic
5	800	4000		
			.53	inelastic
4	900	3600		
			.37	inelastic
3	1000	3000		

  2. This question uses the data in the previous question.

    (a) On the first graph on the next page, plot the demand curve (price vs. quantity demanded). Using the same horizontal scale, on the second graph plot the total revenue curve (total revenue vs. quantity demanded).

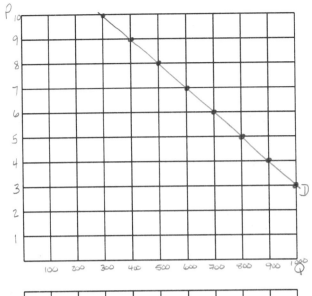

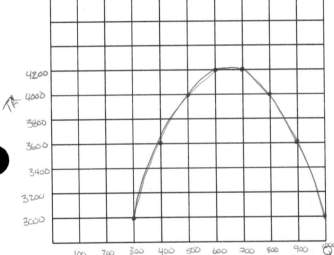

(b) Based on your answers in the previous question, the demand curve is price elastic between the prices __7__ and __10__. In this range, as quantity increases, the total revenue curve is (increasing, decreasing, flat) _increasing_. The demand curve has unitary elasticity between the prices __6__ and __7__. In this area the total revenue curve is __flat__. The demand curve is inelastic between the prices __3__ and __6__. Here the total revenue curve is _decreasing_. These results illustrate that along a straight-line demand curve, price elasticity _increases_ as price increases, and that total revenue is _maximized_ at the point of unit elasticity.

3. For each case below determine whether the demand is elastic, inelastic, or unit elastic.

(a) When the Flin Flon Flyers cut prices by 10%, they sold 20% more tickets to their roller hockey games. _elastic_

(b) When the Internet service provider increased their subscription rate by 15%, their total revenues increased 3%. _inelastic_

(c) Momma's Deli finds that no matter whether they charge a little more or a little less for their bagels, their total revenue from bagels remains the same. _unit elastic_

4. On the following graph are three different supply curves (S_1, S_2, S_3) for a product bought and sold in a competitive market.

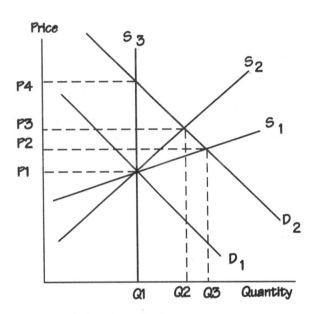

(a) Match the supply curves to the period:
market period — S_2
short run — S_3
long run — S_1

(b) No matter what the period of time under consideration, if the demand for the product were D_1, the equilibrium price of the product would be __P_1__ and the equilibrium quantity would be __Q_1__.

(c) If demand increases from D_1 to D_2 then: (1) in the market period, the equilibrium price would increase to __P_4__ and the equilibrium quantity would be __Q_1__; (2) in the short run, the price of the product would increase to __P_2__ and the quantity would increase to __Q_2__; (3) in the long run, the price of the product would be __P_2__ and the quantity would be __Q_3__.

(d) The longer the period of time allowed for sellers to adjust their outputs, the (more, less) __more__ elastic is the supply of their product.
(e) When demand increases, the more elastic the supply of a product, the (greater, less) __less__ is the effect on equilibrium price, and the __greater__ is the effect on equilibrium quantity.

5. Suppose that your college or university sets a target of increasing annual tuition revenue by 4%. To achieve this, they raise the tuition fee per student by 8%. At the end of the first term after the increase, the president of the school reports to the board of governors that the "tuition fee increases have proven to be even more successful than we had hoped — total tuition revenue is up 5% compared to last fall semester."

(a) Assuming that the *ceteris paribus* condition holds, is the school's demand elastic or inelastic in the short run? __inelastic__
(b) Why might the elasticity of demand be greater over time? __Students may choose a different school.__
(c) If the demand is much more elastic in the long run, what is the significance of that?

6. The graph below shows a supply curve and two hypothetical demand curves. Note that regardless of whether demand is initially given by D_1 or by D_2 the equilibrium price and quantity are the same.

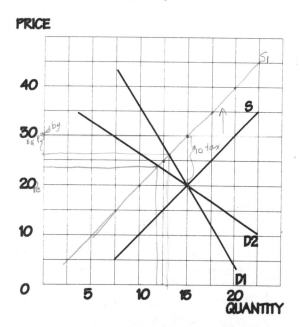

PRICE

(a) Show the effect of a $10 per unit tax.

(b) If demand was initially D_1 the imposition of the tax raises price to $\$26$. The equilibrium quantity falls to __13__. The tax burden is a price increase of __6__ for consumers, and a price decrease of __4__ for producers.
(c) If demand was initially D_2 the imposition of the tax raises price to __24__. The equilibrium quantity falls to __12__. The tax burden is a price increase of __4__ for consumers, and a price decrease of __6__ for producers.
(d) The difference between the results in (b) and (c) illustrates that, in general, a tax will impose a greater burden on consumers, and a lesser burden on producers, the more (elastic, inelastic) __inelastic__ is the demand curve.

7. This problem uses algebra to express demand and supply. Demand is represented by the equation $Q_d = 100 - 3P$ and supply by the equation $Q_s = 10 + 7P$. Price in $ is expressed by P, and quantity is represented by Q.

(a) Equilibrium is found where quantity demanded equals quantity supplied. Therefore, $P^* =$ __9__, and $Q^* =$ __73__.
(b) If government institutes a price floor of $11, $Q_d =$ __67__, $Q_s =$ __87__. Therefore, there is a (shortage, surplus) __surplus__ of __20__ units. To maintain the floor price government may be required to (buy, sell) __buy__ a quantity of __20__ units.

8. In each case below, identify:
(1) which good is the central focus,
(2) which of the four types of elasticity studied in the chapter is relevant,
(3) whether the speaker expects the elasticity to be negative (-) or positive (+), and
(4) whether the speaker is hoping for a large (L) or a small (S) elasticity.

(a) "Our company publishes crossword puzzle magazines. We expect that the falling household incomes that we're seeing in this recession will actually help our sales." (1) __crossword puzzle magazines__ (2) __income elasticity__ (3) __-__ (4) __L__
(b) "We've been having trouble attracting qualified machinists to work at this factory. Now we're going to try offering a higher wage rate." (1) __machinists__ (2) __elasticity of supply__ (3) __+__ (4) __L__
(c) "The frosts in the California orange groves have killed a big portion of their crop. Those of us growing apples in the Okanagan Valley should really benefit." (1) __apples__ (2) __cross__ (3) __+__ (4) __L__

(d) "The city really needs more revenue to fund social programs like the food bank. That's why we need a new tax on hotel rooms." (1) _hotel rooms_ (2) _price elasticity of demand_ (3) ____ (4) _S_

■ TRUE-FALSE

Circle T if the statement is true, F if it is false.

1. If the relative change in price is greater than the relative change in quantity demanded, the price elasticity coefficient is greater than one. T (F)

2. Along a downward sloping linear demand curve, demand tends to be elastic at higher prices and inelastic at lower prices. (T) F

3. If demand for wheat is inelastic, an increase in the harvest will reduce farm incomes from wheat sales. (T) F

4. If the quantity demanded of a product increases from 100 to 150 units when the price decreases from $14 to $10, demand is elastic in this price range. (T) F

5. If the price elasticity of demand coefficient is 3, this means that a one dollar decrease in price will lead to a three unit increase in quantity demanded. T (F)

6. The demand for "necessities" tends to be inelastic, for "luxuries" elastic. (T) F

7. The price elasticity of demand will tend to be greater the less substitutes there are for the good. T (F)

8. Other things being equal, the larger the portion of one's income spent on a good the greater the elasticity of demand for that good. (T) F

9. The demand for a product tends to be more inelastic the longer the time period under consideration. T (F)

10. In the market period the elasticity of supply is effectively zero. (T) F

11. If supply is perfectly inelastic, an increase in demand will not change the equilibrium price. T (F)

12. The supply of a product tends to be more elastic the longer the time period under consideration. (T) F

13. The cross elasticity of demand between a pair of goods that are complements is negative. T F

14. A zero or near-zero coefficient for cross elasticity suggests that the two goods are unrelated or independent goods. T F

15. If the consumption of a good is inversely related to the income level of consumers, that good is a luxury good. T (F)

16. If the bottle depot is willing to pay $2 per dozen bottles, and will buy whatever quantity people bring in, then the depot's demand curve for bottles is perfectly elastic. (T) F

17. Given the supply, the more inelastic is the demand, the greater is the producer's burden of a new excise tax. (T) F

18. Rent controls distort market signals so that resources are misallocated: too many resources are allocated to rental housing, too few to alternative uses. T F

19. When price floors are in place governments sometimes subsidize demand in order to eliminate surpluses. T F

20. An effective minimum wage law will increase the total incomes earned in minimum wage jobs if demand for the workers is inelastic. T F

■ MULTIPLE-CHOICE

Circle the letter that corresponds to the best answer.

1. The price elasticity of demand measures:
(a) the percentage change in quantity demanded as a result of a 1 percent change in supply
(b) the change in quantity demanded as the result of a 1 percent change in price
(c) the percentage change in quantity demanded as a result of a 1 percent change in price
(d) the slope of the demand curve

2. If an increase in the price of a product from $1.50 to $2.00 causes the quantity demanded of the product to decrease from 1,000 to 900, the price elasticity of demand coefficient is:
(a) 3.00

(b) 2.71
(c) .37
(d) .33

3. If a 1 percent fall in the price of a commodity causes the quantity demanded of the commodity to increase 2 percent, demand is:
(a) inelastic
(b) elastic
(c) unit elastic
(d) perfectly elastic

4. If the price elasticity of demand for restaurant meals were 2.0, what would be the effect of a 5% increase in restaurant prices?
(a) quantity demanded will fall by 2.5%
(b) quantity demanded will fall by 2.8%
(c) quantity demanded will fall by 3.0%
(d) quantity demanded will fall by 10.0%

5. Moving down a straight-line demand curve that has a slope of -2:
(a) the elasticity of demand coefficient is a constant equal to 2
(b) the elasticity of demand coefficient always equals 1
(c) the elasticity of demand coefficient declines as the price is lowered
(d) is largest at the intercept value on the quantity axis

6. If sellers' total revenues are the same before and after a price decrease, then demand is:
(a) unit elastic
(b) inelastic
(c) elastic
(d) perfectly inelastic

7. Suppose the only beer outlet in the town of Adanac increased the price of a litre of beer from $2.75 to $3.25. If the number of litres of beer sold decreased by 22 percent, then the elasticity of demand for beer is about:
(a) .67
(b) .90
(c) 1.0
(d) 1.32

8. Since bacon and eggs are complementary goods, the cross elasticity of demand between them would be:
(a) greater than 1
(b) negative

(c) 1
(d) vary between -1 and +1

9. An increase in supply will lead to an increase in total expenditure on a good if:
(a) demand is elastic
(b) demand is unit elastic
(c) demand is inelastic
(d) none of the above

10. If demand is perfectly inelastic, a decrease in supply will result in:
(a) a decrease in the equilibrium price
(b) an increase in the equilibrium quantity
(c) a decrease in equilibrium quantity
(d) no change in equilibrium quantity

11. A perfectly elastic demand curve is:
(a) parallel to the quantity axis
(b) downward sloping with a slope of -1
(c) parallel to the price axis
(d) a "long-run" demand curve

12. If the income elasticity of demand for turnips is -0.2, what is the effect of an 8% decrease in incomes?
(a) quantity demanded will fall by 1.6%
(b) quantity demanded will rise by 1.6%
(c) quantity demanded will fall by 4%
(d) quantity demanded will rise by 4%

13. Which of the following data would be evidence that CDs are a normal good?
(a) price elasticity of demand is 0.3
(b) cross price elasticity with cassette players is −0.8
(c) income elasticity is 0.2
(d) price elasticity of supply is 0.9

14. Which of the following is not characteristic of a good for which the demand is price inelastic?
(a) the good has many good substitutes
(b) the buyer spends a small percentage of his/her total income on the good
(c) the good is regarded by consumers as a necessity
(d) the period of time for which demand is given is very short

15. Which of the following lists correctly ranks the products in descending order of price elasticity of demand (i.e., from most elastic to least elastic)?
(a) soft drinks, colas, Pepsi

(b) colas, soft drinks, Pepsi
(c) colas, Pepsi, soft drinks
(d) Pepsi, colas, soft drinks

16. Generally in the long run the supply curve:
(a) is less elastic than in the short run
(b) is more elastic than in the short run
(c) has the same elasticity as in the short run
(d) is perfectly elastic

17. Suppose the quantity available of a good is fixed. The elasticity of supply would:
(a) be fixed at some positive value
(b) be fixed at some negative value
(c) be zero
(d) change along the supply curve from a small value to a large value

18. If supply is perfectly elastic, an increase in demand will result in:
(a) an increase in the equilibrium price
(b) a decrease in the equilibrium price
(c) a decrease in the equilibrium quantity
(d) an increase in the equilibrium quantity

19. Which of the following pairs of goods would be most likely to have a positive cross price elasticity of demand?
(a) sport sandals and running shoes
(b) skis and ski boots
(c) tea cups and hard-hats
(d) mechanical pencils and lead refills

20. Which of the following pairs of goods would be most likely to have a negative cross price elasticity of demand?
(a) tea and coffee
(b) black jeans and blue jeans ·
(c) camp stoves and tents
(d) steak and hamburger

21. An effective minimum wage law can be expected to:
(a) increase incomes for all workers who previously worked for less than the minimum wage
(b) have no effect on teenage unemployment
(c) create more jobs for teenagers
(d) reduce employment among teenagers

Questions 22 through 24 refer to the following graph.

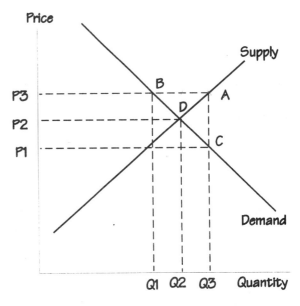

22. If a price floor of P$_3$ is imposed, the quantity demanded will be:
(a) Q$_1$
(b) Q$_2$
(c) Q$_3$
(d) none of the above

23. If a price floor of P$_3$ is imposed, the result will be:
(a) a surplus of AB
(b) a surplus of AC
(c) a shortage of AB
(d) a shortage of BD

24. If the government announces a price ceiling at P$_3$, what is the effect?
(a) a surplus of AB
(b) a shortage of AB
(c) a shortage of BD
(d) there is no effect on the market

25. If government fixes apartment rents below the equilibrium level, there will occur in the long run:
(a) an increase in the supply of apartments
(b) a decrease in the demand for apartments
(c) conversion of condos into rental units
(d) a withdrawal of resources from the apartment market into other sectors of the economy

■ DISCUSSION QUESTIONS

1. Explain the price elasticity of demand concept in terms of: (a) the relative sensitivity of quantity demanded to changes in price; (b) the behaviour of

total revenue when price changes; (c) the elasticity coefficient; (d) the relationship between the relative (percentage) change in quantity demanded and the relative (percentage) change in price.

2. What is meant by perfectly elastic demand? And what is meant by perfectly inelastic demand? What does the demand curve look like in each case?

3. In computing your price elasticity of demand for pizzas between two prices, say $10 and $12, it makes a considerable difference whether the higher price or the lower price is used as the initial reference point. (The same is true of quantities.) How do we eliminate the confusion that would arise if the elasticity coefficient varied and depended upon whether a price rise ($10 to $12) or price fall ($12 to $10) were being considered?

4. It is common to see many vacant seats at movie theatres. Presumably this is no surprise to the theatre owners. Why don't theatre owners drop their prices far enough to fill all seats? Give an explanation based on the concept of price elasticity of demand.

5. What is the relationship, if any, between the elasticity of demand and the slope of the demand curve?

6. What factors determine the price elasticity of demand for a product?

7. Of what practical importance is the price elasticity of demand? Cite examples of its importance to business firms, workers, farmers, and governments.

8. Explain what determines the elasticity of supply of a product.

9. Can you name a few types of businesses whose sales would slump dramatically if a recession were to pull average incomes down? Can you name a few whose sales would rise under the same circumstances? Which of these businesses sell normal goods, and which sell inferior goods?

10. What are some of the unintended consequences that normally result when a price ceiling is implemented? When a price floor is implemented?

11. Ticket-scalping at NHL hockey games and some rock concerts is quite similar to the consequences of government-set price ceilings. Why does ticket scalping occur, and what are its effects? In your opinion, is it a good thing or a bad thing? How would you defend your opinion?

12. Suppose that a college having financial difficulty has more students applying than they have spaces for, but is prevented by a government policy from raising tuition fees to a market clearing level. Based on the theory of price ceilings, what specific predictions can you make about how the college might respond?

■ ANSWERS

FILL-IN QUESTIONS

1. sensitivity, quantity, price

2. 10; 100; 10, 100, 10; 4; 25; 4, 25, 16; 10, 16, 0.63.

3. inelastic, elastic

4. percentage, numerical or absolute, goods

5. average, average

6. Elastic: greater than 1, decrease, increase; Inelastic: less than 1, increase, decrease; Unit elastic: equal to 1, remain constant, remain constant

7. inelastic, vertical; zero; elastic, horizontal; infinity

8. (a) greater than, (b) less than, (c) equal to

9. elastic

10. number of substitutes; proportion of income spent on the good; necessity or luxury; time period under consideration

11. inelastic

12. inelastic; no

13. time; market; vertical; short; up-sloping; long, expand, increase; more

14. inelastic

15. income, 5, quantity demanded

16. positive; negative

17. inelastic; supply, upward, $0.25.

18. below; above

19. rationing; black

PROBLEMS AND PROJECTS

1. Total revenue: 3000, 3600, 4000, 4200, 4200, 4000, 3600, 3000; Elasticity coefficient: 2.71, 1.89, 1.36, 1.00, 0.73, 0.53, 0.37; Character of demand; elastic, elastic, elastic, unit elastic, inelastic, inelastic, inelastic

2. (a) graphs similar to Figure 6-2 in text; b) 7, 10; increasing; 6, 7; flat; 3, 6; decreasing; increases, maximized

3. (a) elastic, (b) inelastic, (c) unit elastic

4. (a) market period = S_3; short run = S_2; long run = S_1; (b) P_1, Q_1 (c)(1) P_4, Q_1; (2) P_3, Q_2, (3) P_2, Q_3; (d) more (e) less, greater

5. (a) inelastic; (b) current students may be unlikely to transfer schools or discontinue their education, but in the long run the school will attract less new students; (c) the 5% increase in total tuition revenue may eventually turn into a decrease

6. (a) the supply shifts vertically parallel by $10; (b) $26; 13; $6, $4; c) $24; 12; $4, $6; d) inelastic

7. (a) 9, 73; (b) 67, 87; surplus, 20; buy, 20

8. (a) crossword puzzle magazines, income elasticity, -, L; (b) machinists, elasticity of supply, +, L; (c) apples, cross price elasticity, +, L; (d) hotel rooms, price elasticity of demand, -, S

TRUE-FALSE

1. F   case elasticity would be less than 1
2. T   unlike the slope – which is constant – elasticity is different at different points on the curve
3. T   because price falls by bigger percentage than quantity increases
4. T   (50/125)/(4/12) = 1.20
5. F   a 1% rise in P leads to 3% drop in Qd
6. T   even if P rises a great deal, necessities are still purchased; luxuries may not be
7. F   opposite is true
8. T   a given P increase affects consumer more if for a product that uses up a big share of consumer's income
9. F   more elastic as substituting becomes easier
10. T   Qs does not change at all
11. F   equilibrium P will rise; equilibrium Q is unchanged

12. T   more time for firms to expand capacity and new firms to enter
13. T   P of one rises; Qd of the other falls
14. T   P change for one has no effect on Qd of other
15. F   negative income elasticity is inferior good
16. T   their demand for bottles is horizontal
17. F   the more is the consumer's tax burden
18. F   too few resources are allocated to rental housing
19. T   the surplus must be dealt with somehow
20. T   earnings per hour rise more than the number of hours of employment falls

MULTIPLE-CHOICE

1.   (c)
2.   (c)   (100/950)/(0.50/1.75)
3.   (b)   2.0 is greater than 1
4.   (d)   x% / 5% = 2... x = 10
5.   (c)
6.   (a)   the effect of P change exactly offset effect of Qd change, because they are the same percentage
7.   (d)   (0.50/3.00) x 100% = 16.7%; 22%/16.7% = 1.32
8.   (b)   if P of eggs rises, Qd for bacon will fall
9.   (a)   Qd increases by bigger proportion than P falls
10.   (d)   supply is vertical
11.   (a)   demand is horizontal
12.   (b)   8% x –0.2 = -1.6%
13.   (c)   normal vs. inferior depends on income elasticity
14.   (a)
15.   (d)   Pepsi is most easily substituted
16.   (b)   as existing firms have time to expand, and new firms have time to enter the industry
17.   (c)   percentage change in Qs is zero
18.   (d)   there is no price change
19.   (a)   substitutes
20.   (c)   complements
21.   (d)
22.   (a)
23.   (a)   Qs exceeds Qd
24.   (d)   the equilibrium price is below the maximum allowed, so the equilibrium price is maintained
25.   (d)   supplying apartments is now less profitable than before

CHAPTER 7

The Theory of Consumer Choice

The law of demand expresses an inverse relationship between price and quantity demanded. This chapter takes a closer look at how consumers make their spending decisions, and offers two complementary explanations for why consumers behave according to the law of demand.

The first explanation, already touched on in Chapter 3, is based on income and substitution effects. If the price of a product increases, the consumer will buy less because: (1) the consumer now has less real income (or buying power) and (2) the product's opportunity cost has increased in terms of other products the consumer could buy.

The second explanation is based on the law of diminishing marginal utility. According to this theory, consumers get less additional utility (or benefit) from each additional unit that they consume of any product. Therefore, the price that the consumer is willing to pay for each additional unit also decreases; hence the downward sloping demand curve. We also find that the more sharply the marginal utility falls as the consumer has more of the good, the more inelastic the consumer's demand curve will be.

Diminishing marginal utility also provides a theory of how a consumer makes his/her spending decisions in order to maximize his/her utility. This model takes four dimensions of the consumer's situation as given: (1) the consumer is rational, (2) the consumer has clear-cut preferences; (3) the consumer has a budget constraint (or fixed, limited income); and (4) the prices of goods are not affected by the consumer. To maximize total utility, the consumer allocates his/her income between products such that the last dollar spent on each product yields the same marginal utility. The numerical example used to illustrate this principle also shows that each point on a consumer's demand curve for a particular good corresponds to a utility maximizing allocation of the consumer's income. Economists do not claim that consumers actually perform such mental gymnastics before making purchases at the grocery store. However, to the extent that consumers behave "as if" they make such calculations, this model will permit us to make correct predictions about how consumer choices respond to price changes or income changes.

The final section of the chapter describes how the theory of consumer choice can be used to explain many real-world phenomena. The examples discussed are the takeover of compact discs from LP records, the diamond-water paradox, the value of time in consumption, and the relative efficiency of cash and noncash gifts.

■ CHAPTER LEARNING OBJECTIVES

In this chapter you will learn:
□ The two explanations for why the demand curve is downward sloping.
□ The theory of consumer choice.
□ About utility maximization and the demand curve.
□ To apply marginal utility theory to real world situations.

■ CHAPTER OUTLINE

1. Both the income effect and the substitution effect can explain the law of demand.
   (a) If the price of a good falls, the consumer's income can purchase more. In the case of a normal good, this income effect leads to increased purchases.
   (b) If the price of a good falls, its relative price (or opportunity cost) measured in other goods

falls. This leads the consumer to substitute in favour of buying more of this good.

2. The utility of a good or service is the satisfaction that a consumer gets from consuming it.
  (a) Utility does not imply usefulness.
  (b) Utility is a subjective notion, because it varies widely from person to person.
  (c) Utility is difficult to quantify, but we assume that consumers can measure utility in units called "utils."

3. Total utility is the total amount of satisfaction a person receives from consuming a specific number of units of a good. Marginal utility is the extra satisfaction a person receives from consuming one extra unit of a good. Marginal utility is also the change in total utility from consuming one extra unit.
  (a) The principle that the marginal utility will decline as the consumer gets additional units of a product is known as the law of diminishing marginal utility. For example, the extra utility from consuming the fifth unit of a good is less than the marginal utility from the fourth unit.
  (b) Diminishing marginal utility provides an explanation for the law of demand: consumers will only wish to purchase more units of a good if the price is lower commensurate with their marginal utility.
  (c) Diminishing marginal utility also explains differing price elasticities of demand: the more sharply a consumer's marginal utility for a good falls as more is consumed, the more inelastic is the consumer's demand for that good.

4. Diminishing marginal utility provides an explanation for how a consumer chooses what to buy. This theory relies on four assumptions about the consumer:
  (a) rational behaviour based on attempting to maximize his or her total utility;
  (b) clear-cut preferences between various goods and services;
  (c) budget constraint (a fixed, limited income);
  (d) prices of goods and services are given and fixed.

5. The consumer spends his or her income so as to maximize the satisfaction received from consuming the goods. Given just two goods, A and B, the consumer is maximizing utility when the last dollar spent on either good yields the same amount of extra utility. This is the utility-maximizing rule, and it can also be summarized as $(MU_A/P_A) = (MU_B/P_B)$. An example is used to show how the consumer could work through allocating his or her income so as to follow this rule.

6. Suppose the consumer is presently consuming amounts of A and B such that the utility-maximizing rule is met. Then the price of A falls while income, tastes, and the price of B remain constant. At the initial amounts of A and B the utility-maximizing rule is no longer met. The consumer, in order to maximize utility at the new price for A, will purchase more of A until the utility-maximizing condition is again fulfilled.

This yields two different prices of A and the two different utility-maximizing quantities of A the consumer will purchase, given that the price of B, income, and preferences are all fixed. Thus, two points on the demand curve for A have been found. Other points can be derived by taking other prices for A and finding new utility-maximizing quantities of A and B.

7. Many real-world phenomena can be explained with the theory of consumer choice in this chapter.
  (a) Compact discs now dominate the market for recorded music because of the change in consumer preferences and the fall in the price of CD players.
  (b) Diamonds are high in price, but of limited usefulness, while water is low in price, but essential for life. This paradox is resolved by explaining the distinction between marginal and total utility. Water is so abundant that its price is very low, causing us to consume it up to the point that its marginal utility becomes nearly zero. Diamonds are so rare that they are very expensive, and so their marginal utility is still very high at our utility-maximizing consumption level of diamonds.
  (c) Marginal utility theory recognizes the fact that consumption takes time, and time is a scarce resource. The full price of any consumer good or service is its market price plus the value of the time taken to consume it (i.e., the income that the consumer could have earned had that time been used for work).
  (d) For recipients, noncash gifts are less efficient than cash gifts. A cash gift allows the recipient to choose whatever goods he or she prefers, whereas with a noncash gift there is no choice.

74 CHAPTER 7

■ **TERMS AND CONCEPTS**

income effect	law of diminishing
substitution effect	marginal utility
utility	rational behaviour
total utility	budget constraint
marginal utility	utility-maximizing rule

■ **HINTS AND TIPS**

1. Utility is a useful abstraction for explaining consumer behaviour. Do not be distracted by the fact that utility is not measurable. It is true that in advanced economics little use is made of this model precisely because of this problem; nevertheless the model is instructive because we can think of consumers making choices "as if" they are applying the utility-maximizing rule, whether or not utility is observable.

2. Master the difference between marginal and total utility. Think of consumers as allocating their incomes one dollar at a time; the next dollar always being allocated to the good that produces the highest marginal utility from one more dollar spent.

■ **FILL-IN QUESTIONS**

1. The law of demand (which states that demand curves are downward sloping) can be explained in terms of the _____ and _____ effects.

2. A fall in the price of a product tends to (increase, decrease) _____ the purchasing power of a consumer. This causes the _____ effect. A fall in price makes the product (more, less) _____ expensive *relative* to other goods. This causes the _____ effect.

3. The extra satisfaction obtained from consuming one more unit of a good is called (marginal, total) _____ utility. The satisfaction obtained from some number of units of a product is called _____ utility. One can calculate _____ utility by summing the _____ figures.

4. The marginal utility theory of consumer behaviour assumes that:
  (a) the consumer is _____
  (b) the consumer has clear-cut _____ for various goods.
  (c) the consumer has a limited and fixed _____.

(d) the consumer faces fixed _____ for various goods.

5. The utility-maximizing rule states that the last dollar spent on each product purchased should yield the same amount of _____. The utility-maximizing condition, for two goods, A and B, can be rewritten as: $MU_A/P_A =$ _____.

6. Suppose the consumer is presently consuming where $(MU_A/P_A > MU_B/P_B)$. The symbol > stands for "greater than." In order to increase utility the consumer should consume less of good _____ and use the money to purchase more of good _____.

7. It is the (marginal, total) _____ utility and not _____ utility that is relevant to the price people are willing to pay for a good. This point explains the _____ paradox.

8. In addition to the monetary price, the opportunity cost of consumption of most goods also includes the value of _____ that is used.

9. Noncash gifts are (more, less) _____ efficient than cash gifts because they yield consumers (more, less) _____ utility.

■ **PROBLEMS AND PROJECTS**

1. Suppose that a consumer's utility levels from consuming goods A, B, and C are given in the table that follows. The utility of the consumer is calculated by adding together the utility obtained from each good. "U" denotes total utility and "MU" denotes marginal utility. Assume the consumer's income equals $17 and the three goods' prices are given by $P_a = \$1$, $P_b = \$2$, and $P_c = \$4$.

Good A				Good B				Good C			
Qa	Ua	MUa	MUa/Pa	Qb	Ub	MUb	MUb/Pb	Qc	Uc	MUc	MUc/Pc
1	6	6	__	1	36	__	__	1	22	__	__
2	11	5	__	2	64	__	__	2	38	__	__
3	15	__	__	3	72	__	__	3	50	__	__
4	18	__	__	4	76	__	__	4	54	__	__
5	20	__	__	5	79	__	__	5	56	__	__

(a) Fill in the blanks for the marginal utility and marginal utility per dollar spent.
(b) Consider the first unit purchased. The individual would choose good B because the mar-

ginal utility per dollar spent for the first unit of good B is _____ as compared to _____ for good A and _____ for good C.

(c) After the consumer has purchased that first unit, the consumer now has $_____ left to spend.

(d) For the next purchase the consumer would take good _____ since the marginal utility per dollar spent on that unit of good _____ is _____ as compared to _____ for good _____ and _____ for good _____.

(e) After the second purchase, the consumer now has $_____ left to spend.

(f) The third item purchased would be good _____ and the marginal utility per dollar spent to get that unit is _____.

(g) To maximize utility the consumer will buy _____ units of good A, _____ units of B, and _____ units of C. Total utility will be _____.

(h) The marginal utility of the last dollar spent on each good will be _____.

(i) The consumer could have purchased 2 units of C, 2 units of B, and 5 units of A, but did not. Why? _____

2. Ms. Thompson's weekly budget is $36. The only two goods she wants to purchase are D and E. The marginal utility schedules for these two goods are shown in the next table.

The price of E is fixed at $4. The marginal utility per dollar from good E at this price is also shown in the table. For good D you are given the marginal utility per dollar spent on D when the price of D is $6, $4, $3, and $2.

	Good D					Good E	
Q	MU	MU/$6	MU/$4	MU/$3	MU/$2	MU	MU/$4
1	45	7.5	11.25	15	22.5	40	10
2	30	5	7.5	10	15	36	9
3	20	3.33	5	6.67	10	32	8
4	15	2.5	3.75	5	7.5	28	7
5	12	2	3	4	6	24	6
6	10	1.67	2.5	3.33	5	20	5
7	9	1.5	2.25	3	4.5	16	4
8	7.5	1.25	1.88	2.5	3.75	12	3

Complete the demand schedule in the table that follows to show how much of good D Ms. Thompson will buy each week at each of these four possible prices of D.

Price of D	Quantity of D demanded
$6	_____
$4	_____
$3	_____
$2	_____

3. Assume that the only two goods a consumer can purchase are R (recreation) and M (material goods). The market price of R is $2 and the market price of M is $1. The consumer spends all her income in such a way that the marginal utility of the last unit of R bought is 12 and the marginal utility of the last unit of M bought is 6.

(a) If we ignore the time it takes to consume R and M, is the consumer maximizing the total utility she gets from R and M? _____

(b) Suppose that it takes 4 hours to consume each unit of R and 1 hour to consume each unit of M; and the consumer can earn $2 an hour by working.

1) The full price per unit of R is $_____.

2) The full price per unit of M is $_____.

(c) If we can take into account the full price of each of the commodities, is the consumer maximizing total utility? _____
How do you know this? _____

(d) If the consumer is not maximizing utility, should she consume more of R or of M? _____
Why should she do this? _____

(e) Will she then use more or less time on R? _____

- **TRUE-FALSE**

Circle T if the statement is true, F if it is false.

1. Utility and usefulness are synonymous.   **T F**

2. Utility is a measure of the satisfaction received from the consumption of goods and services.   **T F**

3. Marginal utility is the extra utility derived from consuming an extra unit of a good or service.   **T F**

4. Decreasing marginal utility means that total utility falls when another unit of the good is consumed.   **T F**

5. When a consumer is maximizing total utility, the marginal utilities of the last unit of every product bought are identical. **T F**

6. When a consumer is maximizing utility, the total utility received from the consumption of each good is equal. **T F**

7. When utility is maximized, the consumer allocates money income so that the last dollar spent on each product purchased yields the same amount of extra utility. **T F**

8. If a good were offered free, consumption would be extended to the point where the marginal utility of the last unit equals zero. **T F**

9. A low market price for a good reflects the low total utility received from the good. **T F**

10. The price of water is low because the marginal utility received from water is low. **T F**

11. Because utility cannot actually be measured, the marginal utility theory cannot really explain how consumers will behave. **T F**

12. High labour productivity gives time a high market value. **T F**

13. The rise of the "fast food" industry is partly due to the increased value of time. **T F**

14. One reason for the shift from record albums to compact discs has been the reduction in price of CD players that are complements to CDs. **T F**

15. For a high-priced criminal lawyer, homegrown vegetables might have a higher full price than vegetables purchased in the most expensive market in Toronto. **T F**

16. If Darrell's grandmother gives him $15 instead of buying him a Lawrence Welk CD for $20, Darrell and his grandmother might both be better off. **T F**

■ **MULTIPLE-CHOICE**

Circle the letter that corresponds to the best answer.

1. Which of the following best expresses the law of diminishing marginal utility?

(a) the more a person consumes of a product, the smaller becomes the utility received from its consumption
(b) the more a person consumes of a product, the smaller becomes the extra utility received as a result of consuming an additional unit
(c) the less a person consumes of a product, the smaller becomes the utility received from its consumption
(d) the less a person consumes of a product, the smaller becomes the extra utility received as a result of consuming an additional unit of the product

2. The substitution effect deals with the change in consumption of a good due to:
(a) the change in the consumer's preferences
(b) the change in the consumer's actual money income
(c) the change in the real buying power of the consumer's money income
(d) the change in the price of the good relative to others

3. Sabina Azula buys only two goods: food and clothing. Both are normal goods for Sabina. If the price of food decreases, Sabina's consumption of clothing will:
(a) increase due to the income effect
(b) increase due to the substitution effect
(c) decrease due to the substitution effect
(d) both (a) and (c)

Questions 4 and 5 use the table below showing total utility data for a consumer of chocolate bars.

Chocolate bars consumed	Total utility
0	0
1	9
2	19
3	27
4	35
5	42
6	42
7	40

4. This consumer begins experiencing diminishing marginal utility after he consumes the:
(a) first chocolate bar
(b) second chocolate bar
(c) sixth chocolate bar
(d) seventh chocolate bar

5. If this consumer can eat chocolate bars free of charge, how many will he eat?
- **(a)** six or seven
- **(b)** five or six
- **(c)** two
- **(d)** as many as possible

6. An individual consumes two products, A and B, with prices P_A, P_B. Utility is maximized when, if all income is spent, the following condition is met:
- **(a)** $MU_A = MU_B$
- **(b)** $MU_A < MU_B$
- **(c)** $MU_A/P_A = MU_B/P_B$
- **(d)** $MU_A/P_B = MU_B/P_A$

7. Suppose the price of A is $3, and the price of B is $2; that Diego is spending his entire income and buying 4 units of A and 6 units of B; and the marginal utility of both the 4th unit of A and the 6th unit of B is 6. It can be concluded that:
- **(a)** Diego is maximizing utility and should not adjust his purchases
- **(b)** Diego should buy more of A and less of B
- **(c)** Diego should buy less of A and more of B
- **(d)** Diego should buy less of both A and B

8. Suppose that the price of A is $3 and the price of B is $6 and the consumer is maximizing utility. If $MU_A = 7$ at this point, it can be concluded that:
- **(a)** the utility received from good A must equal the utility received from good B
- **(b)** the consumer must be purchasing an equal number of units of good A and good B
- **(c)** the two goods are substitutes
- **(d)** $MU_B = 14$

9. A decrease in the price of good X, other things remaining the same, will:
- **(a)** decrease the marginal utility for the last unit of X that will be purchased
- **(b)** increase the total utility from purchases of X
- **(c)** have no effect on total utility from purchases of X
- **(d)** both (a) and (b)

Answer the next three questions on the basis of the following table. The price of good A is $4 and the price of good B is $5, and income is $35. Suppose the utility received from good A is independent of the number of units of good B consumed. Total utility from consumption is obtained by adding the utility from A to the utility from B.

Units of A	Total Utility	MU of A	Units of B	Total Utility	MU of B
1	32	32	1	20	20
2	60	28	2	35	15
3	72	12	3	40	5
4	80	8	4	43	3
5	84	4	5	45	2
6	86	2	6	46	1

10. How many units of A and B will be purchased?
- **(a)** 5 of A and 3 of B
- **(b)** 5 of A and 4 of B
- **(c)** 5 of A and 5 of B
- **(d)** 4 of A and 4 of B

11. What is the total utility for the consumer when the utility-maximizing combination of A and B is purchased?
- **(a)** 120
- **(b)** 124
- **(c)** 126
- **(d)** 118

12. If the consumer's income were reduced to $22, the consumer would maximize satisfaction by consuming:
- **(a)** 2 of A and 2 of B
- **(b)** 3 of A and 3 of B
- **(c)** 2 of A and 3 of B
- **(d)** 3 of A and 2 of B

13. Other things being equal, demand is likely to be inelastic if the marginal utility of the product:
- **(a)** decreases rapidly as additional units are consumed
- **(b)** decreases slowly as additional units are consumed
- **(c)** increases rapidly as additional units are consumed
- **(d)** increases slowly as additional units are consumed

14. The full price of a product to a consumer is:
- **(a)** its market price
- **(b)** its market price plus the value of its consumption time
- **(c)** its market price less the value of its consumption time
- **(d)** the value of its consumption time less its market price

15. If the opportunity cost of the time spent in consumption is added to the market price of a good when making a purchase decision, we can expect:

(a) the same combination of goods will be purchased as when time is ignored

(b) more of the time-intensive good will be purchased

(c) the consumer's demand curve for the good to be upward sloping

(d) none of the above

16. Compared to cash gifts, noncash gifs are:

(a) of greater total utility but of less marginal utility

(b) of less total utility but of greater marginal utility

(c) more efficient because they do not waste resources

(d) less efficient because they do not generally match recipients' preferences

■ **DISCUSSION QUESTIONS**

1. Is it possible to compare the marginal utility received by John and Joe when each consumes a third lobster? How does the subjective nature of utility limit the practical usefulness of the marginal utility theory of consumer behaviour?

2. "The marginal utility of money is diminishing. Therefore society's total utility will be increased by taking money from the rich and giving it to the poor." What is wrong with this argument?

3. What essential assumptions are made about consumers in developing the marginal utility theory of consumer behaviour? What is meant by the "budget constraint"?

4. Mr. Ritz says, "I don't clip cents-off coupons out of the paper — it's not worth it to me." Mr. Brown, who reads the same newspaper, shops at the same store, and buys the same goods, says "I save lots of money by using the coupons from the paper." What concept discussed in this chapter might explain the difference in their behaviours?

5. Suppose you take two hours off work to see the dentist. The dentist charges you $360. What is your full price for this dental service?

6. My doctor always schedules patients 15 minutes apart, even though he knows that it takes more than 15 minutes of his time for most patients. The result is a crowded waiting room and long delays. Why doesn't the doctor schedule patients 20 or 30 minutes apart?

7. If you won a charity golf tournament and could choose between a $1000 cash prize and a new set of golf clubs with a retail value of $1000, which would you prefer? Why? What concept from the chapter is relevant?

■ **ANSWERS**

FILL-IN QUESTIONS

1. income, substitution

2. increase; income; less; substitution

3. marginal; total; total; marginal

4. (a) rational; (b) preferences (tastes); (c) income; (d) prices

5. marginal utility; MU_B/P_B

6. B, A

7. marginal, total; diamond-water

8. time

9. less, less

PROBLEMS AND PROJECTS

1. (a) Blank values, from top to bottom: MU_A: 4, 3, 2; (MU_A/P_A): 6, 5, 4, 3, 2; MU_B: 36, 28, 8, 4, 3; (MU_B/P_B): 18, 14, 4, 2, 1.5; MU_C: 22, 16, 12, 4, 2; (MU_C/P_C): 5.5, 4, 3, 1, 0.5; (b) 18, 6, 5.5; (c) $15; (d) B, B, 14, 6, A, 5.5, C; (e) $13; (f) A; 6 (g) 3, 3, 2; 125 (h) 4 (i) utility would equal 122, which is less than the 125 that can be obtained; or, MU/P would not be equal for all three goods

2. 2, 3, 4, 6

3. (a) yes, because MUr/Pr = MUm/Pm; (b) (1)$10, (2)$3; (c) No; The marginal utility to price ratio is not the same for the two goods: 12/$10 < 6/$3; (d) M; because its MU/P ratio is greater (e) less

TRUE-FALSE

1. F something can provide utility without being useful

2. T

3. T
4. F   total utility may still be rising, but at a decreasing rate
5. F   MU/P is equal for all goods, but not MU
6. F   MU/P is equal for all goods, but not total utility
7. T   in other words, MU/P is equal for all goods
8. T
9. F   it indicates low MU; total utility could be very high
10. T
11. F   consumers may well behave "as if" they make these calculations
12. T   high productivity leads to high hourly wage rates
13. T   to avoid the opportunity cost of time for food preparation, people are willing to pay to have food prepared for them
14. T
15. T   full price includes the monetary value of time which may be several hundred dollars per hour
16. T   if Darrell values the Lawrence Welk CD less than $15 in cash

MULTIPLE-CHOICE

1. (b)
2. (d)
3. (d)   the lower price for food raises her real income, so she consumes more clothing due to the income effect; and the higher relative price for clothing causes a substitution effect that reduces her clothing purchases
4. (b)   MU is 9, 10, 8, 8, 7, 0, -2
5. (b)   MU of the sixth = 0, and MU of the seventh = -2
6. (c)
7. (c) MU_A/P_A =2, MU_B/P_B = 3, so buy more B as it is creating more utility per dollar spent at the margin
8. (d) MU_B/P_B must equal MU_A/P_A
9. (d)   both statements because more X is bought
10. (a)   for each purchase choose the good with higher MU/P until $35 is fully spent
11. (b)   84 + 40
12. (d)   repeat decision process until $22 is spent
13. (a)   when MU drops off sharply, it takes large price cuts to induce more consumption
14. (b)
15. (d)   the law of demand still holds, but consumption patterns would be different
16. (d)   the purchase price of the gift might be used by the recipient to buy something different that would provide more utility

APPENDIX TO CHAPTER 7

Indifference Curve Analysis

This appendix outlines a more advanced approach to the theory of consumer choice. This approach uses the concepts of budget lines (representing what the consumer can buy) and indifference curves (representing what the consumer would prefer to buy).

A consumer's ability to buy goods A and B is limited by his or her fixed income, and by the prices of A and B. These "objective" variables define the budget line, or set of all attainable combinations of goods A and B.

"Subjective" information about the consumer's preferences between A and B is shown by indifference curves. A single indifference curve shows all combinations of these two goods that yield the same level of total utility for this consumer. A complete set of such curves – known as the indifference map – gives a complete picture of how the consumer ranks all possible combinations of A and B. Unlike the marginal utility theory, this approach does not depend on the idea of quantifying how many "utils" of satisfaction the consumer gets from A or B.

When the consumer's indifference map is superimposed on the budget line, we find the equilibrium point where the budget line is tangent to the highest attainable indifference curve. At this tangency the slope of the budget line (which is the opportunity cost of A in terms of B) is equal to the marginal rate of substitution (which is the rate at which the consumer is willing to trade A for B while remaining equally satisfied). If the price of a good changes, the budget line shifts, and a new equilibrium is found on a different indifference curve. We can derive a demand curve, say for A, by finding a series of such tangency points as we vary the price of A.

■ **CHECKLIST**

When you have studied this appendix, you should be able to:
☐ Define the budget line.
☐ Derive a budget line from given data on income and prices of two goods.
☐ Show the effect on the budget line of varying: (a) income only; (b) one price only; (c) both prices only.
☐ Define an indifference curve.
☐ State the two characteristics of an individual indifference curve.
☐ Explain the meaning of an indifference map.
☐ Place both the indifference map and the budget line on a graph to show the combination of goods that maximizes the consumer's utility.
☐ Explain the utility-maximizing rule in terms of the slope of the indifference curve and the slope of the budget line.
☐ Derive the consumer's demand curve for a good using indifference curve analysis.
☐ Compare and contrast the marginal utility and the indifference curve analyses of consumer behaviour.

■ **APPENDIX OUTLINE**

1. A budget line graphs the different combinations of two goods that a consumer can purchase at given prices, with a given money income. Because all the income is spent, the consumer can buy more of one good by giving up some of the other. Therefore the budget line is negatively sloped.

(a) An increase (decrease) in money income will cause a parallel shift of the budget line to the right (left).

(b) A change in one of the prices will change the slope of the budget line. The intercept will increase (decrease) on the axis showing the good whose price has decreased (increased). The intercept will remain unchanged for the good whose price has not changed.

(c) If the two goods are X and Y, with X on the horizontal axis and Y on the vertical axis, the absolute value of the slope of the budget line is written as P_X/P_Y.

2. An indifference curve graphs the various combinations of two goods that give the consumer the same total utility.

(a) An indifference curve is downward sloping: since both goods generate utility, if utility is to remain constant when the quantity of one good increases, the quantity of the other good must decrease.

(b) We assume indifference curves are convex to the origin: the more a consumer has of one good, the smaller is the quantity of the second good that he or she is willing to give up to obtain an additional unit of the first good.

(c) The consumer has an indifference curve for every level of total utility; indifference curves farther to the right on the graph show higher levels of total utility.

(d) The slope of the indifference curve measures the marginal rate of substitution, which is the rate at which the consumer is willing to substitute one good for the other while maintaining a constant utility level.

3. At the point of maximum satisfaction the budget line is tangent to an indifference curve.

(a) This condition also implies that the relative price ratio between the two goods is equal to the consumer's marginal rate of substitution between the two goods.

(b) This condition is identical to the utility-maximizing rule in the marginal utility approach.

4. The budget line and indifference curve approach to explaining consumer choices depends on weaker assumptions than does the marginal utility approach presented in Chapter 7. The approach presented in this appendix depends on the consumer being able to rank and choose between combinations of goods. Unlike the marginal utility approach, it does not depend on measurable utility whereby one can tell by *how much* one combination is preferred over another.

5. To find a demand curve for good X, vary the price of X and note the different quantities of X at which the new budget lines are tangent to an indifference curve.

■ **TERMS AND CONCEPTS**

budget line
indifference curve
marginal rate of substitution (MRS)

indifference map
equilibrium position

■ **HINTS AND TIPS**

1. Because each consumer has different preferences, one consumer's indifference curve map looks somewhat different from another consumer's. Nevertheless, their maps will share the common properties discussed in this appendix.

2. When a consumer moves from one indifference curve to another, this indicates a change in the level of utility achieved, *not* a change in preferences. If the consumer's preferences change, all indifference curves in the consumer's map would change shape or position.

■ **FILL-IN QUESTIONS**

1. A budget line shows all combinations of two products that can be purchased with a given _____, holding constant the _____ of the two goods.

2. When the quantities of X are measured on the horizontal axis, and the quantities of Y on the vertical, the budget line has a slope equal to the ratio of the _____ to the _____.

3. When the consumer's income increases, the budget line moves to the (right, left) _____, and its slope (does, does not) _____ change.

4. If the quantity of X is measured horizontally and the quantity of Y is measured vertically, an increase in the price of X will fan the budget line (inward, outward) _____ around a fixed point on the _____ axis. The budget line becomes (steeper, flatter) _____.

5. An indifference curve slopes (downward, upward) _____; and the slope of an indifference curve measures the marginal _____ of

_____. The indifference curve is (concave, convex) _____ to the origin.

6. As the consumer moves down along the indifference curve (from left to right) the indifference curve becomes (flatter, steeper) _____.

7. The farther from the origin an indifference curve is, the (greater, smaller) _____ is the total utility obtained from the combination of products on that curve.

8. At the consumer's utility maximizing combination of goods, the budget line is _____ to the indifference curve. At this point, the _____ of the budget line and the _____ of the indifference curve are _____.

9. The marginal utility approach to consumer behaviour requires that we assume utility (is, is not) _____ numerically measurable. The indifference curve approach (does, does not) _____ require that assumption.

■ **PROBLEMS AND PROJECTS**

1. Michelle spends all of her income of $200 on gasoline (G) and sandwiches (S). The prices per unit are: $P_G = \$0.50$ and $P_S = \$2$.

(a)   The maximum amount of gasoline that Michelle can consume is _____.

(b)   The maximum number of sandwiches that Michelle can consume is _____.

(c)   Therefore the intercepts of Michelle's budget line are _____ G and _____ S.

(d)   Graph Michelle's budget line on the following graph, showing G on the vertical axis and S on the horizontal.

(e)   Michelle (can, cannot) _____ afford to buy a combination of 200 G and 60 S because this combination of goods is located (outside, inside, on) _____ her budget line.

(f)   The slope of this budget line is _____.

(g)   The opportunity cost of one sandwich is ___ gasoline.

(h)   If Michelle's income drops to $160, the new intercepts of her budget line are _____ G and _____ S.

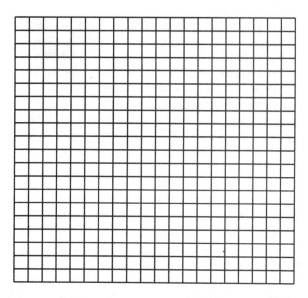

2. Sammy's preferences between bats and gloves are represented by the three indifference curves pictured in the next graph (U1, U2, U3). Several combinations of goods are labelled (*a, b, c, d*). Answer the next few questions based on this graph.

(a)   Which of the four labelled combinations of goods would Sammy prefer? _____

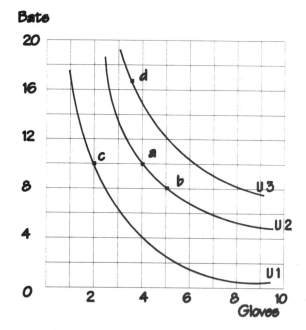

(b)   Which two of the four combinations of goods is Sammy indifferent between? _____ and _____.

(c)   Sammy's marginal rate of substitution is the rate at which he is willing to trade bats for gloves to remain equally satisfied. The MRS calculated between points *a* and *b* is _____ bats per 1 glove.

3. This problem uses Sammy's indifference curves from the previous problem to derive points on Sammy's demand for gloves. Assume that Sammy's income is fixed at $1000, and that the price of a bat is $50.

(a)   Draw in Sammy's budget line if the price of a glove is $125, and label it BL_1. (Hint: use the same technique used in problem 1 to find Michelle's budget line.)

(b)   Where is Sammy's utility-maximizing equilibrium for this budget line? (Hint: the budget line is tangent to one of the given U curves, and at one of the points already labelled.) _____

(c)   Draw in Sammy's new budget line if the price of a glove goes up to $250, *ceteris paribus*, and label it BL_2.

(d)   Where is Sammy's utility-maximizing equilibrium for BL_2? _____

(e)   Use your results above to fill in values for Sammy's demand schedule for gloves:

Price per Glove	Quantity Demanded of Gloves
$125	_____
250	_____

■ **TRUE-FALSE**

Circle T if the statement is true, F if it is false.

1. The slope of the budget line when good X is on the horizontal and Y is on the vertical is: (price of Y/price of X).   **T F**

2. If good Y is on the vertical axis and good X is on the horizontal axis, an increase in the price of Y, *ceteris paribus*, will make the budget line become steeper.   **T F**

3. An indifference curve gives the various combinations of two goods that give the consumer the same level of total utility.   **T F**

4. Indifference curves slope downward because in order to keep utility constant, increases in the consumption of one good must be offset by decreases in the consumption of the second good.   **T F**

5. The following combinations of goods X and Y could not lie on the same indifference curve: (3X and 5Y) and (6X and 7Y).   **T F**

6. An indifference curve exists only for those combinations of goods the consumer can afford.   **T F**

7. A change in tastes can change the slope of an indifference curve.   **T F**

8. If a number of indifference curves are placed on the same graph, the resulting figure is called an indifference map.   **T F**

9. To find a demand curve, change the consumer's income and note the combinations of goods where the budget line and indifference curves are tangent.   **T F**

10. If the price of cheese is $4 and the price of steak is $8, at Philly's equilibrium his marginal rate of substitution is 2 cheese per 1 steak.   **T F**

■ **MULTIPLE-CHOICE**

Circle the letter that corresponds to the best answer.

1. Along a consumer's budget line:
(a)   utility is constant
(b)   income is constant
(c)   prices of the two goods are changing
(d)   marginal rate of substitution is constant

2. A decrease in income will:
(a)   shift the budget line inward and increase its slope
(b)   shift the budget line outward and increase its slope
(c)   shift the budget line outward and have no effect on its slope
(d)   shift the budget line inward and have no effect on its slope

3. If good Y is on the vertical axis and good X is on the horizontal axis, a lower price for X will, *ceteris paribus*:
(a)   rotate the budget line outward, leaving fixed the Y axis intercept
(b)   rotate the budget line inward, leaving fixed the X axis intercept

(c) shift the budget line outward in a parallel fashion

(d) shift the budget line inward in a parallel fashion

4. If the consumer's income is $200, the prices are $10 for good X and $20 for good Y, the budget line can be found by joining the intercept terms, which are:

(a) 10 on the X axis and 5 on the Y axis
(b) 20 on the X axis and 10 on the Y axis
(c) 20 on the X axis and 20 on the Y axis
(d) 10 on the X axis and 20 on the Y axis

5. Suppose that a consumer has an income of $8, the price of R is $1, and the price of S is $0.50. Which combination is on the consumer's budget line?

(a) 8R and 1S
(b) 7R and 1S
(c) 6R and 6S
(d) 5R and 6S

6. When the income of the consumer is $20, the price of T is $5, the price of Z is $2, and the quantity of T is measured horizontally, the slope of the budget line is:

(a) 2/5
(b) 2.5
(c) 4.0
(d) 0.4

7. An indifference curve shows the different combinations of two goods that:

(a) give the consumer equal marginal utilities
(b) cost the same
(c) give a consumer equal total utility
(d) can be purchased with a given income

8. The amount of one good the consumer is willing to give up to get an additional unit of another good is called:

(a) slope of the budget line
(b) the income constraint
(c) marginal rate of substitution
(d) relative price ratio

Use the next diagram to answer questions 9 to 13.

9. Which combination is currently unattainable for this consumer?

(a) A
(b) B

(c) C
(d) D

10. For this consumer it can be said that:
(a) combination A is preferred to combination D
(b) combination A is preferred to combination C
(c) combination B is preferred to combination C
(d) combination B is preferred to combination A

11. Given the preferences and budget line depicted, the consumer will purchase combination:
(a) A
(b) B
(c) C
(d) D

12. Which of the following may allow the consumer to purchase combination C?
(a) a decrease in income
(b) an increase in the price of good I
(c) an increase in the price of good J
(d) a decrease in the price of good I

13. To derive the demand for good I, the price of I is varied. Held constant is:
(a) money income of the consumer
(b) price of good J
(c) consumer's tastes
(d) all of the above

14. The fact that the marginal rate of substitution diminishes along an indifference curve is reflected in:

(a) the convexity of the indifference curve
(b) the negative slope of the indifference curve
(c) the fact that there are many indifference curves
(d) the negative slope of the budget line

Use the next diagram to answer questions 15 and 16.

15. If the budget line shifts from BL1 to BL2, it could be because:
(a) the price of K has increased
(b) the price of K has decreased
(c) the price of L has increased
(d) the price of L has decreased

16. The diagram shows that when the budget line shifts from BL1 to BL2, this consumer will:
(a) buy more of both K and L
(b) buy less of K and more of L
(c) buy less of both K and L
(d) buy more of K and less of L

17. Mike loves his car, and spends all his income on gas and car washes. At his equilibrium, Mike's marginal rate of substitution is 6 car washes per tank of gas. If it costs him $7 to wash his car, what does a tank of gas cost him?
(a) $42
(b) $36
(c) $35
(d) we don't have enough data to know

18. Jamila is consuming at a point on her budget line where her marginal rate of substitution is 3 ap-

ples per 1 cappuccino. The market prices are $0.50 for apples, and $2 for cappuccino. Therefore:
(a) Jamila is in a utility-maximizing equilibrium
(b) Jamila can increase utility by purchasing more apples and less cappuccino
(c) Jamila can increase utility by purchasing less apples and more cappuccino
(d) Jamila can increase utility by purchasing more apples and more cappuccino

19. If at his current consumption levels Kris's marginal utility from hats is 50 utils per hat, and his marginal utility from CDs is 10 utils per CD, then his marginal rate of substitution is:
(a) 5 hats per CD
(b) 40 hats per CD
(c) 5 CDs per hat
(d) 1/5 CD per hat

■ **DISCUSSION QUESTIONS**

1. Explain why the slope of the budget line is negative.

2. Explain why the slope of the indifference curve is negative, and why the curve is convex.

3. Explain why the budget line can be called "objective" whereas the indifference curve is "subjective."

4. Explain how the consumer's indifference map and budget lines are used to derive the consumer's demand for one of the products. In deriving demand what is varied and what is held constant?

5. Sketch an indifference curve-budget line diagram that shows the case of a person buying a combination of goods where the indifference curve cuts down through the budget line. Is the individual getting the maximum possible utility from his or her income? Draw in a new budget line to show that the individual could obtain the same level of utility now being enjoyed with a smaller income.

6. As consumers we don't actually use indifference curves and budget lines to decide what to buy at the grocery store; so how can this theory be useful in explaining consumer behaviour?

7. What is the "important difference between the marginal utility theory and the indifference curve theory of consumer demand"?

■ ANSWERS

FILL-IN QUESTIONS

1. income, prices

2. price of X, price of Y

3. right, does not

4. inward, vertical (Y); steeper

5. downward, rate, substitution; convex

6. flatter

7. greater

8. tangent; slope, slope, equal

9. is; does not

PROBLEMS AND PROJECTS

1. (a) 400; (b) 100; (c) 400, 100; (e) cannot, outside; (f) 4G/1S; (g) 4; (h) 320, 80

2. (a) *d* because it's on the highest indifference curve; (b) *a, b* because they are on the same indifference curve; (c) 2 because he is willing to move from 10 to 8 bats in order to have 5 instead of 4 gloves

3. (b) *a*; (d) *c*; (e) 4, 2 because these are the number of gloves purchased at the equilibrium at each of these two prices

TRUE-FALSE

1. F   it's the reciprocal of this
2. F   because the Y intercept decreases, the budget line becomes flatter
3. T
4. T
5. T   the second basket would be preferred because it has more of both X and Y
6. F   indifference curves exist for all combinations, attainable or unattainable
7. T   if it changes the consumer's willingness to trade between the two goods
8. T
9. F   change the price of the good in question, not income
10. T   because the slope of the budget line must equal the MRS

MULTIPLE-CHOICE

1. (b)
2. (d)   a parallel inward shift
3. (a)   only the X intercept changes because only the price of X changed
4. (b) $200/$10 = 20 and $200/$20 = 10
5. (d)   (5 x $1) + (6 x $0.50) = $8
6. (b)   intercepts are 4T and 10Z, 10/4 = 2.5 Z per T
7. (c)
8. (c)
9. (c)   point C lies outside the budget line
10. (d)   B lies on a higher indifference curve than A
11. (b)   B lies on the highest attainable indifference curve, and the budget line and indifference curve are tangent at this point
12. (d)   this is the only option given that expands the budget line; the other options shrink the budget line
13. (d)   these are among the *ceteris paribus* conditions when we move along a demand curve
14. (a)
15. (b)
16. (a)   the tangency point on BL2 has more L and more K than the tangency point on BL1
17. (a)   MRS = price ratio; X/$7 = 6/1
18. (b)   MRS = 3 A/C and this is lower than relative price ratio = 4 A/C.
19. (c)   5 CDs add as much to his total utility as 1 hat

CHAPTER 8

The Organization and Costs of Production

This important chapter is the first of several that examine the behaviour of business firms that make up the supply side of markets. We begin with a description of the general nature and organization of business firms in Canada, and then discuss production and costs.

While we assume that all firms attempt to maximize profits, firms differ drastically in form and size. The three major legal forms are the sole proprietorship, the partnership, and the corporation. The chapter discusses the advantages and disadvantages of each legal form. A key point is that a corporation offers its owners limited liability. This advantage enables a corporation to raise large sums of financial capital by selling shares to many small investors, and has made the corporation the dominant form of business in Canada.

Much of the chapter examines the nature of the production costs. To reckon economic (opportunity) costs correctly, we must count both explicit and implicit costs. Consequently, economic profits differ from accounting profits. Correct thinking about costs also requires that we clearly distinguish between the short run and long run because there are different costs according to the adjustment options open to the firm within each timeframe.

In the short run the firm's plant is fixed, so the firm is limited to adjusting output by adjusting the amount of variable resources employed (usually labour). When the firm adds labour, beyond some point the firm's production becomes less and less efficient as the plant becomes overcrowded with increasing numbers of workers (who don't have more space or equipment to work with). This is the idea behind the law of diminishing returns, a concept which also affects the shapes of short-run cost curves. Short-run costs can be represented in both "total" and "per unit" terms.

In the long run the firm is not limited by the size of its current plant. There is time to change plant size, and for firms to enter or leave the industry. The key cost curve in the long run is the firm's average cost curve. The shape of this curve depends on the disadvantages and advantages that come into play as the firm expands output. If the advantages dominate, then the firm experiences economies of scale, and the long-run average total cost curve is declining.

Over the next few chapters we will see how a firm's production and cost conditions influence the firm's choices in various market structure settings: how much output to produce, what price to charge, whether to stay in business, whether to expand plant capacity, etc.

■ CHAPTER LEARNING OBJECTIVES

In this chapter you will learn:
□ The various organizational forms a firm can take.
□ The nature of economic costs.
□ About a firm's short-run production relationships.
□ About a firm's short-run production costs.
□ The link between a firm's size and costs in the long run.

■ CHAPTER OUTLINE

1. A plant is a physical establishment where production takes place (e.g., a factory, store, or mine). A firm is a business organization that owns one or more plants where it produces its output. An industry is a group of firms that produce the same or similar products.

2. Multiplant firms can be organized in various ways:

(a)   A horizontally integrated firm owns multiple plants performing much the same function.

(b)   A vertically integrated firm owns plants that operate at different stages of the production process.

(c)   A conglomerate owns plants producing goods across a number of markets or industries.

3. The entrepreneur has three choices of legal forms under which to operate a business firm: sole proprietorship, partnership, or corporation.

(a)   A sole proprietorship is owned and operated by one person, so has the advantages of ease of organization, maximum freedom, and strong individual incentive to operate efficiently. Its drawbacks are lack of financial resources, the burden for a single person to perform all management functions, and unlimited liability for the owner.

(b)   A partnership is owned by two or more owners who pool their resources in order to mobilize more financial resources and take advantage of greater specialization than the sole proprietorship can provide. Partnerships can be hampered by disagreements in management, lack of continuity, and unlimited liability for each partner — even for the consequences of decisions made by their partners.

(c)   A corporation is a legal entity distinct and separate from its owners (or stockholders). Limited liability for investors enables corporations to attract large amounts of financial capital, allowing for the use of mass-production technologies. Disadvantages of the corporation include bureaucracy and expense in organization, and double taxation of income. From a social viewpoint, corporations can shelter business operators from legal consequences of unscrupulous actions.

4. Two main sources of financing for corporations are the sales of stocks and bonds.

(a)   A stockholder is a part owner of the firm, and is entitled to share in any profits.

(b)   A bondholder is a lender to the firm, and is entitled to specified regular interest payments, and when the bond reaches maturity, the return of the original investment.

5. Very large corporations often face the principal-agent problem. The corporation is owned by many, many stockholders (principals) who each have only a small stake, and are not involved in managing the corporation. For this they hire managers (agents).

Unfortunately, the agents' goals may be in conflict with the principals' goals of maximizing profits.

6. Production costs exist because resources are scarce and have alternative uses. The economic cost (or opportunity cost) of resources used in production is measured as their value in their next best use.

7. Economic costs may be explicit or implicit.

(a)   An explicit cost is a direct monetary outlay from a firm to a resource supplier (e.g., wages, payments to suppliers of raw materials).

(b)   An implicit cost is the opportunity cost of using a self-owned, self-employed resource. A key type of implicit cost is "normal profit." Unless the entrepreneur earns a return equal to what his/her skills could command in a different business, he/she will leave to seek the higher return available elsewhere.

(c)   Economic profit (or pure profit) is total revenue received in excess of all explicit and implicit opportunity costs of resources used. In contrast, accounting profit is equal to total revenue less accounting (explicit) costs.

8. The firm's economic costs vary with the firm's output. The specific relationship between costs and output depends upon whether the firm is able to make short-run or long-run changes in the amount of resources it employs.

(a)   In the short run the firm's plant is a fixed resource, so the level of output can be changed only by changing the usage of labour and other variable factors.

(b)   In the long run all resources can be altered, so even plant size is variable.

9. Short-run production relationships show how output varies with labour when the plant size is fixed.

(a)   Total product, TP, shows total output at each level of labour input.

(b)   Marginal product, MP, shows the extra output from adding an extra unit of labour.

(c)   Average product, AP, also called labour productivity, shows total output per unit of labour.

10. The law of diminishing returns states that as successive units of a variable resource (say, labour) are added to a fixed resource (say, capital), beyond some point the marginal product will decline. This law and the input prices together determine the manner in which the costs of the firm change as output varies in the short run.

11. In the short run, the total costs of a firm are the sum of its fixed and variable costs. As output increases:
(a)   the total fixed costs (TFC) do not change;
(b)   the total variable costs (TVC) increase, at first at a decreasing and then at an increasing rate; and
(c)   total costs (TC) at first increase at a decreasing and then at an increasing rate.

12. Average fixed, average variable, and average total cost are equal, respectively, to the firm's fixed, variable, and total cost divided by the output of the firm. As output increases in the short run:
(a)   average fixed cost (AFC) decreases;
(b)   average variable cost (AVC) at first decreases and then increases; and
(c)   average total cost (ATC) also decreases at first and then increases.

13. Marginal cost (MC) is the extra cost incurred in producing one additional unit of output.
(a) Because the marginal product of the variable resources increases and then decreases (according to the law of diminishing returns), MC decreases and then increases as output increases.
(b) At the minimum point on AVC, AVC and MC are equal; and at the minimum point on ATC, ATC and MC are equal.
(c) Given fixed input prices, the MC and AVC curves are mirror images of the MP and AP curves, respectively.

14. Changes in resource prices or technology will cause the cost curves to shift.

15. In the long run all resources employed by the firm are variable resources; therefore all costs are variable costs. The chapter focuses on the long-run average total cost derived from the set of ATC curves for all possible plant sizes.
(a)   The long-run ATC curve shows the lowest per-unit cost that can be achieved at each output level, given that the firm has had time to change to a plant of the most appropriate size.
(b)   If the firm expands its output by expanding its plant, long-run ATC tends to fall at first because of the economies of large-scale production, but if this expansion continues far enough, long-run ATC will begin to rise because of the diseconomies of large-scale production.
(c)   A firm that has constant returns to scale has a flat long-run ATC curve.

16. Economies of scale result from the greater possibilities in larger plants for specialization of labour and management, and the ability to employ more efficient capital equipment. Diseconomies of scale are caused by managerial problems of coordination and control encountered in large firms.
(a)   Examples from startup firms, the Verson metal stamping machine, and the daily newspaper illustrate economies of scale.
(b)   The example of GM illustrates how very large firms encounter diseconomies of scale.

17. Economies or diseconomies of scale are an important determinant of an industry's structure. Minimum efficient scale (MES) is the lowest level of output at which a firm can minimize long-run average costs. The size of MES therefore dictates the minimum size for the firm.
(a)   The concept of MES explains why large and small firms could both be viable in an industry with constant returns to scale over a wide output range.
(b)   In other industries where the long-run average-cost curve declines over a wide range of output, there may be insufficient consumer demand to allow for efficient production by more than a small number of large firms.
(c)   When economies of scale extend beyond the market size, the conditions exist for a natural monopoly, meaning that per-unit costs are minimized only if the product is made by only a single firm.

■   **TERMS AND CONCEPTS**

plant	economic profit
firm	short run
vertical combination	long run
horizontal combination	total product
conglomerate combination	marginal product
industry	average product
sole proprietorship	law of diminishing returns
partnership	fixed costs
corporation	variable costs
stocks	total cost
bonds	average fixed cost
limited liability	average variable cost
double taxation	average total cost
principal-agent problem	marginal cost
	economies of scale
	diseconomies of scale

economic
  (opportunity) cost
explicit costs
implicit costs
normal profit

constant returns to
  scale
minimum efficient
  scale
natural monopoly

■ HINTS AND TIPS

1. This is a difficult and important chapter that requires and deserves more of your time than most
chapters.

2. Many different concepts of productivity and cost
are described in this chapter. Be sure that you understand their definitions, that you also know them
by their abbreviations, and that you know their for-
mulas – forwards and backwards.

3. Make sure that you clearly recognize the difference between *marginal* and *average* relationships.
Marginal always refers to something incremental
(i.e. for one unit more). Average is always a per unit
measure calculated by dividing a total measure by a
number of units.

4. You have not mastered the various concepts
until you can correctly sketch from memory: (1) the
productivity curves, (2) the short-run total cost
curves, (3) the short-run average and marginal cost
curves, and (4) the long-run average cost curve.
You should also be able to explain the relationship
between the curves in each set that you draw.

5. In graphs and tables, marginal product and
marginal cost are always treated as "in between."
For example, the marginal cost value calculated
from data at output levels of 10 units and 20 units
should be graphed at 15 units.

■ FILL-IN QUESTIONS

1. McDonald's is an example of a(n) (plant, firm,
industry) _firm_. The McDonald's restaurant
in Salmon Arm is an example of a(n) _plant_.
McDonald's and all other fast food restaurants together represent a(n) _industry_.

2. A multi-plant firm would be a (vertical, horizontal) _____ combination of plants if each plant
is at the same stage in the production process, and
a _____ combination if each plant is at a different stage in the production process.

3. A firm that owns plants that operate across different markets and industries is termed a
conglomerate.

4. The main legal forms of business enterprise
are: _sole proprietorship_, _partnership_, and _corporation_.

5. Corporations are responsible for most economic
activity due to their superior ability to raise
capital.

6. Double taxation of corporate profit refers to the
fact that corporate income is taxed twice: once as
corporate profit and again, if paid out in dividends, as
part of stockholders' _personal incomes_.

7. The liability for business losses of a sole proprietor or of partners is _unlimited_, but the liability
of stockholders for the debts of a corporation is
limited.

8. A purchaser of a corporate (stock, bond)
stock owns a portion of the corporation,
whereas a purchaser of a corporate _bond_ is
simply lending to the corporation.

9. The separation of ownership and control that is
typical in (large, small) _large_ corporations with
(many, few) _many_ stockholders may create a
principal-agent problem. In this situation the (managers, stockholders) _stockholders_ are the principals,
and the _managers_ are their agents.

10. Costs exist because resources are _scarce_
and have _alternative_ uses. The economic cost of
a resource is also known as its _opportunity_ cost,
measuring its value in its next best use.

11. A monetary payment a firm makes to outside
suppliers is called an (explicit, implicit) _explicit_
cost. An _implicit_ cost is the opportunity cost of
self-owned, self-employed resources.

12. A normal profit is a return for performing the
entrepreneurial function and is an (explicit, implicit)
implicit cost.

13. Accounting profit equals total revenues minus
explicit costs. Economic profit is defined as accounting profit minus _implicit_ costs.

14. The firm's plant capacity is fixed in the (short,
long) _short_ run and variable in the
long run.

15. The change in output as a result of using one more unit of the variable input is called _marginal_ product.

16. The law of diminishing returns is that as successive units of a (fixed, variable) _variable_ resource are added to a _fixed_ resource, eventually the (total, marginal) _marginal_ product of the (fixed, variable) _variable_ resource will decrease. Marginal product ultimately diminishes because too much of the _variable_ resource is being used relative to the _fixed_ resource.

17. When the total product:
(a)   increases at an increasing rate, the marginal product is (rising, falling) _rising_;
(b)   increases at a decreasing rate, the marginal product is (positive, negative, zero) _positive_, but (rising, falling) _falling_;
(c)   is at a maximum, the marginal product is (positive, negative, zero) _zero_;
(d)   decreases, the marginal product is (positive, negative, zero) _negative_.

Questions 18 to 23 are based on the table below:

Units of Labour	Units of Capital	Total Product	Total Cost of Labour	Total Cost of Capital	Total Cost of Production
1	1	10	$15	$30	$45
2	1	27	30	30	60
3	1	40	45	30	75
4	1	50	60	30	90
5	1	56	75	30	105
6	1	58	90	30	120

18. The variable input is _Labour_ and the fixed input is _capital_. When production is 56 units of output, total variable cost is $ _75_ and total fixed cost is $ _30_.

19. The marginal product of the 4th unit of variable input is _10_; the marginal product of the 6th unit of variable input is _2_.

20. The law of diminishing returns (does, does not) _does_ hold in this case because with one (fixed, variable) _fixed_ input, the (average, marginal, total) _marginal_ product of the _variable_ input (increases, decreases) _decreases_.

21. In the table, as output goes from 10 to 27 units, total costs increase from $ _45_ to $ _60_. Therefore marginal cost will be _15_ / _17_ = _0.88_.

22. The decreasing part of the marginal cost curve corresponds to (decreasing, increasing) _increasing_ marginal product and the increasing section corresponds to _decreasing_ marginal product. The minimum point on marginal cost matches the _maximum_ point of marginal product.

23. In the table:
(a)   the average variable cost of 50 units of output is $ _1.20_ (60/50)
(b)   the average fixed cost of 50 units of output is $ _0.60_ (30/50)
(c)   the average total cost of 50 units of output is $ _1.80_ (90/50)

24. Suppose that the average weight of players on the Argonauts football team was 100 kg. If a new player weighing 110 kg were added to the team without anyone being dropped, the average weight would (increase, decrease) _increase_. This example indicates that when the marginal value is (greater, less) _greater_ than the average value, the average value will (increase, decrease) _increase_.

25. When marginal cost is less than average variable cost, average variable cost is (rising, falling, constant) _____.

26. The long-run average total cost curve shows the _lowest_ per unit cost at which any output can be produced after the firm has had time to make all appropriate adjustments in its _plant size_.

27. Economies of scale explain the _downward_ -sloping part of the (long-run, short-run) _long-run_ ATC curve. Diseconomies of scale explain the _upward_ -sloping part of the same curve. If the curve is flat the firm is experiencing _constant_ returns to scale.

28. Three factors that can lead to lower average costs of production as plant size increases are:
(a)   _____
(b)   _____
(c)   _____

29. The smallest level of output at which a firm can minimize long-run average cost is termed

_____. Relatively large and small firms could both be viable an the same industry if there is an extended range of _____ returns to scale.

30. The conditions for a _____ exist when unit costs are minimized if a single firm produces all output for the market.

■ **PROBLEMS AND PROJECTS**

1. Indicate, whether each business characteristic below is associated with the sole proprietorship (PROP), partnership (PART), corporation (CORP), two of these, or all three of these legal forms.
   (a)   Much red tape and legal expense in beginning the firm _____
   (b)   Unlimited liability _____
   (c)   No specialized management _____
   (d)   Has life independent of its owner(s) _____
   (e)   Its owners are called stockholders _____
   (f)   Greatest ability to acquire funds for the expansion of the firm _____
   (g)   Permits some but not a great degree of specialized management _____
   (h)   Possibility of unresolved disagreement among owners over courses of action _____
   (i)   Business owner can avoid responsibility for business losses _____
   (j)   Issues common shares with voting rights _____

2. The Jack of Diamonds Jewellers reports the following results for 2001:

Total sales revenue	$2,000,000
Cost of diamonds	1,500,000
Staff wages and benefits	300,000
Rent	100,000
Forgone wages for owner	45,000
Forgone interest	5,000
Forgone entrepreneurial income	10,000

   (a)   The total explicit cost = $ 1.9m .
   (b)   The accounting profit = $ 100,000 .
   (c)   The total implicit cost = $ 60,000 .
   (d)   The normal profit = $ 10,000 .
   (e)   The economic profit = $ 40,000 .

3. The following table shows the daily production at Texas Style Textiles, a firm that manufactures jeans using labour, capital, and materials. Capital is held constant in the short run.

Labour	Total Production	Average Product of Labour	Marginal Product of Labour
(workers/day)	(jeans/day)	(jeans/worker)	(jeans/worker)
0	0	—	
			80
1	80	80	
			120
2	200	100	
			130
3	330	110	
			70
4	400	100	
			50
5	450	90	
			30
6	480	80	
			10
7	490	70	
			-10
8	480	60	

   (a)   In the parentheses at the head of each column, indicate the units of measurement.
   (b)   Fill in the values for the average product column (AP).
   (c)   Fill in the marginal product column (MP).
   (d)   There are increasing returns to labour from the first to the _3rd_ unit of labour, and diminishing returns from the _3rd_ to the eighth unit.
   (e)   When total production (TP) is increasing, MP is (positive, negative) _____, and when TP is decreasing, MP is _____.
   (f)   When the MP is greater than the AP, AP (increases, decreases) _____.

4. Match each cost concept from the list on the left with the correct formula on the right.
   (a)   TC   (i)   AVC x Q
   (b)   AVC   (ii)   TFC + TVC
   (c)   MC   (iii) TVC / Q
   (d)   ATC   (iv)   change in TC / change in Q
   (e)   TVC   (v)   TFC / Q
   (f)   AFC   (vi) AFC + AVC

5. Centurion Tax Services has a fixed amount of capital (office space and computer equipment). It varies its output of tax returns by varying the number of clerks it employs. The table below shows the relationships between the amount of labour employed, output, marginal product of labour, and average product of labour.

(a) Assume there is a fixed cost of $200 for capital resources. Fill in the TFC column.

(b) Assume each unit of labour costs $50. Compute the cost of labour, or TVC, for each quantity of labour that Centurion might employ, and enter these figures in the table.

(c) Fill in the AVC column.

(d) Fill in the MC column.

(e) When MP increases, the MC (increases, decreases) _____, and when MP decreases, the MC _____ .

(f) When AP increases, the AVC (increases, decreases) _____, and when AP decreases, the AVC _____ .

(g) Fill in the AFC column.

(h) Fill in the ATC column.

(i) In this example, ATC falls and then rises. At the output level closest to the lowest value of ATC, the AFC is (falling, rising) _____ and AVC is _____ .

(j) MC has approximately the same value as AVC and ATC in the vicinity of the _____ values for each.

Labour	Output	Marginal Product of Labour	Avg Product of Labour	Total Variable Cost	Marginal Cost	Avg Variable Cost	Total Fixed Cost	Avg Fixed Cost	Total Cost	Avg Total Cost
clerks	returns	returns/ clerk	returns/ clerk	$	$/return	$/return	$	$/return	$	$/return
0	0									
		5			—					
1	5		5	—		—	—	—	—	—
		6			—					
2	11		5.5	—		—	—	—	—	—
		7			—					
3	18		6	—		—	—	—	—	—
		6			—					
4	24		6	—		—	—	—	—	—
		5			—					
5	29		5.8	—		—	—	—	—	—
		4			—					
6	33		5.5	—		—	—	—	—	—
		3			—					
7	36		5.1	—		—	—	—	—	—
		2			—					
8	38		4.8	—		—	—	—	—	—

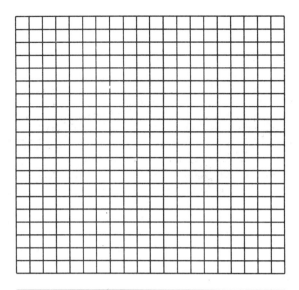

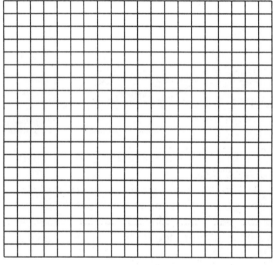

6. Using the graphs above, plot the data from question 5 as follows:

(a) In one graph plot total fixed cost, total variable cost, and total cost.

(b) In the other graph plot average fixed cost, average variable cost, average total cost, and marginal cost.

7. An economic historian has recovered the following table of costs from a 19th century coal mine. The document is crumbling with age, so many of the entries are illegible (marked as blanks). Use your knowledge of cost relationships to fill in the blank values.

	Q = 1	Q = 2	Q = 3	Q = 4	Q = 5
TFC	___	___	___	___	___
TVC	___	___	9.00	___	___
TC	___	25.00	___	___	___
AFC	___	___	___	___	4.00
AVC	3.00	___	___	___	4.00
ATC	___	___	___	8.50	___

8. The diagram below shows the short-run average-total-cost schedules for three different plant sizes. Assume that these are the only possible plant sizes that a firm might build.

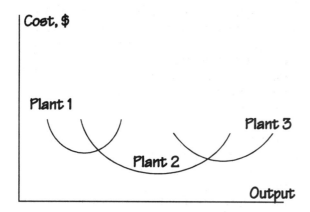

(a)   Draw the firm's long-run average cost curve in this diagram.
(b)   On the output axis, indicate the range of production levels for which Plant 1 is most efficient, the range for which Plant 2 is most efficient, and the range for which Plant 3 is the most efficient.

9. Suppose last year you went into business buying and selling used textbooks. It cost you $10,000 to buy used books from students at the end of the term. The purchase was financed by a bank loan that has been repaid with an interest cost of $665. Part-time help cost $7,000 for the year. You operated the business out of your garage and paid utility expenses of $500 for the year. You bought a cash register, shelves, etc. with $1,200 from your savings account. Your part-time helper happened to be an accounting student who told you that you should make an allowance of $200/year for the wear and tear on the equipment you bought.

You estimate that you worked 500 hours in your store but did not take any wage payment. The previous year you had worked in the campus bookstore and earned $5 per hour. Previously, you had rented your garage to a neighbour for $20 per month. Your savings were earning 10% interest.

(a)   List the explicit and the implicit costs.
(b)   Suppose you sold all the purchased books for $21,600. (1) Did you make an accounting profit? (yes, no) _____; how much? _____; (2) an economic profit? (yes, no); _____; how much? _____.
(c)   If you could sell your equipment for $1,000 and rent out the garage for $20/month, would you continue in business for another year? _____.

■   **TRUE-FALSE**

Circle T if the statement is true, F if it is false.

1. A plant is defined as a group of firms under a single management. **T F**

2. A firm that operates a number of plants at the same stage in the production process would be termed a horizontal combination. **T F**

3. Best Western Hotels would be a conglomerate because it owns plants in a number of different provinces. **T F**

4. Imperial Oil Ltd. would be a horizontal combination since it owns some plants that refine crude oil and other plants that sell the refined product. **T F**

5. The sole proprietorship form of business organization is subject to unlimited liability. **T F**

6. The partnership form of business organization allows for greater specialization in management than the sole proprietorship form. **T F**

7. The death of a partner usually leads to dissolution and complete reorganization of the firm. **T F**

8. A corporation is a legal entity, distinct and separate from its owners. **T F**

9. The owners of a corporation are called bondholders. **T F**

10. When a person purchases a common stock he/she becomes a part owner of the corporation. **T F**

11. The return paid to stockholders by the corporation is called a dividend. **T F**

12. A shareholder is liable for the unpaid debts of the corporation he/she owns. **T F**

13. The economic costs of a firm are the payments it must make to resource owners to attract their resources from alternative employments. **T F**

14. The separation of ownership and control in a corporation means that managers and executives may make decisions contrary to the stockholders' goal of profit-maximization. **T F**

15. Economic or pure profit is a return over and above the alternative cost of all inputs. **T F**

16. Normal profit is an implicit cost. **T F**

17. It is possible for a firm to have an accounting profit but to suffer an economic loss at the same time. **T F**

18. In the short run all factors of production are variable. **T F**

19. In the short run, the reason that marginal product declines is that variable inputs of inferior quality are hired last and produce less. **T F**

20. If marginal product is negative, total output decreases when an extra unit of the variable input is utilized in production. **T F**

21. The larger the output of the firm, the smaller is the firm's average fixed cost. **T F**

22. Marginal cost is the extra cost incurred by hiring one more unit of input. **T F**

23. In the short run marginal cost can be calculated from either the change in total cost or the change in total variable cost. **T F**

24. Minimum efficient scale occurs at the largest level of output at which a firm can minimize long-run average costs. **T F**

25. One explanation of why the long-run average cost curve of a firm rises after some level of output has been reached is the law of diminishing returns. **T F**

26. A firm that is experiencing constant returns to scale can double output by doubling its employment of all inputs. **T F**

27. Diseconomies of scale are caused by problems of coordination and communication that arise in large firms. **T F**

■ **MULTIPLE-CHOICE**

Circle the letter that corresponds to the best answer.

1. A single firm owns and operates three plants: a farm growing wheat, a flour-milling plant, and a bakery. This group of plants is an example of a:
  (a) horizontal combination
  (b) vertical combination
  (c) conglomerate combination
  (d) corporation

2. Which of the following is **not** one of the advantages of a sole proprietorship?
  (a) ease of organization
  (b) ease of decision-making
  (c) strong incentive for the owner
  (d) easy access to capital

3. Which of the following is a disadvantage of a partnership compared to a proprietorship?
  (a) greater access to capital
  (b) greater access to specialized management
  (c) unlimited liability for another partner's decisions
  (d) all of the above

4. Limited liability is associated with:
  (a) sole proprietorships
  (b) partnerships
  (c) corporations
  (d) both proprietorships and partnerships

5. Which form of business organization is most effective in raising financial capital?
  (a) corporation
  (b) partnership
  (c) proprietorship
  (d) vertical combination

6. Double taxation of corporate profits arises because:
  (a) personal income tax must be paid on dividends but not on interest earned

(b) both the federal government and the provinces in Canada levy a corporation profits tax
(c) American-owned corporations in Canada are taxed by both Canadian and American governments
(d) a corporation pays a corporate profits tax and a shareholder also pays a personal income tax on any dividends received from the corporation

7. The separation of ownership and control in corporations raises questions concerning:
(a) accountability of corporate managers to corporate stockholders
(b) dividend policy
(c) managerial benefits
(d) all of the above

8. Normal profit is defined as the cost of obtaining the services of:
(a) management
(b) entrepreneurs
(c) capital
(d) land

9. The revenues of a firm less its explicit costs are defined as the firm's:
(a) normal profit
(b) accounting profit
(c) economic profit
(d) economic rent

Questions 10 through 12 refer to the following table that shows a firm's short-run production relationship between the variable factor (labour) and output. Assume that plant capacity is fixed.

Amount of Labour	Amount of Output
1	3
2	8
3	12
4	15
5	17
6	18
7	17

10. The marginal product of the fourth unit of labour is:
(a) 2 units of output
(b) 3 units of output
(c) 4 units of output
(d) 5 units of output

11. When the firm hires four units of labour, the average product of labour is:
(a) 3 units of output
(b) 3.75 units of output
(c) 4 units of output
(d) 15 units of output

12. Diminishing returns becomes operative when:
(a) the second unit of labour is employed
(b) the third unit of labour is employed
(c) the fifth unit of labour is employed
(d) the seventh unit of labour is employed

13. Because the average product of a variable resource at first increases, and later decreases as a firm increases its output:
(a) AVC at first decreases then later increases
(b) AFC decreases as the output of the firm expands
(c) TVC at first increases by increasing amounts and then increases by decreasing amounts
(d) MC at first increases then later decreases

14. Because the marginal product of a resource at first increases and then decreases as the output of the firm increases:
(a) AFC declines as the firm's output increases
(b) AVC at first increases and then decreases
(c) TVC at first increases by increasing amounts and then increases by decreasing amounts
(d) MC at first decreases and then increases

15. Marginal cost and average variable cost are equal at the output at which:
(a) marginal cost is a minimum
(b) marginal product is a maximum
(c) average variable cost is a minimum
(d) average variable cost is a maximum

The table below refers to a firm with a fixed cost of $500, and variable costs as indicated in the table. Questions 16 through 18 use the given data.

Output	Total Variable Cost
1	$ 200
2	360
3	500
4	700
5	1,000
6	1,800

16. The average variable cost when the firm produces 4 units of output is:
- **(a)** $175
- **(b)** $200
- **(c)** $300
- **(d)** $700

17. The average total cost of 4 units of output is:
- **(a)** $175
- **(b)** $200
- **(c)** $300
- **(d)** $700

18. The marginal cost of the sixth unit of output is:
- **(a)** $200
- **(b)** $300
- **(c)** $700
- **(d)** $800

Questions 19 through 26 are based on the next diagram that shows a firm's short-run cost curves.

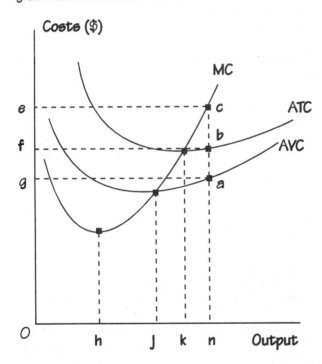

19. The marginal cost of the *n*th unit of output is distance:
- **(a)** 0e
- **(b)** 0f
- **(c)** 0g
- **(d)** 0h

20. The average fixed cost at output 0n is distance:

(a) 0e
(b) 0f
(c) gf
(d) 0g

21. Total fixed cost for 0n units of output is area:
- **(a)** ecfb
- **(b)** 0fbn
- **(c)** 0gan
- **(d)** fgab

22. Total variable cost of 0n units of output is area:
- **(a)** 0nag
- **(b)** 0nfb
- **(c)** 0nec
- **(d)** fbec

23. Total cost of 0n units of output is area:
- **(a)** 0nag
- **(b)** 0nbf
- **(c)** 0nce
- **(d)** fbce

24. Average total cost is at a minimum at output:
- **(a)** 0h
- **(b)** 0j
- **(c)** 0k
- **(d)** 0n

25. The point of diminishing returns for this firm comes at output:
- **(a)** 0h
- **(b)** 0j
- **(c)** 0k
- **(d)** 0n

26. This firm's average product of labour is maximized at output:
- **(a)** 0h
- **(b)** 0j
- **(c)** 0k
- **(d)** 0n

27. Identify the incorrect formula:
- **(a)** ATC = AFC + AVC
- **(b)** AVC = TVC / Q
- **(c)** MC = ATC - AVC
- **(d)** TFC = AFC x Q

28. If a firm has ATC = $5 when output is 100 units, and ATC = $6 when output is 110 units, what is the MC between these two output levels?
- **(a)** $0.10

(b) $1.00
(c) $5.50
(d) $16.00

29. If a firm has TFC = $1000, and TC = $3000 when output is 100 units, how much is the AVC at 100 units of output?
(a) $2.00
(b) $20.00
(c) $30.00
(d) $2000.00

30. If a firm's MC is $12 between output of 3 units and 4 units, and TVC is $100 when output is 3 units, what is AVC when output is 4 units?
(a) $12.00
(b) $25.00
(c) $28.00
(d) $112.00

31. Based on the following table that shows short-run cost schedules for plants of three different sizes, what is the long-run average cost of producing 30 units of output, assuming that the firm can eventually build any one of these plants?
(a) $7
(b) $8
(c) $9
(d) $10

Plant 1		Plant 2		Plant 3	
Output	ATC	Output	ATC	Output	ATC
10	$10	10	$12	10	$14
20	9	20	10	20	11
30	8	30	9	30	9
40	9	40	8	40	7
50	10	50	9	50	9

32. Using the table above, at what output is long-run average cost at a minimum?
(a) 20
(b) 30
(c) 40
(d) 50

33. The minimum efficient scale of plant is:
(a) the size of plant where average fixed cost is a minimum
(b) the size of plant where average variable cost is falling
(c) the smallest level of output at which a firm can minimize long-run total costs
(d) the smallest level of output at which a firm can minimize long-run average cost

34. The long-run average costs of producing a particular product is one of the factors that determines:
(a) the competition among firms producing the product
(b) the number of firms in the industry producing the product
(c) the size of each of the firms in the industry producing the product
(d) all of the above

35. In the short run, which of the following curves will not shift as a result of an increase in the price of labour?
(a) average fixed cost
(b) average variable cost
(c) average total cost
(d) marginal cost

36. In the short run, which of the following curves will shift when total fixed cost increases?
(a) average fixed cost
(b) average variable cost
(c) marginal cost
(d) none of these will shift

37. A sunk cost:
(a) affects decisions in the short run
(b) affects decisions in the long run
(c) affects decisions in the short run and in the long run
(d) is irrelevant for decisions

■ **DISCUSSION QUESTIONS**

1. What is the difference between a plant and a firm? Between a firm and an industry? Which of these three concepts is the most difficult to apply in practice? Why? Distinguish between a horizontal, a vertical, and a conglomerate combination.

2. What are the principal advantages and disadvantages of each of the three legal forms of business organization? Which of the disadvantages of the proprietorship and partnership explain why most big businesses use the corporate form?

3. Explain what "separation of ownership and control" of the modern corporation means. What problems does this separation create for stockholders and the economy?

4. Suppose you start up a courier business, and use your own vehicle. What explicit and implicit costs would you incur? How would you determine what amount to assign to the implicit costs?

5. What is the difference between normal and economic profit? Why is the former an economic cost? How do you define accounting profit?

6. What type of adjustments can a firm make in the long run that it cannot make in the short run? What adjustments can it make in the short run? How long is the short run?

7. State precisely the law of diminishing returns. Is this a short run or a long run phenomenon? Why?

8. Distinguish between a fixed cost and a variable cost. Why are short-run total costs partly fixed and partly variable costs, and why are long-run costs entirely variable?

9. Suppose that you are in a garage band that decides to issue a CD. What might be some of the fixed costs associated with producing and selling the CD, and what might be some of the variable costs?

10. Given that the price of inputs is fixed, what is the connection between marginal product and marginal cost?

11. What happens to the average total cost, average variable cost, average fixed cost, and marginal cost curves when the price of a variable input increases or decreases? Describe what other factor can cause short-run cost curves to shift.

12. What does the long-run average-cost curve of a firm show? What relationship is there between long-run average-cost and the short-run average-total-cost schedules of the different-sized plants a firm might build?

13. Why is the long-run average-cost curve of a firm U-shaped? What is meant by and what are some causes of economies of large scale? What is meant by and what causes diseconomies of large scale?

14. How do the economies and diseconomies of scale influence the size and number of firms in an industry?

■ **ANSWERS**

FILL-IN QUESTIONS

1. firm; plant; industry
2. horizontal; vertical
3. conglomerate
4. sole proprietorship, partnership, corporation
5. capital
6. corporate profits, personal incomes
7. unlimited, limited
8. stock, bond
9. large, many, principal-agent; stockholders, managers
10. scarce, alternative; opportunity
11. explicit; implicit
12. entrepreneurial, implicit
13. explicit; implicit
14. short, long
15. marginal product
16. variable, fixed, marginal, variable; variable, fixed
17. (a) rising, (b) positive, falling (c) zero, (d) negative
18. labour, capital; 75, 30
19. 10; 2
20. does, fixed, marginal, variable, decreases
21. 45, 60; $15/17, $0.88
22. increasing, decreasing; maximum
23. (a) 1.20, (b) 0.60, (c) 1.80
24. increase; greater, increase
25. falling
26. lowest, plant size

27. down, long-run; up, constant

28. labour specialization, managerial specialization, efficient capital

29. minimum efficient scale; constant

30. natural monopoly

PROBLEMS AND PROJECTS

1. (a) CORP; (b) PROP and PART; (c) PROP; (d) CORP; (e) CORP; (f) CORP; (g) PART; (h) PART; (i) CORP; (j) CORP

2. (a) 1,900,000, (b) 100,000, (c) 60,000, (d) 10,000, (e) 40,000

3. (a) jeans/worker; jeans/worker; (b) AP = 80, 100, 110, 100, 90, 80, 70, 60; (c) MP = 80, 120, 130, 70, 50, 30, 10, -10; (d) third, fourth; (e) positive, negative; (f) increases

4. (a)-(ii); (b)-(iii); (c)-(iv); (d)-(vi); (e)-(i); (f)-(v)

5. (a) TFC = 200 at all output levels; (b) TVC = 50, 100, 150, 200, 250, 300, 350, 400; (c) AVC = 10.00, 9.09, 8.33, 8.33, 8.62, 9.09, 9.72, 10.53; (d) MC = 10.00, 8.33, 7.15, 8.33, 10.00, 12.50, 16.67, 25.00; (e) decreases, increases; (f) decreases, increases; (g) AFC = 40.00, 18.18, 11.11, 8.33, 6.90, 6.06, 5.55, 5.26; (h) ATC = 50.00, 27.27, 19.44, 16.66, 15.52, 15.15, 15.27, 15.79; (i) falling, rising; (j) minimum

7. Values (including those already given) from left to right in the table: TFC = 20, 20, 20, 20, 20; TVC = 3, 5, 9, 14, 20; TC = 23, 25, 29, 34, 40; AFC = 20.00, 10.00, 6.67, 5.00, 4.00; AVC = 3.00, 2.50, 3.00, 3.50; ATC = 23.00, 12.50, 9.67, 8.50, 8.00.

8. (a) The curve is made up of segments of the short-run curves, choosing at each output the lowest cost point; (b) Plant 1 is most efficient for all levels of output below where the curve for Plant 1 intersects the curve for Plant 2; Plant 2 is most efficient from that level of output up to the output where the Plant 2 curve intersects the Plant 3 curve; beyond that point, Plant 3 is most efficient.

9. (a) Explicit costs: book purchase $10,000, interest payment $665, wages for part-time help $7000, utilities $500. Implicit costs: forgone own wages $2500, forgone garage rent $240, forgone saving account interest $120, depreciation $200 (b) (1) yes, $3435 (Accounting recognizes depreciation as an explicit cost so the $3435 would be reduced by that amount) (2) yes, $375 (c)An economic profit was realized so you should stay in this business.

TRUE-FALSE

1. F   a plant is a single place of production
2. T
3. F   it would be a conglomerate if it owns plants producing different products
4. F   this describes a vertical combination
5. T
6. T   some degree of specialization is possible
7. T   only in a partnership
8. T
9. F   they are stockholders (or shareholders)
10. T
11. T
12. F   the shareholder can lose his/her investment, but is not personally liable to any extent for the firm's debts
13. T   opportunity costs, in other words
14. T   if managers and executive follow self-interest
15. T   over and above explicit and implicit costs
16. T   because entrepreneurial ability has an opportunity cost
17. T   if implicit costs exceed accounting profit
18. F   at least one factor is fixed in the short run
19. F   the law of diminishing returns does not assume this
20. F   because MP represents the change in TP as one more unit of variable input is added
21. T   "spreading the overhead"
22. F   the extra cost associated with one more unit of output
23. T   since TFC is, of course fixed, TVC and TC vary at exactly the same rate
24. F   lowest level of output to minimize long-run ATC
25. F   diminishing returns is relevant only in the short run, because it deals with one fixed input
26. T   and therefore ATC is constant
27. T

MULTIPLE-CHOICE

1. (b)   three different stages of production
2. (d)   difficult to raise capital beyond proprietor's own savings or personal credit
3. (c)   the others are advantages
4. (c)   others have unlimited liability
5. (a)   able to sell shares to large numbers of investors many of whom wish to invest only small amounts with limited liability
6. (d)
7. (d)   all are issues due to the principal-agent problem
8. (b)
9. (b)   because accountants do not allow for implicit costs
10. (b)   (15-12)/(4-3) = 3
11. (b)   15/4 = 3.75
12. (b)   MP of third L is 4, MP of second L is 5

13. (a) AVC and AP shapes are linked
14. (d) MC and MP shapes are linked
15. (c)
16. (a) 700/4 = 175
17. (c) (500+700)/4 = 300
18. (d) (1800-1000)/(6-5) = 800
19. (a)
20. (c) AFC = ATC - AVC
21. (d) TFC = AFC x Q
22. (a) TVC = AVC x Q
23. (b) TC = TFC + TVC
24. (c)
25. (a) maximum MP occurs at same output as minimum MC
26. (b) maximum AP occurs at same output as minimum AVC
27. (c)
28. (d) ((6 x 110) - (5 x 100))/(110-100)
29. (b) TVC = TC – TFC; AVC = TVC/Q
30. (c) TVC at Q = 4 is 100 +12; AVC = 112/4 = 28
31. (b) this cost can be reached by building Plant 1
32. (c) this cost can be reached by building Plant 3 and producing 40
33. (d)
34. (d) MES is the key concept
35. (a) assuming labour is the variable input
36. (a) AFC = TFC/Q
37. (d) it exists regardless of how much is produced and whether or not the firm shuts down

CHAPTER 9

Pure Competition

Chapters 7 and 8 provide the basic tools for understanding how markets determine the equilibrium prices and quantities for goods and services. Chapter 9 is the first of three chapters that apply these tools to analyze the behaviour of firms operating under different market structures. The goal of any firm is to maximize profit — the difference between revenues and costs. The theory of costs developed in Chapter 8 applies to all firms, but the revenue or demand side of the profit equation depends on the type of market structure in which the firm operates. Therefore, the firm's choices about production levels and pricing depend on such factors as the number of competitors, conditions of entry, the nature of the product, etc. Chapter 9 studies the firm's choices under the market structure called pure competition. The next two chapters analyse the behaviour of firms in the market structures known as pure monopoly, monopolistic competition, and oligopoly.

A purely competitive market has a very large number of firms, all selling a standardized product for a price over which they have no control. It is very easy for firms to enter or exit such a market, and nonprice competition does not exist. Under these conditions, how do firms behave? The key questions that we address are:

(1) How much output should the firm produce to maximize profits?

(2) What will be the market price of the product?

(3) How much output will the entire industry produce?

(4) Under what conditions will the firm decide to shut down production?

(5) Under what conditions will firms enter or leave the industry?

(6) How efficient is the allocation of resources in such a market?

Results are derived using both graphical and numerical examples. Both a "total revenue-total cost approach" and a "marginal revenue-marginal cost approach" are used to find the profit-maximizing output level in the short run. At this output level a firm may be enjoying profits, or be suffering losses. If suffering losses, the firm wants to minimize that loss, so the firm will have to consider shutting down. If the price is below average variable cost, the firm will immediately cease operating.

The market supply curve is found by adding up the individual supply curves of all firms in the industry. Where this market supply curve meets the market demand curve determines the equilibrium price at which all firms will sell their goods.

The industry's long-run equilibrium is reached when the number of firms has stabilized because there is no incentive to enter or leave the industry because economic profits are exactly zero. This point is reached when the market price exactly equals the firm's minimum average total cost. Starting from such a long-run equilibrium, if there is a demand shift that changes the size of the industry in the long run, the effect on the market price will depend on whether the size of the industry affects the costs of individual firms.

The last section of the chapter explains how profit-maximization by purely competitive firms leads to productive and allocative efficiency. Pure competition also provides consumers with the largest possible consumer surplus (the utility surplus measured by the value consumers received above what they had to pay).

■ CHAPTER LEARNING OBJECTIVES

In this chapter you will learn:
- The four basic market structures and how they determine the degree of competition among firms.
- The four conditions required for perfectly competitive markets.
- The profit maximizing output in the short-run for a firm in pure competition.
- About the marginal cost and the short-run supply curve.
- About the firm's profit maximization in the long-run.
- That in competitive markets firms attain both allocative and productive efficiency.

■ CHAPTER OUTLINE

1. The goal of the firm is to maximize profits. The profit-maximizing price and output level for the firm's product depend not only on the demand for the product, and the costs of producing it, but also on the structure of the industry (market) in which the firm sells the product.

2. The defining characteristics of market structure are: number of firms in the industry, type of product (differentiated or standardized), degree of control over price, conditions of entry, and extent of non-price competition.

3. Four different market structures receive the most attention in microeconomics: pure competition, pure monopoly, monopolistic competition, and oligopoly.

4. Pure competition is a situation in which a large number of independent firms, no one of which is able by itself to influence market price, sell a standardized product in a market that firms are free to enter and to leave in the long run.

5. Although pure competition is rare in practice, this market model is highly relevant because some industries more closely approximate this market structure model than any other, and because this model provides an efficiency standard against which to evaluate other market structures.

6. A purely competitive firm is called a "price taker" because it sells only a minute part of the industry output of a standardized good, and the firm cannot influence the market price.

(a) The market demand curve is downsloping, but the individual firm's demand is horizontal (perfectly elastic).
(b) Total revenue increases at a constant rate as the firm increases its output. On a graph TR will be a straight line rising from the origin, with a slope dependent on the price.
(c) Price, average revenue, and marginal revenue are equal and constant at the market price. On a graph all three are the identical horizontal line when plotted against output.

7. There are two complementary ways to analyze the purely competitive firm's choice of output level in the short run.
(a) In the total-revenue and total-cost approach, the firm will produce the output at which total economic profit is the greatest or total loss is the least, provided that the total revenue is greater than or equal to total variable cost. If not, the firm would minimize its losses by closing down and producing no output.
(b) In the marginal-revenue and marginal-cost approach, the firm will produce the output at which marginal revenue (or price) and marginal cost are equal, provided price is greater than average variable cost. If price is less than average variable cost, the firm's loss is greater than its fixed costs, so the firm will minimize losses by closing down.

8. The rules for determining output lead us directly to supply curves:
(a) The short-run supply curve of the individual firm is that part of its short-run MC curve that is above average variable cost. At any price below this shutdown point the firm produces no output.
(b) The supply curve is upward sloping because the law of diminishing returns causes the marginal cost to begin rising after some point.
(c) The firm's break-even point is the point on the supply curve where price equals average total cost.
(d) A short-run supply curve of the industry is found by adding horizontally the supply curves of all individual firms.
(e) The short-run supply curve of the industry and the market demand determine the short-run equilibrium price and output of the industry. At this equilibrium firms may have either economic profits or losses.

9. The existence of economic profits or losses in the short-run equilibrium will trigger long-run adjustments. The analysis makes three simplifying assumptions:

(a) The only long-run adjustment is in the entry or exit of firms.

(b) All firms in the industry have identical costs.

(c) The industry in question has constant costs. That is, the number of firms does not influence resource prices faced by the individual firm.

10. If economic profits exist, new firms will enter in the long run, increasing the total industry supply, and reducing the equilibrium price until it equals the minimum average total cost at which firms can supply the product. The adjustments continue until the firms in the industry make only normal profits (zero economic profits).

11. If losses occur, some firms will leave the industry in the long run, reducing total industry supply, and raising equilibrium price until it equals the minimum average total cost. The adjustments continue until all remaining firms earn enough revenue to cover their opportunity costs, making normal profits (zero economic profits). At that point, price and minimum average total cost are equal.

12. When firms enter (leave) the industry, the demands for the inputs used in the industry increase (decrease). How these demand shifts change the prices of the inputs will define whether the industry is one of increasing costs, decreasing costs, or constant costs. This will also dictate the slope of the industry's long-run supply curve.

(a) In a constant-cost industry, entry or exit of firms does not affect input prices, so the ATC curves of firms in the industry are unchanged. Therefore, there is no change in the minimum price at which firms can cover their opportunity costs. Because the long-run equilibrium price is unchanged, and the industry can supply larger quantities at a constant price, the long-run supply curve is horizontal at the price level equal to the minimum average total cost.

(b) In an increasing-cost industry, the entry of new firms pushes input prices upwards, and so increases firms' ATC curves. The minimum price at which firms can cover their costs is increased. Therefore, an increase in demand will raise the long-run equilibrium price, so the industry can supply larger quantities only at higher prices. The long-run industry supply curve is upward sloping.

(c) In a decreasing-cost industry, the entry of new firms pushes input prices downwards, and so decreases firms' ATC curves. Firms can now cover their costs at lower prices, so the long-run equilibrium price will fall and the industry will supply more output at lower prices. The long-run supply curve will be downward sloping.

13. Productive efficiency is achieved when the average total cost of producing goods is at its minimum. In the long run, competition forces the firm to produce at a zero profit equilibrium where average total cost is at a minimum.

14. Allocative efficiency is achieved when society's resources are used to produce the combination of goods that will maximize consumers' total satisfaction. This occurs when the price of each good — which also reflects its marginal benefit to consumers — is equal to its marginal cost. The equilibrium in pure competition satisfies this condition. As shown in the "Last Word," consumers receive more utility from the goods than their total expenditures on those goods. This gain in utility or satisfaction is known as consumer surplus. The amount of consumer surplus is maximized under the pure competition equilibrium, as can be shown on a demand and supply graph.

15. A purely competitive market restores efficiency when disrupted by changes in the economy. For example, a change in consumer preferences or a change in production technology will throw the market out of its zero profit equilibrium, triggering entry or exit of firms until zero profits and output at the ATC minimum are restored.

16. Competition in the economy drives firms who seek only their own interests to promote the best interest of society, and leads to the achievement of both allocative and productive efficiency. Competition results in an economy being on its production possibilities curve at a point determined by consumers.

■ **TERMS AND CONCEPTS**

pure competition	**MR = MC rule**
pure monopoly	**short-run supply curve**
monopolistic competition	**long-run supply curve**
oligopoly	**constant-cost industry**
imperfect competition	**increasing-cost industry**

price-taker
average revenue
total revenue
marginal revenue
break-even point

decreasing-cost indus-
    try
productive efficiency
allocative efficiency

■   **HINTS AND TIPS**

1. The purely competitive model is the standard against which other market models — pure monopoly, monopolistic competition, and oligopoly — are compared for economic efficiency. Therefore you need a thorough understanding of this chapter to fully understand the next two chapters.

2. You can think of the firm as making its short-run output decision in two steps: (1) find the output where marginal cost equals marginal revenue; (2) produce this output if price is high enough to cover average variable cost, otherwise cease production.

3. Consider the case of a firm suffering losses. A very common mistake is to believe that the firm continues to produce in the short run only if it earns enough revenue to cover fixed costs. It is variable costs that must be covered to justify continued operation. Fixed costs are unavoidable, so they should not affect the decision.

4. The absolutely essential idea for understanding long-run equilibrium in a purely competitive market is that economic profit must be zero. Firms do not set out to make zero profit, but they are forced by competition to sell at a price at which zero economic profit is the very best they can achieve. This is the point where price equals minimum average total cost.

FILL-IN QUESTIONS

1. The four basic market models examined in this and the next two chapters are:
   (a) _pure competition_
   (b) _monopoly_
   (c) _monopolistic competition_
   (d) _oligopoly_

2. The basic market models or market structures differ in terms of the _number_ of firms; type of _products_; control over _price_; conditions of _entry_; and _non-price_ competition.

3. The four distinct characteristics of pure competition are: (a) a _large_ number of independent firms; (b) each firm has (no, some) _no_ control over the market price; (c) the product is _standardized_ (d) there are (no, some) _no_ barriers to entry of new firms.

4. In pure competition the industry demand curve is _downward_-sloping, but the demand curve for the individual firm is perfectly (elastic, inelastic) _elastic_, so that the firm's marginal revenue is constant and (less than, greater than, equal to) _equal to_ the price of the product.

5. Economic profit is calculated as _TR_ minus _TC_. The firm's maximum profit is found at the output level where (marginal, total) _Total_ revenue minus _total_ cost is the greatest. Equivalently, the firm's maximum profit is found at the output level where _marginal_ revenue is equal to _marginal_ cost.

6. A firm should produce in the short run only if it can obtain a _profit_ or suffer a loss no greater than its _avc_. Provided it produces any output at all, it will produce that output at which its profit is a (maximum, minimum) _maximum_ or its loss is a _minimum_.

7. In the short run the firm is suffering a loss if price is below _ATC_, but should continue to produce if price is higher than _AVC_.

8. The short-run supply curve of the firm is that part of the _mc_ curve that is above its _AVC_ curve. The short-run market supply curve is the _horizontal sum_ of the individual firms' supply curves.

9. In the short run there is a fixed number of _firms_ in the industry, each with a _fixed_ size of _plant_.

10. If firms in an industry are obtaining economic profits, firms will (enter, leave) _enter_ the industry, the industry will employ (more, fewer) _more_ resources and produce (more, less) _more_ output, the price of the industry's product will (rise, fall) _fall_, and the industry's economic profits will (increase, decrease) _decrease_ until they are equal to _zero_.

11. When a purely competitive industry is in long-run equilibrium, the price that the firm receives for its product is equal not only to marginal revenue but to <u>marginal</u> cost and to <u>average total</u>cost; and average cost is a (maximum, minimum) <u>minimum</u>.

12. If the entry of new firms into an industry tends to raise the costs of all firms in the industry, the industry is a(n) (constant-, increasing-, decreasing-) <u>increasing</u> cost industry; and its long-run supply curve is (horizontal, downsloping, upsloping) <u>upsloping</u>.

13. The long-run supply curve of a constant-cost industry is (perfectly elastic, perfectly inelastic, unit elastic) <u>perfectly elastic</u>.

14. The supply curve in a decreasing-cost industry has a (positive, negative, zero) <u>negative</u> slope because an increase in industry output causes the prices of industry inputs to (increase, decrease, stay the same) <u>increase</u>.

15. The purely competitive industry achieves allocative efficiency where price and <u>marginal cost</u> are equal. It will achieve productive efficiency where price and <u>ATC</u> are equal and the latter is at a (minimum, maximum) <u>minimum</u>.

■ **PROBLEMS AND PROJECTS**

1. Slot the following into the appropriate spaces in the table below. (Hint: two answers are used more than once.)

one	considerable
few	very easy
many	blocked
a very large number	fairly easy
standardized	fairly difficult
differentiated	none
some	~~unique~~

Market characteristics	Pure Competition	Monopoly	Monopolistic Competition	Oligopoly
Number of firms	a very lg #	one	many	few
Type of product	standardized	unique	differentiated	stand or diff
Control over price	none	consid.	some	consid
Conditions of entry	very easy	blocked	fairly easy	fairly difficult
Nonprice competition	none	cons.	consid.	consid

2. The following table shows data for Blue Lite, a match maker, who sells their product in a purely competitive market.

Output (boxes/yr)	Total Cost ($/yr)	Total Revenue ($/yr)	Profit ($/yr)
0	200	0	
1000	250	160.00	
2000	275		
3000	325		
4000	400		
5000	500		
6000	625		
7000	775		
8000	950		

(a) Assume that the market price for matches is $0.16 per box. Fill in the total revenue column.
(b) Fill in the profit column.
(c) What level of output maximizes profits for Blue Lite? <u>7000</u>
(d) In the next table, in the TR1 and Profit 1 columns, recompute the results for Blue Lite assuming that the price of matches is now $0.09 per box.

Output	TC	TR 1	Profit 1	TR 2	Profit 2
0	$200	$0	$(200)	$0	$-200
1000	250	90	(160)	30	-220
2000	275	180	(95)	60	-215
3000	325	270	(55)	90	-235
4000	400	360	(40)	120	-280
5000	500	450	(50)	150	-350
6000	625	540	(85)	180	-445
7000	775	630	(145)	210	-565
8000	950	720	(230)	240	-710

(e) If Blue Lite chooses to produce at this price, they would produce <u>4000</u> boxes/year. Their loss at this output is $<u>40</u> per year. Because Blue Lite's total fixed cost is $<u>200</u> per year, they (should, should not) <u>should</u> continue in the short run to produce matches at a price of $0.09. Their loss by continuing to produce is $<u>40</u> per year (less than, more than) <u>less than</u> their loss if they close down and incur only their total fixed cost.
(f) Recompute the results in the TR2 and Profit 2 columns assuming that the price of matches is now $0.03 per box.
(g) If Blue Lite does produce at this price, they would produce <u>2000</u> boxes/year. Blue Lite (should, should not) <u>should not</u> continue in the short run to produce matches at this price. Their

loss by producing at this price is $ _215_ per year, compared to a total fixed cost of $ _200_ per year.

3. A purely competitive firm faces the following demand schedule and marginal cost schedule.

(a)   Compute the average revenue (AR) and marginal revenue (MR) schedules from the demand schedule data.

(b)   If the P, AR, and MR schedules were graphed as a function of Qd, all three would be the same horizontal line at price = $ _10_ .

(c)   Given the MC and MR data, the profit-maximizing quantity is _5_ . The last unit produced adds $ _10_ to revenues and adds $ _9_ to costs. Therefore, it adds $ _1_ to profits. If one more unit would be produced it would add $ _10_ to revenues, and $ _13_ to costs, therefore reducing profits by $ _3_ . Therefore, at the optimum, every unit has been produced that can contribute anything to profit.

Q d	P	AR	MR	MC
1	$10	$ 10	$ 10	$4
2	10	10	10	3
3	10	10	10	4
4	10	10	10	6
5	10	10	10	9
6	10	10	10	13
7	10	10	10	18

4. The firm whose cost curves are shown in the next graph sells vitamins in a purely competitive market. Output is measured in bottles per day, and costs are in $ per bottle. The AVC curve includes costs for labour and ingredients. The firm also pays fixed costs for their production facility and machinery.

(a)   If the market price of vitamins is $19 per bottle, how many bottles will this firm wish to sell?
_1500.00_

(b)   On the graph show the rectangle of profit earned at $19 per bottle.

(c)   What is the firm's break-even price? _min ATC = 11.00_

(d)   What is the firm's short-run shutdown price?
_8_

Treat the remaining questions as separate cases.

(e)   If there is an unexpected increase in the demand for vitamins, which of the results (a) through (d) would change, and why?

(f)   If there is an increase in the rent on the production facility, which of the results (a) through (d) would change, and why?

(g)   If there is an increase in the price of ingredients, which of the results (a) through (d) would change, and why?

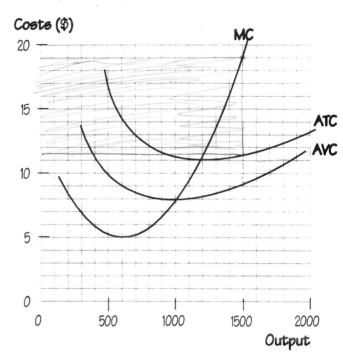

Costs ($)

5. The pumpkin industry is purely competitive, and consists of 100 identical firms, each with costs as shown in the schedule below.

Output	ATC	MC
20	$7.00	
		$2.00
40	4.50	
		3.00
60	4.00	
		4.00
80	4.00	
		5.00
100	4.20	
		6.00
120	4.50	

(a)   Plot the average total costs and marginal costs for a typical firm on the left-hand panel of the following graphs. Remember to plot MC at

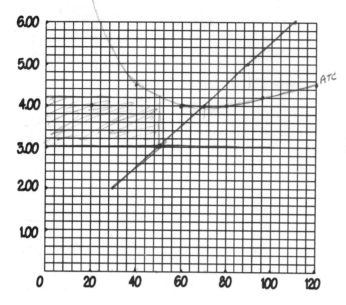

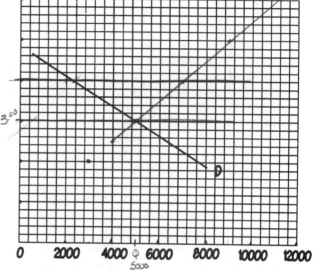

the midpoints of the output ranges. (For example, plot $3 at quantity = 50.)

(b)   Suppose that the minimum average variable cost for this firm is $2.50. Based on this, the firm's supply curve is its ___mc___ curve above $ _2.50_.

(c)   The right-hand panel shows the market demand for pumpkins. Derive and plot the short-run market supply (Hint: the industry consists of 100 firms with supply curves identical to the one shown in your left-hand graph).

(d)   From the short-run equilibrium now shown in the industry graph, the market price is $ _3_ , and the market quantity is _5000_.

(e)   Based on the market price from the industry graph, and the individual firm's supply curve, the firm will maximize profits (or minimize losses) by producing an output of _50_ . $P=mc$

(f)   We can show that the industry result and the firm result are consistent by multiplying the firm's output by the number of firms. This gives _5000_ (which should equal the industry output).

(g)   On the diagram show the area that represents the firm's short-run profit (or loss) at this equilibrium. $3.00 - 4.20 \times 50 = (60.00)$ Loss

6. This question uses the pumpkin market graphs in the previous question. Assume that the short-run average total cost and marginal cost data also represent long-run ATC and MC. Also assume that pumpkins are produced in a constant-cost industry.

(a)   Since each firm is suffering losses at the short-run equilibrium, there is an incentive for firms to (enter, exit) ___exit___ the industry.

(b) The long-run equilibrium price is found at the _minimum_ point of the ATC, which is where ATC = $ _4._ .

(c)   At the industry level, this long-run equilibrium price will result only if the market supply curve intersects the existing market demand curve at a quantity of _2000_.

(d)   At this long-run equilibrium price, each firm will wish to produce a quantity of _70_ (by the P = MC rule).

(e)   Given the equilibrium quantity for the industry, and the optimum quantity for the firm, the long-run equilibrium number of firms is approximately _29_ (divide the two). Therefore, about _71_ firms must leave the industry.

(f)   Draw in the new short-run industry supply curve after the number of firms has changed.

(g)   Because this is a constant-cost industry, the long-run industry supply is a _horizontal_ line, which is located at a price equal to the individual firm's minimum ATC. Draw in this supply curve.

7. Skeena Mills and Stikine Forest Products are hypothetical firms in a purely competitive lumber market. They have different cost structures. At normal price ranges for lumber they produce the same quantity of lumber, but Stikine makes a larger short-run profit than Skeena does. However, when lumber prices fall temporarily, Stikine closes down temporarily, while Skeena continues producing. Sketch a pair of diagrams showing ATC, AVC and MC for each firm consistent with the facts presented.

8. Several guitarists are in the market for a new guitar. Each has a different maximum willingness to pay for a guitar of a certain high quality brand:

Jimi $5000
Eric $4000
Bonnie $3200
Wayne $500

(a) If the market price of this particular guitar is $3000, how many of the four guitarists will choose to buy one? *3*

(b) What is the amount of consumer surplus gained by each guitarist at this price? *2000, 1000, 200*

■ TRUE-FALSE

Circle T if the statement is true, F if it is false.

1. There are no barriers to industry entry or exit in a purely competitive market. **T** F

2. Extensive advertising and annual model changes indicate that the automotive industry is purely competitive. T **F**

3. If there are many firms in an industry, then the industry is purely competitive. T **F**

4. The demand curve for the individual purely competitive firm is horizontal at the market price. **T** F

5. Purely competitive producers cannot make economic profits in the short run. T **F**

6. In the short run a purely competitive firm maximizes profits by producing where price equals average total cost. **T** F

7. The competitive firm will shut down in the short run if fixed costs cannot be met at all possible output levels. T **F**

8. The break-even point is found in the short run where the firm's total revenue equals total costs. **T** F

9. A firm that is suffering losses may be wise to continue to produce in the short run even if they never expect to earn economic profits. **T** F

10. In the long run the competitive firm that spends most on research and development will earn economic profits. T **F**

11. When a purely competitive firm is in a long-run equilibrium, product price will be exactly equal to the firm's minimum average total cost. **T** F

12. Given sufficient time for entry or exit, the economic profits in a purely competitive industry will tend to disappear. **T** F

13. In an increasing-cost industry the long-run supply curve is upward-sloping. **T** F

14. The long-run supply curve for an industry could be downward-sloping. **T** F

15. In a constant-cost industry the long-run supply curve is infinitely elastic. **T** F

16. Consumer surplus equals the total utility value received less the total expenditures on the product. **T** F

■ MULTIPLE-CHOICE

Circle the letter that corresponds to the best answer.

1. The four market structure models differ in their assumptions concerning:
   (a) the number of firms in the industry
   (b) the ease or difficulty for new firms in entering the industry
   (c) whether the product is standardized or differentiated
   (d) all of the above

2. Which of the following is not one of the four market models?
   (a) pure competition
   (b) monopoly
   (c) monopolistic competition
   (d) imperfect competition

3. In which of the following market models is the seller of a product a "price taker"?
   (a) pure competition
   (b) monopoly
   (c) monopolistic competition
   (d) oligopoly

4. Entry is blocked in:
   (a) pure competition
   (b) monopoly
   (c) monopolistic competition

(d) oligopoly

5. Examples of oligopolistic industries in Canada would include all but:
(a) commercial banking
(b) steel
(c) airlines
(d) wheat farming

6. The market model in which there is considerable interdependence among firms is:
(a) pure competition
(b) monopoly
(c) monopolistic competition
(d) oligopoly

7. Which of the following is not characteristic of pure competition?
(a) large number of sellers
(b) advertising by individual sellers
(c) easy entry
(d) standardized products

8. The demand schedule or curve confronted by the individual purely competitive firm is:
(a) perfectly inelastic
(b) inelastic but not perfectly inelastic
(c) perfectly elastic
(d) unit elastic

9. For the purely competitive firm, price equals:
(a) marginal revenue
(b) average revenue
(c) both marginal revenue and average revenue
(d) none of the above

10. Using the total-revenue and total-cost approach the competitive firm should produce, given total variable costs are covered, the level of output where:
(a) total revenue is a maximum
(b) total revenue equals total cost
(c) a normal profit is realized
(d) the difference between total revenue and total cost is maximized

11. Using the marginal-revenue and marginal-cost approach the competitive firm should produce, given average variable cost is covered, the level of output where:
(a) average cost equals price
(b) average variable cost equals price

(c) marginal cost equals price
(d) marginal cost equals average variable cost

12. A firm would be earning an economic profit in the short run if it is producing the quantity where marginal cost equals price and:
(a) average fixed cost is less than price
(b) average variable cost is greater than price
(c) average total cost is greater than price
(d) average total cost is less than price

13. A firm will be willing to operate at a loss in the short run if:
(a) the loss is no greater than its average fixed costs
(b) the loss is no greater than its total fixed costs
(c) the loss is no greater than its total variable costs
(d) the loss is no greater than its average variable costs

14. Which of the following is an incorrect formula for calculating economic profit?
(a) TR - TC
(b) TR - ATC
(c) (P – ATC) x Q
(d) both (a) and (c)

15. Suppose at the present rate of output a competitive firm finds that marginal cost is less than price. To maximize profits this firm should:
(a) close down
(b) reduce output
(c) increase output
(d) reduce the price

16. An increase in a firm's fixed cost would:
(a) lower the firm's shutdown price in the short run
(b) raise the firm's shutdown price in the short run
(c) have no effect on the firm's shutdown price
(d) force the firm to immediately cease production

17. An increase in the wage rate that a firm must pay its variable factor (labour) would:
(a) lower the firm's shutdown price in the short run
(b) raise the firm's shutdown price in the short run
(c) have no effect on the firm's shutdown price

(d) force the firm to immediately cease production

Questions 18 through 24 are based on the following cost data for a firm that sells in a purely competitive market.

Output	AFC	AVC	ATC	MC
1	$300	$100	$400	$100
2	150	75	225	50
3	100	70	170	60
4	75	73	148	80
5	60	80	140	110
6	50	90	140	140
7	43	103	146	180
8	38	119	157	230

18. The total fixed costs for this firm are:
- **(a)** $100
- **(b)** $200
- **(c)** $300
- **(d)** $400

19. If the market price for the product is $140, this firm will produce:
- **(a)** 0 units
- **(b)** 6 units
- **(c)** 7 units
- **(d)** 8 units

20. If the market price for the firm's product is $180, the firm's maximum profit in the short run will be:
- **(a)** an economic profit of $238
- **(b)** an economic profit of $592
- **(c)** an economic profit of $1,071
- **(d)** an economic profit of $0

21. If the market price is $60, this firm will:
- **(a)** produce 3 units and lose $330
- **(b)** produce 3 units and lose $300
- **(c)** close down and break even
- **(d)** close down and lose $300

22. If the market price is $110, this competitive firm will:
- **(a)** close down
- **(b)** produce 5 units at a loss of $150
- **(c)** produce 5 units at a profit of $150
- **(d)** produce 7 units and break even

23. This firm's shut-down price is:
- **(a)** $38
- **(b)** $40

- **(c)** $70
- **(d)** $140

24. This firm's break-even price is:
- **(a)** $38
- **(b)** $40
- **(c)** $70
- **(d)** $140

Questions 25 through 31 are based on the next diagram showing the short-run costs of a purely competitive firm.

25. Given that the price is 0e the profit-maximizing competitive firm should produce:
- **(a)** cn units
- **(b)** 0n units
- **(c)** 0k units
- **(d)** 0h units

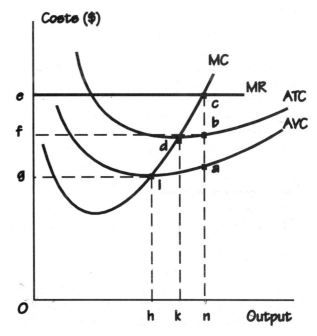

26. The marginal cost at the profit-maximizing rate of output is:
- **(a)** an dollars
- **(b)** nb dollars
- **(c)** 0f dollars
- **(d)** 0e dollars

27. Total revenue at the profit-maximizing rate of output is given by the area
- **(a)** 0nbf
- **(b)** 0ecn
- **(c)** 0gan

(d) *efab*

28. Total cost at the profit-maximizing rate of output is given by the area:
- **(a)** *ecn0*
- **(b)** *0gan*
- **(c)** *fbag*
- **(d)** *fbn0*

29. Economic profit is given by the area:
- **(a)** *ecbf*
- **(b)** *fbag*
- **(c)** *ecag*
- **(d)** *ecdf*

30. The firm's short-run supply curve is represented by:
- **(a)** the ATC curve above point *d*
- **(b)** the AVC curve above point *i*
- **(c)** the MC curve above *i*
- **(d)** the MR curve

31. The lowest price at which this firm will continue to produce output in the short run is:
- **(a)** *0e*
- **(b)** *0f*
- **(c)** *0g*
- **(d)** the firm will produce at any price

32. In a competitive firm, technological progress that increases the productivity of labour would:
- **(a)** shift the MC curve downward
- **(b)** shift the MC curve upward
- **(c)** shift the AFC curve downward
- **(d)** reduce the profit-maximizing output level

33. If each firm in a purely competitive market is experiencing economic losses, then in the long run we can expect:
- **(a)** the market supply curve to shift to the right
- **(b)** the demand curve to increase
- **(c)** the market supply curve to shift to the left
- **(d)** the demand curve to decrease

34. The long-run supply curve under pure competition is upward sloping when increased product demand leads to:
- **(a)** more firms entering the market
- **(b)** firms building bigger plants
- **(c)** input price increases
- **(d)** economies of scale

35. Productive efficiency is achieved in the long run in a competitive industry because competition forces each firm to produce where:
- **(a)** marginal cost equals price
- **(b)** fixed cost is zero
- **(c)** economic profits are positive
- **(d)** long-run average total cost is minimized

36. An economy is producing the goods most wanted by society when for each and every good:
- **(a)** price and average cost are equal
- **(b)** price and marginal cost are equal
- **(c)** economic profit is positive
- **(d)** the amount sold equals the amount produced

■ DISCUSSION QUESTIONS

1. Explain why all firms in a purely competitive market must charge exactly the same price.

2. If pure competition is so rare in the real world, why is it covered in this course?

3. Suppose the market for macaroni is purely competitive. Since consumers' demand for macaroni is surely downward-sloping, how can it be that the individual producer faces a horizontal or perfectly elastic demand curve?

4. Why is the firm willing to produce at a loss in the short run if the loss is no greater than fixed costs? At what point does a firm drop out of the industry?

5. Suppose a firm has determined that they should leave the industry in the long run. How does the firm decide when, practically speaking, they should wind up their business? If all firms were experiencing losses, would they all drop out of the industry at the same time?

6. What factors determine the short-run supply for an individual purely competitive firm, and for its industry?

7. What determines the equilibrium price and output of a purely competitive industry in the short run?

8. Why must economic profits be zero in long-run equilibrium for a purely competitive industry? What forces the purely competitive firm into this position?

9. If economic profits end up at zero in long-run equilibrium, why should entrepreneurs bother starting up businesses in purely competitive industries?

Consider the difference between normal profits and economic profits.

10. What is a constant-cost industry? What is an increasing-cost industry? Under what economic conditions is each likely to be found? What will be the nature of the long-run supply curve in each of these industries?

11. Why would a restaurant industry in a large city likely be a constant-cost industry? Why would a hotel industry on a very small island likely be an increasing-cost industry?

12. What two kinds of efficiency are necessary if the economy is to make the best use of its resources?

■ **ANSWERS**

FILL-IN QUESTIONS

1. (a) pure competition; (b) pure monopoly; (c) monopolistic competition; (d) oligopoly

2. number, product, price, entry, nonprice

3. (a) large; (b) no; (c) standardized; (d) no

4. downward, elastic, equal to

5. total revenue, total cost; total, total; marginal, marginal

6. profit, total fixed cost; maximum, minimum

7. ATC; AVC

8. MC, AVC, horizontal sum

9. firms, fixed, plant

10. enter, more, more, fall, decrease, zero

11. average total, marginal, minimum

12. increasing, upsloping

13. perfectly elastic

14. negative, decrease

15. MC; ATC, minimum

PROBLEMS AND PROJECTS

1. Number of firms: very large number, one, many, few; Type of product: standardized, unique, differentiated, standardized or differentiated; Control over price: none, considerable, some, considerable; Conditions of entry: very easy, blocked, fairly easy, fairly difficult; Nonprice competition: none, considerable, considerable, considerable.

2. (a) 0, 160, 320, 480, 640, 800, 960, 1120, 1280; (b) -200, -90, 45, 155, 240, 300, 335, 345, 330; (c) 7000; (d) TR1 = 0, 90, 180, 270, 360, 450, 540, 630, 720; Profit 1 = -200, -160, -95, -55, -40, -50, -85, -145, -230; (e) 4000, 40, 200; should, 160, less than; (f) TR2 = 0, 30, 60, 90, 120, 150, 180, 210, 240; Profit 2 = -200, -220, -215, -235, -280, -350, -445, -565, -710; (g) 2000; should not; 215, 200

3. (a) AR and MR both $10 at all Q values; (b) 10; (c) 5; 10, 9; 1; 10, 13, 3

4. (a) 1500; (b) Rectangle shows (P - ATC) x Q = (19-11.5) x 1500; (c) minimum ATC = $11; (d) minimum AVC = $8; (e) Q* increases because P = MC at higher Q, Profit rectangle becomes larger because Q increases and (P-ATC) increases; (f) Profit rectangle becomes smaller because ATC shifts up, so (P-ATC) decreases; the break-even point increases because ATC shifts up; (g) MC, ATC, AVC all shift up, so Q* falls, profit decreases, break-even price and shutdown price both rise.

5. (b) MC, $2.50; (d) about $3, about 5000; (e) 50; (f) 5000; (g) rectangle: (P - ATC) x Q

6. (a) exit; (b) minimum, $4.00; (c) about 2000; (d) 70; (e) 29; 71; (g) horizontal

7. Skeena's ATC is higher than Stikine's, but Stikine's AVC is higher than Skeena's, so Stikine's shutdown price in the short run is higher.

8. (a) Only those with willingness to pay that is higher than the market price will buy a guitar and gain consumer surplus: Jimi, Eric and Bonnie. (b) For each, subtract the market price of $3000 from each guitarists marginal utility: Jimi: $2000; Eric: $1000; Bonnie $200; Wayne gets none.

TRUE-FALSE

1. T
2. F   product differentiation and other nonprice competition does not occur in pure competition
3. F   not necessarily; it could also be monopolistic competition
4. T   therefore the individual firm is a "price taker"
5. F   profits are competed away in the long run, but may exist in the short run
6. F   profit-maximization occurs where P = MC
7. F   it is variable costs that must be met in order for the firm to continue operating

8. T
9. T   they may minimize losses this way
10. F   there are no economic profits in the long run in this market structure
11. T
12. T   as more firms enter, the industry supply increases, and price falls
13. T   as the industry grows, firms' cost curves are shifted up as resources become more scarce
14. T   in the case of a decreasing-cost industry
15. T   horizontal, in other words
16. T

MULTIPLE-CHOICE

1. (d)
2. (d)   imperfect competition refers to more than one market structure model
3. (a)   only pure competition does the firm have no control whatsoever over price
4. (b)
5. (d)   there are far too many wheat farmers for an oligopoly
6. (d)
7. (b)   no individual seller would have any incentive to advertise since his product is identical to any other sellers' products
8. (c)   price-taking behaviour
9. (c)   price-taking behaviour
10. (d)   economic profit is this difference
11. (c)
12. (d)   profit = (P − ATC) x Q
13. (b)   since the total fixed cost would become the loss if the firm chooses to shutdown rather than produce
14. (b)
15. (c)   since MC is rising as output rises, increase output until MC rises enough to equal P
16. (c)   fixed costs have no affect on decisions in the short run
17. (b)   the AVC curve (and MC and ATC) would shift upwards
18. (c)   TFC = AFC x Q
19. (b)   set Q where P = MC
20. (a)   set Q at 7 where P = MC; (P − ATC) x Q = (180-146) x 7
21. (d)   close down because P is below AVC, and lose TFC = 300
22. (b)   set Q = 5 where P = MC; (P − ATC) x Q = (110-140) x 5
23. (c)   the minimum value for AVC
24. (d)   the minimum value for ATC
25. (b)   where P = MC
26. (d)   P = MC
27. (b)   P x Q
28. (d)   ATC x Q
29. (a)   (P − ATC) x Q
30. (c)   MC above AVC
31. (c)   minimum AVC is the shutdown price

32. (a)   lower production costs at all output levels
33. (c)   as some firms exit
34. (c)   increasing-cost industry
35. (d)   production occurs at lowest possible cost
36. (b)   allocative efficiency

CHAPTER 10

Pure Monopoly

This chapter, on pure monopoly, is the second of three chapters dealing with specific market structure models. Pure monopoly exists when there is only one seller of a product for which there are no close substitutes, and where other potential sellers are blocked from entering the market. Under these conditions the seller is a "price maker." We study pure monopoly because there are some important examples in the Canadian economy (especially in local markets), and because some characteristics of monopoly will help us to understand the market models of monopolistic competition and oligopoly (to be studied in Chapter 11).

Sooner or later, the monopoly firm will lose its exclusive position in the market unless there are obstacles preventing other firms from entering. Barriers to entry can stem from economies of scale, legal protection (patents and licences), ownership or control of essential resources, or pricing and other strategic behaviour. None of these barriers are likely to be impenetrable in the long run, except perhaps barriers sanctioned by government.

The analysis in Chapter 10 identifies key similarities and differences between pure monopolies and firms in pure competition:

1. In pure monopoly, as in pure competition, firms maximize profits by setting output where marginal cost and marginal revenue are equal.
2. The purely competitive firm faces a perfectly elastic demand curve at the going market price because it is only one of many firms in the industry. Because the monopolist is the whole industry, the monopolist faces a downsloping market demand and must therefore simultaneously choose price as well as output.
3. In pure competition the firm's demand is perfectly elastic, so price is constant and equal to marginal revenue. The monopoly firm's demand is not perfectly elastic, so marginal revenue is below price, and both fall as output rises.
4. Whereas the pure competitor has a supply curve defined by its marginal cost curve (above average variable cost), the monopolist has no supply curve.
5. Entry automatically erodes any profits in a purely competitive industry. In pure monopoly barriers to entry can protect profits indefinitely.
6. Unlike pure competition, pure monopoly will not achieve either productive efficiency or allocative efficiency.

Most comparisons between pure competition and pure monopoly are based on the assumption that costs are identical. In fact, costs could be either higher or lower under pure monopoly. If extensive economies of scale exist, the market may be served most efficiently by one firm (a natural monopoly). On the other hand, the lack of competitive discipline in a pure monopoly may permit costs to drift upwards (X-inefficiency), or the quest for monopoly profits may lead to wasteful rent-seeking expenditures. Monopolies often have the financial ability – but not the incentive – to be technologically progressive. But in some cases being technologically progressive is a strategy for the monopoly to maintain market dominance. Overall, monopoly is believed to be inefficient, and governments have several policy options for controlling the behaviour of monopolies.

The final sections of the chapter deal with the practice and consequences of price discrimination by a pure monopolist, and the practice and consequences of government regulation of natural monopolies.

■ CHAPTER LEARNING OBJECTIVES

In this chapter you will learn:
□ The necessary conditions required for monopoly to arise.
□ How the monopolist determines the profit-maximizing price and output.
□ About the economic effects of monopoly.
□ Why a monopolist prefers to charge different prices in different markets.

■ CHAPTER OUTLINE

1. Pure monopoly is a market structure in which a single firm sells a product for which there are no close substitutes. There are no immediate competitors because entry to the market is totally blocked. A monopoly is a "price maker." While pure monopoly is not very common, some important examples exist: public utilities, professional sports teams, and even gas stations in small, remote towns. The study of pure monopoly also helps us to understand firms that are "almost" monopolies.

2. Pure monopoly (and oligopoly) can exist in the long run only as long as barriers to entry prevent other competitors from entering the market. There are several types of barriers:
(a) Economies of scale can bar entry and produce the conditions for "natural monopoly" if the firm's long-run average-cost curve declines over a wide range of output.
(b) Governments create legal barriers by awarding firms patents and licences.
(c) Ownership or control of a specific resource critical to the production of a good can bar competitors.
(d) Strategic price-cutting or advertising campaigns specifically aimed at making new competitors unprofitable may also deter entry.

3. The analysis of pure monopoly behaviour makes three assumptions: (1) patents, economies of scale, or resource ownership secure the firm's monopoly position; (2) the firm is not regulated by government; and (3) the firm charges a single price for all units, to all consumers.

4. The monopolist is the entire industry, so its demand curve is the downsloping industry demand curve. Therefore:
(a) More output can be sold only by reducing price. Therefore, marginal revenue will be less than price for every level of output except for the first unit.
(b) The monopolist chooses some price-quantity point along the industry demand curve and is, therefore, a "price maker."
(c) The monopolist will set price in the elastic part of the demand curve, because marginal revenue is negative in the inelastic portion.

5. The monopolist selects the combination of price and output that maximizes the difference between total revenues and costs.
(a) We assume that a monopolist hires inputs in a purely competitive market and utilizes the same technology as a competitive firm, as described in Chapter 9.
(b) The monopolist chooses the output level at which the marginal cost and marginal revenue are equal, and charges the price corresponding to this output on the demand curve.
(c) The monopolist has no supply curve because no unique relationship exists between price and quantity supplied. Different demand conditions can bring about different prices at the same output level.
(d) Three common misconceptions about monopolists are that they charge as high a price as possible, that they seek the maximum profit *per unit* of output, and that monopoly status is a guarantee of profitability.

6. The existence of pure monopoly has significant effects on society as a whole.
(a) Because output is set below the level at which P = MC, monopoly does not achieve allocative efficiency. Because it fails to produce at the point of minimum ATC, monopoly does not achieve productive efficiency. On both counts pure monopoly fails to measure up to the standard of pure competition.
(b) As compared to a purely competitive system, monopoly transfers income from consumers to the owners of the firm, tending to increase inequality of incomes.

7. Contrary to what is assumed throughout most of the chapter, a pure monopoly may face higher or lower costs of production as compared to a firm in pure competition.
(a) If there are economies of scale in production, the monopolist can produce at a lower long-run average cost than a large number of small pure competitors. Simultaneous consumption and

network effects create extensive economies of scale in some firms in information technology industries.

(b) Lack of competition makes the monopolist more susceptible to X-inefficiency (operation at greater than lowest cost for a particular level of output).

(c) Firms may incur rent-seeking expenditures (such as lobbying fees, and public relations expenditures), to gain or preserve monopoly position. These expenditures increase costs but add nothing to society's output.

(d) Monopoly *may* produce more cost-saving technological advances than pure competition does. A monopoly, however, does not have a strong incentive to innovate, except perhaps to reinforce barriers to entry.

8. The various types of inefficiency that are possible under pure monopoly cause society to consider what action government might take in the public interest. Three general policy options are available: prosecute monopoly power gained through anticompetitive actions, regulate natural monopolies, or simply allow monopoly to exist (especially in cases where the monopoly power seems unsustainable in the long run).

9. To increase profits, a pure monopolist may engage in price discrimination by selling the same product at different prices (where the price differences are not justified by cost differences). This practice is common in Canada.

(a) To price discriminate, the seller must have some monopoly power, be able to segregate buyers into groups having different elasticities of demand, and be able to prevent the resale of the product.

(b) The seller charges a higher price to the group with the more inelastic demand.

(c) Perfect price discrimination increases the monopoly profits; surprisingly, it also increases output and thereby reduces allocative inefficiency of monopoly.

10. Natural monopolies are often subject to rate (price) regulation as governments try to reduce the misallocation of resources.

(a) A natural monopoly exists when economies of scale are so extensive that one firm can supply the entire market at lower average cost than could a number of competing firms.

(b) In Canada many important examples of natural monopolies involve public utilities (such as retail distributors of natural gas, electricity, and local phone service).

(c) To achieve the socially optimal price, where P = MC, the regulatory agency could set a ceiling price at the level where the demand curve is cut by the marginal cost. This would achieve allocative efficiency.

(d) Because the optimal social price may force the firm to produce at a loss, government may set the ceiling at a level where the average total cost and demand intersect, thus allowing the monopolist a "fair return" where opportunity costs are recouped, but no economic profit is gained.

(e) The dilemma of regulation is that the optimal social price may cause losses for the monopolist, and that a fair-return price results in a less efficient resource allocation. Nevertheless, either of these alternatives is more efficient than the unregulated monopoly price.

■ **TERMS AND CONCEPTS**

pure monopoly
barriers to entry
X-inefficiency
rent-seeking
 behaviour

price discrimination
socially optimal price
fair-return price

◘ **HINTS AND TIPS**

1. How narrowly or broadly a market is defined will affect what degree of monopoly power a firm has in its market. The Vancouver Canucks may be the only NHL-level live hockey entertainment in British Columbia, which sounds like a monopoly! But for a consumer who is willing to substitute televised NHL hockey, or live junior A games, or perhaps some other sport, the Canucks have much less monopoly power.

2. In a monopoly, the demand and marginal revenue curves are distinct. The MR curve is twice as steep as the demand curve, so the MR curve lies, at all points, halfway between the demand and the price axis. This is handy to know when sketching a graph. Draw the demand curve first, and then sketch in the MR curve.

3. The monopolist's price is *on the demand curve*. First locate the monopolist's profit-maximizing output where MR = MC. Then go up to the demand curve to find the maximum price that consumers are willing to pay for this quantity.

4. When displaying the monopolist's data in a table (e.g., Table 10-1), it is customary to show MR and MC "between the lines" because MR and MC are calculated going from one quantity to another. To follow the same principle when graphing, be sure to plot each point on MR and MC at the quantity right in the middle between the two quantities from which the calculation was made.

■ FILL-IN QUESTIONS

1. Pure monopoly is a market structure in which a single firm is the sole seller of a product for which there are no _subs._ and into which entry in the long run is _difficult_.

2. Legal barriers to entry include _patents_ and _licences_.

3. An industry in which the long-run average cost declines over the range of possible demand levels would be termed a _natural_ monopoly.

4. The demand schedule confronting the pure monopolist is _downward_ sloping; this means that marginal revenue is (greater, less) _less_ than price and that both marginal revenue and price (increase, decrease) _decrease_ as output increases.

5. Suppose a car dealer can sell 5 cars at $20,000 each, or 6 cars at $19,000 each. The revenue from the sale of the sixth car would be $_19000_, but to sell the sixth car the dealer would have to cut the price and lose a total of $_5,000_ on the _5_ cars that he could otherwise have sold at the higher price. Therefore, the marginal revenue from the sixth car is the gain of $_19000_ minus the loss of $_5000_, for an overall change in total revenue of $_14000_.

6. The profit-maximizing monopolist will always want to choose a price-quantity combination somewhere in the (elastic, inelastic) _elastic_ segment of its demand curve. The monopolist will avoid the _inelastic_ segment, because there the (total, marginal) _marginal_ revenue is (negative, positive) _negative_.

7. Like the pure competitor, the pure monopolist sets profit-maximizing output at the level where marginal cost equals _MR_. For the pure competitor, marginal cost is (above, below, equal to) _equal_ the price, whereas for the monopolist marginal cost is _below_ the price.

8. Given the same costs, the monopolist will find it profitable to sell (more, less) _less_ output and to charge a (higher, lower) _higher_ price than would a purely competitive firm.

9. A monopoly that spends money lobbying the government to impose tariffs that would keep foreign competitors out of the Canadian market is said to be engaging in _rent seeking_ behaviour.

10. There is price discrimination whenever a product is sold at different _prices_ and these differences are not justified by differences in the _costs_ of supplying the product.

11. Price discrimination is possible only when the following three conditions are found:
(a) _monopoly power_
(b) _product cannot be resold_
(c) _market segregation._

12. Charging different prices in segmented markets can increase a monopolist's profits if the _elasticity_ of demand differs between the markets.

13. The misallocation of resources that results from monopoly can be eliminated if a ceiling price for the monopolist's product is set equal to _marginal cost_. However, since such a price is often _less_ than average total cost, the regulation will cause the monopolist to suffer a loss.

14. If a regulated monopolist is allowed to earn a fair return, the ceiling price for the product is set equal to _ATC_.

■ PROBLEMS AND PROJECTS

1. Billy Bob is a pure monopolist selling hot dogs outside a bar at closing time. His demand schedule and total cost schedule are given in the table that follows.
(a) Complete the table by computing total revenue, marginal revenue, and marginal cost.
(b) Why would Billy Bob never sell more than 5 hot dogs no matter what the level of costs?
Because this results in a loss

(c)   Use the marginal-revenue and marginal-cost approach to find the profit-maximizing output. (In numerical examples it can happen that there is no output level where marginal revenue and marginal cost are equal. In that case the extra unit should be produced as long as marginal revenue is greater than marginal cost.) 4

(d)   What price will Billy Bob charge for a hot dog? $6

(e)   How much economic profit will he make? $16

(f)   Plot price, marginal revenue, marginal cost, and average cost on the blank graph below. (Remember to plot MR and MC at the "midpoints" of the quantity ranges over which they are calculated.)

(g)   Indicate on the graph the monopoly output, price and total profit.

Qd	P	TR	MR	TC	MC
0	$10	$0	--	$4.00	--
1	9	9	$9	4.25	$0.25
2	8	16	7	5.00	0.75
3	7	21	5	6.25	1.25
4	6	24	3	8.00	1.75
5	5	25	1	10.25	2.25
6	4	24	<1>	13.00	2.75
7	3	21	<3>	16.25	3.25

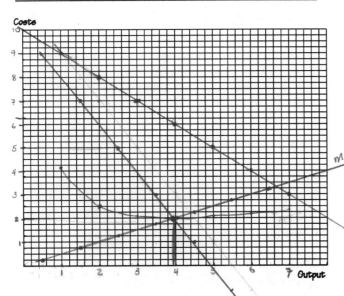

2. Assume that Billy Bob (from the previous question) is able to engage in perfect price discrimination (selling each hot dog at the maximum price that a buyer is willing to pay).

   (a) Complete the following table by computing total revenue at each quantity and the marginal revenue this discriminating monopolist obtains for

each additional unit sold. [The total and marginal revenue will not be the same as in the table in the previous question.]

Qd	P	TR	MR
0	$10	$0	--
1	9	9	$9
2	8	17	8
3	7	24	7
4	6	30	6
5	5	35	5
6	4	39	4
7	3	42	3

(b) The table shows that Billy Bob's marginal revenue as a discriminating monopolist is equal to the __price__.

(c) Assuming the costs are as given in the previous question, as a discriminating monopolist Billy Bob would produce __6__ hot dogs, charge the buyer of the last one produced a price of $__4__, and obtain a total economic profit of $__26__.

(d) Compared to the situation where he charges each buyer the same price, perfect price discrimination (increases, decreases) __increases__ profits, and __increases__ output.

(e) In the situation described, do you think that Billy Bob would be successful in price discriminating? Why?

3. Trogg is thinking about building a raft to carry passengers from his island to the mainland. It would cost him 60 clams to build, and the raft would last for one season. Marginal costs are zero. The demand for raft trips for the season is given by the following table:

Qd (trips)	P (clams/trip)	TR (clams)	Profit (clams)
0	8	0	<60>
5	7	35	<25>
10	6	60	0
15	5	75	15
20	4	80	20
25	3	75	15
30	2	60	0
35	1	35	<25>
40	0	0	<60>

(a) Trogg (should, should not) __should__ build the raft because the best he can do is a (profit, loss) __profit__ of __20__ clams. At this optimum he charges __4__ clams per trip and sells __20__ trips.

(b) The optimal social price for raft rides is __0__ clams, because at this price the condition for allocative efficiency is met: __P__ = __mc__.

(c) The problem with the optimal social price is that Trogg would lose __60__ clams.

(d) If the Cave Clan Council regulates Trogg in order to allow the whole society to benefit as much as possible from the raft service without driving Trogg out of business, then a fair-return price would be __6__ clams.

4. Use the next graph that shows a profit-maximizing pure monopolist to fill in these blanks:

(a) output __80__
(b) marginal revenue at this output __8__
(c) marginal cost at this output __8__
(d) price at this output __13.50__
(e) total revenue at this output __1080__
(f) average cost at this output __11__
(g) total cost of this output __880__
(h) profit per unit of output __2.50__
(i) total profit __200__

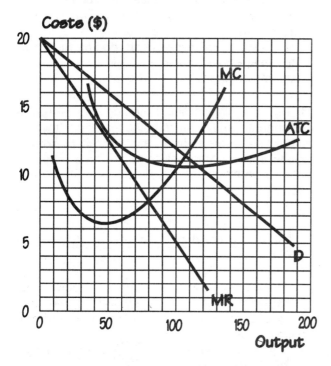

5. One-Eyed Jack's is the only saloon in Dry Gulch. The demand for Jack's whiskey is given by: $Q = 100 - P$ where Q is the number of shots sold per day, and P is the price in cents per shot. Jack's only variable costs are for the whiskey itself: a constant 20 cents per shot. (Therefore the MC and AVC curves are horizontal at 20 cents.) Jack's fixed costs are $12 per day for building rental and wages for himself, the barmaid and the piano player. There are no other costs.

(a) To maximize profits, how much whiskey should One-Eyed Jack's sell per day? (Hint: Start by graphing the demand curve, the MR curve, and MC curve.) $mR = mc$

(b) What price will be charged?

(c) What is the total daily profit?

■ **TRUE-FALSE**

Circle T if the statement is true, F if it is false.

1. In the monopoly model the firm and the industry are one and the same. **(T)** F

2. Barriers to entry normally cannot prevent entry in the long run. T **(F)**

3. A natural monopoly is defined to be a firm that holds a government-granted franchise. T **(F)**

4. A purely competitive firm is a price taker, but a monopolist is a price maker. **(T)** F

5. On a graph the marginal revenue curve is half as steep as the demand curve. T **(F)**

6. Marginal revenue is less than price for downsloping demand curves because in order to sell an extra unit the firm must lower the price of all previous units sold. **(T)** F

7. In Canada a new patent gives an inventor monopoly power for twenty years. **(T)** F

8. A monopoly may attempt to establish an entry barrier through a policy of dramatic price-cutting whenever it appears another firm might enter the market. **(T)** F

9. If a pure monopoly is losing money it can always make a profit by raising the price of its product. T **(F)**

10. At the profit-maximizing monopoly output, price is greater than marginal cost. **(T)** F

11. If a monopolist sets marginal revenue equal to marginal cost, yet stills suffers a loss, then at this point price must be less than average cost. **(T)** F

12. When a monopolist is maximizing its total profit, it is also maximizing its per unit (or average) profit. **T** **F**

13. Since a monopoly sets price equal to marginal cost, at the profit-maximizing rate of output, resources are allocated efficiently. **T** **F**

14. A monopolist has no supply curve. **T** **F**

15. When there are substantial economies of scale in production, the monopolist may charge a price that is lower than the price that would prevail if the product were produced by a purely competitive industry. **T** **F**

16. Rent-seeking behaviour adds to the inefficiency of monopoly. **T** **F**

17. The inefficiencies of monopoly may be somewhat offset by economies of scale and technological progress. **T** **F**

18. Whenever a monopolist simultaneously sells the same product at two or more different prices, then price discrimination occurs. **T** **F**

19. Price discrimination is fairly unusual in Canada. **T** **F**

20. If a movie theatre sells tickets to students at 25% below the regular adult price, then this is an example of price discrimination, assuming students and adults are equally costly to serve. **T** **F**

21. The price that achieves allocative efficiency is called the socially optimal price. **T** **F**

22. A "fair-return" price for a regulated utility would set price equal to average cost. **T** **F**

■ **MULTIPLE-CHOICE**

Circle the letter that corresponds to the best answer.

1. Which of the following is the best example of a pure monopoly?
 (a) a neighbourhood grocer in Saskatoon
 (b) the only gas station in a remote town
 (c) the manufacturer of Crest toothpaste
 (d) a bank in downtown Winnipeg

2. For the monopolist:
 (a) price equals marginal revenue
 (b) price is greater than marginal revenue
 (c) price is less than marginal revenue
 (d) price and marginal revenue are unrelated

3. In order to maximize profits the monopolist should set output at the level where:
 (a) price equals marginal cost
 (b) price equals average cost
 (c) marginal revenue equals marginal cost
 (d) marginal revenue equals average cost

4. Reasons for the existence of monopoly include all but:
 (a) patents
 (b) declining long-run average costs over a large range of output relative to industry demand
 (c) control of a raw material
 (d) inelastic demand for the product

5. Which of the following is the key characteristic of a natural monopoly?
 (a) economies of scale throughout the range of market demand
 (b) it is a public utility
 (c) it has low fixed costs
 (d) profits are large

6. Because the monopolist is the sole producer in the industry:
 (a) the demand curve for the monopolist is the industry demand curve
 (b) the monopolist's demand curve will be inelastic
 (c) the monopolist will not lose sales when price is raised
 (d) the marginal revenue will be greater than price at all levels of output

7. At its present output a monopolist determines that its marginal cost is $18 and its marginal revenue is $21. The monopolist will maximize profits or minimize losses by:
 (a) increasing price while keeping output constant
 (b) decreasing price and increasing output
 (c) decreasing both price and output
 (d) increasing both price and output

8. If a monopolist's MC curve shifts up, how will the monopolist respond?
   (a)   increase price and increase output
   (b)   decrease price and increase output
   (c)   decrease price and decrease output
   (d)   increase price and decrease output

Answer questions 9 through 11 on the basis of the demand and cost data for a monopolist given in the following table.

Output	Price	Total Cost
0	$80	$50
1	70	60
2	60	72
3	50	86
4	40	102
5	30	120

9. The marginal revenue of the third unit of output is:
   (a) $10
   (b) $20
   (c) $30
   (d) $40

10. The profit-maximizing monopolist would produce:
   (a)   1 unit
   (b)   2 units
   (c)   3 units
   (d)   4 units

11. The profit-maximizing monopolist would set its price at:
   (a) $20
   (b) $30
   (c) $40
   (d) $50

12. At the output which maximizes profits, the monopoly may not be productively efficient because:
   (a)   the average total cost of producing is not a minimum
   (b)   the marginal cost of producing the last unit is less than its price
   (c)   marginal cost may not be at its minimum value
   (d)   average revenue exceeds the cost of producing an extra unit of output

Use the diagram that follows to answer questions 13 through 15.

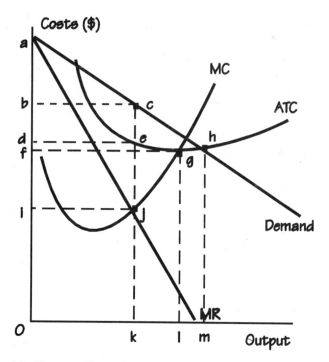

13. The profit-maximizing monopolist would produce:
   (a)   0*k* units
   (b)   0*l* units
   (c)   0*m* units
   (d)   zero units

14. The profit-maximizing monopolist would set a price of:
   (a)   0*a*
   (b)   0*b*
   (c)   0*f*
   (d)   0*i*

15. The profit-maximizing monopolist would earn an economic profit of:
   (a)   *deji*
   (b)   *bck0*
   (c)   *abc*
   (d)   *bced*

16. The concept of "simultaneous consumption" would be most applicable for which firm's product?
   (a)   a newspaper
   (b)   a dentist
   (c)   a tanning salon
   (d)   an apple grower

17. Kim would have more fun with her hockey cards if more of her friends also enjoyed collecting and trading cards. This is an example of which economic concept?

   (a)   economies of scale
   (b)   network effects
   (c)   barriers to entry
   (d)   X-inefficiency

18. Which of the following is probably not an example of price discrimination?

   (a)   a plumber charging a higher hourly rate for customers who live in bigger houses
   (b)   a taxicab charging more for longer trips
   (c)   a university charging higher tuition for executive MBA students than for other students in the same courses
   (d)   a ski hill charging different lift fees for local residents than for tourists

19. Which is not one of the conditions for successful price discrimination?

   (a)   the buyer must be unable to resell the product
   (b)   the product must be a service
   (c)   the seller must have some monopoly power
   (d)   the seller must be able to segment the market

20. As compared to a competitive industry with the same costs, a monopolized industry will have:

   (a)   more output and a higher price
   (b)   more output and a lower price
   (c)   less output and a lower price
   (d)   less output and a higher price

Questions 21 through 25 are based on the next graph.

21. The monopoly depicted is:

   (a)   a natural monopoly because the demand curve is downward sloping
   (b)   a natural monopoly because ATC is still falling where it intersects demand
   (c)   a natural monopoly because MR and MC intersect at an output level below the social optimum
   (d)   not a natural monopoly

22. If unregulated, which price and output combination would this monopolist choose?

   (a)   *Pa* and *Qa*
   (b)   *Pd* and *Qa*
   (c)   *Pb* and *Qb*
   (d)   *Pc* and *Qc*

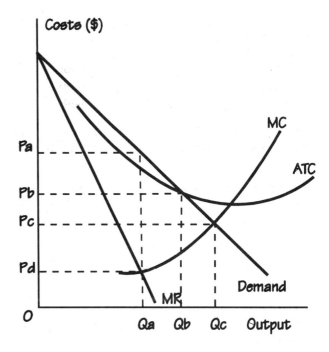

23. If the government regulates this monopolist so as to avoid allocative inefficiency, the price and output combination should be:

   (a)   *Pa* and *Qa*
   (b)   *Pd* and *Qa*
   (c)   *Pb* and *Qb*
   (d)   *Pc* and *Qc*

24. The problem with the regulated solution found in question 23 is that:

   (a)   the monopolist incurs a loss
   (b)   the monopolist still earns excessive profits
   (c)   the monopolist produces too little output
   (d)   the monopolist produces too much output

25. A regulatory compromise is to charge a price that allows the monopolist a "fair return" but also results in an output level close to the social optimum. Such a price and output combination is:

   (a)   *Pa* and *Qa*
   (b)   *Pd* and *Qa*
   (c)   *Pb* and *Qb*
   (d)   *Pc* and *Qc*

26. A firm experiencing X-inefficiency would likely:

   (a)   pay managers salaries above the going market rate
   (b)   produce more output than is optimal
   (c)   earn unusually high profits
   (d)   experience economies of scale

27. The DeBeers company enforced their diamond monopoly for many years by:
   (a) convincing independent producers to market through one central agency
   (b) cutting prices to discipline producers who sold outside the cartel
   (c) buying and stockpiling diamonds produced by independent mines
   (d) all of the above

■ **DISCUSSION QUESTIONS**

1. Describe the characteristics of the purely monopolistic market structure. Why is it included in the text if it is fairly rare in practice?

2. What is meant by a barrier to entry? What are the different kinds of barriers to entry? How important are they in pure competition, pure monopoly, monopolistic competition, and oligopoly?

3. For each type of barrier to entry, give an example of a firm in your community that has some monopoly power by virtue of this type of barrier.

4. Why are most natural monopolies also public utilities? What does government hope to achieve by granting exclusive franchises to and regulating such natural monopolies?

5. If you owned a National Hockey League franchise in Charlottetown, you would have more of a monopoly than if you owned the New York Rangers NHL franchise. Why? Would you have a natural monopoly in Charlottetown? Would you be able to make a profit?

6. The lone movie theatre in Jasper, Alberta, presumably has some monopoly power. What factors limit this monopoly power?

7. How do patent laws contribute to monopoly power? In 1995 the GATT extended patent protection from 17 years to 20 years. How could such an increase in the duration of a patent be justified considering that monopoly leads to allocative and productive inefficiency?

8. Compare the pure monopolist and the individual pure competitor with respect to:
   (a) the demand schedule
   (b) the marginal-revenue schedule
   (c) the relationship between marginal revenue and the price
   (d) the condition that must be met at the profit-maximizing output
   (e) the ability to set price
   (f) long-run economic profits
   (g) long-run efficiency

9. Explain why marginal revenue is always less than price when demand curves are downsloping.

10. Suppose you are a pure monopolist and discover you are producing and selling an output at a point on the inelastic part of the demand curve. Explain why a decrease in output accompanied by a price increase must improve your profits.

11. For what reasons might a monopolist have lower or higher average costs than purely competitive firms?

12. What are some symptoms of X-inefficiency?

13. What is meant by price discrimination and what conditions must be realized before it is workable? In what ways might price discrimination be considered socially harmful or beneficial?

14. How do public utility regulatory agencies attempt to eliminate the misallocation of resources that results from monopoly? Explain the dilemma that almost invariably confronts the agency in this endeavour; and explain why a fair-return price only reduces but does not eliminate misallocation.

■ **ANSWERS**

FILL-IN QUESTIONS

1. close substitutes, blocked

2. patents, licences

3. natural

4. downward, less, decrease

5. 19,000, 5,000; 19,000, 5,000, 14,000

6. elastic; inelastic, marginal, negative

7. marginal revenue; equal to, below

8. less, higher

9. rent-seeking

10. prices, cost

11. (a) monopoly power; (b) market segregation; (c) no resales

12. elasticity

13. marginal cost; less

14. average total cost

PROBLEMS AND PROJECTS

1. (a) Total revenue: $0, 9, 16, 21, 24, 25, 24, 21; Marginal revenue: $9, 7, 5, 3, 1, -1, -3; Marginal cost: $.25, .75, 1.25, 1.75, 2.25, 2.75, 3.25; (b) Total revenue falls after 5 hot dogs so it would never pay to sell 6 or more; (c) 4 hot dogs (MR > MC up this point, and MR < MC thereafter); (d) $6; (e) $16

2. (a) Total revenue: $0, 9, 17, 24, 30, 35, 39, 42. Marginal revenue: $9, 8, 7, 6, 5, 4, 3. (b) price; (c) 6, $4, $26; (d) increases, increases; (e) probably not; segregating groups of buyers and preventing resale would be nearly impossible

3. (a) should; profit; 20; 4.20; (b) 0; P = MC; (c) 60; (d) 2 because Trogg's TR = TC = $60

4. (a) 80 (b) $8.00 (c) $8.00 (d) $13.50 (e) $1080 (f) $11.00 (g) $880 (h) $2.50 (i) $200

5. (a) 40 (b) $0.60 (c) $4.

TRUE-FALSE

1. T
2. T   except perhaps government sanctioned barriers (patents and licences)
3. F   key is economies of scale
4. T
5. F   twice as steep
6. T
7. T
8. T
9. F   monopoly power is no guarantee of economic profit
10. T
11. T   profit = (P – ATC) x Q
12. F   total profit is objective, and isn't typically maximized where per unit profit is maximized
13. F   P > MC
14. T
15. T   so monopoly can be more efficient than pure competition
16. T   resources are wasted on lobbying, etc.
17. T
18. F   not if price differences are explained by cost differences
19. F   very common; text gives many examples
20. T
21. T
22. T   when P = ATC, economic profit = 0, but normal profit still exists

MULTIPLE-CHOICE

1. (b) competition or substitutes seem to exist in the other cases
2. (b) P is on demand curve; MC = MR below demand curve
3. (c) this is the same rule as for pure competition
4. (d)
5. (a) a firm with significant economies of scale, often with high fixed costs
6. (a)
7. (b) expand output until MC = MR; to sell more output, price must decrease
8. (d) new MC will intersect MR at lower output; this will correspond to a higher price on the demand curve
9. (c) 150 – 120 = 30
10. (c) for third unit, MR = 30, MC = 14; for fourth unit MR = 10, MC = 16, so profit would fall by 6 if output = 4
11. (d) P = 50 corresponds to Qd = 3 in the demand schedule
12. (a) ATC is not usually minimum where MC = MR
13. (a) MC = MR
14. (b) up to the demand curve from where MC = MR
15. (d) (P – ATC) x Q
16. (a) once the newspaper is written, laid out and typeset, the MC to print additional copies is very low
17. (b) the consumer's benefits or value for the good depends on how many others consume the same good
18. (b) longer trips entail more cost
19. (b) price discrimination can be used for goods or services
20. (d) hence allocative inefficiency
21. (b)
22. (a)
23. (d) where P = MC
24. (a) at Qc, ATC is above P
25. (c) P = ATC, so economic profit = 0
26. (a) insufficient incentive to minimize costs
27. (d) see the Last Word

CHAPTER 11

Monopolistic Competition and Oligopoly

This, the last of three chapters on market structure models, deals with monopolistic competition and oligopoly. These two market structures fall between the extremes of pure competition (Chapter 9) and pure monopoly (Chapter 10), and are the most prevalent market structures in the Canadian economy.

As its name suggests, monopolistic competition is a blend of pure competition and pure monopoly. The number of firms and the entry and exit conditions are similar to pure competition, but because each firm offers a version of the product that is differentiated from other sellers' versions, each firm has some monopoly power, or control over price. The firm's demand curve is downsloping, but quite elastic. Advertising, product differentiation, and other forms of nonprice competition are the outstanding features of monopolistic competition. Control over price is quite limited because close substitutes are sold by many other sellers. To maximize profits, the monopolistic competitor juggles three factors: price, product, and advertising. Given the product quality and level of advertising, the price-output analysis of the monopolistic competitor in the short run is straightforward and identical to that outlined in Chapter 10 for the pure monopolist. The monopolistic competitor may earn an economic profit (or incur a loss) in the short run, but in the long run firms will enter or leave the industry until only normal profits remain.

Though it is clear that monopolistic competitors achieve neither productive efficiency nor allocative efficiency in long-run equilibrium, an evaluation of the welfare effects of this market structure is more complicated than this. Monopolistic competition produces both socially beneficial and detrimental effects related to product differentiation, development, and advertising. Because these have no counterpart

in pure competition, which is the standard for efficiency comparisons, an overall evaluation of monopolistic competition is difficult.

Oligopoly is closer to pure monopoly than to pure competition. An oligopoly is a market dominated by a few large sellers, and difficult for new sellers to enter. The degree to which a market is controlled by a few firms can be measured using a concentration ratio or Herfindahl index. These measures are useful, but also imperfect because it is difficult to exactly define a market or industry.

Because each of the dominant firms in an oligopoly has a significant market share, each firm's pricing and sales strategies will have a noticeable impact on their rivals' sales. Oligopolists are then "price makers" who are also mutually interdependent; because each firm holds a large market share, if one firm sells more by cutting price, advertising more, or developing new products, rivals will lose sales, and might respond with competitive strategies of their own. A firm contemplating a competitive action is well aware of this, and will choose its action with such reactions in mind. Economists have a variety of models of oligopoly behaviour that incorporate this mutual interdependence. The chapter presents a simple game theory model that succinctly illustrates two fundamental points about oligopoly behaviour: firms have incentive to collude, and they have incentive to cheat on collusive agreements!

Three other specific oligopoly models are presented in Chapter 11. The first is the kinked demand curve model, which assumes no collusion, and different reactions from rivals depending on whether the firm raises or lowers price. The firm expects that rivals will match price cuts, but will not respond to price increases. The kinked demand curve model explains why prices tend to be relatively inflexible in an oligopoly, but fails to explain how oligopoly prices are set in the first place. The second model assumes pricing based on collusion between oligopolists. Whether overt (cartel agreement) or covert (illegal conspiracy), collusion produces price and industry output levels that correspond to the pure monopoly outcome. Though OPEC provides an example of a very successful cartel, there are many obstacles to effective collusion that make cartels difficult to establish and even more difficult to sustain. In the price leadership model, a dominant firm takes the initiative for changing prices and other firms follow the leader. Instead of risking price wars, oligopolists often compete through advertising and other forms of nonprice competition. Advertising can have both positive and negative effects for society as a whole.

Most economists agree that there is allocative and productive inefficiency in most oligopolistic industries. There is disagreement over the degree to which oligopolists collude and thereby exploit their monopoly power. Oligopoly may be the market structure most conducive to technological advances that can improve society's range of products and reduce the costs of production. Chapter 12 looks at these issues.

■ CHAPTER LEARNING OBJECTIVES

In this chapter you will learn:
☐ The necessary conditions required for monopolistic competition to arise.
☐ How the profit-maximizing price and output are determined in monopolistic competition.
☐ The necessary conditions for oligopoly to arise.
☐ About monopolistic competition and nonprice competition.
☐ How game theory can help explain the behaviour of oligopolists.
☐ About three oligopoly models.
☐ About the debate of the impact of advertising on consumers and firms.
☐ Why oligopoly achieves neither productive nor allocative efficiency.

■ CHAPTER OUTLINE

1. A monopolistically competitive industry has a relatively large number of independent firms, differentiated products, and easy entry and exit in the long run. Many Canadian industries are monopolistically competitive.

2. Product differentiation is the hallmark of monopolistic competition. The main elements on which firms compete are: product attributes, service, location, brand names and packaging, advertising, and pricing.

3. Assume that each firm is selling a product of given quality and characteristics, and is engaged in a given amount of advertising.
   (a) The demand curve facing each firm is highly, but not perfectly, elastic. Because each firm sells a unique product, the firm has price making power, but not very much, because many rivals offer closely substitutable products. The firm's demand is less elastic than a pure competitor's, but more elastic than a pure monopolist's.
   (b) In the short run, the individual firm will produce the output at which marginal cost and marginal revenue are equal and charge the price at which the output can be sold. In the short run the firm may realize profits or incur losses.
   (c) If short-run profits exist, entry of new firms in the long run will *tend* to decrease the demand curve for the product of the individual firm until economic profits are eliminated (price and average cost are made equal to each other). If short-run losses exist, some firms will exit, *tending* to increase the demand curves of surviving firms until economic profits are once again zero.

4. In monopolistic competition firms end up with excess capacity, and neither allocative nor productive efficiency is reached. Because the price is at least slightly above marginal cost, the monopolistic competitor will produce too little output to achieve allocative efficiency. Excess capacity exists because there are so many firms that each firm cannot sell enough to reach its minimum-ATC output.

5. In an effort to exceed the normal profit that they will tend to earn in long-run equilibrium, monopolistic competitors continually try to make their products more appealing and develop better advertising. If these strategies are successful, the demand curve shifts to the right and becomes more inelastic. To the extent that such nonprice competition leads to new product innovations and quality improvements that consumers value, the wastes of monopolistic competition may be offset.

6. An oligopoly is a market dominated by a few large producers of a homogeneous or differentiated

product. Firms are "price makers" but are also mutually interdependent. Oligopoly is a common industry structure in Canada.

7. An oligopoly is usually the result of economies of scale, other barriers to entry, or a merger of two or more rivals.

8. The degree of market domination by large firms can be measured by a concentration ratio or the Herfindahl index. One standard for defining oligopoly is a 40% four-firm concentration ratio (that is, 40% of the market is held by the largest four firms). Any numerical measure of industry concentration is subject to criticism because the relevant market can be very difficult to define. Markets can be localized, national, or international.

9. A simple game theory model illustrates the strategic problem every oligopolist faces because each firm's profits depend on their own actions and those of their rivals. An example of two rival producers, each deciding whether to set price high or low, leads to three conclusions.

    (a)   An oligopoly has few enough firms that one firm's actions effect a rival's profits enough that the rival is likely to react. The initial action should be based on what reaction is anticipated. This is known as mutual interdependence.

    (b)   Mutual interdependence creates an incentive to collude rather than to compete, because competition simply erodes potential profits for all firms in the industry.

    (c)   If a collusive agreement is made, each firm has an incentive to cheat on the agreement.

10. Oligopolies vary so much that no single model can adequately explain behaviour in all oligopolies. Even so, most models fit with the observation that oligopolies generally have inflexible prices, and that when prices do change, firms tend to change their prices together. This is a feature of the three models presented in this chapter: the kinked demand curve model, collusive pricing model, and price leadership model.

11. In the kinked demand curve model, which is a noncollusive model, each firm believes that when it lowers its price, rivals will lower their prices, and when it increases its price, rivals will not increase their prices. Therefore the firm is reluctant to change its price, and even if its variable costs change, it may not change price unless the cost shift is large.

This model, while providing a theory for price inflexibility, does not explain how prices are set initially. Also, when the macroeconomy is unstable, oligopoly prices are not as rigid as predicted by this theory.

12. In the collusive pricing model, firms jointly set their price and their combined output at the same level that a pure monopolist would select. Firms may reach such an equilibrium through overt collusion in a formal cartel, through a covert collusive conspiracy, or through a tacit understanding. Numerous obstacles make collusive agreements difficult to maintain: demand and cost differences, entry of new firms and growth of firms that are outside the agreement, cheating on the agreement, recession, and legal prohibitions. Even the highly successful OPEC cartel has been vulnerable to many of these problems.

13. In the price leadership model the dominant firm in the industry (usually the biggest or most efficient) initiates all price changes, and other firms follow. The outcome is similar to collusion, but price leadership does not depend on formal agreements. Price changes, which are often publicly signalled by the leader, are infrequent and occur only in response to significant changes in cost or demand conditions. In some cases the leader chooses a price designed to maximize long-run profits by deterring entry, rather than maximize short-run profits.

14. Oligopolists tend to compete through product development and advertising. Such forms of competition are preferred to price cutting because: 1) price cuts are easily duplicated by rivals and can spark price wars, and; 2) oligopolists usually have enough resources to engage in advertising and product development.

15. Advertising has both positive and negative effects for the economy:

    (a)   Where advertising provides information, it reduces search costs, promotes competition by enabling new products and brands to gain market share, and therefore helps firms to obtain economies of scale.

    (b)   Where advertising is mainly persuasive, it promotes brand loyalty and monopoly power, acting as a barrier to entry for new firms. If advertising is self-cancelling, it is inefficient.

16. Oligopoly is like pure monopoly in failing to generate either allocative or productive efficiency. Evidence of sustained profits in many oligopolies supports this view. On the brighter side, three mitigating factors work to limit the extent of the inefficiency:

(a) Recently, more oligopolies are facing competition from foreign producers.

(b) Through "limit pricing," some oligopolies hold prices down somewhat to deter entry.

(c) Sustained profits may give oligopolists more incentive and ability to invest in research and development than firms in other market structures.

■ **TERMS AND CONCEPTS**

monopolistic competition	interindustry competition
product differentiation	import competition
nonprice competition	Herfindahl Index
excess capacity	game theory model
oligopoly	collusion
homogeneous oligopoly	kinked demand curve
differentiated oligopoly	price war
mutual interdependence	cartel
concentration ratio	tacit understandings
	price leadership

■ **HINTS AND TIPS**

1. This is quite a long, action-packed chapter. Because it deals with important classes of business behaviours, and some of the topics are difficult, you should allocate extra time to studying this chapter.

2. After reading this chapter, make sure to review Table 9-1 on the four basic market structure models. Everything in that table should be clear to you by now. It should also help you to avoid a common but disastrous mistake: that of confusing pure monopoly with monopolistic competition. These are two distinct market structures!

3. If you have trouble seeing why monopolistic competition *must* result in excess capacity in the long-run equilibrium, try to sketch a diagram that shows all of the following: 1) a downward sloping demand, 2) output set where MC = MR, 3) this output also at the minimum of ATC, *and* 4) losses being incurred at every other possible output level. Such a diagram is impossible to draw.

4. There is no standard model of oligopoly. Be sure to know the different assumptions that give rise to each of the four models presented in this chapter.

■ **FILL-IN QUESTIONS**

1. In a monopolistically competitive market, a (few, relatively large number of) _relatively large_ producers sell (standardized, differentiated) _diff_ products; these producers behave (independently, collusively) _ind._; and in the long run, entry into the market is (difficult, easy) _easy_.

2. The demand curve faced by a monopolistic competitor will be (more, less) _more_ elastic than the demand facing a monopolist and (more, less) _less_ elastic than the demand facing a pure competitor. The elasticity of the monopolistic competitor's demand curve will depend upon the number of _firms_ and the degree of _prod. diff._.

3. In the long run, the entry of new firms into a monopolistically competitive industry will (expand, reduce) _reduce_ the demand for the product produced by each firm in the industry and (increase, decrease) _increase_ the elasticity of that demand.

4. In the long run, the price charged by the individual firm in monopolistic competition will tend to equal _ATC_, its economic profits will tend to equal _zero_, and its average cost will be (below, equal to, above) _above_ the minimum average total cost.

5. In monopolistic competition, allocative efficiency is not achieved because _price_ is (less than, equal to, greater than) _greater than_ marginal cost. Productive efficiency is not achieved because production does not take place at the minimum point of the _ATC_ curve.

6. In the long run, the monopolistic competitor attempts to protect and increase profits by various forms of nonprice competition including further product _diff._, and better _adver_.

7. Oligopoly exists when a _few_ large firms, producing a _stand._ or _diff._ product, dominate a market that is difficult for new firms to _enter_.

8. A four-firm concentration ratio is calculated by dividing the sales of the _4 larges_ firms in the industry by the sales of the _whole ind._. An industry is usually considered an oligopoly when this concentration ratio is at least _40_ %.

9. The basics of strategic behaviour by oligopolists can be understood from a _game_ theory perspective. A payoff matrix for two oligopolists indicates the _profits_ generated when the two firms charge various _prices_. The payoff matrix calls attention to three key characteristics of oligopoly: (1) mutual _interdependence_ (2) _collusive_ tendencies, and (3) the incentive to _cheat_.

10. Oligopolists are mutually _interdep_ because one firm's actions have (significant, insignificant) _sign_ impacts on the profits of rival firms. This means that when setting price each producer must consider the _reaction_ of rivals.

11. Oligopoly prices tend to be (flexible, inflexible) _inflexible_ and oligopolists tend to change their prices (independently, simultaneously) _simul_, preferring instead to fight for market share through _non-price_ competition.

12. The kinked demand model reflects the assumption that if the oligopolist raises its price, its rivals (will, will not) _will not_ raise their prices, and if it lowers its price its rivals _will_ lower their prices. Thus, the individual oligopolist sees a demand curve that is relatively (elastic, inelastic) _elastic_ at prices above the current price, and relatively _inelastic_ at prices below the current price.

13. When oligopolists collude, the price they set and their combined output tend to be the same as would be set in a _pure monopoly_ industry.

14. A cartel is a formal agreement among _sellers_ to fix the _price_ of the product, _divide_ up the market, or otherwise restrict _competition_ among them. A cartel is an example of a (collusive, noncollusive) _collusive_ oligopoly.

15. A successful cartel, or _collusive_ agreement, is *more* likely to be successful when: (a) firms have (similar, different) _similar_ costs and demand curves; (b) there are (many, few) _few_ firms in the industry, (c) cheating is (easy, difficult) _easy_ to detect; (d) the

level of demand is (shrinking, growing) _growing_; (e) it is (easy, difficult) _diff._ to enter the industry; and (f) price-fixing collusion is (illegal, legal) _legal_.

16. When one firm in an oligopoly is usually the first to change its price and the other firms follow with similar price changes, there is probably a type of (overt, tacit) _tacit_ collusion called _price leadership_.

17. A strategy of setting price at a level that will discourage new entry is called _limit_ pricing.

18. The ability of advertising to provide consumers with _information_ about new products, increases the ability of new firms to enter markets, thereby (increasing, decreasing) _decreasing_ the price-making power of established firms. On the other hand, advertising by established firms (raises, lowers) _raises_ the ATC curve for new entrants, thereby _increasing_ the price-making power of established firms.

■ PROBLEMS AND PROJECTS

1. For each market situation described below, explain which market structure model seems to fit best: monopolistic competition or oligopoly.

(a) Grocery Stores: two food stores serve a town of 5,000 inhabitants. These stores feature some of the same brands, but also some different ones. They tend to have slightly different prices on specific items, but discount their prices at the same times. _oligopoly_

(b) Tourist Accommodations: About one hundred hotels, motels, and lodges compete for tourists seeking accommodation in a resort town in the Rockies. Most of these firms advertise widely. All are required by local regulations to belong to the Tourist Bureau that does some collective advertising and promotional work for all members. Each year there is some turnover in the group of firms operating in this market. _m.c._

(c) Banking: A country has numerous financial institutions, big and small, but a few banks issue the vast majority of loans. These banks have nearly identical interest rates, and tend to change their rates within days of one another. _Olig._

2. Roma Pizza is a restaurant operating as a monopolistic competitor near the campus of a major university. Their most popular pizza now sells for a price of $14, and is being produced for an average total cost of $12. If Roma could sell enough pizzas, they could reduce this cost to $10.

(a)   Sketch Roma's short run situation on a graph like those used in this chapter.

(b)   How and why is Roma's demand curve likely to change in the long run?

(c)   What will be the effect of this demand change on Roma's profits if the restaurant continues to produce the same pizzas and engage in their current promotional activities?

(d)   What happens to Roma's demand curve and average total cost curve if Roma introduces new varieties of pizzas, or higher quality pizzas, or if Roma increases advertising? Will these measures necessarily improve Roma's profits?

(e)   Will Roma ever be able to sell enough pizzas to push average total cost down to $10?

3. The following are hypothetical sales data for firms that manufacture DVD players in Canada:

Firm	1999 Sales million $	1999 Market Share	2002 Sales million $	2002 Market Share
Alpha	15	6%	30	6
Beta	20	8	40	8
Delta	10	4	20	4
Poseidon	40	16	60	12
Gamma	60	24	90	18
Omicron	75	30	200	40
Omega	25	10	50	10
Epsilon	5	2	10	2

250   500

(a)   Calculate the four-firm concentration ratio for 1999 and use the result to determine what type of market structure these firms operate in.

(b)   Calculate the Herfindahl index for 1999.

(c)   Give at least two reasons why the concentration ratio or Herfindahl index might overstate the amount of monopoly power held by these Canadian manufacturers of DVD players.

(d)   Recalculate the concentration ratio and Herfindahl ratio using 2002 data. What shortcoming of the concentration ratio calculation does comparing the 1999 and 2002 results on these two indicators of market power reveal?

4. Suppose that two manufacturers, Apogee and Bristol, control the whole market for a particular computer chip. There is no brand loyalty, so each firm's profit depends only on their pricing strategy, and that of their rival. Each firm can set a high or low price, and neither firm knows what strategy its rival will follow. If both charge a high price, the profits will be $25 million for Apogee and $18 million for Bristol. If both charge a low price, profits will be $6 million for Apogee and $5 million for Bristol. If Apogee charges a high price and Bristol a low price, Apogee's profits will be $2 million and Bristol's profits will be $30 million. If Apogee charges a low price and Bristol charges a high price, Apogee's profits will be $35 million and Bristol's will be $3 million.

(a)   Set up a payoff matrix showing each firm's profits for the four possible pricing outcomes.

(b)   If Bristol sets a high price, Apogee gets a higher profit by setting a (high, low) _low_ price. If Bristol sets a low price, Apogee gets a higher profit by setting a _low_ price. Therefore, if there is no collusion, Apogee will set a _low_ price.

(c)   If Apogee sets a high price, Bristol gets a higher profit by setting a (high, low) _low_ price. If Apogee sets a low price, Bristol gets a higher profit by setting a _low_ price. Therefore, without collusion, Bristol will set a _low_ price.

(d)   if the two firms do not collude, Apogee will get a profit of $_6_ and Bristol will get a profit of $_5_. Their combined profits will be $_11_. These profits (are, are not) _are not_ the maximum possible.

(e)   Given the result in (d), Apogee and Bristol (will, will not) _will_ have an incentive to collude. If they collude they would choose a _high_ price, resulting in a combined profit of $_43_.

(f)   If a collusive agreement is formed, Apogee (will, will not) _will_ have an incentive to cheat on the agreement. If Apogee cheats — and Bristol does not — Apogee's profits would (increase, decrease) _increase_ by $_10_. Similarly, if Bristol cheats — and Apogee does not — Bristol's profits would (increase, decrease) _increase_ by $_12_. Therefore, it is quite likely that the collusive agreement, if formed, (would, would not) _would not_ last long.

5. Mammoth Enterprises competes in homogeneous oligopoly in which all firms set price at $15. At this price Mammoth sells 10 units. Mammoth believes that if they raise their price their rivals will still charge $15. Mammoth also believes that if they cut

their price their rivals will match the price cut. Accordingly, Mammoth expects to sell 2 units less for every $1 price increase above $15, 1 unit more for every $1 cut in price.

Price	Qd	TR	MR	MC
$18	4	$ 72		
			$ 15	$6
17	6	102		
			13	7
16	8	128		
			11	8
15	10	150		
			4	9
14	11	154		
			2	10
13	12	156		
			-	11
12	13	156		
			-2	12
11	14	154		

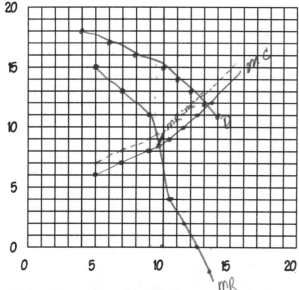

(a) Fill in the table showing Mammoth's demand schedule, total revenue, marginal revenue, and marginal cost.

(b) In the graph above, plot Mammoth's demand, marginal revenue, and marginal cost curves. Be sure to plot the marginal revenue and marginal cost curves at the midpoint of the two quantities involved in the calculation for each.

(c) Use the graph to confirm that Mammoth's profit-maximizing price is $15 and output is 10 under these assumptions about costs and demand.

(d) Use the graph to confirm that if Mammoth's marginal cost curve shifts up by $1 (parallel to original MC), that Mammoth will not change their output or their price.

(e) Use the graph to confirm that if Mammoth's marginal cost curve shifts up by $4 (parallel to original MC), that Mammoth will change their output and price.

■ **TRUE-FALSE**

Circle T if the statement is true, F if it is false.

1. Monopolistic competitors have no control over the price of their products. T (F)

2. In monopolistic competition each firm determines its policies after considering the possible reactions of rival firms. (T) F

3. The smaller the number of firms in an industry and the greater the extent of product differentiation, the greater will be the elasticity of the individual seller's demand curve. T (F)

4. In the short run, a monopolistic competitor may earn economic profits or losses. (T) F

5. In the long run, barriers to entry in monopolistically competitive industries usually result in sustained economic profits. T (F)

6. Productive efficiency is achieved in the long run in a monopolistically competitive industry since economic profits tend to be zero for the firm. T (F)

7. In long-run equilibrium the monopolistically competitive firm operates where its long-run average cost is tangent to its demand curve. (T) F

8. Monopolistically competitive industries tend to be overcrowded with firms, with each firm producing below its capacity output. (T) F

9. Economists agree that from a social perspective the positive effects of advertising outweigh the negative effects. T (F)

10. Advertising by established firms can contribute to monopoly power by making entry more difficult and expensive for new firms. (T) F

11. Differences between individual firms' products have economic significance whether the differences are real or merely imagined by consumers. **T** F

12. The products produced by oligopolistic firms may be either homogeneous or differentiated. **T** F

13. A four-firm concentration ratio of 64 percent in oil refining would mean that the largest four firms accounted for 64% of the industry's shipments. **T** F

14. The larger the Herfindahl index the greater the degree of market power in the industry. **T** F

15. Two industries can have the same concentration ratio yet have different Herfindahl index values. **T** F

16. Mergers increase market concentration. **T** F

17. Oligopolistic prices tend to be inflexible. **T** F

18. Collusion to fix prices is illegal under Canadian law. T **F**

19. Price leadership is almost always based on a formal written or oral agreement. T **F**

■ **MULTIPLE-CHOICE**

Circle the letter that corresponds to the best answer.

1. Which of the following is not characteristic of monopolistic competition?
(a) product differentiation
(b) a relatively large number of firms
(c) collusive agreements among firms
(d) relatively easy industry entry in the long run

2. A similarity between a pure monopoly firm and a monopolistically competitive firm is that both:
(a) earn economic profits in the long run
(b) operate where P = MC in the short run
(c) operate at the minimum point of their long-run average cost in the long run
(d) face downward sloping demand curves

3. Which of the following is not an example of product differentiation and other nonprice competition under monopolistic competition?
(a) an economics textbook publisher offering a free website to supplement the text

(b) an athletic shoe store in Toronto brings Vince Carter in to sign autographs
(c) a motel chain in Vancouver begins offering free airport limousine service
(d) all of the above

Questions 4 through 7 are based on the following graph showing a monopolistically competitive firm in short-run equilibrium.

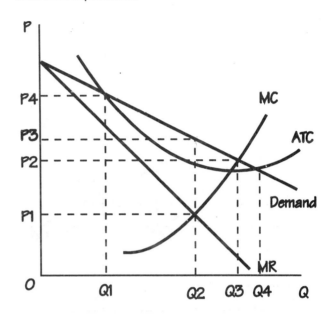

4. The equilibrium output for this firm will be:
(a) Q1
(b) Q2
(c) Q3
(d) Q4

5. The firm's profit-maximizing price will be:
(a) P1
(b) P2
(c) P3
(d) P4

6. At this equilibrium the firm will:
(a) realize an economic profit
(b) suffer an economic loss and eventually exit
(c) suffer an economic loss and remain in business
(d) break even and eventually exit

7. If this is an increasing cost industry, and firms enter this industry in the long run:
(a) the ATC curve will shift up and demand will decrease

(b) the ATC curve will shift up and demand will increase

(c) the MR curve will shift up and demand will decrease

(d) the MR curve will shift up and demand will increase

Questions 8 through 12 are based on this graph of a monopolistic competitor in long-run equilibrium.

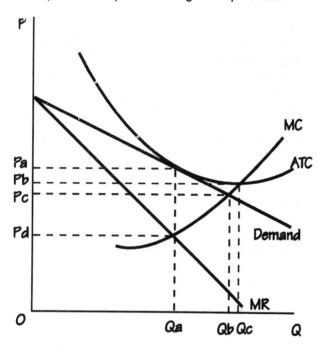

8. Long-run equilibrium output will be:
(a) Qa
(b) Qb
(c) Qc
(d) 0

9. Long-run equilibrium price will be:
(a) Pa
(b) Pb
(c) Pc
(d) Pd

10. This firm is:
(a) earning an economic profit
(b) covering its explicit costs but not its implicit costs
(c) earning a normal profit
(d) operating at the minimum average total cost of production

11. In order to meet the productive efficiency criterion this firm would have to produce an output of:

(a) Qa
(b) Qb
(c) Qc
(d) above Qc

12. The amount of excess capacity in this firm is:
(a) Qb-Qa
(b) Qc-Qb
(c) Qc-Qa
(d) there is no excess capacity

13. Even though prices may be higher under monopolistic competition than pure competition, consumers benefit from:
(a) lower prices than in the purely competitive model
(b) greater output than in the purely competitive model
(c) greater product variety than in the purely competitive model
(d) less advertising expenses than in the purely competitive model

14. Economic profits tend to be driven to zero in monopolistic competition. However, some firms may be able to sustain economic profits due to:
(a) especially effective product differentiation
(b) an exceptionally well-known brand name
(c) a one-of-a-kind superior location
(d) any of the above

15. How many firms are there in an oligopoly?
(a) one
(b) a few
(c) many
(d) very many

16. Concentration ratios take into account:
(a) interindustry competition
(b) import competition
(c) the existence of separate local markets
(d) none of the above

17. Which of the following does not contribute to the existence of oligopoly?
(a) the economies of large-scale production
(b) the gains in profits that result from mergers
(c) high barriers to entry
(d) the profits that result from cheating on a cartel agreement

Questions 18 through 21 are based on the following payoff matrix for a two-firm oligopoly. The numbers in the matrix represent the profits for a high-price or low-price strategy.

		Firm A	
		High-price	**Low-price**
Firm B	**High-price**	A = 600 B = 600	A = 875 B = 200
	Low-price	A = 200 B = 875	A = 350 B = 350

18. If the firms collude to maximize joint profits, the total profits for the two firms will be:
- **(a)** $700
- **(b)** $1075
- **(c)** $1200
- **(d)** $1475

19. If Firm A always pursues a high-price strategy, the best strategy for Firm B is:
- **(a)** a low-price strategy for earnings of $875
- **(b)** a low-price strategy for earnings of $350
- **(c)** a high-price strategy for earnings of $600
- **(d)** a high-price strategy for earnings of $275

20. Suppose the firms collude and agree to keep prices high. If Firm B cheats, and cuts price, it will:
- **(a)** gain an extra $400
- **(b)** gain an extra $275
- **(c)** decrease its profit by $675
- **(d)** decrease its profit by $150

21. If both firms act independently and do not collude, the most likely result is:
- **(a)** $600 for Firm A and $600 for Firm B
- **(b)** $875 for Firm A and $200 for Firm B
- **(c)** $200 for Firm A and $875 for Firm B
- **(d)** $350 for Firm A and $350 for Firm B

22. Mutual interdependence means that:
- **(a)** each firm sells a product similar but not identical to the products sold by its rivals
- **(b)** each firm sells a product identical to the products sold by its rivals
- **(c)** each firm must consider the reactions of its rivals when it determines its price policy
- **(d)** each firm faces a perfectly elastic demand for its product

23. The oligopolist's demand curve has a kink at the going price if the oligopolist believes that:
- **(a)** competitors will match both price cuts and price increases

- **(b)** competitors will match neither price cuts nor price increases
- **(c)** competitors will not notice either price cuts or price increases
- **(d)** competitors will match price cuts but not price increases

24. In the kinked demand curve model, an individual oligopolist's demand curve is:
- **(a)** more inelastic above the going price than below the going price
- **(b)** more elastic above the going price than below the going price
- **(c)** elastic above the going price and inelastic below the going price
- **(d)** of unitary elasticity at the going price

25. In the oligopolistic market structure the kinked demand analysis provides an explanation of:
- **(a)** barriers to entry
- **(b)** "sticky" prices
- **(c)** price leadership
- **(d)** mergers

Use the next diagram for questions 26 and 27.

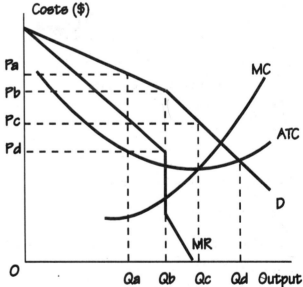

26. The profit-maximizing price and output for this oligopolistic firm is:
- **(a)** P_a and Q_a
- **(b)** P_b and Q_b
- **(c)** P_c and Q_c
- **(d)** P_d and Q_d

27. How would this firm respond to a small rise in their MC curve?

(a) reduce output, raise price, and maintain profits
(b) maintain output, maintain price, and have smaller profits
(c) maintain output, raise price, and maintain profits
(d) none of the above

28. Which of the following is a shortcoming of the kinked demand curve model?
(a) the model suggests that prices are relatively inflexible under oligopoly
(b) the model suggests that costs fluctuate unpredictably
(c) the model assumes product differentiation
(d) the model does not explain how price is determined in the first place

29. For collusion to be successful, oligopolists must be able to:
(a) keep prices and profits as low as possible
(b) block or restrict the entry of new producers
(c) engage in technological improvements of their products
(d) reduce legal obstacles that protect market power

30. When oligopolists collude, the results are generally:
(a) greater output and higher price
(b) greater output and lower price
(c) smaller output and lower price
(d) smaller output and higher price

31. Another name for a "gentlemen's agreement" as applied to oligopolists is:
(a) limit pricing
(b) joint-profit maximization
(c) tacit understanding
(d) illegal conspiracy

32. Which of the following is an obstacle to collusion among oligopolists?
(a) a general business recession
(b) a small number of firms in the industry
(c) a homogeneous product
(d) the patent laws

33. The prices of products produced in an industry characterized by price leadership tend to be:
(a) quite flexible and when firms change prices they are apt to change them at the same time

(b) quite inflexible and when firms change prices they are not apt to change them at the same time
(c) quite inflexible and when firms change prices they are apt to change them at the same time
(d) quite flexible and when firms change prices they are not apt to change them at the same time

34. The price leader in an oligopolistic industry:
(a) necessarily sets the price that maximizes industry profit
(b) determines production quotas for each firm
(c) is usually the largest or most efficient firm in the industry
(d) is assured that other firms will initiate similar price changes

35. Market shares in oligopolistic industries are usually determined on the basis of:
(a) tacit collusion
(b) nonprice competition
(c) gentlemen's agreements
(d) joint profit maximization

36. According to the positive view of advertising, advertising does all of the following with the exception of:
(a) providing useful information to consumers
(b) promoting monopoly power
(c) diminishing monopoly power by calling attention to an array of substitute goods or services
(d) facilitating the introduction of new products and, hence, enabling technological progress

37. According to the negative view of advertising:
(a) advertising has no effect on costs or output
(b) advertising lowers both costs and output
(c) advertising raises costs and makes entry more difficult
(d) advertising raises costs but raises output substantially

■ **DISCUSSION QUESTIONS**

1. What are the three chief characteristics of monopolistic competition? In what sense is there competition and in what sense is there monopoly in such a market? Does product differentiation create competition or does it create monopoly?

2. What is meant by product differentiation? By what methods can products be differentiated? What

methods are used in the markets for breakfast cereals, perfumes, rock music, and jeans?

3. What is the difference between the elasticity of the demand curve faced by the monopolistically competitive firm and the purely competitive firm? What two factors determine just how elastic that demand curve will be?

4. Why will the monopolistic competitor produce a long-run output smaller than the most "efficient" output? In answering this question, assume that the firm is producing a given product and selling it with a given amount of promotional activity.

5. Using a graph that includes the average total cost curve and the demand curve, show why it is impossible for a monopolistic competitor who is both maximizing profit and making zero economic profit to also be producing at the minimum point on the average total cost curve.

6. What strategies, other than price cutting, could an individual monopolistic competitor try in order to protect and increase its profits in the long run?

7. How do product differentiation and product development tend to offset the "wastes" associated with monopolistic competition?

8. Is advertising simply a waste of resources, or does it promote a more efficient use of resources? What arguments support the claim that it is wasteful and detrimental, and what arguments support the view that it is beneficial to the economy?

9. Why does it make sense for a monopolistic competitor to advertise, and why does it not make sense for a pure competitor?

10. What are the essential characteristics of an oligopoly? How does oligopoly differ from monopolistic competition? How is oligopoly like a chess game whereas monopolistic competition is not?

11. Explain how the concentration ratio and the Herfindahl Index in a particular industry are computed. How do these indicators measure monopoly power? What are the shortcomings of these indicators as measures of the extent of competition in an industry?

12. What are the underlying causes of oligopoly, and what is the essential "mutual interdependence" that drives the strategies of oligopolists?

13. What assumptions give rise to the kinked demand curve? How can the kinked demand curve be used to explain why oligopoly prices are relatively inflexible? Under what conditions will an oligopolist who believes it faces a kinked demand choose to change price?

14. Why do producers find it advantageous to collude? What are the obstacles to collusion?

15. Why do oligopolists engage in little price competition and in extensive nonprice competition?

■ **ANSWERS**

FILL-IN QUESTIONS

1. relatively large number of, differentiated; independently; easy

2. more, less; rival firms, product differentiation (or substitutability)

3. reduce, increase

4. average total cost, zero, above

5. price, greater than, average total cost

6. differentiation, advertising

7. few, homogeneous, differentiated, enter

8. largest four, whole industry; 40

9. game; profits; prices; (1) interdependence, (2) collusive, (3) cheat

10. interdependent, significant; reactions

11. inflexible, simultaneously, nonprice

12. will not, will; elastic, inelastic

13. pure monopoly

14. sellers, price, divide, competition; collusive

15. collusive; (a) similar; (b) few; (c) easy; (d) growing; (e) difficult; (f) legal

16. tacit, price leadership

17. limit

18. information, decreasing; raises, increasing

PROBLEMS AND PROJECTS

1. (a) Oligopoly: number of firms, clear mutual inter-dependence, timing of price changes; (b) Monopolistic competition: number of firms, product differentiation, entry and exit; (c) Oligopoly: few firms are dominant, pattern of price changes.

2. (a) See Figure 11-1(a); (b) Economic profits will attract new firms, shifting Roma's demand curve to the left as market share falls, and making it more elastic as the number of substitutes increases; (c) Roma's profits will tend towards zero; (d) If these nonprice competition strategies are successful, Roma's demand curve will decrease less than otherwise (or could even increase). Their demand will not become as elastic as otherwise. Advertising costs raise ATC curve, so Roma's profits may not improve; (e) No; entry of competitors will prevent Roma from gaining market share, and in long-run equilibrium Roma's output will have excess capacity.

3. (a) 200/250 = 80% oligopoly; (b) Convert each firm's sales into a percentage of whole market (for Omega, 25/250 = 10%); square that number (10 x 10 = 100); add up these values for all firms: end result = 1952; (c) import competition is not reflected, competition from VCRs or other potentially substitutable products is not reflected; (d) 80%, 2288; The concentration ratio does not reflect distribution of market shares among firms. The total market share held by the largest firms did not change from 1999 to 2002, but Omicron grew larger relative to other large firms.

4. (a)

		APOGEE	
		High-price	Low-price
BRISTOL	High-price	A = 25 B = 18	A = 35 B = 3
	Low-price	A = 2 B = 30	A = 6 B = 5

(b) low, low, low; (c) low, low, low; (d) 6 million, 5 million; 11 million; are not; (e) will; high; 43 million; (f) will; increase, 10 million; increase, 12 million; would not.

5. (a) Quantity demanded: 4, 6, 8, 10, 11, 12, 13, 14; Total Revenue: $72, 102, 128, 150, 154, 156, 156, 154; Marginal Revenue: $15, 13, 11, 4, 2, 0, -2; (b) Like Figure 11-4(b) but with a single MC curve; (c) the MC = MR in the vertical break section where Q = 10; on demand curve, P = 15 at Q = 10; (d) MC would still = MR in the vertical break section; (e) MC would now = MR in the upper downsloping section of MR.

TRUE-FALSE

1. F   they have a degree of monopoly power because their products are differentiated
2. F   firms in this market model behave independently
3. F   the less will be the elasticity
4. T
5. F   this market structure has few, if any, barriers
6. F   productive efficiency is not achieved, because minimum ATC is not reached
7. T   this is the defining characteristic of long-run equilibrium
8. T
9. F   there is no such consensus
10. T   new firms may also have to advertise extensively, raising their ATC unless their output is large
11. T   if these differences are the basis for consumer choices of different brands
12. T
13. T
14. T   a pure monopoly has a value of 10,000 and a purely competitive industry has a value approaching 0
15. T   it depends on the relative market shares of the top four firms
16. T   by reducing the number of firms
17. T   fear of price wars, preference for nonprice competition
18. T
19. F   more often tacit understanding

MULTIPLE-CHOICE

1. (c)   firms behave independently, not collusively
2. (d)   because their products have no perfect substitutes
3. (d)   all are competitive strategies by firms with numerous competitors
4. (b)   where MC = MR
5. (c)   on the demand curve at the Q where MC = MR
6. (a)   P3 is above ATC
7. (a)   ATC shifts up as competition for resources drives up their prices, and demand decreases as market share shrinks
8. (a)   where ATC is tangent to demand, so economic profit is zero
9. (a)
10. (c)   P = ATC implies zero economic profit, but a normal profit is included in ATC
11. (c)   where ATC is minimized
12. (c)   the difference between minimum efficient scale and actual output
13. (c)
14. (d)   if new entrants cannot match these advantages
15. (b)

16. (d) therefore a concentration ratio can be a misleading indicator of monopoly power

17. (d) these profits are a consequence not a contributing cause

18. (c)

19. (a) 875 > 600

20. (b)

21. (d)

22. (c) this is the essence of oligopoly

23. (d) this is the key assumption in the model

24. (b) for the reasoning in the previous question

25. (b) cost changes, unless major, tend not to lead to price changes

26. (b) where MC = MR

27. (b) the MC will still intersect MR at the same Q

28. (d)

29. (b) otherwise, as the cartel raises prices, new competitors will offer lower prices and take market share

30. (d) as prices are increased Qd decreases

31. (c)

32. (a) cartel members would experience falling sales and excess capacity, tempting them to cut price

33. (b)

34. (c) and therefore has the credibility to lead

35. (b) collusion is not the norm, but neither is vigorous price competition

36. (b) promoting monopoly power would be negative

37. (c) by increasing the minimum output at which new firms can be viable

CHAPTER 12

Technology, R&D, and Efficiency

The last few chapters have examined the firm's decisions over the short run and the long run. However, over both of these time horizons the firm is limited to operating with the same basic technology. This chapter discusses the very long run: a period in which technology can change and in which firms can introduce entirely new products. We learn about the nature of technological advance, the firm's decision-making regarding research and development (R&D), the relationship of market structure to technological advance, and the connection between technological progress and efficiency.

Technological advance is a three-step process: (1) invention, (2) innovation, (3) diffusion. In the modern view, all three steps occur in response to economic incentives, making technological advance an internal process, rather than something that happens randomly — or because of non-economic forces. Accordingly, we examine the roles of the economic agents at the center of this process. Entrepreneurs and other innovators (intrapreneurs) combine resources in unique ways to produce new products. Such activities are carried on within very small "startup" companies, within large established firms, and within the non-profit sector including government and university labs and research departments.

Investment in R&D should — as with any other economic activity — continue up to the point where its marginal benefit equals its marginal cost. Because the benefits are so uncertain, it is difficult to know exactly what the optimal level is. No matter how the R&D investment is financed, it will always have an implicit or explicit opportunity cost. This cost is reflected in the interest-rate cost-of-funds curve. The marginal benefit of R&D is represented in the expected return from the marginal dollar spent on R&D, as shown in the expected-rate-of-return curve. Where the two curves intersect defines the optimal level of R&D expenditures.

Innovation can increase the firm's profits through adding revenue or reducing costs. Revenue can be added via product innovation (the invention of entirely new products or significant improvements to existing products) and costs can be reduced via process innovation (reducing the costs of producing existing products).

If innovation creates opportunities for imitation by rivals, why not simply wait for other firms to innovate first? One reason is that the original innovator acquired valuable property rights: patents, copyrights and trademarks. Incentives also include brand-name recognition, trade secrets and learning by doing, time lags for imitation, and the chance of profits through a buyout by a larger firm.

Is there one particular market structure best suited to technological progress? Examining the incentives and opportunities for innovation in each of the four market structures studied in previous chapters leads to the inverted-U theory that indicates that R&D effort is highest in oligopolies.

Process innovation improves productive efficiency by lowering average total costs for the producer. Product innovation contributes to allocative efficiency by providing a more-preferred mix of goods and services. These conclusions are tempered by the fact that innovation can either create and entrench monopoly power, or destroy monopoly power (through a process that Schumpeter called "creative destruction"). Where innovation creates monopoly power the efficiency benefits of innovation are reduced or even negated.

Consumer surplus and producer surplus offer another way to understand allocative efficiency. Consumer surplus is the difference between what consumers are willing to pay for a product and its market price. Producer surplus is the difference between the revenue a producer is paid for a product and the marginal cost of producing it. Allocative efficiency is reached when the sum of consumer surplus and producer surplus is maximized. At this point, every possible unit is being produced for which any consumer is willing to pay at least the marginal cost of production. Producing more or less than this would result in a deadweight loss.

■ **CHAPTER LEARNING OBJECTIVES**

In this chapter you will learn:
☐ The distinction between an invention, an innovation, and technological diffusion.
☐ About the role of entrepreneurs and other innovators.
☐ A firm's optimal amount of R&D.
☐ About the role of market structure on technological change.
☐ How technological advance enhances both productive and allocative efficiency.
☐ About consumer surplus and producer surplus.

■ **CHAPTER OUTLINE**

1. Technological advance consists of the provision of new and better goods and services and new and better ways of producing or distributing them. Technological advance is possible within the time period called the very long run.

2. Technological advance is a three-step process of invention, innovation, and diffusion.
(a) Invention is the first discovery of a product or process through the use of imagination, ingenious thinking, and experimentation and the first proof that it will work.
(b) Innovation, which draws on invention, is the first successful commercial introduction of a new product, the first use of a new method, or the creation of a new form of business enterprise. We distinguish between product innovations and process innovations.
(c) Diffusion is the spread of an innovation through imitation or copying.

3. Research and development (R&D) includes direct efforts at invention, innovation, and diffusion. Compared to other industrial nations, Canadian firms and governments spend relatively little on R&D (measured as a percentage of GDP).

4. Technological advance was once seen as a process external to the economy: a random outside force. In the modern view, technological advance is an internal process driven by the market economy. Invention, innovation, and diffusion are not predictable in their specifics, but they occur in response to incentives in our economic system.

5. The role of entrepreneurs and other innovators is central to the process of technological advance.
(a) Entrepreneurs (or entrepreneurial teams) take on the role of initiator, innovator, and risk-bearer.
(b) Intrapreneurs are also innovators who carry some of the same roles, but do not bear personal financial risk.
(c) Entrepreneurs often form startups: new firms trying to create and introduce new products or processes of production or distribution.
(d) Innovation also occurs within existing firms, large and small. Often the R&D is housed within a separate division of a corporation.
(e) Successful innovators have an ability to anticipate the future.
(f) Most nations, including Canada, rely on government and universities for much basic scientific research.

6. The firm chooses its optimal amount of expenditures on R&D by expanding the activity until its marginal benefit equals its marginal cost.
(a) R&D can be financed through bank loans, bonds, retained earnings, venture capital, or the personal savings of entrepreneurs.
(b) Whatever the source of the R&D financing, we assume that its opportunity cost can be represented in a constant interest rate. The horizontal interest-rate cost-of-funds curve thus captures the marginal cost of R&D.
(c) The marginal benefit from R&D is reflected in the firm's expected profit (or return) from the last dollar spent on R&D. Because the firm would first pursue those R&D projects with bigger payoffs, this expected-rate-of-return curve slopes downward.
(d) A higher interest rate will reduce the optimal level of R&D expenditures; an overall increase in expected profitability will raise the optimal level of R&D expenditures.

7. Innovation can increase a firm's profits by raising revenues or by lowering costs.

(a)   Revenue increases can result from product innovation that allows consumers to increase their total utility.

(b)   Cost reductions result from process innovations. The total product curve shifts up, enabling the firm to produce the same goods with fewer resources, and shifting down the average total cost curve.

8. Any innovator is subject to the problem of innovation by rivals. Some firms may rely on reverse engineering or a fast-second strategy instead of systematically investing in their own R&D. Given these options, what incentive is there to bear R&D expenses?

(a)   Patents legally protect the inventor against imitation.

(b)   Copyrights (for books, software, videos, etc.) and trademarks (for product names, logos, etc.) prevent direct copying.

(c)   Brand-name recognition may give a major marketing advantage for many years.

(d)   Some innovations involve trade secrets on unique processes or products. A head-start through innovation may yield cost advantages through learning-by-doing.

(e)   Time lags before imitation can occur give a window of opportunity to make profits.

(f)   An innovator has the chance to be bought out at a profit by a larger rival.

9. Is there some market structure or firm size that generates the most technological advance? This question must be considered in any full evaluation of the efficiency of different market structures. Therefore, we survey the strengths and shortcomings of each market structure in relation to technological advance.

(a)   Pure competitors appear to have strong reason and desire to innovate, but easy entry would quickly erode potential profits. Ability to finance R&D is also an obstacle.

(b)   Monopolistic competitors have a strong incentive to innovate in order to differentiate their products and gain market share. Impediments to R&D are very similar to those found in pure competition.

(c)   Oligopolists are often large enough to finance R&D, and barriers to entry can sustain profits long enough to pay off R&D investments. On the other hand, the market power and entry barriers may create some complacency among oligopoly firms.

(d)   Pure monopolists rarely have much incentive to innovate, except as a defensive strategy. They have already gained control over their markets, so there seems little reason to take risks on R&D spending.

(e)   This comparison of market structures led to the inverted-U theory of the relationship between market structure and technological advance. This theory suggests that R&D activity is very weak in the least concentrated industries (pure competition) and in the most concentrated (pure monopoly), but strongest in "loose" oligopolies. In such markets, where concentration ratios are around 50%, firms typically have strong incentives for innovation and good access to financing.

10. Technological advance plays a role in the efficiency of our economy.

(a)   Process innovations improve productive efficiency, thereby shifting upwards the firm's production function, and shifting downward the firm's average total cost curve.

(b)   Product innovations add to allocative efficiency because they increase consumer utility by expanding the range of product choices.

(c)   However, where a process or product innovation creates monopoly power, society may lose part of the benefit of the innovation because the monopolist restricts output to maximize profits.

(d)   Joseph Schumpeter argued that innovation leads to "creative destruction" as a new product or process explodes the monopoly of one firm and replaces it with a new temporary monopoly. However, this process seems to be neither automatic nor inevitable.

11. Consumer surplus and producer surplus offer another way to understand allocative efficiency.

(a) Consumer surplus is the difference between what consumers are willing to pay for a product and its market price. The downsloping demand curve indicates that willingness to pay is maximum at first, and then declining. Therefore, the amount of consumer surplus created is maximum for the first unit and declines until the last unit purchased creates no further consumer surplus.

(b) Producer surplus is the difference between the revenue a producer is paid for a product and the marginal cost of producing it. Given that marginal costs are rising, producer surplus per unit decreases up to the final unit produced (on which there is no surplus because price equals marginal cost).

(c) Allocative efficiency is achieved when consumer surplus plus producer surplus is maximized. This occurs at the intersection of the demand curve and the supply curve in pure competition. In other words, this occurs where the marginal cost equals the marginal benefit.

(d) Graphically, consumer surplus is shown as the area under the demand curve and above the market price. Producer surplus is shown as the area above the supply curve and below the market price.

(e) If insufficient resources are allocated to producing the product, then the consumer surplus and producer surplus will not be maximized. The potential surplus that is lost is called deadweight loss. Such a loss – or allocative inefficiency – arises under pure monopoly, for example.

■ TERMS AND CONCEPTS

technological advance	expected-rate-of-return
venture capital	curve
invention	optimal amount of
patent	R&D
innovation	imitation problem
product innovation	fast-second strategy
process innovation	inverted-U theory of
diffusion	R&D
start-ups	creative destruction
venture capital	consumer surplus
interest-cost-of-funds	producer surplus
curve	deadweight loss

■ HINTS AND TIPS

1. No brand new technical tools are introduced in this chapter. The choice of optimal level of expenditures on R&D is merely another application of the already familiar "marginal benefit equals marginal cost" model. Consumer surplus and producer surplus were first introduced in Chapter 9's Last Word, and are based on supply and demand curves.

2. The potentially contradictory effects of innovation on efficiency are important. An innovation creates potential benefits for society, but if the innovation gives the firm monopoly power that it can exploit to restrict output, then economic efficiency may not increase.

■ FILL-IN QUESTIONS

1. In the _____ run the firm must work with fixed plant, equipment, and technology. In the _____ run the firm can adjust its plant and equipment but must still work with the same technology. In the _____ run the firm has the opportunity to change also the technology.

2. When McDonald's discovered how to cook hamburgers so that they were ready when customers ordered them, this was an example of a _____ innovation. When Sony discovered how to make a small portable personal stereo, this was an example of a _____ innovation.

3. The three steps in technological advance are:
(a) _____; (b) _____; (c) _____

4. _____ are like entrepreneurs, except that they do not carry personal financial risk.

5. Small new companies formed by entrepreneurs to introduce innovations are called _____.

6. The rate of spending on R&D will decrease if the interest rate (falls, rises) _____. The rate of R&D spending will also decrease if the expected-rate-of-return curve (falls, rises) _____.

7. Xerox, Kleenex, and Levis are such leaders in their product groups that they have historically enjoyed a huge _____ recognition advantage.

8. Studies of the relationship between market structure and technological advance tend to show that the market structure most conducive for innovation is the _____, with a concentration ratio in the _____% to _____% range.

9. Innovators enhance society's _____ efficiency when they find new production processes that lower the _____ curve. Innovators enhance _____ efficiency when they introduce new products that expand choices for consumers. However, _____ efficiency can also be compromised if the innovation increases the amount of _____ power held in a market.

■ PROBLEMS AND PROJECTS

1. Sort the following events as either: invention (INV), innovation (INN), or diffusion (DIF).

(a)   A pen manufacturer becomes the first to commercially manufacture rolling ball pens with replaceable cartridges. _____
(b)   After a European automaker introduces a special shoulder harness, an "after market" manufacturer begins selling harnesses that can be installed in any car. _____
(c)   A computer manufacturer patents a new computer hard disk drive the size of a box of matches. _____
(d)   A mountain bike maker "reverse engineers" the new suspension design of a leading competitor. _____
(e)   A retailer creates the first big box store concept for home health care products. _____

2. The Great White Northern Sporting Goods Company has five different R&D projects for potential investment as listed below.

Project	R&D Cost, million $	Expected Rate of Return %
A. Graphite hockey sticks	3	8
B. Perma-sharp skates	16	9
C. Lightweight helmets	10	11
D. Clear-vue visors	7	7
E. Extra-flex gloves	8	5

(a)   Use the list to fill in the expected-rate-of-return schedule below. Hint: at each level of rate of return, determine which projects (and how many dollars of R&D investment) will produce at least this rate of return. The correct results are already filled in at a 9% return.

Expected Rate of Return %	R&D Cost, million $	Projects Undertaken
5	_____	_____
6	_____	_____
7	_____	_____
8	_____	_____
9	26	C, B
10	_____	_____
11	_____	_____

(b)   If Great White Northern can acquire any amount of financing at a constant interest rate of 7.5%, which projects would they undertake, and what would be their optimal level of R&D spending?

Projects: _____; R&D Spending: _____

3. Match the product on the left with the type of protection for innovation on the right.

(i) instant camera (a) trademark
(ii) seven secret herbs and spices (b) copyright
(iii) famous product name (c) trade secret
(iv) recorded music (d) patent

4. The table below shows the demand and supply schedules for a purely competitive market. This market would come to equilibrium at 3 units of output.
(a) At this equilibrium price is $_____.
(b) For each of the three units produced, fill in the consumer surplus (CS).
(c) The total consumer surplus at equilibrium is $_____.
(d) For each of the three units produced, fill in the producer surplus (PS).
(e) The total producer surplus at equilibrium is $_____.
(f) If this industry produced only 1 unit, consumer surplus would decrease by $_____, and producer surplus would decrease by $_____, so the deadweight loss would be $_____.
(g) If this industry produced 4 units, there would also be inefficiency, because what consumers are willing to pay for the fourth unit is $_____ less than the marginal cost of producing the fourth unit.

Qd	Price ($)	CS ($ / unit)	Qs	Price ($)	PS ($ / unit)
0	9		0	3	
1	8	_____	1	4	_____
2	7	_____	2	5	_____
3	6	_____	3	6	_____
4	5		4	7	

■ TRUE-FALSE

Circle T if the statement is true, F if it is false.

1. As a percentage of the nation's GDP, Canada spends significantly less on R&D than do most industrial nations. T F

2. It is optimal for a corporation to engage in as much R&D as they can afford. T F

3. It is rational to invest in R&D only if the returns are guaranteed. **T F**

4. New products can entice consumers to switch from existing products in order to increase their total utility. **T F**

5. One potential incentive for a small firm to innovate is a buyout by a larger firm. **T F**

6. A firm pursuing a fast-second strategy will be content to allow other firms to produce the innovations. **T F**

7. The diffusion stage for ballpoint pens occurred when the first prototype ballpoint pen was manufactured. **T F**

8. Typical firms in both pure competition and monopolistic competition would have difficulty raising enough capital to finance an R&D program. **T F**

9. Most economists agree that monopoly is the market structure most conducive to stimulating technological advance. **T F**

10. Lengthening periods of patent protection would give inventors greater incentive to create new products and processes. **T F**

11. Consumer surplus occurs when more is being supplied than buyers are willing to purchase. **T F**

12. Allocative efficiency is achieved if the sum of consumer surplus and producer surplus is maximized. **T F**

■ **MULTIPLE-CHOICE**

Circle the letter that corresponds to the best answer.

1. Which one of the following is not considered one of the three steps in technological advance?
(a) invention
(b) innovation
(c) diffusion
(d) exclusion

2. An "innovator" is defined as an entrepreneur who:
(a) makes basic policy decisions in a business
(b) combines factors of production to produce a good or service

(c) invents a brand new product or production process
(d) introduces new products on the market or employs a new method of production

3. Which of the following sectors are important sources of technological advance in Canada?
(a) business firms
(b) universities
(c) government
(d) all of the above

4. Reverse engineering is:
(a) a strategy used in imitation
(b) a process used in getting a patent
(c) the opposite of technological advance
(d) the process of moving to labour intensive production

5. The modern view of technological advance is that:
(a) technological advance happens randomly and unpredictably
(b) governments can directly control technological advances
(c) technological advance occurs at a consistent and predictable pace
(d) technological advance occurs in response to economic incentives

6. The firm should increase spending on R&D if:
(a) MB > MC
(b) MC > MB
(c) MB = MC
(d) the firm has any more new ideas

7. An investor purchase of shares in a new high-risk business is an example of what kind of financing?
(a) bank loans
(b) bonds
(c) retained earnings
(d) venture capital

8. For a company that has invented a new migraine drug, the expected-rate-of-return curve will shift up if:
(a) the cost of manufacturing the drug increases
(b) more people begin experiencing migraine headaches
(c) other companies create similar drugs
(d) none of the above

9. If a firm becomes more efficient through experience, they are likely gaining from:
   (a) learning by doing
   (b) fast-second strategy
   (c) brand-name recognition
   (d) trade secrets

10. The inverted-U theory refers to the relationship between:
   (a) the interest rate and the expected rate of return
   (b) the amount of R&D expenditures and the expected rate of return
   (c) the market concentration ratio and the amount of R&D expenditures
   (d) the amount of R&D expenditures and the interest rate

11. Identify the true statement:
   (a) purely competitive firms that innovate can enjoy the profits for a long time
   (b) monopolistic competitors that innovate can differentiate their products more effectively
   (c) oligopolists are generally too small to raise the financing needed to innovate
   (d) monopolists generally have the strongest incentives to innovate

12. Process innovation will:
   (a) shift the TP curve upwards and the ATC curve downwards
   (b) shift the TP curve downwards and the ATC curve upwards
   (c) shift the TP curve downwards and the ATC curve downwards
   (d) shift the TP curve upwards and the ATC curve upwards

13. The idea that innovation may generate "creative destruction" is attributed to:
   (a) Bill Gates
   (b) Karl Marx
   (c) Joseph Schumpeter
   (d) Adam Smith

14. Which is the best description of consumer surplus?
   (a) the value a consumer gets from a product over and above what he was willing to pay
   (b) the amount a consumer was willing to pay for a product over and above what he had to pay

   (c) the amount a consumer had to pay for a product over and above the value he placed on it
   (d) none of the above

15. If demand for a product increases:
   (a) both consumer surplus and producer surplus will increase
   (b) consumer surplus will increase and producer surplus will decrease
   (c) consumer surplus will decrease and producer surplus will increase
   (d) both consumer surplus and producer surplus will decrease

16. If a firm implements a process innovation:
   (a) both consumer surplus and producer surplus will increase
   (b) consumer surplus will increase and producer surplus will decrease
   (c) consumer surplus will decrease and producer surplus will increase
   (d) both consumer surplus and producer surplus will decrease

■ **DISCUSSION QUESTIONS**

1. What is meant by technological advance, and what are its three steps?

2. How are product innovations different from process innovations?

3. What is the firm's incentive to invest in technological advantage? What risks are there to such investment?

4. How is the firm's optimal level of R&D spending chosen? What can the government do to influence this optimal level?

5. Draw the graph showing the optimal level of R&D, explain each of the two curves, and explain how a shift up or down in either would shift the R&D level.

6. What are some key reasons why firms may choose to imitate rather than innovate? What defenses against imitation exist in our economy?

7. If you had a great idea for an innovation, but insufficient financing on your own, what would be the advantages and disadvantages of the different types of financing that you might arrange?

8. Analyze the incentives and opportunities for R&D and technological advance that exist under each of the four basic market structures.

9. What is the evidence on the relation between market structure and innovation?

10. Explain why technological advance does not necessarily improve the efficiency of our economy.

11. What is measured by consumer surplus and producer surplus? What is the connection between these concepts and allocative efficiency?

■ ANSWERS

FILL-IN QUESTIONS

1. short; long; very long

2. process; product

3. (a) invention; (b) innovation; (c) diffusion

4. intrapreneurs

5. startups

6. rises; falls.

7. brand-name

8. oligopoly; 40, 60

9. productive, ATC; allocative; allocative, monopoly

PROBLEMS AND PROJECTS

1. (a) INN; (b) DIF; (c) INV; (d) DIF; (e) INV

2. (a) top to bottom: R&D cost: 44, 36, 36, 29, 26, 10, 10, Projects: C,B,A,D,E; C,B,A,D; C,B,A,D; C,B,A; C,B; C; C; (b) C,B,A; $29 million.

3. (i)-(d); (ii)-(c); (iii)-(a); (iv)-(b)

4. (a) 6; (b) 2, 1, 0; (c) 3; (d) 2, 1, 0; (e) 3; (f) 1, 1, 2; (g) 2

TRUE-FALSE

1. T   see Global Perspective 12-1
2. F   only up to where marginal benefit = marginal cost
3. F   by its nature, the benefits of R&D are almost always uncertain
4. T
5. T   the small firm may come up with an invention that it doesn't have the capital to exploit
6. T
7. F   a prototype is a basic working model at the invention stage
8. T
9. F   oligopoly, according to the inverted-U theory, and supporting evidence
10. T   they could enjoy the economic profits for a longer period of time
11. F   consumer surplus should not be confused with a surplus in the sense of excess supply
12. T

MULTIPLE-CHOICE

1. (d)
2. (d)   an inventor and an innovator play different roles
3. (d)
4. (a)   imitation based on careful study of rival's new product to learn how it is made
5. (d)
6. (a)   increase until MB has fallen, and MC risen, to the point that they are equal
7. (d)   venture capital because it is quite speculative, or risky
8. (b)   demand for the product would then rise
9. (a)
10. (c)
11. (b)   product differentiation is the main form of competition in monopolistic competition
12. (a)
13. (c)
14. (a)
15. (a)   equilibrium P and Q both increase, and the CS and PS triangles will expand
16. (a)   equilibrium P will decrease, and Q will increase, and the CS and PS triangles will expand

CHAPTER 13

Competition Policy and Regulation

This chapter deals with three areas of government policy meant to modify the behaviour of businesses for the benefit of society as a whole: anti-combines policy, industrial regulation, and social regulation.

By the late 1800s the Canadian government had become concerned with adverse effects on consumers and competitors of firms exploiting their monopoly power. Monopoly power exists where there is industrial concentration: the situation of a single firm or a few firms selling most of the output in a market. Concentration implies the opportunity for firms to set output where MC = MR, and raise price above marginal cost, causing allocative inefficiency.

Canada's earliest legislation to control monopoly was passed in 1889. By 1892 it was a criminal offence to restrict trade or competition. In 1910 the Combines Investigation Act established a specific mechanism for investigating and prosecuting alleged combines (conspiracies between firms to restrict competition). Despite numerous changes to the legislation over several decades, very few prosecutions occurred under this Act, largely because of the heavy burden of proof for prosecution under the Criminal Code. In 1986, the Competition Act replaced the Combines Investigation Act, and jurisdiction was shifted from the criminal law to civil law, making it easier to prosecute monopolies and mergers harmful to the public interest.

Another theme of the recent changes in legislation has been to recognize certain trade-offs between the goal of competition in the Canadian economy and other goals such as efficiency justifications for mergers and monopolization, and international competitiveness considerations. The 1999 airline merger, and the bank mergers proposed in 1998 have brought these concerns to the forefront. In many of these cases government faces difficult policy dilemmas indeed.

In industries that are natural monopolies, anti-combines policy to prevent monopoly is not the appropriate mechanism of control. Other policy alternatives include public ownership or industrial regulation. The public interest theory of regulation holds that a natural monopoly should be subjected to price regulation that allows the monopoly to charge a price high enough to cover their opportunity costs, including a normal profit (or "fair return"). Because the price allowed is based on costs, the regulated monopolist has little incentive to minimize costs, and is prone to X-inefficiency. A second problem is the risk that regulation may itself perpetuate monopoly by protecting the monopolist from competitors. The legal cartel theory of regulation reflects a third area of concern. In this theory the regulated firms end up "capturing" the regulators, as they put into effect a system of rules that creates conditions much like an illegal cartel.

Beginning in the 1970s, these various problems with regulation led to a backlash of deregulation in many industries. In most cases deregulation led to lower prices and improved efficiency.

Since the 1960s, government has introduced many regulations aimed at improving health, safety, and environmental conditions. Because such interventions usually apply across industries, they are called social regulations — as opposed to industrial regulations, which are directed at particular industries. Social regulations have improved our quality of life, but not without opportunity costs. While there is general agreement that we should have social regulation, the appropriate level is controversial. Some critics claim that at current levels there are enough administrative costs, unintended side effects, and inappropriate uses of social regulation to raise consumer prices, slow the rate of technological innovation, and reduce competition.

■ CHAPTER LEARNING OBJECTIVES

In this chapter you will learn:
- [ ] The definition of industrial concentration.
- [ ] About the evolution of Canadian competition (anti-combines) policy and its current aims.
- [ ] What social regulations are and what their goals are.
- [ ] What a natural monopoly is and why governments regulate natural monopolies.

■ CHAPTER OUTLINE

1. "Industrial concentration" occurs when one firm or a few firms control the major portion of the output of an industry. "Industrial concentration" in this chapter refers to firms that are large in an absolute sense and in relation to their own industry.

2. In response to combines (cartels) that began to emerge in various Canadian industries in the 1880s, the Canadian government has implemented anti-combines policy and regulatory agencies to protect society from harmful effects of monopolization and industrial concentration. The goals of this government intervention include promotion of competition and the achievement of allocative efficiency. As we learned in Chapter 10, monopolies restrict output and raise price above marginal cost, resulting in allocative inefficiency.

3. A merger occurs when two or more firms join together to form one firm. There are three types of mergers, with the horizontal merger having the most potential to create industrial concentration and monopoly power:

   (a) A horizontal merger occurs when the merging firms are competitors selling the similar products in the same market (e.g., two daily newspapers serving the same city).

   (b) A vertical merger occurs when the merging firms are at different stages of the production process in the same industry (e.g., a magazine publisher and a printing company).

   (c) A conglomerate merger occurs when the merging firms produce unrelated goods in different industries (e.g., a diamond mine and a fast-food restaurant chain).

4. Canadian anti-combines legislation began in 1889. This law and its successor, the Combines Investigation Act of 1910, were enacted to restrain the growth and exploitation of monopoly power. The anti-combines legislation was periodically amended and updated in the light of court decisions, the emergence of new marketing strategies, and changing perceptions of the benefits and costs of particular business practices.

5. The effectiveness of the anti-combines law in preventing monopoly and maintaining competition was questionable, especially in the monopoly and merger areas. Convictions were difficult to obtain because what the law prohibited was fairly vague, and the burden of proof is very heavy under criminal law.

6. The Competition Act of 1986, designed to tighten the rules for corporate behaviour, replaced the Combines Investigation Act. The new Act views competition not as an end in itself but as one means to promote efficiency. A quasi-judicial body called the Competition Tribunal replaces the criminal courts for adjudication of prosecutions of mergers and monopolies under the civil law. The conspiracy provisions now provide for larger fines, and allow for prosecutions based on circumstantial evidence.

7. Among the most important recent cases dealt with by the Competition Tribunal under the Competition Act are the merger of Air Canada and Canadian Airlines (which was allowed), and two proposed mergers of major banks (which were denied). These cases illustrate the trade-off between the efficiency effects of mergers and the anti-competitive effects of mergers. Government also weighs trade-offs between maximizing competition and maximizing the ability of Canadian producers to export goods (and improve our balance of trade), and between maximizing competition and fostering the implementation of new technologies.

8. In industries where cost and demand conditions dictate that efficiency in production is compatible with having only one producer (a natural monopoly), anti-combines is not appropriate. Instead, government often employs a policy of public ownership or of industrial regulation.

9. The objective of industrial regulation is embodied in the public interest theory of regulation, according to which the goal is to capture for society some of the cost savings from natural monopoly without suffering the output restriction and price increase typical under unregulated monopoly. Regulators attempt to allow the monopolist to charge a

price that will cover production costs and provide a "fair" return.

10. Not everyone agrees that industrial regulation is effective. There are least two major criticisms:

(a) Regulated monopolists are prone to X-inefficiency because, with the regulated price being based on the firm's costs, there is little incentive to minimize costs.

(b) Regulators often protect firms from competition based on a mistaken diagnosis of natural monopoly. Thus, monopolies can be perpetuated by regulation.

11. The legal cartel theory of regulation sees regulation as being "supplied" by politicians to firms who fear competition. Such regulation often works to block entry and divide the market up among existing firms, creating a legal cartel. Unlike illegal cartels, these cartels can be very durable. Occupational licensing is a prime example.

12. By the 1970s, the many problems with industrial regulation had created much pressure for deregulation. Many transportation and utility industries have since been opened to competition, despite considerable controversy. Based on numerous studies, economists believe that regulation overall has been beneficial to consumers and the economy by lowering prices and costs, and raising output.

13. In the 1960s governments began to enact social regulations governing such things as health and safety conditions in the workplace, environmental impacts of production activities, product quality and safety standards, etc. Many new regulatory agencies were formed. Social regulation usually applies across all industries.

(a) The central aim of social regulation is to improve the quality of life for Canadians.

(b) The aim of social regulation is uncontroversial, but the costs to the economy are high. Some critics argue that we are now overregulated; that regulation's marginal cost now exceeds its marginal benefits. Furthermore, argue the critics, social regulation tends to be based on inadequate information and administered by overzealous personnel.

(c) This regulation raises prices (as costs of compliance are passed on to consumers), slows the rate of innovation (because producers are reluctant to take risks), and reduces competition (because compliance is harder for small firms).

(d) The supporters of social regulation contend that the benefits outweigh the costs, though the benefits are often underestimated and may only become apparent over time. Supporters believe that many serious and neglected social problems can be attacked only with such regulations.

14. The Microsoft case is an enormously important example of government action against a monopoly. U.S. courts decided that Microsoft had acted illegally – not because it is a monopoly – but because it abused its monopoly position, using anticompetitive strategies to prevent Netscape from gaining any toehold in the operating system market.

■ **TERMS AND CONCEPTS**

anti-combines legislation	vertical merger
industrial concentration	conglomerate merger
industrial regulation	natural monopoly
social regulation	public interest theory of regulation
horizontal merger	legal cartel theory of regulation

■ **HINTS AND TIPS**

1. This chapter shows that to understand thoroughly many aspects of the modern Canadian economy, one requires some knowledge of our economic history and of how we are influenced by developments elsewhere in the world. For example, the present Competition Act and regulatory framework reflect not only current economic and legal thinking, but also many decades of experience with previous laws and regulatory mechanisms in Canada and elsewhere.

2. In any discussion of regulation it is important to be clear on the type of regulation. The purposes, methods, and effects of industrial regulation and social regulation are quite different.

■ **FILL-IN QUESTIONS**

1. In this chapter the term "_____" refers to industries in which firms are large in absolute terms and in relation to the total market.

2. Mergers are of three basic types: _____, _____, and _____.

3. Canadian anti-combines legislation was initially administered under a (civil, criminal) _____ law framework. Under this legislative framework there were (few, many) _____ successful prosecutions.

4. The Combines Investigation Act was replaced in 1986 by the _____ Act. Under the new law, mergers and monopolies (now called abuse of dominant position) are offenses only where they result in an unacceptable _____ of competition. Mergers that result in gains in _____ may be allowed even though they result in a _____ of competition.

5. Mergers and monopoly (abuse of dominant position) are now adjudicated by the Competition _____, which can issue _____ orders to restore and maintain market competition.

6. The basic reason for social regulation and the creation of the new regulatory agencies has been the desire to improve the _____ of life in Canada. This type of regulation (is, is not) _____ usually directed at specific firms or industries.

7. Critics claim that social regulation (increases, decreases) _____ product prices, reduces worker _____ by reallocating investment funds, causes a (slower, more rapid) _____ rate of innovation, and (more, less) _____ competition in the economy.

8. (Industrial, Social) _____ regulation tends to cause X-inefficiency because the regulated firm has little incentive to reduce _____.

■ **PROBLEMS AND PROJECTS**

1. Match the item in List A with the item in List B.
List A:
    (a) balance of trade versus competition
    (b) civil law versus criminal law
    (c) "fair" rate of return
    (d) perpetuating monopoly
List B
    (i)   legal cartel theory
    (ii)   tradeoffs among goals
    (iii)   burden of proof
    (iv)   public interest theory of regulation

2. Go to your library and find a copy of the Competition Act. Identify the specific section of the Act that applies to each of the following:
    (a)   a price-fixing agreement among five companies controlling 97 percent of the business of the compressed gas market
    (b)   the purchase of a controlling interest in a group of 38 community and real estate newspapers in the lower mainland region of British Columbia by a firm that controlled the dominant dailies in that area
    (c)   the purchase of waste disposal firms so that 87 percent of the waste disposal market in three Vancouver Island areas was brought under the control of one firm
    (d)   a merger of two major firms in the oil refining industry
    (e)   misleading representation as to the price at which a product is ordinarily sold

3. Magna Carta and Maps for All are two retail chains that specialize in selling maps. Cartographica is a company that prints maps. Dogwood & Blandie is a restaurant chain.
    (a)   If Magna Carta merged with Maps for All it would be a _____ merger.
    (b)   If Magna Carta merged with Cartographica it would be a _____ merger.
    (c)   If Magna Carta merged with Dogwood & Blandie it would be a _____ merger.
    (d)   Of these mergers, the one most likely to be prohibited under the Competition Act is the _____ merger.

■ **TRUE-FALSE**

Circle T if the statement is true, F if it is false.

1. Since most wheat in Canada is produced on the Prairies, there is a high degree of industrial concentration in the wheat growing industry.   **T F**

2. Although competition is beneficial to an economy, monopoly power benefits an individual firm.   **T F**

3. A horizontal merger is a merger between firms selling similar products in the same market.   **T F**

4. A merger of Air Canada and Canadian International Airlines would be an example of a vertical merger.   **T F**

5. A merger of Imperial Oil and Zellers would be an example of a conglomerate merger.   **T F**

6. The latest major revision to Canada's anti-combines laws was passed in 1986.   **T F**

7. The Competition Act makes some allowances for trade-offs between the goal of competition and other goals.   **T F**

8. Under the Competition Act mergers and monopolies are no longer violations of Canada's Criminal Code.   **T F**

9. The Competition Bureau recommended that Air Canada and Canadian Airlines be permitted to merge on the condition that the Canadian market is opened to foreign airlines.   **T F**

10. Examples of social regulation are health, safety, and environmental laws.   **T F**

11. Those who favour social regulation believe that it is needed in order to improve the quality of life in Canada.   **T F**

12. Economists' overall assessment is that in most industries that have been deregulated, consumers have suffered.   **T F**

13. Social regulation has resulted in significant reductions in highway fatalities.   **T F**

■ **MULTIPLE-CHOICE**

Circle the letter that corresponds to the best answer.

1. "Industrial concentration" in this chapter refers to which one of the following?
  (a) firms that are absolutely large
  (b) firms that are relatively large compared to others in their industry
  (c) firms that are either absolutely or relatively large compared to others in their industry
  (d) firms that are both absolutely and relatively large compared to others in their industry

2. Which of the following is not a part of the case against industrial concentration?

  (a) firms in highly concentrated industries are larger than they need to be to take advantage of economies of scale
  (b) firms in highly concentrated industries earn economic profits that they use for research and technological development
  (c) monopoly power leads to the misallocation of resources
  (d) monopoly power leads to greater income inequality

3. Which kind of merger is anti-combines policy mostly concerned with?
  (a) horizontal
  (b) vertical
  (c) conglomerate
  (d) all of the above

4. The Competition Tribunal is a quasi-judicial body that:
  (a) has jurisdiction to determine cases on mergers and monopoly
  (b) has recommended removal of interprovincial barriers to trade
  (c) regulates agricultural marketing boards
  (d) was replaced by the Restrictive Trade Practices commission in 1986

5. Suppose that two Canadian firms each produce a large furnace and a small furnace. How would the Competition Tribunal treat an agreement to split the market, with each firm specializing in one type of furnace?
  (a) the Tribunal would have no jurisdiction over such an agreement
  (b) the Tribunal must deny such an agreement
  (c) the Tribunal would not care about such an agreement
  (d) the Tribunal might allow such specialization if it allowed the firms to reduce average costs

6. Which one of the following has not tended to reduce competition?
  (a) occupational licensing
  (b) natural monopoly
  (c) legal cartels
  (d) the Competition Act

7. Critics of the deregulation of industry argue that (among other things) deregulation can lead to:
  (a) higher prices for the products produced by the industry

(b) the monopolization of the industry by a few large firms

(c) a decline in the quantity or the quality of the product produced by the industry

(d) all of the above

8. Which of the following is not a concern of social regulation?

(a) the prices charged for goods

(b) the physical characteristics of goods produced

(c) the conditions under which goods are manufactured

(d) the environmental impact of production processes

9. Which of the following is not one of the criticisms levelled against social regulation?

(a) it results in higher prices

(b) it is too slow in achieving its objectives

(c) it will slow the rate of innovation in the economy

(d) it is anti-competitive

10. Which theory predicts that regulation will sometimes perpetuate monopoly by creating barriers to entry in the regulated industry?

(a) legal cartel theory

(b) public interest theory of regulation

(c) natural monopoly theory

(d) economies of scale theory

11. Which of the following is not among Canada's main regulatory agencies?

(a) Canadian Wheat Board

(b) National Energy Board

(c) Bank of Canada

(d) Canadian Grain Commission

12. What would the critics of deregulation have predicted would happen when the airline industry was deregulated?

(a) destructive price wars

(b) improved safety

(c) improved customer service

(d) all of the above

■ DISCUSSION QUESTIONS

1. What is the difference between the way the term "monopoly" is used in this chapter and the way it is used in Chapter 10? What is "industrial concentration"?

2. When and why was Canadian anti-combines policy born?

3. Why was it difficult under the Combines Investigation Act to convict firms for forming a monopoly or a merger?

4. Section 1.1 of the Competition Act begins: "The purpose of this Act is to maintain and encourage competition in Canada in order to promote the efficiency and adaptability of the Canadian economy...." Why might there be a conflict between encouraging competition and efficiency? Which goal is emphasized more in the Act?

5. Find the Competition Act in your library and read Section 45. Now explain why the Ottawa Senators in the NHL had to pay millions of dollars to other NHL teams to be allowed to serve fans willing to pay for hockey entertainment.

6. Explain the role of the Bureau of Competition Policy in a hypothetical merger of Labatt's and Molson's brewing companies.

7. Why is the definition of the market an important issue in the application of anti-combines laws?

8. Give examples of how strict enforcement of anti-combines laws could conflict with other key social goals.

9. How does social regulation differ from industrial regulation? The critics of social regulation argue that it has resulted in overregulation. How so? If there is overregulation, what are its more important implications?

10. Why did industrial regulation give way in many industries to deregulation? What did critics of deregulation fear? What were the results of deregulation?

■ ANSWERS

FILL-IN QUESTIONS

1. industrial concentration

2. horizontal, vertical, conglomerate

3. criminal; few

4. Competition; lessening; efficiency, lessening

5. Tribunal, remedial

6. quality; is not

7. increases, productivity, slower, less

8. Industrial, costs

PROBLEMS AND PROJECTS

1. (a) (ii); (b) (iii); (c) (iv); (d) (i)

2. (a) section 45(1)(b); (b) section 79(1); (c) section 79(1); (d) section 79(1); (e) section 36(1)

3. (a) horizontal; (b) vertical; (c) conglomerate; (d) horizontal.

TRUE-FALSE

1.	F	wheat is produced by a larger number of firms
2.	T	
3.	T	
4.	F	horizontal; they compete in the same market
5.	T	they produce in unrelated markets
6.	T	entitled the Competition Act
7.	T	
8.	T	they are now handled under civil law
9.	T	
10.	T	
11.	T	
12.	F	in most industries consumers have enjoyed lower prices
13.	T	

MULTIPLE-CHOICE

1. (d)
2. (b) this is a defense for industrial concentration
3. (a) this type of merger increases monopoly power
4. (a)
5. (d) efficiencies can be a justification for anticompetitive behaviours like specialization agreements
6. (d)
7. (d)
8. (a) prices are the concern of industrial regulation
9. (b) if anything, critics complain that it moves too swiftly (before costs and benefits are understood)
10. (a)
11. (c)
12. (a) the others would have been predicted by advocates of deregulation

CHAPTER 14

The Demand for Resources

Chapter 14 studies markets for resources employed by the firms that we have studied in recent chapters. When a firm chooses how many units output to produce, it simultaneously chooses how many units to employ of its various resource inputs (labour, land, capital and entrepreneurial ability). Most of the discussion in the chapter is in terms of labour, but the general principles apply equally well to the other resources. Chapters 15 and 16 examine particular resources in detail.

Resource markets are important because resource prices determine households' incomes, because the efficient operation of these markets is vital for the overall efficiency of the economy, and because there are many important ethical and policy issues related to these markets.

The demand for inputs is derived from the demand for the firm's product because the firm demands inputs so that it may profit from selling the products of these inputs. The chapter stresses the simplest case: a firm selling its product in a purely competitive market, and hiring its inputs in a purely competitive market. The firm is thus a "price taker" and a "wage taker."

Marginal revenue product (MRP) is the change in the firm's total revenue resulting from using one more unit of input. It depends on the productivity of the resource and the price of the output. Marginal resource cost (MRC) is the change in the firm's total cost resulting from hiring one more unit of input. In order to maximize profits, a firm will hire an extra unit of input if the added revenue earned exceeds the added cost. Therefore, the firm hires additional units of a resource until MRP = MRC. By hiring up to this point, the firm is also choosing the output level where MR = MC. Therefore, the input demand decision and output supply decision are one and the same.

The MRP curve is the firm's resource demand curve. In the short run, the law of diminishing returns guarantees that this curve must eventually slope downward. For firms that are "price makers" in the output market there is a second reason the MRP curve falls: as more units of the input are hired the firm must lower its output price to sell the increased output. Just as found for product demand curves, input demand curves can shift, and can vary with changes in their elasticity. The MRP curve shifts with changes in: demand for the product, productivity of the resource, and prices of substitute or complementary resources. Elasticity of the demand curve depends on: the rate of decline in the marginal productivity of the resource, the ease with which the resource can be substituted for other resources, the elasticity of demand for the product, and the proportion of total production costs accounted for by the resource.

In the long run the firm can vary its employment of all resources. Thus, long-run resource demand decisions depend on the substitutability or complementarity of resources. Two key concepts are the "least-cost rule" and the "profit-maximizing rule," which address the interrelated issues of finding the optimal mix of inputs and producing the optimal amount of output.

The marginal productivity theory of income distribution holds that resource owners are paid according to the marginal product that their resources contribute to society's output, and that therefore the distribution of income is fair and equitable. This view of economic justice is flawed, however, by the very unequal distribution of resources among society's members, and by the fact that resource markets are far from purely competitive.

■ CHAPTER LEARNING OBJECTIVES

In this chapter you will learn:
☐ How resource prices are determined.
☐ What determines the demand for a resource.
☐ What determines the elasticity of resource demand.
☐ How to arrive at the optimal combination of resources to use in the production process.

■ CHAPTER OUTLINE

1. The firms whose output supply decisions we have discussed in recent chapters simultaneously make input demand decisions. These decisions are the subject of this chapter. Most of the examples use labour as the input, though land, capital, or entrepreneurial ability could be used equally well.

2. The study of resource pricing is important because resource prices: 1) influence households' incomes and the distribution of income, 2) allocate scarce resources and affect the economy's efficiency, 3) affect how firms combine resources to minimize costs and maximize profits, and 4) raise ethical questions and policy issues about the distribution of income.

3. The basic analysis assumes the firm's output market is purely competitive, and so is the resource market. Therefore, the firm is both a "price taker" and a "wage taker."

4.   The demand for a resource is a derived demand because it flows from the demand for the product that the resource helps to produce.
   (a)   The demand for a resource depends upon its marginal productivity and the market price of the product it helps to produce. Marginal revenue product (MRP) combines the two factors of marginal product and output price into a single variable that indicates the amount that an extra unit of input adds to the firm's revenue.
   (b)   Marginal resource cost (MRC) is the addition to the firm's costs from hiring one more unit of the input.
   (c)   A profit-maximizing firm will hire a resource up to the quantity at which MRP = MRC.
   (d)   The firm's MRP curve is their demand curve for the resource. In the short run this curve is downsloping because of the law of diminishing returns.
   (e)   The MRP curve for an imperfectly competitive producer falls more steeply (is less elastic) than that of a purely competitive producer. The reason is that such a firm's MRP curve is downsloping for two reasons: diminishing returns and the fact that the firm's output price falls as the firm produces more output.
   (f)   The market (or total) demand for a resource is found by summing horizontally the individual demands of all firms employing the resource.

5.   Shifts in the demand for a resource can be caused by changes in the demand for the product (which changes the output price); changes in the productivity of the resource (which changes its marginal product); or changes in prices of other resources.
   (a)   If demand for the product changes, the firm's demand for the resource will change in the same direction.
   (b)   If the productivity of a resource changes (caused by an increase in the quantity of other resources, technological progress, or improvement in resource quality), the firm's demand for the resource will change in the same direction.
   (c)   If the price of a substitute resource changes, the demand for the resource will change in the same direction if the substitution effect outweighs the output effect, and in the opposite direction if the output effect outweighs the substitution effect. (The substitution effect occurs when a firm uses more of a resource that has become relatively less expensive, and less of resources that have become relatively more expensive. The output effect occurs when a change in the price of a resource leads to a change in output, and therefore, in input usage.)
   (d)   If the price of a complementary resource changes, this will change the demand for a resource in the opposite direction because of the output effect. (There is no substitution effect.)

6.   The elasticity of resource demand measures the sensitivity of the demand to changes in the price of the resource. It depends on four

factors: rate of marginal product decline, ease of resource substitutability, elasticity of product demand, and ratio of resource cost to total cost.

(a)   The less rapidly marginal product of the resource falls as more units are hired, the more elastic the demand.

(b)   The easier it is to find other resources to substitute in the production process, the more elastic the demand.

(c)   The more elastic the product demand, the more elastic the resource demand.

(d)   The larger the ratio of the resource cost to the firm's total cost represented by a resource, the more elastic the resource demand.

7.   Most products can be produced with various combinations of resources, and in the long run the profit-maximizing firm will vary their mix of resources in order to find the cost-minimizing resource combination for producing the chosen level of output.

(a)   The firm is hiring the least-cost combination of resources when the last dollar spent on each resource yields the same marginal product. Expressed another way, the ratio of the marginal product to resource price is the same for all resources.

(b)   The firm is hiring resources in the most profitable combination if it hires resources to the point where the MRP of each resource is equal to the price of that resource.

(c)   A firm that is hiring resources in the most profitable combination is also using a least-cost combination of inputs.

8.   Some people contend that a competitive market system produces a fair and just distribution of income. The marginal productivity theory is taken to support this claim because each unit of a resource receives a payment equal to its marginal contribution to the firm's revenue. However, the theory has at least two serious faults.

(a)   The distribution of income is unequal because individuals own radically different amounts of resources in the first place.

(b)   Incomes of resource suppliers are not based on their marginal productivities if there is monopoly power in resource markets.

■   TERMS AND CONCEPTS

derived demand
marginal product

elasticity of resource
   demand

marginal revenue
   product
marginal resource
cost
MRP = MRC rule
substitution effect
output effect

least-cost combination
   of resources
profit-maximizing
   combination of
   resources
marginal productivity
   theory of income
   distribution

■   HINTS AND TIPS

1.   Recall the production function that related inputs and outputs. Given that relationship, it should come as no surprise that decisions about output levels simultaneously imply decisions about levels of input usage.

2.   When we view the firm's profit-maximizing decisions from the output perspective, marginal revenue and marginal cost are calculated with respect to changes in output, so we plot output on the horizontal axis of graphs. When the same decisions are viewed from the input perspective, marginal revenue product and marginal resource cost are calculated with respect to changes in input usage, so we plot input on the horizontal axis.

3.   The marginal revenue product (MRP) of a resource is simply the marginal product of the resource (MP) times the marginal revenue from the sale of the product of that resource (MR), or MRP = MP x MR. Under pure competition in the firm's output market, MP falls as employment increases, but MR is constant and equal to output price. Under imperfect competition in the firm's output market, price falls as the firm hires more resources and produces more output, so MR also falls.

4.   The profit-maximizing rule for combining resources is easy enough to remember. Since the price of any resource must equal its marginal revenue product at the profit maximum, the ratio must equal one for every resource.

■   FILL-IN QUESTIONS

1.   Resource prices allocate _____ and are a main determinant of household (costs, incomes) _____ and business _____.

2.   The demand for a resource is _____ from the demand for the _____ of the resource.

3. The impact of an additional unit of input on the firm's production is called the marginal _____, while the impact on the firm's total revenues is called the marginal _____.

4. The marginal revenue product schedule is obtained by multiplying the _____ of each unit of input by the _____ of the output.

5. The marginal resource cost is the change in the firm's _____ due to the hiring of _____ more unit of a(n) _____.

6. A firm will find it profitable to hire units of a resource up to the quantity at which the _____ equals _____.

7. A firm's demand schedule for a resource is the firm's _____ schedule for that resource because both indicate the quantities of the resource the firm will employ at various resource _____.

8. The marginal revenue product of the imperfectly competitive seller falls for two reasons: both _____ and _____ fall as output increases. As a consequence, the MRP (or demand) schedule for the resource is (more, less) _____ elastic than it would be if the output were sold in a purely competitive market.

9. The demand for a resource will shift if the demand for the _____ changes, if the _____ of the resource changes, or if the _____ of other resources change.

10. For each of the following, indicate whether the change would tend to increase (+), decrease (-), or have an uncertain effect (?) upon a manufacturer's demand for conveyor machines.
(a) an increase in the price of the manufacturer's product _____
(b) a decrease in the number of workers employed to run conveyor machines _____
(c) an increase in the productivity of conveyor machines _____
(d) an increase in the price of a substitute resource when the output effect is greater than the substitution effect _____
(e) a decrease in the price of a complementary resource _____

11. Holding constant the output of the firm, a decrease in the price of resource A will induce the firm to hire (more, less) _____ of resource A and _____ of other resources; this is called the _____ effect. But if the decrease in the price of A results in lower total costs and an increase in output, the firm may hire _____ of both resources; this is called the _____ effect.

12. A firm's demand for labour will be *less* elastic: 1) the more (rapidly, slowly) _____ the marginal product of labour falls, 2) the (less, more) _____ elastic is the demand for the product the labour produces, 3) the (more, less) _____ difficult it is to substitute other resources in place of labour, 4) the (larger, smaller) _____ the percentage of the firm's total costs represented by labour costs.

13. Suppose a firm employs resources in purely competitive markets. If the firm wishes to produce any given amount of its product in the least costly way, the ratio of the _____ of each resource to its _____ must be the same for all resources. In order to maximize _____, the firm must not only minimize costs, but also produce the optimal level of output. At this level, the firm employs the combination of resources where the ratio of the _____ of each resource to its _____ is equal to _____ for all resources.

■ **PROBLEMS AND PROJECTS**

1. The following table shows production and input cost data for a firm buying and selling competitively. The firm uses one variable input and has fixed costs of $20. Complete the table and then use the information to answer the fill-in questions.

Input Units	Q	MP	Unit Input Price $	Price of Q $	MRP $	TR $	TC $	Profit $
1	17	__	20	2	__	__	__	__
2	32	__	20	2	__	__	__	__
3	45	__	20	2	__	__	__	__
4	56	__	20	2	__	__	__	__
5	65	__	20	2	__	__	__	__
6	72	__	20	2	__	__	__	__
7	77	__	20	2	__	__	__	__

(a)   The firm's marginal resource cost is $_____.

(b)   For the first unit of input marginal revenue product is $_____ and is found by multiplying _____ and _____.

(c)   The firm should hire the first unit of input since the _____ is greater than the _____.

(d)   For the second unit of input the MRC is $_____ and the MRP is $_____. The firm should hire the second unit of resource since the _____ is greater than the _____.

(e)   To maximize profits the firm should hire _____ units of input and obtain profits of $_____.

(f)   Suppose the firm was using 4 units of input and was considering using one more unit. For the 5th unit of input the increase in the firm's revenue is $_____ and the increase in the firm's costs is $_____. The firm (should, should not) _____ hire the 5th unit of input.

(g)   Another way to show whether the firm should hire the 5th unit of input is to compare the marginal revenue and marginal cost of an additional unit of output. Suppose the firm was using 4 units of input and decided to use 5 units. Total output would increase by _____ units and total cost would increase by $_____. Marginal cost of the extra output is defined as: (change in total cost/change in output) and equals $_____. Since this is a competitive firm, MR is the same as the _____ and equals $_____. Since MR of the output is (greater, less) _____ than its MC, the firm (should, should not) _____ undertake the extra production.

2.   The table below refers to the same firm as in problem 1 (above).

Unit Input Price	Qd of Input (Output P = $2)	Qd of Input (Output P = $3)
15	_____	_____
20	_____	_____
25	_____	_____
30	_____	_____
35	_____	_____
40	_____	_____

(a)   In the first blank column, fill in this firm's short-run input demand schedule if their product sells in a purely competitive market for $2 (the same price as assumed in Problem 1).

(b)   In the second blank column, fill in the input demand schedule if the price of their product rises to $3.

3.   Use the graph below to plot two input demand curves for the firm represented in Problems 1 and 2 above.

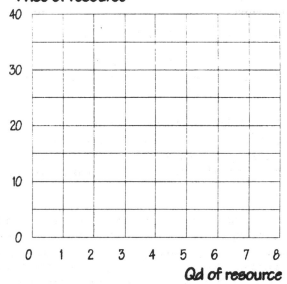

4.   A manufacturer of toy wagons uses, among other resources, four wheels and one steel box to make a wagon. If there is an increase in the price of steel boxes, what will happen to the firm's demand for wheels? Is this a result of a substitution effect, an output effect, or both?

5.   A food processing firm combines carrots, corn, and other ingredients to produce tins of soup. The same vegetables are included in every tin, but the proportions can be varied according to cost and availability of specific vegetables. In 1994 the firm paid a lower price for carrots than they did in 1993. The price of corn was the same in both years. The firm participates in competitive markets for inputs and output.

(a)   For this firm, are corn and carrots complementary resources or substitute resources?

(b)   How would the typical contents of a can of this firm's soup have changed from 1993 to 1994?

(c)   How would the firm's output level have changed?

(d)   Would the firm be buying more or less carrots in total in 1994 than in 1993? Explain in terms of the substitution effect and the output effect.

(e)   Would the firm be buying more or less corn in total in 1994 than in 1993? Explain in terms of the substitution effect and the output effect.

6.   The next two tables show the marginal product and marginal revenue product schedules for a particular firm's employment of resource C and resource D. Both resources are variable, and the productivity of one is independent of the level of usage of the other. The price of C is $2 and the price of D is $3.

Units of C Employed	Marginal Product of C	Marginal Revenue Product of C
1	10	$5.00
2	8	4.00
3	6	3.00
4	5	2.50
5	4	2.00
6	3	1.50
7	2	1.00

Units of D Employed	Marginal Product of D	Marginal Revenue Product of D
1	21	$10.50
2	18	9.00
3	15	7.50
4	12	6.00
5	9	4.50
6	6	3.00
7	3	1.50

(a)   The least-cost combination of C and D that would enable the firm to produce:
  (1) 64 units of output is _____ C and _____ D;
  (2) 99 units of output is _____ C and _____ D.

(b)   The profit-maximizing combination of C and D is _____ C and _____ D.

(c)   When the firm employs the profit-maximizing combination of C and D, it is also employing C and D in the least-cost combination because _____ equals _____.

(d)   The figures in the table show that the firm sells its product in a _____ competitive market at a price of $_____.

(e)   Employing the profit-maximizing combination of C and D, calculate the firm's:
  (1) total output: _____
  (2) total revenue: $_____
  (3) total cost: $_____
  (4) total profit: $_____

7.   The table below shows three separate cases of a firm using two inputs and operating in competitive output and input markets. For each case, determine whether or not the firm is:
  (a) minimizing costs at current input levels;
  (b) maximizing profits at current input levels.

	Case 1	Case 2	Case 3
Output Price	$1	$2	$3
MP of Labour	12	3	6
MP of Capital	8	2	6
Price of Labour	$6	$6	$6
Price of Capital	$4	$4	$4
Cost Minimization ?	Yes No	Yes No	Yes No
Profit Maximization ?	Yes No	Yes No	Yes No

■   **TRUE-FALSE**

Circle T if the statement is true, F if it is false.

1. Resources are demanded by business firms and supplied by households.   **T F**

2. The demand for resources is derived from the demand for the goods and services the resources produce.   **T F**

3. Marginal resource cost is the extra resource cost of producing an extra unit of output.   **T F**

4. Marginal revenue product is the extra revenue the firm obtains from selling one more unit of output.   **T F**

5. For a firm that is a "price taker," the marginal revenue product is found by multiplying the marginal product of the extra input by the price of the output.   **T F**

6. If the price of the product increases, the firm's demand curve for a resource will shift to the left.   **T F**

7. If the productivity of computer programmers rises because they are given faster computers to use, the demand for programmers will shift to the right.   **T F**

8. An increase in the wage rate for berry pickers will decrease the demand for berry pickers.   **T F**

9. A firm's demand schedule for a resource will be more elastic if it sells its product in a purely competitive market than it would be if it sold the product in an imperfectly competitive market.   **T F**

10. When two resources are substitutable for each other, both the substitution effect and the output effect of a decrease in the price of one of these resources operate to increase the quantity the firm employs of the other resource.   **T F**

11. Consider two inputs termed i and j. If an increase in the price of j results in a decrease in the use of i, then i and j are called complements.   **T F**

12. If a firm wishes to produce any level of output at least-cost, resources should be combined so that their marginal products are equal.   **T F**

13. If a factory's marginal product of labour falls sharply as more workers are hired, the factory's demand for labour will be quite elastic.   **T F**

14. *Ceteris paribus*, a construction company that hires hundreds of labourers and only a few supervisors will have a higher elasticity of demand for supervisors than for labourers.   **T F**

15. If there are no close substitutes for haircuts, but many close substitutes for massages, then the demand for hair stylists will be less elastic than the demand for masseurs, *ceteris paribus*.   **T F**

16. If labour is less expensive in India than in Canada, and capital is about equally expensive in India and Canada, the theories of this chapter predict a tendency towards the use of more labour-intensive production methods in India.   **T F**

17. If individuals are paid according to the marginal products of their resources, society's income distribution will be fair and equal.   **T F**

18. The existence of monopoly power helps resource suppliers gain a larger share of the income from their production.   **T F**

■   **MULTIPLE-CHOICE**

Circle the letter that corresponds to the best answer.

1.   The price paid for resources affects:
   (a)   the money incomes of households in the economy
   (b)   the allocation of resources among different firms and industries in the economy
   (c)   the quantities of different resources employed to produce a particular product
   (d)   all of the above

2.   The demand for a resource depends on:
   (a)   the marginal productivity of the resource and price of the good or service produced from it
   (b)   the marginal productivity of the resource and the price of the resource
   (c)   the price of the resource and the price of the good or service produced from it
   (d)   the price of the resource and the quantity of the resource demanded

3.   The resource demand curve for a competitive firm slopes downward because of:
   (a)   the law of downsloping demand
   (b)   the law of diminishing returns
   (c)   decreasing returns to scale
   (d)   the reduction in output price required to increase sales

4.   All but one of the following would shift the demand curve for a resource. Which one?
   (a)   a change in technology
   (b)   a change in the price of the other inputs used in production
   (c)   a change in the price of the resource
   (d)   a change in the price of the output

5.   Which of the following would increase a firm's demand for a particular resource?
   (a)   an increase in the prices of complementary resources used by the firm
   (b)   a decrease in the demand for the firm's product
   (c)   an increase in the productivity of the resource

(d) an increase in the productivity of a substitutable resource

6.   Marginal resource cost is:
(a)   the price paid for an input
(b)   the slope of the input supply curve
(c)   the increase in total cost when one more unit of the input is hired
(d)   the increase in total cost when one more unit of output is produced

7.   A firm is a "wage taker" if:
(a)   it hires so little of a particular type of labour that it has no effect on the price of this labour
(b)   it has all of the power in the employment relationship and can therefore determine the wage
(c)   it earns wage income rather than paying wages
(d)   it sells its output in a purely competitive market

8.   A profit-maximizing firm will hire an input up to the point where:
(a)   the law of diminishing returns no longer holds
(b)   average cost of production is minimized
(c)   marginal product begins to fall
(d)   marginal revenue product equals marginal resource cost

9.   If a firm hires resources up to the point where marginal resource cost equals marginal revenue product, then the firm must also be operating where:
(a)   marginal revenue equals marginal cost
(b)   the marginal products of all inputs are equal
(c)   the elasticity of resource demand equals 1
(d)   marginal revenue is greater than the output price

10.   As a firm that sells its product in an imperfectly competitive market hires more units of a resource, the marginal revenue product of that resource falls because:
(a)   the price paid for the resource falls
(b)   the marginal product of the resource falls
(c)   the price of the firm's product falls
(d)   both the marginal product and the price at which the firm sells its product fall

11.   A firm that is a "price maker" in output market will, as compared to a firm that is a "price taker":

(a)   employ more labour and produce more output
(b)   employ less labour and produce less output
(c)   employ more labour and produce less output
(d)   employ less labour and produce more output

12.   To maximize profits a competitive firm should hire additional units of a resource so long as:
(a)   marginal resource cost is greater than output price
(b)   input price is greater than marginal revenue product
(c)   each successive resource unit adds more to the firm's revenues than to its costs
(d)   the firm is earning economic profits

Using the following schedules showing total product and marginal product for a resource, answer questions 13 through 15. Assume that the firm employs constant quantities of other resources.

Units of Resource	Total Product	Marginal Product
1	8	8
2	14	6
3	18	4
4	21	3
5	23	2

13.   If the firm's product sells for a constant $3 per unit, the marginal revenue product of the 4th unit of the resource is:
(a) $3
(b) $6
(c) $9
(d) $12

14.   If the firm's product sells for a constant $3 per unit and the price of the resource is a constant $15, how many units of the resource will the firm hire?
(a)   2
(b)   3
(c)   4
(d)   5

15.   If the firm can sell 14 units of output at a price of $1 per unit and 18 units of output at a price of $0.90 per unit, the marginal revenue product of the third unit of the resource is:

(a) $4
(b) $3.60
(c) $2.20
(d) $0.40

16.   A firm operating in competitive input and output markets pays $6 per unit for a certain input. If the last unit of this input hired produces $16 worth of output, the firm:
(a)   is maximizing profits
(b)   should hire more units of the input
(c)   should reduce employment of the input
(d)   should raise the price paid to the input

17.   A computer disk manufacturer is employing resources so that the MRP of the last unit hired for resource X is $240 and the MRP of the last unit hired for resource Y is $150. The price of resource X is $80 and the price of resource Y is $50 and both of these prices are constant. The firm should:
(a)   hire more of resource X and less of resource Y
(b)   hire less of resource X and more of resource Y
(c)   hire less of both resource X and resource Y
(d)   hire more of both resource X and resource Y

18.   A firm that hires resources in competitive markets is not necessarily maximizing its profits when:
(a)   the marginal revenue product of every resource is equal to 1
(b)   the marginal revenue product of every resource is equal to its price
(c)   the ratio of the marginal revenue product of every resource to its price is equal to 1
(d)   the ratio of the price of every resource to its marginal revenue product is equal to 1

19.   The effect on the employment of a resource when its price or the price of other inputs changes can be broken down into a substitution effect and an output effect. In finding the substitution effect which of the following is assumed to be constant?
(a)   the total output of the firm
(b)   the total expenditures of the firm
(c)   the employment of all other resources
(d)   the marginal products of all resources

20.   Suppose resource A and resource B are substitutable and the price of A increases. If the output effect is greater than the substitution effect:

(a)   the quantity of A employed by the firm will increase and the quantity of B employed will decrease
(b)   the quantity of both A and B employed by the firm will decrease
(c)   the quantity of neither A nor B employed will decrease
(d)   the quantity of A employed will decrease and the quantity of B employed will increase

21.   If decreases in the price of computers have decreased the employment of secretaries in medical clinics, then:
(a)   computers and medical secretaries are complements
(b)   there is no substitution effect on the demand for medical secretaries
(c)   there is no output effect on the demand for medical secretaries
(d)   the substitution effect on the demand for medical secretaries outweighs the output effect

22.   Which of the following has no effect on the elasticity of demand of an input?
(a)   the rate at which the marginal product of that resource declines
(b)   the elasticity of demand for the product that the resource helps to produce
(c)   the ratio of the resource cost to total costs
(d)   the marginal resource cost of the input

23.   Which of the following is the best example of a pair of complementary inputs?
(a)   tractors and fertilizer in agriculture
(b)   bricks and lumber in house-building
(c)   cars and drivers in the taxi business
(d)   computers and telephones in offices

24.   A firm is allocating its expenditure on resources so as to minimize the total cost of producing any given output when:
(a)   the amount the firm spends on each resource is the same
(b)   the marginal revenue product of each resource is the same
(c)   the marginal product of each resource is the same
(d)   the marginal product per dollar spent on the last unit of each resource is the same

25.   A competitive firm is currently using two inputs, A and B, and is producing its output at least cost. The input prices are $4 and $6 respectively. If

the marginal product of A is 12 units, then the marginal product of B must be:
- **(a)** 6 units
- **(b)** 12 units
- **(c)** 18 units
- **(d)** 24 units

26. A business is using inputs such that the MP of labour is 20 and the MP of capital is 45. The price of labour is $10 and the price of capital is $15. If the business wants to minimize cost, then it should:
- **(a)** use more labour and less capital
- **(b)** use less labour and more capital
- **(c)** use less labour and less capital
- **(d)** make no change in resource use

27. At present levels of resource usage, a firm's MP of labour is 4, MP of capital is 12, and the prices are $1 per unit of labour, and $4 per unit of capital. 15. Given this, the firm is:
- **(a)** minimizing cost and maximizing profit
- **(b)** minimizing cost but not maximizing profit
- **(c)** maximizing cost but not minimizing cost
- **(d)** not minimizing cost or maximizing profit

28. For a firm hiring resources in an imperfectly competitive market to maximize profit, the marginal revenue product of each resource must equal:
- **(a)** its marginal product
- **(b)** its marginal resource cost
- **(c)** its price
- **(d)** one

29. A major criticism of the marginal productivity theory of income distribution is that:
- **(a)** markets are subject to imperfect competition
- **(b)** the theory predicts that there will be equality in incomes
- **(c)** the theory does not allow for losses in the short run
- **(d)** in order to maximize profits, firms will pay their inputs as little as possible and not their marginal revenue product

30. Individuals' incomes vary because of differences in:
- **(a)** the amounts of resources they own
- **(b)** the productivity of resources they own
- **(c)** the amounts of market power they have in resource markets
- **(d)** all of the above

■ DISCUSSION QUESTIONS

1. Why is resource pricing an important topic?

2. Why is the demand for a resource a derived demand, and upon what two factors does the strength of this derived demand depend?

3. What constitutes a firm's demand schedule for a resource? Why? What determines the total, or market, demand for a resource?

4. Explain why firms that wish to maximize their profits will follow the MRP = MRC rule.

5. Explain the difference in the derivation of the resource demand curve for a competitive and imperfectly competitive firm.

6. Explain the factors that will cause the demand for a resource to increase or decrease.

7. Suppose that there is an increase in the price of lumber used to build houses. Explain how the "substitution effect" and the "output effect" might affect the total use of lumber, and of bricks.

8. What determines the elasticity of the demand for a resource? Explain the relationship between each of these four determinants and elasticity.

9. Considering the four determinants of elasticity of resource demand, which would be more elastic, a hospital's demand for heart surgeons, or its demand for nurses? Explain your reasoning.

10. Assuming a firm employs resources in purely competitive markets, explain the rule for combining inputs so that it can produce a given output for the least total cost.

11. If highway engineers in Mexico have the same knowledge and expertise as Canadian engineers, why might they build highways using more labour-intensive methods than are used in Canada?

12. What is the marginal productivity theory of income distribution? What ethical proposition must be accepted if this distribution is to be fair and equitable? What are the two major shortcomings of the theory?

THE DEMAND FOR RESOURCES 165

■ ANSWERS

FILL-IN QUESTIONS

1. resources, incomes, costs

2. derived, product

3. product, revenue product

4. marginal product, marginal revenue (or price, in pure competition case)

5. total costs, one, input

6. marginal revenue product, marginal resource cost

7. marginal revenue product, prices

8. marginal product, output price; less

9. product, productivity, prices

10. (a) +; (b) -; (c) +; (d) -; (e) +

11. more, less, substitution; more, output

12. 1) rapidly, 2) less, 3) more, 4) smaller

13. marginal product, price; profits; marginal revenue product, price, one

PROBLEMS AND PROJECTS

1. Marginal Product: 17, 15, 13, 11, 9, 7, 5; Marginal Revenue Product: 34, 30, 26, 22, 18, 14, 10; Total Revenue: 34, 64, 90, 112, 130, 144, 154; Total Cost: 40, 60, 80, 100, 120, 140, 160; Profit: -6, 4, 10, 12, 10, 4, -6
(a) 20; (b) 34, marginal product, output price; (c) MRP, MRC; (d) 20, 30; MRP, MRC; (e) 4, 12; (f) 18, 20; should not; (g) 9, 20; 2.22; price, 2.00; less, should not

2. (a) Qd at P = $2: 5, 4, 3, 2, 0, 0; (b) Qd at P = $3: 7, 6, 5, 4, 3, 2.

3. plot the unit input prices and Qd values at P = $2, and P = $3.

4. output effect leads to decreased demand for wheels; no substitution effect because input proportions are fixed

5. (a) substitutes; (b) more carrots and less corn in 1994; (c) lower costs lead to increased output; (d) more

because of both effects; (e) less due to substitution effect, more due to output effect; net effect is unknown

6. (a) (1) MP/P = 5 where C=1, D=3; (2) MP/P = 3 where C = 3, D = 5; (b) MRP = P where C = 5, D = 6; (c) MPc/Pc; MPd/Pd; (d) purely, 0.50 because MRP/MP = MR; (e) (1) 114 by summing MP's of C and D; (2) 57; (3) (5x2)+(6x3) =28; (4) 57-28=29

7. Case 1: Yes, No; Case 2: Yes, Yes; Case 3: No, No

TRUE-FALSE

1. T
2. T
3. F extra resource cost of hiring an additional unit of input
4. F extra revenue from hiring an additional unit of input
5. T
6. F demand will shift right
7. T increase in marginal productivity increases demand
8. F this is a movement along the demand curve for berry pickers
9. T
10. T
11. T
12. F the ratio MP/P should be equal for each resource
13. F quite inelastic
14. F lower elasticity for supervisors because they represent a smaller share of the firm's total costs
15. T elasticity of demand for an input is directly related to the elasticity of demand for its product
16. T due to the least-cost rule
17. F resources are not equally distributed among individuals
18. T

MULTIPLE-CHOICE

1. (d)
2. (a) the price of the resource determines the point on the demand curve, but not the position of the whole demand
3. (b)
4. (c) this causes a movement along the resource demand curve, not a shift in the curve
5. (c)
6. (c)
7. (a) so it faces a horizontal supply of labour
8. (d)
9. (a) MRP = MRC implies MR = MC
10. (d)

11. (b) output is restricted; therefore so is the amount of labour hired to produce the output

12. (c)

13. (c) 3 x 3

14. (a) MRP > MRC for the first 2 units, after that MRP < MRC

15. (c) (18 x 0.90) – (14 x 1)

16. (b) hire more of an input whenever MRP > MRC

17. (d) the firm is minimizing cost at the current output level, but profits could be increased by producing more

18. (b) at this point costs are minimized, but profits are not maximized unless MP/P = 1 for each resource

19. (a) the effect of output change is captured in the "output effect"

20. (b) employment of A falls due to both effects; employment of B rises because of substitution effect, but falls due to output effect, and in this case output effect is stronger

21. (d) substitution effect: less secretaries; output effect: more secretaries

22. (d) costs have no effect on demand curve

23. (c) cars and drivers are used in fixed proportions

24. (d)

25. (c) 12/4 = 3; 18/6 = 3

26. (b) this will cause MP of L to rise and MP of K to fall, until MP/P is equal for L and K

27. (d)

28. (b) exactly as for firms in purely competitive markets

29. (a) and this distorts relative prices of inputs and incomes of their owners

30. (d)

CHAPTER 15

Wage Determination, Discrimination and Immigration

This chapter explores how labour demand and labour supply interact to determine wage rates in purely competitive markets and in markets where there are market imperfections (e.g., unions, monopsonies, discrimination), or government intervention to modify market outcomes (e.g., the minimum wage law, immigration policy).

The chapter begins with a discussion of trends in the general level of wages, stressing that high real wages are found where and when the demand for labour is high relative to its supply, and the demand depends crucially on the productivity of labour. A number of reasons are given for international variations in productivity and wages.

Earlier chapters showed that determination of prices and quantities in a product market depends very much on the structural conditions of that market. This is equally true in the labour market. The analysis of a purely competitive market for labour parallels very closely the analysis of purely competitive product markets. Employers and workers are "wage takers," and the equilibrium wage rate is determined where the market supply of labour intersects the market demand for labour. At this point, each firm's marginal revenue product is equal to their marginal resource cost.

Monopsony involves market power on the labour demand side of the market because there is only one employer in a labour market. Such an employer is a "wage maker" because it faces an upsloping labour supply curve and must simultaneously select an employment level and a wage rate. The monopsonist restricts employment in order to hold the wage rate down, and ends up paying a wage rate below the marginal revenue product, or competitive wage rate.

When workers are unionized, market power exists on the supply side of the market. The chapter presents three models of unions: (1) a demand enhancement model in which the union benefits workers by raising wages and employment; (2) an exclusive or craft union model in which wages are raised through supply reduction, and; (3) an inclusive or industrial union model in which the union attempts to organize all available workers and then impose an above equilibrium wage on the employers. Evidence suggests that unions have managed to raise wages, but also at the expense of employment.

A bilateral monopoly exists when labour is supplied by a union and hired by a monopsonist. The model alone cannot predict where the equilibrium wage will end up because it depends on relative bargaining power and skill.

The chapter then discusses some policy issues, controversies, and research relating to labour markets in Canada. These include: (1) the pros and cons of minimum wage legislation; (2) the reasons for wage differentials between different workers; (3) the effects of compensation schemes that tie pay to performance; (4) models of different types of labour market discrimination and their effects; (5) antidiscrimination policies; and (6) immigration policy.

■ CHAPTER LEARNING OBJECTIVES

In this chapter you will learn:

☐ That wages are determined by demand and supply forces.

☐ About the effects of monopoly power on the demand and supply of labour.

☐ The pros and cons of a minimum wage.

☐ The effects of labour market discrimination.
☐ The effects of immigration on domestic labour markets.

■ **CHAPTER OUTLINE**

1. The wage rate is the price paid per unit of labour, for a given period of time. It can be measured in nominal terms, or in real terms, but it is real wages that determine living standards. Earnings are equal to the wage multiplied by the amount of time worked.

2. The general level of wages in Canada is relatively high because the demand for labour in Canada has been strong relative to the supply of labour. The strong demand for labour in Canada has been the result of high labour productivity in Canada, which can be traced back to:
(a) plentiful capital for workers to work with
(b) abundant natural resources
(c) advanced technology
(d) high quality labour through investment in training, education, and health
(e) intangible factors related to Canada's strong economic and social institutions

3. The real hourly wage rate in Canada rises at about the same rate as the output per hour of labour input. Rapid productivity growth over the decades has caused the demand curve for labour to grow faster than the supply of labour, leading to secular growth in real wages in Canada.

4. The wage rate earned by a specific type of labour depends on the demand and supply of that labour and on the competitiveness of the markets in which that labour is hired and its output is sold.

5. In a purely competitive labour market, employers and workers are "wage takers." The market demand curve is the horizontal sum of the marginal revenue product curves for all individual firms. The market supply is the sum of the supply curves from all individual workers. It is upward sloping as higher wage rates draw more workers in from other places or other occupations. At the equilibrium the marginal revenue product of labour is equal to the firm's marginal resource cost. From the individual employer's perspective, the supply of labour is perfectly elastic at the wage rate determined by the market demand and supply.

6. In a monopsony (one employer), with pure competition on the supply side, the firm faces an upsloping labour supply curve, so the marginal resource cost exceeds the wage rate. The firm hires the amount of labour at which marginal resource cost and the marginal revenue product of labour are equal. The wage rate is set on the labour supply curve at the equilibrium employment level, and this is below the marginal resource cost and the marginal revenue product. Both the wage rate and level of employment are less than they would be under purely competitive conditions.

7. Where a union represents workers collectively, the union attempts to raise wage rates by:
(a) increasing the demand for labour by increasing the demand for the products made by union workers, by increasing the workers' productivity, and by increasing prices of resources that are substitutes for union labour;
(b) exclusive, or craft unionism, which is based on reducing the supply of labour by forcing employers to hire union members, and sometimes by controlling the number of workers allowed into the union;
(c) inclusive, or industrial unionism, which is based on organizing as many workers as possible, and then imposing upon employers wage rates that are higher than the equilibrium wage rate that would prevail in a purely competitive market.

8. Union members on average enjoy a 10 to 15 percent wage advantage over nonunion workers. Unions are aware of the tradeoff between wage increases and employment for their members. They may, therefore, limit their demands for higher wages. But the unemployment effect of higher wages could be lessened by increases in labour productivity or a relatively inelastic demand for labour.

9. In a labour market that is a bilateral monopoly, the wage rate depends, within certain limits, on the relative bargaining power of the union and of the employer. Bilateral monopoly may be more socially desirable than a situation of market power on only one side of the market because having market power on both sides of the market may cancel out the effect of that power. The wage rate and employment level could end up near the purely competitive level.

10. A minimum wage law is normally imposed as a way to provide a "living wage" for less-skilled workers and their households, but may not be effective.

(a) Opponents of minimum wage laws argue that employers are simply pushed back up their demand curves for unskilled labour, causing a loss of employment for these workers. Secondly, many of the workers that do benefit from a wage increase are not members of low-income households.

(b) Advocates argue that in monopsonistic firms both wages and employment may be increased by the minimum wage. Also, if forced to pay higher wages, employers may be shocked into using workers more efficiently, therefore improving their productivity.

(c) Recent evidence suggests that increases in the minimum wages cause small or negligible decreases in employment. At the same time, the law is not as strong an anti-poverty tool as hoped because many of its benefits go to workers from nonpoverty households.

11. Wage differentials between workers exist for three major reasons related to supply and demand.

(a) Workers differ in terms of their marginal revenue productivity for their employers.

(b) Workers are not homogeneous, so they fall into noncompeting groups with differing wages because of differences in ability, skill, and in human capital investment through education, training, or work experience.

(b) Compensating differences in wages exist because of differences in nonmonetary aspects of jobs. Some of these aspects are location, health risks, and working conditions.

(c) Market imperfections impede the mobility of workers due to such factors as: (1) lack of job information; (2) geographical immobility; (3) union and government restraints; (4) gender and race discrimination.

12. Many workers are not paid on a fixed basis, but have their compensation tied directly to performance.

(a) A principal-agent problem arises when the interests of principals (firms) do not match the interests of their agents (workers). The workers may increase their own utility by shirking on the job.

(b) Firms may combat shirking by monitoring (supervision), but this is sometimes ineffective, and always costly. Another solution is an incen-

tive pay plan. Some examples are: piece rates, commissions and royalties, bonuses, stock options, profit sharing, and efficiency wages.

(c) Poorly designed incentive pay systems may eliminate shirking but introduce unexpected negative side effects.

13. Labour market discrimination occurs when equivalent labour resources are paid or treated differently even though their productive contributions are equal. Such discrimination may be based on gender, race, ethnicity, or other minority status, and takes four main forms.

(a) Wage discrimination occurs when members of one group receive lower wages than members of another group doing the same work.

(b) Employment discrimination occurs when one group experiences inferior treatment in hiring, promotion, layoffs, etc.

(c) Occupational discrimination occurs when members of one group are arbitrarily restricted from entering certain desirable occupations.

(d) Human capital discrimination occurs when members of one group enjoy less access to investments in education and training.

14. Labour market discrimination imposes a cost on its victims, but also on society as a whole. Because some labour resources are not allocated to their most productive uses, our nation's output ends up below its potential (inside our production possibilities curve).

15. Several models of discrimination are presented.

(a) In the taste-for-discrimination model, prejudiced employers behave as if employing visible minority workers involves an extra cost (captured in the concept of the discrimination coefficient). In the equilibrium, minority workers are employed by prejudiced employers only if their wage rate is lower than that paid to other workers. Competition should eventually work to reduce this type of discrimination, but the results to date are not encouraging.

(b) Statistical discrimination occurs when workers are judged on the basis of average characteristics of the group with which they are associated, rather than on their individual characteristics or productivity. This sort of discrimination is not malicious, but is profitable, so tends to persist.

(c) In the crowding model, or occupational segregation model, members of one group are segregated into less desirable occupations, which also end up lower-paying because of the large supply of labour crowded there.

(d) Each of these models appears to explain some of the labour market discrimination faced by women and visible minorities in Canada, and some of the inefficiency in our economy due to misallocation of labour resources.

16. Government can attack labour market discrimination in a number of ways.

(a) In a healthy growing economy, demand for labour is high, so it is expensive for employers to indulge in tastes for discrimination against women and minorities.

(b) Education and training opportunities can be improved for women and minorities.

(c) An affirmative action plan would require employers to give preferential treatment to women and minorities in hiring and promotion decisions. This, the most direct strategy for addressing the problem, is also the most controversial. Advocates argue that labour market discrimination is so deeply entrenched that extreme measures are necessary to make any progress, and that the social benefits in terms of efficiency will outweigh the costs. Opponents argue that affirmative action amounts to reverse discrimination and ends up making the economy less efficient.

17. What immigration policy should Canada adopt, and what are the economic effects of immigration?

(a) When workers migrate from low-wage nations to a high-wage nation such as Canada, they increase Canada's labour supply, and decrease the labour supply in their original countries. This tends to move wages nearer together, and results in more efficient overall allocation of the world's labour. It is also beneficial for Canadian businesses that employ immigrant workers.

(b) Costs of migration (monetary and non-monetary) impede migration to some extent, and prevent immigration totally closing the wage differential between nations.

(c) Remittances by immigrants to their families at home cause some of the benefits to be captured by the nation the migrants have left.

(d) Whether Canada benefits from immigration depends both on the number of immigrants each year, and on their characteristics (e.g., highly educated investors vs. long-term welfare recipients).

■ **TERMS AND CONCEPTS**

nominal wage	marginal revenue pro-
real wage	ductivity
purely competitive	noncompeting groups
labour market	investment in human
monopsony	capital
exclusive unionism	compensating differ-
occupational licens-	ences
ing	incentive pay plan
inclusive unionism	affirmative action
bilateral monopoly	reverse discrimination
minimum wage	legal immigrants
wage differentials	illegal immigrants

■ **HINTS AND TIPS**

1. To clarify the differences between the various wage determination models presented in this chapter, it might help to see that there are four fundamental scenarios in a labour market:

(a) pure competition in both labour demand and supply

(b) pure competition in labour demand, and market power in supply (union)

(c) pure competition in labour supply, and market power in demand (monopsony)

(d) market power in both demand and supply (bilateral monopoly)

2. You should be able to draw and interpret the supply and demand diagram to illustrate each model in the chapter. By the way, have you noticed how much more competent you have become at using supply and demand tools? You should feel real satisfaction in that!

■ **FILL-IN QUESTIONS**

1. A nominal wage is an amount of _____ received per time period, while a real wage is an amount of _____ that can be purchased with the nominal wage. The percentage change in real wages is found by subtracting the percentage change in the price level from the percentage change in _____. Thus, a 3.5% increase in the nominal wage over the same period that the price level rose by 2% yields a _____ real wage increase for that period.

2. The general level of wages is determined by the _____ for and the _____ of labour in an economy. In the previous chapter it was stated that the demand for labour depends upon its marginal revenue product, which, in turn, depends upon the _____ of the output and the _____ of the input.

3. The general level of wages is (higher, lower) _____ in Canada than in most nations. The demand for labour in Canada is (great, small) _____ relative to its supply. The demand for Canadian labour has been strong because of its high productivity, which results from: (a) plentiful _____; (b) abundant _____; (c) advanced _____; (d) labour _____; and, (e) _____ factors.

4. In a purely competitive labour market, the demand for labour services is the horizontal _____ of the labour demand curves of all _____ hiring this type of labour.

5. A monopsonist faces an _____-sloping supply curve of labour and has to pay a _____ wage rate to hire more labour.
  (a) The extra cost of hiring an extra input is (greater than, less than) _____ the wage rate paid to that input. To the monopsonist the _____ is greater than the wage rate.
  (b) The monopsonist hires labour up to the point where _____ equals _____.
  (c) Other things being equal, the monopsonist hires (more, fewer) _____ workers and pays a (higher, lower) _____ wage than would a competitive employer.

6. The most important economic goal of a labour union is to _____. The union attempts to accomplish this goal either by increasing the _____ for labour, restricting the _____ of labour, or imposing demands for wages _____ their competitive equilibrium value.

7. Craft unions, which are examples of _____ unionism, typically try to increase wages by _____ the supply of labour. Industrial unions, which are examples of _____ unionism, try to increase wages by _____ the demand for labour.

8. If craft unions are successful in restricting the supply of labour,
  (a) the wage rate (rises, falls, remains the same) _____ and employment in the craft or industry _____.

(b) This effect on the employment of their members may lead unions to (increase, restrain) _____ their wage demands.
(c) Unions will worry less about the tradeoff between wages and employment if the economy is (growing, declining, stationary) _____ or if the demand for labour is relatively (elastic, inelastic) _____.

9. A wage difference between two jobs that exists because one job is more hazardous than the other is an example of a _____ differential.

10. The firm is the (agent, principal) _____, and the worker is the _____. The principal-agent problem arises because the objectives of the two are _____. Specifically, it may be in the worker's interest to _____ on the job. To control this problem, the firm may implement some sort of _____ pay plan.

11. Mike sells magazine subscriptions door-to-door and is paid $50 a day. On an average day he sells 10 subscriptions. If Mike was paid by commission instead of a wage, and if his productivity is unchanged, a commission of $_____ per subscription would leave Mike with the same average daily income. However, a commission is an example of an _____ pay plan, and it would probably (decrease, increase) _____ Mike's productivity by reducing his incentive to _____ at his employer's expense.

12. Discrimination imposes economic costs (only, not only) _____ on those who are discriminated against. Overall, discrimination (decreases, increases) _____ the output and income of our economy.

13. If some workers from India relocate to Canada in search of better job opportunities, the supply of labour in India will (increase, decrease) _____ and the wage rate will _____, whereas in Canada the supply of labour will _____ and the wage rate will _____. National output will increase in _____ and decrease in _____.

■ PROBLEMS AND PROJECTS

1. One farm has, for a certain type of labour, the marginal-revenue-product schedule in the first table below.

(a) Assume there are 100 farms with the same MRP schedules. Compute the total or market demand for this labour by completing the first column of the second table below.

(b) Combining the total demand for labour with the total supply given in the same table, the equilibrium wage rate is $_____, and _____ units of labour will be hired in this market.

Units of Labour	MRP of Labour
1	$15
2	14
3	13
4	12
5	11
6	10
7	9

Quantity of Labour Demanded	Wage Rate	Quantity of Labour Supplied
_____	$15	850
_____	14	800
_____	13	750
_____	12	700
_____	11	650
_____	10	600
_____	9	550

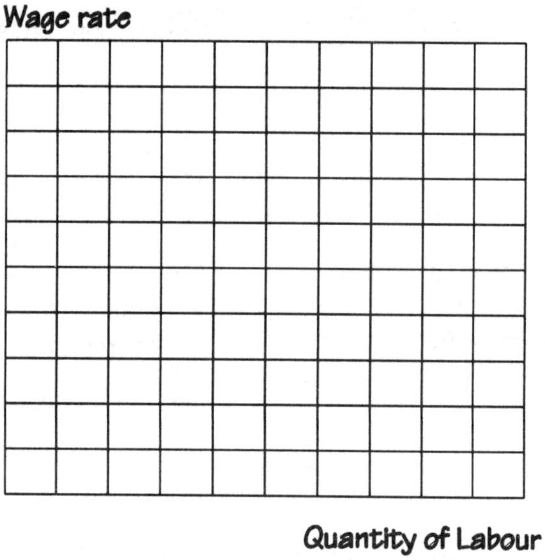

Wage rate

Quantity of Labour

(c) At the equilibrium found in (b), the individual firm will have a marginal labour cost of $_____, will employ _____ units of labour, and will pay a wage of $_____.

(d) On the graph above, plot the market demand and supply curves for labour and indicate the equilibrium wage rate and the total quantity of labour employed.

(e) On the graph below, plot the individual firm's demand for labour, supply of labour, and MRC curve. Indicate the quantity of labour the firm will hire and the wage it will pay.

(f) The imposition of a $12 minimum wage rate would change the total amount of labour hired in this market to _____.

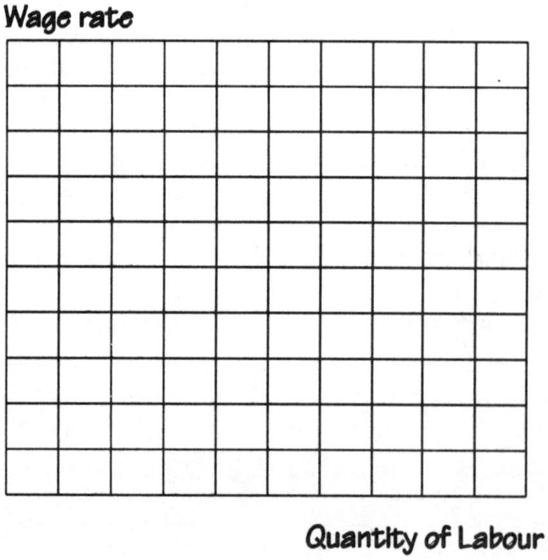

Wage rate

Quantity of Labour

2. A monopsonist has the marginal-revenue-product schedule for labour given in columns 1 and 2 of the next table, and faces the supply schedule for this labour as given in columns 1 and 3.

(1) Units of Labour	(2) MRP of Labour	(3) Wage Rate	(4) Total Labour Cost	(5) Marginal Resource Cost
0		$2	$_____	
1	$36	4	_____	_____
2	32	6	_____	_____
3	28	8	_____	_____
4	24	10	_____	_____
5	20	12	_____	_____
6	16	14	_____	_____
7	12	16	_____	_____
8	8	18	_____	_____

Wage rate

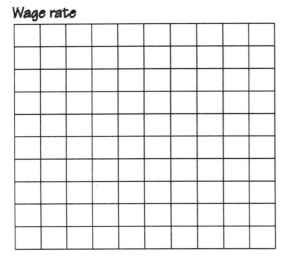

Quantity of Labour

(a) Compute the firm's total labour costs at each level of employment and the marginal resource cost of each unit of labour, and enter these figures in columns 4 and 5 of the table.

(b) The firm will hire _____ units of labour, pay a wage of $ _____, and have a marginal revenue product for labour of $_____ for the last unit of labour employed.

(c) Plot the MRP curve, the supply curve for labour, and the MRC curve on the graph above. Indicate the quantity of labour the firm will employ and the wage it will pay.

(d) If this firm hired labour in a competitive labour market, it would hire _____ units and pay a wage of $_____.

3. The next graph represents the market for iron miners in an isolated Labrador community. The local iron mine is the only employer, and the miners are not unionized.

(a) If the employer behaves as a monopsonist, _____ miners will be employed at a wage rate of $_____.

(b) Suppose that the miners now unionize and demand a wage rate of $8 per hour. This labour market scenario is known as _____ monopoly.

(c) On the graph identify the new supply curve of labour.

(d) Why is the wage rate outcome uncertain when the union deals with the monopsony employer?

Wage ($/hour)

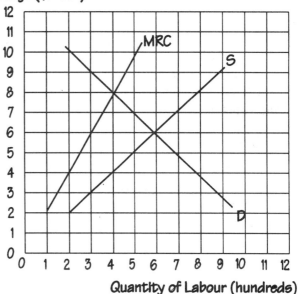

Quantity of Labour (hundreds)

4. Match each example in the first list with the appropriate model or concept in the second list.

List 1:

(a) hospital workers earn a higher hourly wage on night shift than on the day shift

(b) a chemical company hires women for secretarial positions and men for technical and engineering positions

(c) a university promotes male professors more readily than female professors with similar academic qualifications, teaching performance, and research productivity

(d) a law firm hires male lawyers over female lawyers because females are more likely to go on parental leave

List 2:
(i) statistical discrimination
(ii) employment discrimination
(iii) compensating differentials
(iv) occupational discrimination

5. Suppose the economy consists of 100 workers; 50 men and 50 women. Men and women are equally productive workers, but at present the two groups are completely segregated in the labour market. All men are employed in the finance industry where the marginal revenue product is given by MRP = 100-L. All women are employed in the retail industry with a marginal revenue product given by MRP = 80-L. Each sector is purely competitive.

(a) The wage rate for men will be $_____, and the wage rate for women will be $_____ in this complete segregation situation.

(b) If the causes of segregation are eliminated, and men and women are both free to work in either sector, women will move into finance. The result will be a (rise, drop) _____ in the wage rate in finance, and a _____ in the wage rate in retail, until wages are equalized in both sectors.

(c) In equilibrium it turns out that employment in finance will now be 60 workers, meaning that at least _____ women will be employed in this sector. Employment in retail will now be 40 workers. The wage rates will be $_____ in both sector A and sector B.

(d) This question is an example of the _____ model which shows that immobility of workers can lead to job _____ and lower wages for the group concentrated in a sector with lower productivity.

(e) Removing the impediments to mobility would definitely (decrease, increase) _____ the output of this society, because at the equilibrium found in part (a), the marginal revenue product of the 50th woman working in retail is only $_____, whereas if she were working in finance, her MRP would be $_____. Therefore, reallocating even just this one worker from retail to finance would (decrease, increase) _____ society's output by $_____.

■ **TRUE-FALSE**

Circle T if the statement is true, F if it is false.

1. The general level of real wages is lower in Canada than in foreign countries because the supply of labour in Canada is great relative to the demand for labour. **T F**

2. In the long run, the real income per worker can only increase at about the same rate as output per worker. **T F**

3. Nominal wages measure the purchasing power of wages. **T F**

4. If the price level falls, a person's real wage could rise even if the nominal wage falls. **T F**

5. If an individual firm employs labour in a competitive market, its marginal resource cost for labour is equal to the wage rate. **T F**

6. Given a competitive employer's wage rate, the more productive the workers, the more will be hired. **T F**

7. For a monopsonist, the extra cost of hiring one more unit of labour is greater than the wage paid to that additional worker. **T F**

8. Both a monopsonist and a firm hiring labour in a competitive market hire labour up to the point where the marginal revenue product of labour and wage rate are equal. **T F**

9. The most important economic objective of unions is job security for their members. **T F**

10. Restricting the supply of labour is a means of increasing wage rates more commonly used by craft unions than by industrial unions. **T F**

11. Unions attempt to increase the demand for the products their workers produce by lobbying for reduced import quotas and higher tariffs. **T F**

12. Craft unions are composed of members who possess specialized skills. **T F**

13. Occupational groups sometimes use licensing requirements as a method to artificially restrict entrance to specific occupations. **T F**

14. Industrial unions are also considered exclusive unions. **T F**

15. The imposition of an above-equilibrium wage rate will cause employment to drop more when demand for labour is inelastic than when demand is elastic. **T F**

16. A bilateral monopoly in a labour market involves a union and a monopsonist. **T F**

17. In the bilateral monopoly model the market power of the employer and the union are offsetting. **T F**

18. In a competitive labour market, the imposition of an effective minimum wage will increase the wage rate and decrease employment. **T F**

19. The labour force is considered to be divided into noncompeting groups of workers because of the differences between workers in their abilities, talents, training, etc. **T F**

20. The principal-agent problem exists in labour markets because workers do not understand employers' objectives. **T F**

21. If Zippy's is the only gas station in the city paying its attendants an efficiency wage, Zippy's can expect to have higher employee turnover than other gas stations. **T F**

22. In the taste-for-discrimination model, if employers discriminate against women, then the higher the employer's discrimination coefficient, the higher women's wages relative to men's wages.

T F

23. An employer using statistical discrimination is probably sacrificing profits as a result of his prejudice. **T F**

24. Women suffer human capital discrimination if they must have higher grades than men in order to be admitted to the same university programs. **T F**

25. Advocates of affirmative action argue that preferential treatment for women and visible minorities is necessary in order to allow these disadvantaged groups to catch up to white men.

T F

26. If workers are completely free to move between nation A and nation B, they will do so until the wage rates are equalized between the two nations. **T F**

■ **MULTIPLE-CHOICE**

Circle the letter that corresponds to the best answer.

1. Real wages would decline if the:
(a) prices of goods and services rose more rapidly than nominal wage rates
(b) prices of goods and services rose less rapidly than nominal wage rates
(c) prices of goods and services fell while nominal wage rates rose
(d) prices of goods and services and nominal wage rates both increase by the same percent

2. Which of the following is not among the reasons for the generally high productivity of Canadian workers?
(a) the high level of real wage rates in Canada
(b) the superior quality of the Canadian labour force
(c) the advanced technology used in Canadian industries
(d) the large quantity of capital available to assist the average worker in Canada

3. The market supply of labour is upward sloping because a higher wage rate will:
(a) attract workers from other industries and occupations
(b) attract workers from other locations
(c) attract workers back into the labour force
(d) all of the above

4. Which of the following is not true of a firm that hires labour in a purely competitive market?
(a) the firm is a "wage taker"
(b) the firm's marginal resource cost equals the wage rate
(c) the firm's marginal resource cost is constant
(d) the firm's labour supply curve is upward sloping

5. The key characteristic of the monopsony model is:
(a) many buyers and sellers of resources
(b) a single seller of resources
(c) a single seller of the product of the resources
(d) a single buyer of the resource

6. A monopsonist pays a wage rate that is:
(a) greater than the marginal revenue product of labour
(b) equal to the marginal revenue product of labour
(c) equal to the firm's marginal labour cost
(d) less than the marginal revenue product of labour

7. Higher wage rates and a higher level of employment are the usual consequences of:
(a) inclusive unionism
(b) exclusive unionism
(c) an above-equilibrium wage rate
(d) an increase in the productivity of labour

8. A craft union is composed of workers who:
(a) work for the same employer
(b) work in the same industry
(c) possess the same skill
(d) are members of noncompeting wage groups

9. Industrial unions typically attempt to increase wage rates by:
(a) imposing an above-equilibrium wage rate upon employers
(b) increasing the demand for labour
(c) decreasing the supply of labour
(d) forming a bilateral monopoly

10. The demand for labour can be increased by all but which one of the following?
(a) increasing labour productivity
(b) increasing the demand for products labour produces
(c) increasing the price of substitute resources
(d) occupational licensing

11. Which policy would be opposed by a union of Canadians who make wooden hockey sticks?
(a) strict quotas on imported hockey sticks
(b) elimination of federal subsidies to municipal governments to help with construction of hockey rinks
(c) tax deductions for children's hockey registration fees
(d) stringent safety regulations that would apply to hockey sticks made of graphite or new materials

12. Which of the following could not be considered to be a union attempt to restrict the labour supply?
(a) support for compulsory retirement
(b) long apprenticeships
(c) support for higher minimum wages
(d) seeking to have the employer hire only union members

13. Which of the following has been a consequence of unionization?
(a) higher wage rates for unionized workers
(b) greater employment of unionized workers
(c) greater employment of the workers in the entire labour force
(d) a higher level of real wages in the economy

Use the data in the following table to answer questions 14, 15 and 16.

Wage Rate	Quantity of Labour Supplied	Marginal Resource Cost	Marginal Revenue Product of Labour
$10	0	---	$18
11	100	$11	17
12	200	13	16
13	300	15	15
14	400	17	14
15	500	19	13
16	600	21	12

14. If the firm employing labour were a monopsonist, the wage rate and the quantity of labour employed would be, respectively:
(a) $15 and 300
(b) $13 and 400
(c) $14 and 400
(d) $13 and 300

15. If the market for this labour were competitive, the wage rate and the quantity of labour employed would be, respectively:
(a) $14 and 300
(b) $13 and 400
(c) $14 and 400
(d) $13 and 300

16. The fact that a star baseball player receives a wage of $15,000,000 a year can best be explained in terms of:
(a) noncompeting labour groups
(b) equalizing differences
(c) labour immobility
(d) imperfections in the labour market

17. Compensating wage differentials are paid to:
(a) firefighters because they work in hazardous situations
(b) garbage collectors because they work under unpleasant conditions
(c) offshore oilrig workers because they work in isolated locations
(d) all of the above

18. Which of the following is not an example of an incentive pay plan utilized to overcome shirking on the job?
(a) piece rates
(b) commissions and royalties
(c) a wage premium for overtime work
(d) bonuses and profit-sharing

Questions 19, 20, and 21 use the next graph.

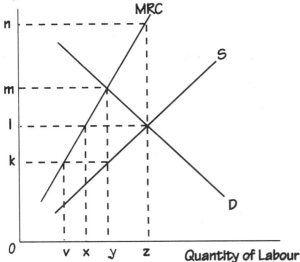

19. If this is a purely competitive labour market, the number of workers hired and the wage rate in equilibrium are:
- (a) 0z and 0*l*
- (b) 0z and 0n
- (c) 0y and 0m
- (d) 0y and 0n

20. If this is a monopsonistic labour market, the employment level and wage rate in equilibrium are:
- (a) 0x and 0*l*
- (b) 0v and 0k
- (c) 0y and 0m
- (d) 0y and 0k

21. If the market is a bilateral monopoly, the number of workers hired and the wage rate in equilibrium are:
- (a) 0x and 0*l*
- (b) 0v and 0k
- (c) 0y and 0m
- (d) indeterminate

22. Efficiency wage theory suggests:
- (a) the most efficient workers prefer to be paid piece rates
- (b) gains in efficiency from using large size plants allow the payment of higher wages
- (c) in any group of workers the more efficient should receive higher wages
- (d) it may be profitable to pay workers a higher wage than they can find elsewhere

23. Those who have suggested the crowding hypothesis assert that the crowding of women into certain occupations:
- (a) is the result of occupational discrimination
- (b) results in the misallocation of resources
- (c) causes lower wage rates for women relative to men
- (d) all of the above

24. If a retailer prefers to hire people from a certain ethnic group because they are more polite, he is engaging in:
- (a) statistical discrimination
- (b) a taste for discrimination
- (c) occupational segregation
- (d) human capital discrimination

25. The discrimination coefficient is a factor in which model?
- (a) taste-for-discrimination
- (b) occupational discrimination
- (c) statistical discrimination
- (d) all of the above

26. If women are rarely sent to training seminars, whereas the men they work with are often sent to the seminars, the women are experiencing:
- (a) statistical discrimination
- (b) occupational segregation
- (c) human capital discrimination
- (d) employment discrimination

27. A defining characteristic of the taste-for-discrimination model is that the employer:
- (a) selects employees on the basis of average group characteristics
- (b) behaves as if employing minority workers adds a cost
- (c) denies minority workers access to certain categories of jobs
- (d) will not hire minority workers

28. Policies for combating labour market discrimination include:
- (a) promoting a strong economy with tight labour markets
- (b) affirmative action
- (c) improve opportunities for training and education for women and minorities
- (d) all of the above

29. Migration of people from low-wage countries to high-wage countries is associated with:

(a) falling wages in the countries from which people emigrate
(b) rising wages in the countries to which people immigrate
(c) increased output in both high-wage and low-wage nations
(d) an overall increase in world output

■ **DISCUSSION QUESTIONS**

1. Why is the general level of real wages higher in Canada than in most nations? Why has the level of real wages continued to increase even though the supply of labour has continually increased?

2. Explain why the productivity of the Canadian labour force increased in the past to its present high level. And why has productivity stagnated recently? Or has it?

3. In the competitive model, what determines the market demand for labour and the wage rate? What kind of supply situation is faced by all firms as a group? Why? What kind of supply situation does the individual firm face? Why?

4. In the monopsony model, what determines employment and the wage rate? What kind of supply situation does the monopsonist face? Why? How do the equilibrium wage and level of employment compare with what would result if the market were competitive?

5. In what sense is a worker who is hired by a monopsonist "exploited," while one who is employed in a competitive labour market "justly" rewarded? Why does a monopsonist wish to restrict employment?

6. When the supply curve of labour is upward sloping, marginal labour cost is greater than the wage rate. Why?

7. What methods might labour unions employ to increase the demand for labour? If these methods are successful, what effect do they have upon wage rates and employment?

8. What strategies can a labour union use to restrict the supply of labour, and why is it in their interest to do so? Are there circumstances under which supply restriction would be pointless, or even detrimental to members' interests?

9. Both exclusive and inclusive unions are able to raise the wage rates received by their members. Why might unions limit or temper their demands for higher wages?

10. What is bilateral monopoly? Do you know of any examples of bilateral monopoly in labour markets? What determines wage rates in a labour market of this type?

11. What is the effect of minimum wage laws upon wage rates and employment in (a) competitive labour markets, and (b) monopsony labour markets?

12. Why do wage rates differ across workers in different occupations, across workers in the same occupations, and across workers in different localities?

13. What are the aspects or forms of discrimination that contribute to a substantial earnings gap when comparing Canadian women and men? Other than discrimination, what factors might explain the gap?

14. What is the principal-agent problem, as applied to labour markets? How do incentive pay plans help address the problem? Discuss the reasons for, and the drawbacks of, using incentive pay schemes in some jobs that you have held, or that students typically hold (restaurant worker, retail clerk, etc.).

15. How does an affirmative action plan work, and what are the arguments for and against addressing discrimination in this way?

16. In what ways, and under what conditions, will Canada as a whole benefit from increased immigration? What will be the effects on the nations that the immigrants stem from?

17. What is the role of remittances and backflows in understanding the costs and benefits of immigration?

■ **ANSWERS**

FILL-IN QUESTIONS

1. money, goods and services, nominal wages, 1.5%

2. demand, supply, price, productivity

3. higher; great; (a) capital; (b) natural resources; (c) technology; (d) quality; (e) intangible

4. sum, firms

5. upward, higher; (a) greater than; MRC; (b) MRP, MRC; (c) fewer, lower

6. increase wages, demand, supply, above

7. exclusive, restricting, inclusive, increasing

8. (a) rises, falls; (b) restrain; (c) growing, inelastic

9. compensating

10. principal, agent, different, shirk, incentive

11. 5, incentive, increase, shirk

12. not only, decreases

13. decrease, increase, increase, decrease, Canada, India

PROBLEMS AND PROJECTS

1. (a) Qd of Labour Demanded: 100, 200, 300, 400, 500, 600, 700; (b) 10, 600; (c) 10, 6, 10; (f) 400

2. (a) Total Labour Cost: 0, 4, 12, 24, 40, 60, 84, 112, 144; Marginal Labour Cost: 4, 8, 12, 16, 20, 24, 28, 32; (b) 5, 12, 20; (d) 6, 14

3. (a) 400, 4; (b) bilateral; (c) horizontal at $8 to 800 miners, and then following the supply curve; (d) equilibrium is uncertain because of countervailing market power

4. (a) (iii); (b) (iv); (c) (ii); (d) (i)

5. (a) 50; 30; (b) drop, rise; (c) 10, 40; (d) crowding, segregation; (e) increase, 30, 49; increase, 19

TRUE-FALSE

1. F   Canadian wages are higher because labour supply is small relative to demand
2. T
3. F   real wages measure purchasing power
4. T   if price level falls by larger percentage than nominal wage
5. T
6. T   because the MRP curve, which is the demand curve, will shift rightward
7. T   because the wage rate for other worker also must be increased
8. F   the monoponist ceases hiring additional labour before this point is reached
9. F   increasing wages is the key objective
10. T

11. T   these tactics can help increase demand for domestically produced products as prices of imports rise
12. T   e.g., an electricians' union or steamfitters' union
13. T   licences can be limited in number or be very difficult to qualify for
14. F
15. F   employment will fall more if demand is elastic
16. T
17. T
18. T   employers move back up along their demand curve for labour
19. T
20. F   the issue is lack of incentive, not of understanding
21. F   Zippy's will pay more than other stations, and therefore have less turnover
22. F   the lower women's wages will be
23. F   statistical discrimination is often profitable
24. T   thus, they have poorer opportunities to create acquire human capital
25. T
26. F   the wages will not completely equalize so long as there are nonmonetary factors and moving costs

MULTIPLE-CHOICE

1. (a)
2. (a)   real wages are high because of high productivity, not the other way around
3. (d)
4. (d)   the firm's labour supply is horizontal (infinitely elastic)
5. (d)   such as the mine in an isolated mining village
6. (d)   MRP = MRC, but MRC > wage
7. (d)   shifting the demand curve to the right
8. (c)   such as plumbers or nurses
9. (a)
10. (d)   this is a strategy for reducing supply
11. (b)   less hockey rinks would mean less demand for sticks, and less demand for their labour
12. (c)
13. (a)
14. (d)   where MRC = MRP
15. (c)   where wage = MRP
16. (a)   very few workers have comparable skills that his employer could substitute instead
17. (d)
18. (c)   the other result in higher pay for higher effort or productivity
19. (a)   where supply and demand intersect
20. (d)   employment is found where MRC = demand, and the wage at this employment level is found from supply curve
21. (d)
22. (d)   giving them the incentive to work especially hard to avoid losing the high-paying job
23. (d)

24. (a) he is using a stereotype (based on group characteristics rather than the actual characteristics of the individual)

25. (a) the bigger this coefficient is, the stronger the taste for discrimination

26. (c)

27. (b) the size of this cost determines the discrimination coefficient

28. (d)

29. (d) the workers move from a place where their marginal productivity was lower to a place where it is higher

CHAPTER 16

Rent, Interest, and Profit

This chapter concludes our study of resource prices by examining the incomes that are earned from land, capital and entrepreneurial ability. Various concepts from the past two chapters are now applied to the study of rent, interest, and profits. In particular, you should recall that the marginal revenue product of a resource determines the demand for that resource.

The market for land is unique in that the supply is perfectly *inelastic*: changes in rent do not change how much land is supplied. Therefore, given the quantity of land available, demand is the only active determinant of rent. Differences in land rents reflect productivity differences between pieces of land. Land rents serve no function in creating an incentive to supply the land. This fact led Henry George in the nineteenth century to suggest government raise all of its tax revenue by taxing land. Land rents do serve an allocative function by determining how the land will be allocated between alternative uses.

Capital, as economists define it, means real capital goods such as machinery and equipment. Is the rate of interest, then, the price paid for the use of capital goods? No; interest is the price paid for the use of money that can be used to invest in real capital goods. The loanable funds theory of interest is a demand and supply explanation of interest rate determination. As the interest rate increases, households with money to spend find it worthwhile to defer some of their spending, and lend some of their money for a time in exchange for interest income. As the interest rate increases, businesses seeking financing to enable them to purchase capital goods will find it preferable to reduce or defer some of their planned capital spending. They make the decision by comparing the interest rate with the expected rate of return on their capital spending projects. There is an equilibrium interest rate that will balance the supply of loanable funds with the demand. The interest rate allocates available funds to those investment projects expected to produce the highest rate of return.

At any given time there is a range of interest rates to account for differences between loans in the level of risk, term to maturity, loan size, and market imperfections. It is also important to distinguish between the nominal interest rate and the real (or inflation-adjusted) interest rate.

Entrepreneurs earn profit, part of which is a "normal" profit covering the opportunity cost of the entrepreneur's time, energy, and ability. This part is necessary to keep the entrepreneur in the current business. Any residual return after the normal profit is called "economic" profit, or pure profit, and this can be positive or negative. Economic profit is a payment for taking uninsurable risks, and for the uncertainty in undertaking innovation. It is also a return on monopoly power. Economic profits are the lure that makes entrepreneurs willing to take the risks that lead to greater efficiency and progress.

The chapter closes with a brief assessment of how the nation's income is shared between wages, interest, rent, and profit. Perhaps surprisingly, labour's share has been a fairly stable share of about 80% ever since the 1920s.

■ CHAPTER LEARNING OBJECTIVES

In this chapter you will learn:
☐ How the price of land is determined
☐ How the interest rate is determined
☐ What economic profit is, and how profits, along with losses, allocate resources among alternative uses in an economy.
☐ What the share of income going to each of the factors of production is in Canada.

■ CHAPTER OUTLINE

1. Economic rent is the price paid for the use of land or other natural resources that are completely fixed in total supply (perfectly inelastic).

(a) Demand is the active determinant of economic rent because supply changes cannot occur. Economic rent is, therefore, a surplus payment that is not necessary to ensure that land is available to the economy as a whole. The rent serves no incentive function.

(b) Rent is not a surplus payment from the viewpoint of a single firm. To the firm, rent is a cost that must be paid to attract the land away from other potential users. Therefore, rent does serve an allocative function in ensuring land is allocated for the most valuable uses.

2. Some people have argued that land rents are unearned, so land should be nationalized or its rents taxed away.

(a) In 1879, Henry George advocated a single tax on land, arguing that government could raise all the revenue needed with such a tax, and that it would not harm resource allocation.

(b) Critics have noted several disadvantages to such a tax:

(1) A land tax alone could not bring in enough tax revenue.

(2) Most rents are combined payments for land and the improvements on the land.

(3) It is unfair to tax only landowners since they are not the only recipients of "unearned" incomes.

(4) It is unfair to tax only current owners of the land given that they have typically paid high prices for their land.

3. Economic rents on different types of land vary because land differs in its productivity. Land of very low productivity may be a free good, attracting no rent at all.

4. The interest rate is the price paid for the use of money.

(a) The interest rate is stated as a percentage annually of the amount borrowed.

(b) Money itself is not a resource, but it can be used to buy physical capital resources such as factories, machinery, etc.

5. Interest rates are determined by the demand for and supply of loanable funds. Graphically, the interest rate is measured on the vertical axis, and the quantity of loanable funds is measured on the horizontal axis.

(a) The supply curve of loanable funds is upward sloping. As interest rates rise, households are more willing to defer present consumption and to save more money, which can then be supplied (through the financial system) as loans to businesses.

(b) The demand curve for loans is downward sloping. As interest rates rise, fewer investment projects that firms are considering will have rates of return that exceed the interest rate, hence firms will wish to borrow less funds to finance investment projects.

(c) The equilibrium interest rate is found where the quantity supplied and the quantity demanded are equal in the market for loanable funds.

(d) Shifts in the supply or demand of loanable funds will change the interest rate.

6. For convenience we speak as if there is only a single interest rate. In reality, there are numerous interest rates. Rates vary because of four factors:

(a) Loans with a higher risk of default carry higher interest rates.

(b) Loans with longer terms to maturity usually carry higher interest rates.

(c) Loans for smaller amounts carry higher interest rates.

(d) Market imperfections, or monopoly power considerations, can also affect interest rates.

7. The pure rate of interest is approximated by the interest rate on long-term, virtually risk-free securities, such as Government of Canada bonds.

8. The interest rate plays three roles.

(a) Because a lower interest rate will stimulate the demand for capital goods, there is an inverse relationship between the interest rate and the level of total output of the economy.

(b) The interest rate rations (allocates) loanable funds, and therefore real capital, among competing firms and industries, thereby determining what kinds of capital are produced.

(c) The interest rate determines the level and composition of R&D spending.

(d) When there is inflation we must adjust the nominal interest rate to find the real interest rate, which is expressed in purchasing power terms. The real interest rate, not the nominal rate, affects investment and R&D spending decisions.

9. Usury laws specify maximum interest rates on loans. These laws exist in some U.S. jurisdictions, and are sometimes lobbied for in Canada. Usury laws typically have the following effects:
    (a)   nonmarket rationing occurs;
    (b)   creditworthy borrowers gain at the expense of lenders; and
    (c)   capital is allocated inefficiently.

10. Economic or pure profit is the residual after all explicit and implicit costs are deducted from a firm's total revenues.
    (a)   The entrepreneur's return includes a normal profit that is the minimum payment necessary to keep the entrepreneur in the current business.
    (b)   Any return (positive or negative) after allocating the normal profit is economic profit. In a static, competitive economy, there is no economic profit. Such profit arises from three sources:
        (1) compensation for assuming the uninsurable risks of business that are inherent in a dynamic economy;
        (2) compensation for dealing with the uncertainties inherent in innovation; and
        (3) surpluses obtained from the exploitation of monopoly power.
    (c)   The expectation of economic profits motivates business firms to innovate; and profits (and losses) guide business firms to produce products and to use resources in the ways most desired by society.

11. Canada's national income is divided between wages, rent, interest, and profit. Using a broad definition of labour income that includes net income of farmers and unincorporated businesses, labour's share has been fairly stable around 80%, so the share going to capitalists (through rent, interest, and profits) has been about 20% of national income.

■ **TERMS AND CONCEPTS**

economic rent	**usury laws**
incentive function of	**explicit costs**
price	**implicit costs**
single-tax movement	**economic (pure) profit**
loanable funds theory	**normal profit**
of interest	**static economy**
pure rate of interest	**insurable risks**
nominal interest rate	**uninsurable risks**
real interest rate	

■ **HINTS AND TIPS**

1. You may be confused by different uses of the term "rent." Usually it applies to income from land, but sometimes it refers to other incomes. In every case, rent pertains to a surplus earned when a resource earns more than it would take to retain that resource in its current use.

2. To understand clearly the difference between normal profit and economic profit, focus on the difference between a static, competitive economy and a dynamic economy with market power. Remember that it is the expectation, not the certainty, of profit that drives the entrepreneur. Economic profit is never certain. In order to generate profit, the entrepreneur must take risks. You should distinguish between risks that are insurable and risks that are uninsurable. Bearing uninsurable risk is a major source of profit in a dynamic and unpredictable market economy.

■ **FILL-IN QUESTIONS**

1. Rent is the price paid for the use of _____ and other _____ resources with a completely (horizontal, vertical) _____ supply curve. Their supply can also be described as perfectly _____.

2. The active factor in determining rent is (demand, supply) _____.

3. When the demand for a fixed resource changes there is a large (price, quantity) _____ effect and no _____ effect.

4. From society's perspective, rent is a _____, because the supply of land is fixed. From a single firm's perspective, a rent payment is a _____ that must be paid in order to attract land away from alternate uses.

5. Henry George argued that land rents are (earned, unearned) _____ incomes and that land should be _____ so that these incomes can benefit society as a whole. Proponents of the _____ tax argue that economic rent could be completely taxed away without changing how much land is available for productive purposes.

6. Interest is the price paid for the use of _____. Money itself is not an economic resource, but when firms borrow money for invest-ment they are ultimately purchasing the use of real _____ goods.

7. In the simplified theory of loanable funds pre-sented in the chapter, loanable funds are supplied by _____, and are demanded by _____. In reality, loanable funds are chan-nelled through banks and other _____.

8. The individual firm is willing to continue invest-ing in capital, and therefore (lending, borrowing) _____, up to the point where the rate of _____ and the expected rate of _____ on capital are equal.

9. The firm's demand for loanable funds is _____ sloping because lower interest rates mean (higher, lower) _____ investment costs so (more, fewer) _____ investment projects will be profitable.

10. The firm's demand for loanable funds will shift rightward as a result of _____ improvements or an increase in _____ for the firm's prod-uct.

11. The supply curve of loanable funds is _____-sloping because (higher, lower) _____ interest rates are required to induce households to _____ more.

12. The interest rate helps determine how much _____ will occur in the economy and also _____ financial and real capital among firms.

13. Normal profits are paid to the human resource called _____ ability. This resource performs four functions: combining the other _____ to produce goods and services; making (routine, non-routine) _____ decisions for the firm; (invent-ing, innovating) _____ products and produc-tion processes; and bearing the economic _____ associated with the other three func-tions.

14. Economic profits promote efficient _____ of resources in the economy unless the profits are the result of (competition, monopoly) _____.

■ PROBLEMS AND PROJECTS

1. Assume that there are 300,000 hectares avail-able of a certain type of farmland, which has no other use but farming. The demand for this land is given in the following table:

Land Rent ($/hectare)	Land Demanded (hectares)
$125	100,000
100	200,000
75	300,000
50	400,000
25	500,000

(a) _____ hectares will be rented.
(b) The rent will be $_____ per hectare.
(c) If the government placed a $50 per hectare tax on this farmland, there would be _____ hectares available.
(d) A tax of $50 per hectare would reduce the landowners' net income to $_____ per hectare.

2. There are three grades of land (A, B, and C) on which wheat is grown with the use of no other inputs but labour. The table gives the output for various amounts of labour applied.

Labour	Output by Land Grade (bushels)		
	Grade A	Grade B	Grade C
1	50	45	20
2	90	75	30
3	120	95	37
4	140	105	41
5	150	110	43
6	155	112	44

If the price is a constant $1 per bushel, complete the following table showing the marginal revenue prod-uct for the various levels of labour input.

Labour	Marginal Revenue Product ($)		
	Grade A	Grade B	Grade C
1	_____	_____	_____
2	_____	_____	_____
3	_____	_____	_____
4	_____	_____	_____
5	_____	_____	_____
6	_____	_____	_____

Labour costs $20 per unit and is purchased in a perfectly competitive input market.

(a) A profit-maximizing firm would employ _____ units of labour on Grade A land; _____ units of labour on Grade B land; and _____ units of labour on Grade C land.

(b) The net income earned: on Grade A land is $_____; on Grade B land is $_____; and on Grade C land is $_____.

(c) In a competitive market for land, Grade A land would rent for up to $_____, Grade B land for $_____, and Grade C land for $_____.

(d) Suppose that the price of wheat increased to $2 a bushel. The rent on Grade A land becomes $_____; on Grade B land $_____; on Grade C land $_____.

(e) Assuming the price of wheat remains at $1 per bushel, Grade B land would command no rent whatsoever if the price of labour rises to at least $_____.

3. The graph below shows the market for loanable funds.

(a) The equilibrium interest rate is _____% per year.

(b) At this interest rate households save $_____ billion per year, and firms borrow $_____ billion per year.

(c) If a usury law set a maximum interest rate of 5% per year, households would save $_____ billion per year, and firms would wish to borrow $_____ billion per year, leaving a (shortage, surplus) _____ of $_____ billion per year.

Interest rate (%/yr)

Quantity of Loanable funds ($ billion /yr)

■ **TRUE-FALSE**

Circle T if the statement is true, F if it is false.

1. Rent is a surplus because it does not perform an incentive function. **T F**

2. Demand is the sole active determinant of land rent. **T F**

3. Because the supply of land is fixed, rent does not change when demand increases. **T F**

4. The demand for land, and therefore the rent on land, would increase if there were an increase in the demand for the product obtained from the land. **T F**

5. Rent, which is a surplus from the viewpoint of society, is a cost from the viewpoint of the firm that pays the rent. **T F**

6. If the demand curve for land lies entirely to the left of the supply curve for land, the land will be free. **T F**

7. Money is an economic resource, and the interest rate is the price paid for this resource. **T F**

8. A decrease in the supply of loanable funds would tend to increase the interest rate and to decrease investment spending and national output and employment. **T F**

9. An individual who borrows at a financial institution is a demander of loanable funds. **T F**

10. Charging different interest rates to individuals for loans of equal size is a form of discrimination and is illegal in Canada. **T F**

11. The pure rate of interest is the nominal rate of interest minus the rate of inflation. **T F**

12. One reason to oppose a merger of major Canadian banks is that such a merger would increase monopoly power in the lending industry, and possibly increase interest rates. **T F**

13. A normal profit is the return required by the entrepreneur to prevent her from transferring her service to another firm. **T F**

14. One of the reasons why entrepreneurs earn economic profits is they are smart enough to buy insurance to cover insurable risks. **T F**

15. Uninsurable risks are the business risks that can be predicted and for which no insurance is required. **T F**

16. The expectation of profits is the basic motive for innovation, while actual profits and losses aid in the efficient allocation of resources. **T F**

17. Economic profits are guaranteed to exist only in a static economy with pure competition. **T F**

18. Growing corporate profits have resulted in a slow but steady growth of capital's share of the national income. **T F**

19. Growth of labour unions has caused labour to take a growing share of Canada's national income.
T F

■ **MULTIPLE-CHOICE**

Circle the letter that corresponds to the best answer.

1. The supply of land to society is:
(a) perfectly inelastic
(b) of unitary elasticity
(c) perfectly elastic
(d) elastic but not perfectly elastic

2. From the viewpoint of society, an increase in the demand for land results in:
(a) an increase in the supply of land
(b) an increase in the quantity supplied of land
(c) an increase in rent and an increase in the quantity supplied of land
(d) an increase in rent only

3. If an input, such as land, is fixed in supply:
(a) rent is supply determined
(b) rent is determined by the owner of that fixed supply
(c) rent is demand determined
(d) in some provinces rent payments are determined by a Rental Review Board

4. The payment to a resource performs an incentive function if:

(a) the supply curve of the resource is perfectly inelastic
(b) the price of the resource is fixed
(c) the demand curve for the resource is downward sloping
(d) the supply curve of the resource is upward sloping

5. Economists consider rent to be a surplus because:
(a) no matter what the level of rent payment the same quantity of land is available to the economy
(b) agricultural products are grown from seeds using land and so a surplus results
(c) landowners are monopolists and charge a price greater than the competitive price
(d) there is a large quantity effect and little price effect when the demand for land changes

6. Which of the following is *not* characteristic of the tax proposed by Henry George?
(a) it would be equal to 100% of all land rent
(b) it would be the only tax levied by government
(c) it would not affect the supply of land
(d) it would distort the allocation of resources

7. Which of the following is *not* among the criticisms of Henry George's single tax proposal?
(a) a land tax alone would not raise enough revenue
(b) a land tax would be unfair to current landowners who bought land at fair market prices
(c) it is hard to separate land rents from payments for buildings and other improvements on land
(d) a land tax would reduce the supply of land available to society

8. Differential rent payments can be due to:
(a) differences in land fertility
(b) differences in land location
(c) differences in the purity of natural resource deposits
(d) all of the above

9. Which of the following statements about differential interest rates is true?
(a) interest rates tend to be lower on riskier loans
(b) interest rates tend to be lower on smaller loans

(c) interest rates tend to be lower on shorter-term loans

(d) all of the above

10. The supply of loanable funds is provided by all of the following except:

(a) borrowers at a commercial bank

(b) business savings

(c) buyers of Canada Savings Bonds

(d) credit creation by financial institutions

11. Which of the following would shift the supply of loanable funds to the right?

(a) an increase in thriftiness of households

(b) an increase in tax rates on interest income

(c) a technological advance

(d) an increase in consumer demands

12. Usually the smaller the rate of interest on a loan:

(a) the greater the risk involved

(b) the shorter the length of the loan

(c) the smaller the amount of the loan

(d) the greater the imperfections in the money market

13. The rate of interest does all of the following except:

(a) affect the total amount of investment in the economy

(b) affect the aggregate level of domestic output and employment

(c) allocate money and physical capital to those industries in which it will be most productive

(d) guarantee that there will be full employment in the economy

14. The profit-maximizing amount of financial and real capital an individual firm would employ is the amount at which the interest rate is equal to the:

(a) expected rate of return

(b) marginal physical product of capital

(c) marginal cost of capital

(d) marginal resource cost of capital

15. If the rate of interest is 12% and a firm expects that a new warehouse investment would yield a rate of return of 14%, the firm would:

(a) not build the new warehouse

(b) build the new warehouse

(c) have to toss a coin to decide whether to build the new warehouse

(d) not be able to determine, from these figures, whether to build the warehouse

16. The pure rate of interest is the interest rate on:

(a) a basic Visa card

(b) a fixed rate mortgage

(c) a savings account

(d) long term government bonds

17. Which of the following is an economic cost?

(a) business profit

(b) normal profit

(c) economic profit

(d) windfall profit

18. Uninsurable risks can stem from:

(a) changes in the general economic environment

(b) changes in the structure of the economy

(c) changes in government policy

(d) all of the above

19. Identify the uninsurable risk from the following list:

(a) shoplifting losses

(b) injuries to employees

(c) technological change

(d) fire damage

20. Which of the following is *not* a basic function of the entrepreneur?

(a) to introduce new products to the market

(b) to supply loanable funds

(c) to incur uninsurable risks

(d) to combine resources to produce a good or service

21. Business firms obtain profits because:

(a) not all risks are insurable

(b) not all markets are competitive

(c) the economy is dynamic

(d) all of these

22. Capital's share of national income is around 20%, and includes:

(a) rent

(b) interest

(c) profit

(d) all of the above

23. If the inflation rate is 2% and the nominal rate of interest is 8%, then the real rate of interest is:

(a) -6%

(b) 4%

(c) 6%

(d) 10%

■ **DISCUSSION QUESTIONS**

1. Explain what determines the economic rent paid for the use of land. What is unique about the supply of land?

2. Why is land rent a "surplus"? What economic difficulties would be encountered if the government adopted Henry George's single-tax proposal as a means of confiscating this surplus?

3. Even though land rent is an economic surplus, it is also an economic cost for the individual user of land. How can it be both an economic surplus and an economic cost?

4. How would a decrease in the supply of loanable funds affect: (a) the interest rate; (b) investment spending; (c) national output and employment?

5. Why are there many different interest rates in the economy at any given time?

6. What is the pure rate of interest and how does it differ from the real rate of interest?

7. Why does the amount of business investment increase when the interest rate falls?

8. What two important functions does the rate of interest perform in the economy?

9. What are economic profits? Why would there be no economic profits in a purely competitive static economy?

10. "The risks an entrepreneur assumes arise because of uncertainties that are external to the firm and because of uncertainties that are developed by the initiative of the firm itself." Explain.

11. What two important functions do profits or the expectations of profits perform in the economy? Why could monopoly power, such as that created by a patent, both impede and enhance the effective performance of these functions?

12. What part of Canada's national income is wages and salaries and what part is labour income? Why do your answers to these two questions differ? What part of the national income do capitalists receive? What kinds of income is capitalist income?

■ **ANSWERS**

FILL-IN QUESTIONS

1. land, natural, vertical, inelastic
2. demand
3. price, quantity
4. surplus, cost
5. unearned, taxed, single
6. money, capital
7. households, firms, financial institutions
8. borrowing, interest, return
9. downward, lower, more
10. technological, demand
11. upward, higher, save
12. investment, allocates
13. entrepreneurial, resources, nonroutine, innovating, risks
14. allocation, monopoly

PROBLEMS AND PROJECTS

1. (a) 300,000; (b) 75; (c) 300,000; (d) 25

2. Grade A: 50, 40, 30, 20, 10, 5; Grade B: 45, 30, 20, 10, 5, 2; Grade C: 20, 10, 7, 4, 2, 1; (a) employing labour up to where MRP = MRC: 4, 3, 1; (b) (P x Q) – (wage x L) = 60, 35, 0; (c) 60, 35, 0; (d) 200, 130, 20; (e) 45

3. (a) 7; (b) 5, 5: (c) 3, 7, shortage, 4

TRUE-FALSE

1. T
2. T
3. F   rent does change; quantity does not
4. T   the MRP of the land rises
5. T
6. T   the equilibrium price is zero
7. F   money is not an economic resource
8. T

9. T
10. F   this a legal and common practice
11. F   this describes the real rate of interest, not the pure rate
12. T   monopoly power does tend to raise interest rates
13. T
14. F   profits pertain to uninsurable risks, not insurable risks
15. F   uninsurable risks are unpredictable
16. T
17. F   in such an economy there would be no economic profits
18. F   capital's share has remained fairly stable at about 20%
19. F   labour's share has remained fairly stable at about 80%

MULTIPLE-CHOICE

1.   (a) supply is vertical
2.   (d)
3.   (c)
4.   (d) an upward sloping supply means quantity supplied responds to price changes
5.   (a)
6.   (d) because supply is fixed, it would be unaffected by such a tax
7.   (d) supply is fixed; the others are practical problems with the tax
8.   (d)
9.   (c)
10.   (a) borrowers are demanders of loanable funds
11.   (a) increased thriftiness means more savings available to lend
12.   (b)
13.   (d) a flexible interest helps, but does not guarantee, the economy will maintain full employment
14.   (a)
15.   (b) the return exceeds the opportunity cost of the interest, so the warehouse would be profitable
16.   (d)
17.   (b) this covers the opportunity cost of the entrepreneurial input
18.   (d) the probability and specifics of any of these cannot be assessed with any certainty
19.   (c) shoftlifting, injuries, and fires are predictable and insurable
20.   (b)
21.   (d)
22.   (d)
23.   (c) in purchasing power terms, the return is 6%

CHAPTER 17

Income Inequality and Poverty

This chapter deals with the facts about income inequality and poverty in Canada, including how these variables are measured and interpreted. There is significant and growing inequality of incomes between Canadian households, and a substantial percentage of Canadians live in poverty. To some extent, these important problems are inherent to any market economy, but in Canada there is a consensus that government should play a role in modifying the distribution of income. The chapter presents some of the basic principles and issues behind our public policies designed to alter the distribution of income.

The Lorenz curve, which plots the percent of the nation's income versus the percent of Canadian families, is a useful device to show that the distribution of income is unequal. However, the fact that households move from one income group to another over time makes it difficult to draw simple conclusions from the Lorenz curve of other data at one point in time. There are many causes of inequality, ranging from very individual circumstances, to social trends, and policies.

How much our governments should redistribute incomes, and what the effects are of present income redistribution mechanisms, are both highly controversial. The basic case for an equal distribution of income — and therefore for income taxes and transfer payments — is that income equality is necessary for consumer utility to be maximized for society as a whole.

The case for inequality is based on the idea that the potential of earning higher incomes provides people with an incentive to work hard, save, invest, and take risks. All of these actions contribute to the nation's output. In summary, then, there is a tradeoff between equality and efficiency if redistribution for the purpose of greater equality reduces incentives and therefore reduces production.

The definition of poverty is necessarily subjective. Nevertheless, no matter where the line is drawn, and no matter whether one considers absolute poverty or relative poverty, poverty is not randomly distributed. For example, unattached individuals, households headed by women, and households with more children are much more likely to live in poverty.

Canada's income maintenance system consists of many component programs including social insurance elements and public assistance (welfare) elements. Important tradeoffs exist in these programs.

■ CHAPTER LEARNING OBJECTIVES

In this chapter you will learn:
☐ The facts about income inequality in Canada and how to measure it.
☐ The causes of income inequality.
☐ That there is a tradeoff between income equality and economic efficiency.
☐ The distinction between absolute and relative poverty.
☐ About the extent of relative poverty in Canada.
☐ About Canada's income maintenance system.

■ CHAPTER OUTLINE

1. Considerable inequality of household incomes is a persistent state of affairs in Canada.

 (a) A table of distribution of personal incomes by families shows the extent of the inequality.

 (b) The Lorenz curve is a geometric device for portraying the extent of inequality at a particular point in time.

2. Several factors must be considered when interpreting the data on income inequality.

(a)   Canada's Lorenz curve has not shifted significantly since World War II.

(b)   Income mobility means that the degree of income inequality is less if viewed over a lifetime. Earnings for most workers start at a low level in youth, peak during middle age, and then decline, meaning that most people move between income quintiles over the life cycle.

(c)   Government redistribution through taxes and transfer payments serves to reduce – modestly – the degree of income of inequality in Canada. Transfers have more impact than taxes in this regard.

(d)   Over time economic growth has raised the absolute dollar incomes of all income classes in Canada, but the relative distribution of personal incomes has been relatively stable since 1951 (the first year for which the data is available).

(e)   In recent years there has been a slight increase in inequality, as shown by a drop in the percentage of total income received by the lower quintiles and a rise in the percentage received by the higher quintiles.

3. The impersonal market system does not necessarily result in a distribution of income that we would consider just. Income inequality can be explained by individual differences in at least seven areas:

(1)   ability
(2)   education and training
(3)   discrimination
(4)   preferences and risk
(5)   unequal distribution of wealth
(6)   market power
(7)   luck, connections, and misfortune

4. Several factors are contributing to the growing inequality of incomes over the last three decades.

(a)   The demand for workers is shifting strongly towards the more highly skilled and educated, creating a larger wage gap between more and less skilled workers.

(b)   Demographic changes are leading to higher proportions of less skilled and less experienced workers, higher proportions of households headed by unmarried or divorced mothers, and a growing tendency for men and women with high earnings to marry each other.

(c)   Wages in certain Canadian industries are suffering because of growing competition from imports produced in low-wage countries, immigration of unskilled workers, and a decline in unionism.

5. An important question society must answer is what degree of income inequality to aim for, given the tradeoff between equality and efficiency.

(a)   A case for equality is made on the basis of maximizing total consumer utility in our society. Since there is diminishing marginal utility to income, redistributing some income from a higher-income individual to a lower-income individual will increase the amount of utility produced by that amount of income.

(b)   A case for inequality is based on the argument that if all income were distributed equally, individuals would lack incentive to work hard, take risks, etc., in order to produce more income. Therefore, society would have much less income to distribute.

(c)   In principle, economic research can shed light on the equality-efficiency tradeoff by determining how much output is sacrificed by choosing redistribution policies to produce a particular degree of equality.

6. Poverty is a significant and persistent problem in Canadian society.

(a)   Absolute poverty exists when basic material needs (food, clothing, and shelter) of a household are not met. Relative poverty exists when a household's income is low relative to others in the society.

(b)   Statistics Canada defines poverty by a "low income cut-off" (revised in 1992, whereby a family spending at least 54.7% of their income on food, shelter, and clothing are considered to be living in poverty). In 1997, 14% of families and 40% of unattached individuals in Canada were living in poverty.

(c)   While the poor are found in all regions, age groups, ethnic groups, and rural and urban populations, poverty is far from randomly distributed. Unattached individuals, households with children, and households headed by women, younger people, or the unemployed are much more likely to be low income.

(d)   Poverty in Canada tends to be invisible because there is significant income mobility, because the "permanent poor" are increasingly isolated geographically, and because the poor lack political voice or organization.

7. About half of federal government spending is on transfer payments, but the bulk of these expenditures are not targeted at the poor. Major programs in Canada's income-maintenance system include:

(a) The Old Age Security (OAS) Pension, payable to everyone reaching the age of 65, and the Guaranteed Income Supplement (GIS), for those over 65 and with incomes below a certain level.

(b) The Canada Pension Plan (CPP) and Quebec Pension Plan (QPP), payable at age 65 based on individuals' contributions made out of earnings during year in the labour force.

(c) Employment Insurance (EI) benefits, paid as temporary support to unemployed workers on the basis of previous contributions.

8. An ideal social assistance (welfare) program should achieve three goals:

(a) It should get people out of poverty.

(b) It should provide adequate incentives for able-bodied, nonretired people to work.

(c) It should have a reasonable cost.

9. Conflicts of the three goals are illustrated in a comparison of three hypothetical welfare plans. All have a minimum annual income, and a benefit-reduction rate (or rate at which the recipients' benefits are reduced as a result of earned income).

(a) Lower minimum annual incomes keep costs down but reduce the ability of the plan to move people out of poverty.

(b) Lower benefit-reduction rates protect the incentive to work but raise the cost of the plan.

■ **TERMS AND CONCEPTS**

income inequality
Lorenz curve
income mobility
noncash transfers
tradeoff between equality and efficiency
absolute poverty

relative poverty
Canada Pension Plan (CPP)
Old Age Security (OAS)
Guaranteed Income Supplement (GIS)
employment insurance

■ **HINTS AND TIPS**

1. Given how strongly people feel about income distribution issues, and given the current political turmoil over the overhaul of Canada's income maintenance programs, it is easy to lose track of the distinction between positive and normative statements. It is important that you keep the positive vs. normative distinction in mind in order to get the most out of this chapter.

2. The most interesting concept in this chapter is probably the equality-efficiency tradeoff. It is at the centre of many public policy debates about our income maintenance programs.

■ **FILL-IN QUESTIONS**

1. Over time, household incomes in Canada have risen in (absolute, relative) _____ terms, but the _____ distribution has been roughly stable since 1951.

2. Income inequality can be portrayed graphically by drawing a _____ curve.

(a) When such a curve is plotted, the cumulative percentage of (income, families) _____ is plotted on the horizontal axis and the cumulative percentage of _____ is plotted on the vertical axis.

(b) The curve that would show a completely equal distribution of income is a diagonal line, which would run from the (lower, upper) _____ left to the _____ right corner of the graph.

(c) The more unequal the distribution of income, the (less, more) _____ the curve "sags" below the diagonal. Thus, the degree of income inequality is measured by the area that lies between the curve and the _____.

3. Those who argue for:

(a) equal distribution of income contend that it results in the maximization of total (income, utility) _____ in the economy;

(b) unequal distribution of income believe income distribution is an important determinant of _____.

4. There is an important tradeoff between _____ and _____. This means that:

(a) less income inequality leads to a (greater, smaller) _____ total output; and

(b) a larger total output requires (more, less) _____ income inequality.

5. Under the Canadian income maintenance system, basic material needs can be met for almost everyone. Therefore, the poverty problem is one of

_____ poverty rather than _____ poverty.

6. Poverty tends to be concentrated:
 (a) among the (young, old) _____;
 (b) among (families, unattached individuals) _____;
 (c) in families headed by _____;
 (d) among those who are poorly _____;
 (e) in (large, small) _____ families.

7. What do the following abbreviations stand for?
 (a) OAS: _____
 (b) GIS: _____
 (c) CPP: _____
 (d) EI: _____

8. The two critical elements of any welfare, or public assistance, program are a _____ income below which a family's income would not be allowed to fall, and a _____ rate that specifies the rate at which the subsidy would be reduced if earned income increases.

9. The three goals of any public assistance (welfare) program include:
 (a) getting families out of _____; (b) providing _____ to work; and (c) assuring the _____ of the program are reasonable. These goals are (complementary, conflicting) _____.

■ PROBLEMS AND PROJECTS

1. The distribution of household incomes in a hypothetical economy is shown in the table below.
 (a) Complete the table by computing, beginning with the lowest income families:
 (1) the percentage of all families in each income class and all lower classes. Enter these figures in column 4.
 (2) the percentage of total income received by each income class and all lower classes. Enter these figures in column 5.
 (b) From the distribution of income data in columns 4 and 5 it can be seen that:
 (1) families earning less than $15,000 a year constitute the lowest _____% of all families and receive _____% of the total income.
 (2) families earning at least $50,000 a year constitute the highest _____% of all families and receive _____% of the total income.

(1) Personal Income Class	(2) % of All Families in This Class	(3) % of Total Income Received by This Class	(4) % of All Families in This and All Lower Classes	(5) % of Total Income Received by This and All Lower Classes
Under $10,000	18	4	_____	_____
$10,000-14,999	12	6	_____	_____
$15,000-24,999	14	12	_____	_____
$25,000-34,999	17	14	_____	_____
$35,000-49,999	19	15	_____	_____
$50,000-74,999	11	20	_____	_____
$75,000 and over	9	29	_____	_____

 (c) Use your figures in columns 4 and 5 to draw a Lorenz curve on the graph below. (Plot the seven points and the zero-zero point and connect them with a smooth curve.)
 (1) On the same graph draw a diagonal line that would indicate complete equality in the distribution of income.
 (2) Shade the area of the graph that shows the degree of income inequality.

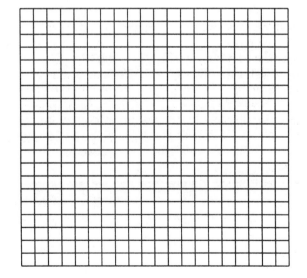

2. Following is a table containing different possible earned incomes for a family of a certain size.

Earned Income	Transfer Payment	Total Income
$0	$5,000	$5,000
5,000	_____	_____
10,000	_____	_____
15,000	_____	_____
20,000	_____	_____
25,000	_____	_____

(a) Assume that $5,000 is the minimum annual income per family and that the benefit-loss rate is 20%. Enter the transfer payment and the total income at each of the five remaining earned-income levels.

(1) This welfare program retains strong incentives to work because whenever the family earns an additional $5,000, its total income increases by $_____.

(2) The family receives a transfer payment until its earned income equals the break-even income of $_____.

(b) To reduce the break-even income, the government raises the benefit-loss rate to 50%. Complete the next table.

Earned Income	Transfer Payment	Total Income
$0	$5,000	$5,000
2,500	_____	_____
5,000	_____	_____
7,500	_____	_____
10,000	_____	_____

(1) This program is less costly than the previous one because the family only receives a transfer payment until it earns the break-even income of $_____.

(2) But the incentives to work are less because, whenever the family earns an additional $5,000, its total income increases by only $_____.

(c) Both of the previous two welfare programs guaranteed an income of only $5,000. Assume the minimum annual income is raised to $7,500 and that the benefit-loss rate is kept at 50%. Complete the table below.

Earned Income	Transfer Payment	Total Income
$0	$7,500	$7,500
3,000	_____	_____
6,000	_____	_____
9,000	_____	_____
12,000	_____	_____
15,000	_____	_____

(1) This program is more costly than the previous one because the break-even income has risen to $_____.

(2) The incentives to earn additional income are no better in this program than in the previous one. But to improve these incentives by reducing the benefit-loss rate to 40% would raise the break-even income to $_____. (Hint: Divide guaranteed income by the benefit-loss rate.)

(d) To summarize:

(1) given the guaranteed income, the lower the benefit-loss rate, the (greater, less) _____ is the incentive to earn additional income and the (greater, less) _____ is the break-even income and the cost of the welfare program;

(2) and given the benefit-loss rate, the greater the minimum annual income, the (greater, less) _____ is the break-even income and the cost of the program;

(3) but to reduce the break-even income and the cost of the program requires either a(n) (increase, decrease) _____ in the benefit-loss rate or a(n) _____ in the minimum annual income.

■ **TRUE-FALSE**

Circle T if the statement is true, F if it is false.

1. There is considerable income inequality in Canada.   **T F**

2. The long-run trend has been for family incomes in Canada to rise in absolute terms.   **T F**

3. In Canada there is considerable mobility between income classes from one year to the next.   **T F**

4. The progressive tax system in Canada has made the after-tax income distribution much more equal than the before-tax income distribution.   **T F**

5. Differences in personal characteristics explain some of the differences in earned income common in the market economy.   **T F**

6. In the tradeoff between equality and economic efficiency, an increase in efficiency requires a decrease in inequality.   **T F**

7. Relative poverty refers to an individual's or family's low income as compared to the incomes of others in society.   **T F**

8. In Canada the "low income cutoff" for defining poverty is set by Statistics Canada on a relative rather than an absolute basis.   **T F**

9. Developing countries typically have relatively equal income distributions.   **T F**

10. In the Lorenz curve analysis, a quintile refers to 20% of the population   **T F**

11. In Canada, the top quintile of the population earns about 10 times as much as the bottom quintile of the population.   **T F**

12. The argument that redistributing income will increase society's well-being is based on the assumption of diminishing marginal utility of income.   **T F**

13. The lower is the benefit-loss rate in an income assistance plan, the smaller are the incentives to earn additional income.   **T F**

14. All Canadians over the age of 65 are eligible to receive OAS and GIS benefits.   **T F**

■   **MULTIPLE-CHOICE**

Circle the letter that corresponds to the best answer.

1. In 1997, roughly what percentage of Canadian families had annual incomes of at least $75,000?
   (a)   5%
   (b)   11%
   (c)   25%
   (d)   38%

2. In 1997, approximately what percentage of all Canadian families had annual incomes below $20,000?
   (a)   1%
   (b)   11%
   (c)   18%
   (d)   32%

3. Which of the following applies to how the Canadian distribution of income has changed over time?
   (a)   incomes have fallen in absolute terms
   (b)   inequality has decreased in relative terms
   (c)   the relative distribution of income has been fairly stable since 1951
   (d)   income mobility has decreased

4. Which of the following would be evidence of a decrease in relative income inequality in Canada?
   (a)   a decrease in the percentage of total income received by the lowest quintile
   (b)   an increase in the percentage of total income received by the highest quintile
   (c)   an increase in the percentage of total income received by the four lowest quintiles
   (d)   a decrease in the percentage of total income received by the four lowest quintiles

5. When a Lorenz curve has been drawn, the degree of income inequality in an economy is measured by:
   (a)   the slope of the diagonal that runs from the southwest to the northeast corner of the diagram
   (b)   the slope of the Lorenz curve
   (c)   the area between the Lorenz curve and the axes of the graph
   (d)   the area between the Lorenz curve and the southwest-northeast diagonal

6. Which of the following is *not* one of the causes of the unequal distribution of income in Canada?
   (a)   the unequal distribution of property
   (b)   the income tax system
   (c)   the inability of the poor to invest in human capital
   (d)   luck and the unequal distribution of misfortune

7. The case for income inequality is primarily made on the basis that income inequality:
   (a)   is reduced by the transfer payment programs for the poor
   (b)   is necessary to maintain incentives to work and produce output

(c) depends on luck and chance, which cannot be corrected by government action
(d) is created by education and training programs that distort the distribution of income

8. The debate over income redistribution focuses on the tradeoff between equality and:
(a) efficiency
(b) unemployment
(c) economic growth
(d) economic freedom

9. Suppose that Carla obtains 5 units of utility from the last dollar of income received by her and that Robert obtains 8 units of utility from the last dollar of his income. Those who favour an equal distribution of income would:
(a) advocate redistributing income from Robert to Carla
(b) advocate redistributing income from Carla to Robert
(c) be content with this distribution of income between Carla and Robert
(d) argue that any redistribution of income between Carla and Robert would decrease total utility

10. Which of the following measures would tend to reduce income inequality?
(a) eliminating the Employment Insurance program
(b) increasing tax deductions for making investments
(c) taxing all personal income at a flat rate
(d) levying large taxes on inheritances

11. Which of the following is a major part of the Canadian income-maintenance system?
(a) public housing
(b) agricultural subsidies
(c) Employment Insurance
(d) minimum-wage laws

12. Which of the following is designed to provide a nationwide income for all those aged 65 and over?
(a) Canada Pension Plan
(b) Guaranteed Income Supplement
(c) Canada Assistance Plan
(d) Old Age Security

13. Which of the following programs is most specifically targeted at alleviating poverty?
(a) Canada Pension Plan

(b) Guaranteed Income Supplement
(c) Canada Assistance Plan
(d) Old Age Security

14. Under a public assistance (welfare) plan the break-even income is:
(a) the level of income at which income and consumption expenditure are equal
(b) the level of income at which income tax payments equal zero
(c) the level of income equal to the low income cutoff as calculated by Statistics Canada
(d) the level of income at which the transfer payment equals zero

15. Which of the following is not among the reasons that the poor are invisible in Canada?
(a) the poor are increasingly isolated in ghettos, slums, and depressed regions
(b) the poor are politically weak
(c) many of the poor are able to escape poverty for only a year or two
(d) there are relatively few poor people

■ **DISCUSSION QUESTIONS**

1. How does the degree of income inequality in Canada compare with other nations, such as the United States, South Africa, or Norway? What factors do you think explain the differences?

2. Has the distribution of income changed much in Canada during the past 40 years? What does this imply about the efficiency of Canada's schemes for income redistribution?

3. If a nation's Lorenz curve becomes more sharply bowed over time, what does that indicate?

4. In your view, is there any difference between a 19-year-old college student being below the low income cutoff, and a 39-year-old retail clerk, working full-time, and parent of three, being below the cutoff? Do these cases present different implications for policy-makers attempting to combat poverty?

5. State the case for an equal distribution of income and the case for an unequal distribution. What are the assumptions underlying each point of view?

6. How is poverty currently defined in Canada? What are the reasons for defining poverty in this way? What are the problems with this definition?

7. What characteristics — other than the small incomes they have to spend — do the greatest concentrations of the poor families of the nation tend to have?

8. Why does poverty in Canada tend to be invisible or hidden?

9. What are the three goals or objectives of any welfare plan? Explain why these goals are in conflict.

10. Suggest some policies that the Canadian government might adopt to significantly reduce income inequality. For each of your suggestions, would you support such a change? Are your reasons normative or positive?

■ **ANSWERS**

FILL-IN QUESTIONS

1. absolute, relative

2. Lorenz; (a) families, income; (b) lower, upper; (c) more; diagonal

3. (a) utility; (b) output (or income)

4. equality, efficiency (either order); (a) smaller; (b) more

5. relative, absolute

6. (a) young; (b) unattached individuals; (c) females; (d) educated; (e) large

7. (a) Old Age Security; (b) Guaranteed Income Supplement; (c) Canada Pension Plan; (d) Employment Insurance

8. minimum annual, benefit-loss

9. (a) poverty; (b) incentives; (c) costs,; conflicting

PROBLEMS AND PROJECTS

1. (a) (1) Column 4: 18, 30, 44, 61, 80, 91, 100; (2) Column 5: 4, 10, 22, 36, 51, 71, 100; (b) (1) 30, 10; (2) 20, 49

2. (a) Transfer payment: 4,000, 3,000, 2,000, 1,000, 0; Total Income: 9,000, 13,000, 17,000, 21,000, 25,000; (1) 4,000, (2) 25,000; (b) Transfer payment: 3,750, 2,500, 1250, 0; Total Income: 6,250, 7,500, 8,750, 10,000; (1)

10,000, (2) 2,500; (c) Transfer payment: 6,000, 4,500, 3,000, 1,500, 0; Total Income: 9,000, 10,500, 12,000, 13,500, 15,000; (1) 15,000, (2) 18,750; (d) (1) greater, greater, (2) greater, (3) increase, decrease

TRUE-FALSE

1. T
2. T
3. F there is significant income mobility, but over periods longer than one year
4. F somewhat more equal, but not much more
5. T ability and luck, for example
6. F more inequality would go with increased efficiency
7. T
8. T it is based on a percentage of income spent on food, clothing, and shelter
9. F they are most often very unequal
10. T
11. T in before tax income, this is about the correct ratio
12. T
13. F a low benefit-loss ratio means that a small percentage of the benefit is deducted when additional income is earned
14. F OAS is universal whereas GIS is received only by those with lower incomes

MULTIPLE-CHOICE

1. (c)
2. (b)
3. (c) considering that 50 years have passed, the data is remarkably stable
4. (c) this would also imply lower share of income for top quintile
5. (d)
6. (b) the income tax system (moderately) reduces income inequality
7. (b)
8. (a)
9. (b) the last dollar taken from Carla and given to Robert would change utility in the society by +3 (8 − 5)
10. (d) inherited wealth is a source of inequality, so taxing such wealth would reduce one advantage
11. (c)
12. (d) the others are not universal
13. (d) because it is subject to a means test
14. (d) because of the benefit reduction as a function of earned income
15. (d) 14% of families, and 40% of unattached individuals are below the low income cutoff

CHAPTER 18

Government and Market Failure

Market failure is said to occur when private markets do not result in an allocation of resources that is optimal from society's perspective. In such cases, there may be a role for government intervention to improve upon market outcomes. This chapter studies three types of market failure: public goods, externalities, and information asymmetries.

We saw in Chapter 4 that a private good is divisible and subject to the exclusion principle, whereas a public good is indivisible and not subject to exclusion. This chapter elaborates on that difference, showing how the demand for a public good is derived. Due to the free rider problem, too little will be produced unless there is direct government involvement. Using benefit-cost analysis, government can determine which public goods to provide, and what level to provide. Public goods should be supplied up to the point at which the marginal benefit equals the marginal cost of providing the good or service.

This chapter also revisits externalities, or spill-overs. An externality occurs when a benefit or cost impacts upon a third party that is external to a market transaction. When spillover costs occur, there is overproduction and overallocation of resources; when spillover benefits occur, there is underproduction and underallocation of resources. There are several solutions, depending on the circumstances. The Coase theorem suggests that individual bargaining can settle externality problems where property rights are clearly defined, the number of people involved is small, and bargaining costs are low. In other cases, lawsuits, trade in externality rights, or government intervention via direct controls, taxes, and subsidies are the best solutions. Much of the focus is on our worst externality problem – that of pollution – and how it arises from a "tragedy of the commons" situation.

The third class of market failure is asymmetric information. A market will not function efficiently if sellers in a market have critical information that is unavailable to buyers, or vice versa. For example, consumers are vulnerable to being cheated on the quantity or quality of products if sellers are dishonest and exploit their information advantage. The consequences range from opting out of markets, in the gasoline example, to outright life-threatening situations, in the surgery example. Sellers are vulnerable to being cheated by buyers in other cases. For example, sellers of insurance are subject to adverse selection and moral hazard, and workers (suppliers of labour) are vulnerable to working under unsafe conditions. Again, the consequences range from collapse of markets to risks of workplace injuries and deaths. The appropriate role for government depends on the situation, but regulation of quality and safety standards, information disclosure rules, policing of measurement standards, etc., are typical solutions.

The common message throughout this chapter is that, in many diverse circumstances, markets can fail to operate efficiently and in the best interests of society unless government plays some strategic role. That role may involve taxes or subsidies, standards, regulations, prohibitions, or the definition and enforcement of property rights so that market participants can solve problems through private contracts and agreements.

■ **CHAPTER LEARNING OBJECTIVES**

In this chapter you will learn:
☐ To distinguish between a public and private good.
☐ How to determine the optimal amount of a public good.

☐ The nature of externalities and the ways of dealing with them.
☐ About information failures.

■ CHAPTER OUTLINE

1. A public good is indivisible and not subject to exclusion — once it is provided for one person it is available for all. The market system does not allocate enough resources to the production of public goods.

(a) Individuals have an incentive to conceal their preferences for public goods, since they can be "free riders" on the benefits if someone else pays to provide the good. Thus, the market demand curve will understate the collective benefit from provision of the good.

(b) If the true demand by each individual for the public good is known, a collective demand schedule is found by adding the prices that people are willing to pay for the last unit of the public good at each possible quantity demanded. Another way of expressing this is to vertically sum the demand curves (or willingness to pay curves) for all individual consumers.

(c) The optimal production of a public good is given at the intersection of the collective demand (or marginal benefit) curve and the supply (or marginal cost) curve.

(d) If the marginal benefit exceeds the marginal cost, there is an underallocation of resources to the public good. This is likely to be the case in the absence of government intervention.

2. Government may use cost-benefit analysis to decide whether a project is worth undertaking, and if so, to what extent. Additional resources should be allocated only so long as the marginal benefit to society from using the additional resources for the project exceeds the marginal cost to society of the additional resources.

3. Market failure can arise from externalities or spillovers, where a benefit or cost accrues to some third party that is external to a market transaction.

(a) Negative externalities, such as pollution, cause external costs. Because these costs are ignored by the producer responsible for the externality, too many resources are devoted to the production activity, and there is overproduction.

(b) Positive externalities, such as inoculations against communicable diseases, cause external benefits. Because these benefits are ignored by the decision-maker responsible for the externality, too few resources are allocated to the activity, resulting in underproduction.

4. Various approaches are used to solve externality problems. Some of these solutions do not directly involve government.

(a) Individual bargaining can be used to correct externalities. The Coase theorem suggests that private bargaining can overcome the externality problem where (1) property rights are clearly defined, (2) the number of people involved in bargaining is small, and (3) costs of bargaining are negligible. For many important externalities (e.g. global warming), these conditions are not met, so this approach will not work.

(b) The legal system, which specifies liability rules and defines property rights, can also be used to adjudicate claims arising from externalities. Expense, length of time required, and uncertainty of the outcomes are deterrents to using the courts to resolve externalities.

5. When there is potential for severe harm to community interests, or when a large number of people are involved, direct government intervention may be necessary.

(a) Direct controls ban or limit the activities that produce negative externalities. The goal is to reduce the supply of an externality-creating product to the level of allocative efficiency.

(b) Specific taxes can curb activities that produce negative externalities. By increasing the cost per unit of production, taxes can decrease supply so that equilibrium output occurs at the level of allocative efficiency.

(c) When there are large spillover benefits, especially if spread over many people, direct government actions may be necessary to correct for the underallocation of resources.

(1) Government can offer subsidies to buyers to encourage consumption of a good. Such subsidies shift demand to the right.

(2) Government can offer subsidies to producers to encourage production of a good. Such subsidies shift supply to the right.

(3) When spillover benefits are extremely large, government may itself produce a good.

6. The problem known as the "tragedy of the commons" arises when a resource that we own in common is ruined or wasted because the lack of private ownership gives people an incentive to abuse or neglect this common property resource. Prime examples are pollution of air and water, and overuse of fishing grounds and parks.

7. One solution to the pollution problem is to create a market for externality rights.

(a)   Government might set a maximum permitted amount of pollution, and then allocate rights or permits based on willingness to pay.

(b)   The permitted amount of pollution would be rationed to those polluters who are willing to pay the most.

(c)   It is not economically efficient to eliminate totally a negative externality such as pollution. For society the optimal reduction occurs where the marginal cost to society and the marginal benefit of reducing the externality are equal (MB = MC).

8. Solid waste disposal is a large and growing problem that stems from the law of conservation of matter and energy: matter can be transformed to other matter or energy, but can never vanish. The high opportunity costs of land and the negative externalities created by dumps had led governments to encourage recycling. Government can use a variety of taxes or subsidies as demand or supply incentives to stimulate the market for recycled products.

9. Global warming due to excessive carbon dioxide and other gas emissions led industrially advanced nations to agree to the 1997 Kyoto Protocol to cut greenhouse gas emissions. There are still many contentious issues that threaten the successful implementation of the agreement. In any case, economists stress that even measures to fight global warming should be weighed in terms of costs and benefits to society.

10. Market failure can occur because of asymmetric information — unequal knowledge possessed by the parties to a market transaction.

(a)   When information about sellers is incomplete, inaccurate, or very costly, then there will be market failure. For example, consumers need accurate information about product quality of automobiles and assurance about the credentials of physicians. The cost would be prohibitive if each buyer had to verify the claims made by auto manufacturers and alleged physicians, so the market economy would be much less effective. Government can remedy such information fail-

ures by establishing measurement standards, testing requirements, and licensing bureaus.

(b)   Markets can also fail if sellers have inadequate information about buyers. For example, insurance providers are vulnerable to problems of moral hazard and adverse selection, and workers are vulnerable to injury and other workplace hazards because they lack information about the risks. Governments can address such problems by requiring information disclosure, by implementing regulations, and by defining standards that are legally enforced.

11. Government does not always need to interfere in the private market to address information problems. Businesses have devised strategies to overcome the lack of information. Some businesses, such as credit bureaus and consumer product testing agencies, exist specifically to profit from providing information to other businesses.

■   **TERMS AND CONCEPTS**

cost-benefit analysis	optimal reduction of
marginal cost = marginal benefit (MC = MB rule)	an externality
	law of conservation of
	matter and energy
externalities	asymmetric
Coase theorem	information
tragedy of the commons	moral hazard problem
	adverse selection
market for externality rights	problem

■   **HINTS AND TIPS**

1.   A review of Chapter 4 would be very useful because you might not have seen the concepts of externalities and public goods for quite some time.

2.   Table 18-3 is a useful summary of methods of dealing with externality problems. Note the variety of interventions available to government, including imaginative ways to harness market incentives.

3.   In your work with this chapter, give careful thought to the role of government. One lesson of the chapter is that one should not underestimate the market's ability to provide private solutions to market failures (as the Coase theorem indicates). However, another lesson is clearly that market failure problems create very important roles for government.

■ FILL-IN QUESTIONS

1. A public good is one which is _____ and which is not subject to the _____ principle. Once a public good is produced, the benefits flowing from the good cannot be confined to the purchaser and result in a _____ effect. Because benefits can be obtained if someone else purchases the good, buyers (will, will not) _____ reveal their true preferences. The market demand curve for a public good will be significantly _____.

2. If individual demand curves for a public good were known, a market demand curve could be constructed by adding the _____ people are collectively willing to pay for the last unit of the public good at each quantity demanded. The collective demand curve indicates the combined _____ for the individuals from consuming an extra unit of the public good, and is constructed as a (horizontal, vertical) _____ sum of all the individual demand curves.

3. In applying benefit-cost analysis, government should employ more resources in the public sector if the _____ from the additional public goods exceed the _____ of providing the goods.

4. Spillovers occur when benefits or costs associated with the production or consumption of a good impact on a _____ party. Spillovers are also called _____.

5. In the event of spillover benefits accompanying the production of a good, resources will be (overallocated, underallocated) _____ to the production of that good by the market economy. In the event of spillover costs, resources will be _____ to the production of that good.

6. The Coase theorem suggests that when there are externalities in situations where _____ are clearly defined, the number of people involved is _____, and bargaining costs are _____, then government intervention (is, is not) _____ required because the parties involved can _____ privately.

7. The legal system is important for settling externality disputes between parties because it specifies _____ rights and specifies _____ rules that can be used for lawsuits.

8. One method to remedy a negative externality such as pollution is to create a market for _____.

9. Eliminating all pollution (may, may not) _____ be economically desirable even if it were technologically possible as the optimal amount of externality reduction occurs where, for society, the _____ of reduction equals the _____.

10. The pollution problem stems from the law of _____ of matter and energy. Matter used for the production of goods and services ultimately gets transformed into _____, which is another form of matter or energy that the environment may not be able to _____.

11. A specific tax on a pollution-producing substance would shift its supply curve to the (left, right) _____, raise equilibrium _____, and _____ the equilibrium output.

12. Garbage dumps and incineration are becoming increasingly expensive due to the high _____ cost of landfill sites and the (positive, negative) _____ externalities created by dumps. An alternative to dumps or burning is _____. Government policies can be enacted to provide incentives on the _____ side or the _____ side of the market.

13. Government can encourage recycling by stimulating the market for recycled inputs by (subsidizing, taxing) _____ the use of recycled inputs, and _____ the use of original inputs.

14. Markets can produce information failures when information about sellers is incomplete or obtaining the information is very _____. To overcome these deficiencies, government establishes _____ for measurement or quality. In the medical market, the government protects consumers by _____ physicians.

15. Inadequate information about buyers can lead to two problems. First, if after a contract is signed, a buyer alters her or his behaviour in a way that is costly to the seller, then a _____ problem has arisen. Second, if buyers withhold information from sellers that would impose a large cost on sellers, then an _____ problem has been created. The first problem occurs (at the time, after) _____ a person signs a contract, but the second problem occurs _____ the person signs a contract.

16. The _____ problem eliminates the pooling of high and low risk, which is the basis for profitable _____. Governments overcome this problem by requiring _____ participation in social insurance schemes.

17. Another example of information failure occurs in labour markets where there is incomplete or inadequate information about workplace _____. The government will intervene in these situations to publish _____ or to enforce _____.

■ **PROBLEMS AND PROJECTS**

1. Given below are schedules of three individuals' willingness to pay for mosquito control (a public good). Assume these three people are the only ones in society.
(a) Fill in the collective willingness to pay schedule in column (5).
(b) Given the marginal cost schedule (6), would any of the individuals buy any mosquito control on their own? _____
(c) The optimal quantity of mosquito control is _____.
(d) The total net gain to this society is $_____ if the optimal quantity of mosquito control is undertaken.

(1) Quantity	(2) Pa	(3) Pb	(4) Pc	(5) Price	(6) MC
1	$15	$8	$10	$___	$16
2	12	7	8	___	18
3	8	6	6	___	20
4	6	5	4	___	22
5	5	4	3	___	24
6	4	3	2	___	26

2. Imagine that the city of Moose Jaw is considering the construction of a new arena for its Junior A hockey team. The city's estimate of the total costs and the total benefits of arenas with various different seating capacities are shown below. (All figures are in millions of dollars.)

Seats	Total Cost	MC	Total Benefit	MB	Total Net Benefit
No arena	$0	- -	$0	- -	$0
3000	12	$___	20	$___	___
4000	15	___	26	___	___
5000	17	___	29	___	___
6000	20	___	31	___	___

(a) Fill in the marginal cost, marginal benefit, and total net benefit of 3000, 4000, 5000, and 6000 seat arenas.
(b) Will it benefit the city to allocate resources to construct an arena? _____
(c) If Moose Jaw builds an arena:
  (1) it should be the _____ seat version
  (2) the total cost will be $_____
  (3) the total benefit will be $_____
  (4) the net benefit to the city will be $_____.

3. Assume the atmosphere of Metropolitan Toronto is unable to reabsorb more than 1,500 tonnes of pollutants per year. The following schedule shows the price polluters would be willing to pay for the right to dispose of pollutants, and the total quantity of pollutants they would wish to dispose of annually at each price.

Price (per tonne of pollution rights)	Total Quantity of Pollution Rights Demanded (tonnes)
$ 0	4,000
1,000	3,500
2,000	3,000
3,000	2,500
4,000	2,000
5,000	1,500
6,000	1,000
7,000	500

(a) If there were no emission fee, polluters would put _____ tonnes of pollutants in the air each year; this quantity of pollutants would exceed the ability of nature to reabsorb them by _____ tonnes.
(b) To reduce pollution to the capacity of the atmosphere to recycle pollutants, an emission fee of $_____ per tonne should be set.
(c) Were this emission fee set, the total emission fees collected would be $_____.

(d) Were the quantity of pollution rights demanded at each price to increase by 500 tonnes, the emission fee could be increased by $_____ and total emission fees collected would increase by $_____.

4. The marginal cost of pollution abatement differs between two industrial firms. The data for the Acrid Acid Co. and the Smoky Smelter Ltd. are shown below:

Acrid Acid		Smoky Smelter	
Unit of Abatement	MC	Unit of Abatement	MC
1	$1	1	$1
2	3	2	2
3	7	3	3
4	12	4	4
5	18	5	5
6	25	6	6

(a) The second unit of pollution abatement by Acrid would cost it $_____.
(b) The third unit of pollution abatement by Smoky would cost it $_____.
Suppose the government decides to reduce pollution by 6 units and demands a 3-unit reduction by both firms:
(c) the total cost to Acrid will be $_____,
(d) the total cost to Smoky will be $_____,
(e) the total cost of the 6-unit reduction will be $_____.
Instead of the above division, suppose that Acrid was required to reduce pollution by 2 units and Smoky by 4 units:
(f) the total cost to Acrid will be $_____
(g) the total cost to Smoky will be $_____.
(h) the total cost of the 6-unit reduction will be $_____. By requiring equal reductions by both firms, the cost of pollution reduction (will, will not) _____ be minimized.
Suppose the government, instead of demanding a 6-unit reduction in pollution, placed a tax of $3.50 on each unit of pollution:
(i) Acrid would reduce pollution by _____ units.
(j) Smoky would reduce pollution by _____ units.
(k) With the tax each firm (will, will not) _____ reduce pollution by the same amount. The firm with the highest marginal cost of pollution abatement will reduce pollution the

(most, least) _____, and this (is, is not) _____ socially efficient.

5. In question 4, suppose each firm was causing 6 units of pollution and the government wanted to reduce pollution to a total of 6 units by issuing 3 transferable pollution rights to each firm.
(a) Without trading, Acrid must abate pollution by _____ units. If it obtained one more pollution right, it would have to abate pollution by _____ units and would save $_____. If Acrid could get a pollution right for less than $_____, it would (increase, decrease) _____ net income.
(b) Without trading, Smoky must abate pollution by _____ units. By giving up one of its pollution rights, Smoky will have to abate pollution by _____ units at an extra cost of $_____. If Smoky could get more than $_____ for a pollution right, it would (increase, decrease) _____ its net income.
(c) Both firms would benefit if the pollution unit sold for more than $_____ but less than $_____.
(d) Explain why only one pollution right would be exchanged between the two profit-maximizing firms.

6. Singh has a tree that blocks Cohen's view of English Bay. The only way to clear the view is to fall the tree.
(a) What would the Coase theorem suggest as a way to determine whether the tree should be cut down or not? Does the Coase theorem seem applicable in this case?
(b) Why would the Coase theorem be less useful if Singh's tree obstructs the angle of view for 10 or 15 different houses in the neighbourhood?

7. The graph below shows the demand for glue (D), the glue producers' supply curve (S), and the full-cost curve (St) that includes external cost to neighbours who suffer the smell from the factory.
(a) If glue producers ignore the external costs of their operations, the output of glue will be _____ and the market price will be $_____.
(b) However, this equilibrium represents an (underallocation, overallocation) _____ of resources to glue, because the optimal output is _____.
(c) Use the graph to show that if producers were taxed $2 per unit of glue, their supply curve would shift and the initial misallocation of resources would be corrected.

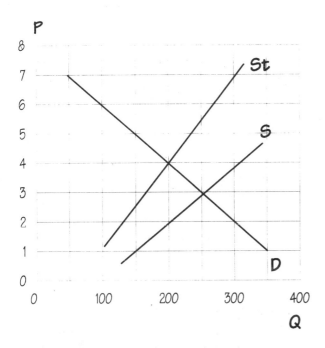

8. The next graph shows a situation of an externality, with the full-benefit demand curve represented by Dt.

   (a)   What type of externality is illustrated here?

   (b)   Will the market tend to overallocate or underallocate resources to production of this good?

   (c)   What policy would solve this misallocation?

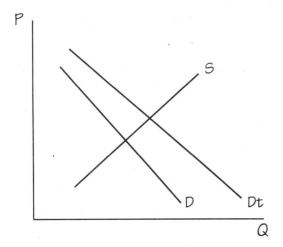

■ TRUE-FALSE

Circle T if the statement is true, F if it is false.

1. For public goods the free-rider problem occurs when people can receive benefits without contributing to the cost of providing the good. **T F**

2. When determining the demand for a public good, we add the prices various individuals are willing to pay for the last unit at each quantity demanded. **T F**

3. Benefit-cost analysis is a method of evaluating public projects by comparing the marginal benefits and marginal costs attributed to the project. **T F**

4. When spillover costs exist, private costs do not fully reflect all the costs flowing from the transaction. **T F**

5. In private markets, resources are overallocated to the production of goods that confer spillover benefits. **T F**

6. A tax could be used to correct the misallocation of resources that results when spillover benefits are present. **T F**

7. The Coase theorem states that as long as private property rights exist, the market system will correct for the presence of externalities without government interference. **T F**

8. The optimal amount of pollution abatement occurs when the marginal benefit from further pollution reduction is zero. **T F**

9. The market system penalizes the socially conscious firm in comparison to its polluting competitors. **T F**

10. Taxes imposed on products that create pollution will lower the marginal cost of production and increase supply. **T F**

11. The "tragedy of the commons" results from an incentive problem when private property rights do not exist. **T F**

12. When governments allow pollution rights to be bought and sold, the governments have created a form of property. **T F**

13. In the market for pollution rights, if a government sets a fixed level for pollution, the supply curve of pollution rights will be perfectly elastic.   **T F**

14. The economically efficient level of pollution is zero, so the government is pursuing an inefficient solution when it issues pollution rights.   **T F**

15. If the government mandates that newspapers must be made of at least 50% recycled paper, the demand for used newsprint will shift to the left. **T F**

16. If the government mandates that newsprint must be made up of 50% recycled products, the price of a newspaper would rise, other things being equal.   **T F**

17. Quality inspection of meat products by the government may be justified on the grounds that it reduces the costs of obtaining information in the marketplace.   **T F**

18. If the provision of deposit insurance encourages banks to invest in more risky business ventures, then it has created a moral hazard.   **T F**

■ **MULTIPLE-CHOICE**

Circle the letter that corresponds to the best answer.

1. A spillover cost exists when:
  (a)   a part of the cost of a transaction is placed on an uninvolved third party
  (b)   a part of the cost of a transaction is paid for by the government
  (c)   the private and social costs of production are equal
  (d)   marginal cost is greater than average cost

2. If external benefits accompany the production of a good:
  (a)   resources will be overallocated to the production of the good
  (b)   resources will be underallocated to the production of the good
  (c)   a tax on the production of the good will result in the optimum production of the good
  (d)   the market demand curve for the good overstates the total benefit flowing from the consumption of the good

3. The government could promote the optimal output when the production of a good causes spillover costs by:
  (a)   banning production of the good
  (b)   taxing the production of the good
  (c)   subsidizing consumers of the good
  (d)   subsidizing producers of the good

4. According to the Coase theorem:
  (a)   government intervention is required to overcome the misallocation of resources when spillovers are present
  (b)   the best way to remedy negative externalities is to create pollution rights
  (c)   public goods should be financed by the government with tax revenue generated by a progressive tax
  (d)   negative externalities can be solved through bargaining — as long as one party to the dispute has clearly defined property rights, affected parties are few, and bargaining costs are small.

5. An emission fee levied against polluters will:
  (a)   encourage the use of pollution-abatement equipment
  (b)   eliminate pollution
  (c)   reduce the revenues of governments that levy the fee
  (d)   externalize the internal costs of pollution

6. An increase in the demand for a fixed quantity of pollution rights will:
  (a)   increase both the quantity of pollutants discharged and the market price of pollution rights
  (b)   increase the quantity discharged and have no effect on the market price
  (c)   have no effect on the quantity discharged and increase the market price
  (d)   have no effect on either the quantity discharged or the market price

7. User charges imposed on those who drive on urban expressways would tend to:
  (a)   relieve congestion on the expressways
  (b)   discourage the use of public transportation facilities

  (c)   reduce the funds available for the expansion of the expressway system
  (d)   do all of the above

8. Public goods differ from private goods in that public goods are:
   (a) divisible
   (b) subject to the exclusion principle
   (c) not subject to the free-rider problem
   (d) not divisible and not subject to exclusion

Answer the next four questions on the basis of the following information for a public good. Q_{d1} and Q_{d2} represent the quantities of the public good demanded at each price by individuals 1 and 2, the only two people in society. Q_S represents society's supply curve for the public good.

Price	$Q_{d\ 1}$	$Q_{d\ 2}$	Q_S
$7	0	0	6
6	0	1	5
5	1	2	4
4	2	3	3
3	3	4	2
2	4	5	1
1	5	6	0

9. This society is willing to pay what amount for the third unit of the public good?
   (a) $7
   (b) $6
   (c) $5
   (d) $4

10. Given the supply Q_S, the optimal price and quantity of the public good in this society will be:
   (a) $7 and 5 units
   (b) $5 and 4 units
   (c) $4 and 3 units
   (d) $3 and 2 units

11. If this good were a private good instead of a public good, the total quantity demanded at the $2 price would be:
   (a) 9 units
   (b) 8 units
   (c) 7 units
   (d) 6 units

12. The "tragedy of the commons" applies to what situation?
   (a) where individuals overuse and abuse common resources
   (b) where individuals tend to "free ride" on public goods

(c) where the harm from externalities tends to affect common people rather than wealthy people
   (d) none of the above

13. The Kyoto Protocol dealt with what problem?
   (a) global warming
   (b) oil spills
   (c) endangered species
   (d) nuclear power

14. The ultimate cause of pollution is:
   (a) profit-seeking in the market economy
   (b) the law of conservation of matter and energy
   (c) rising incomes
   (d) the greenhouse effect

15. The optimal amount of pollution control occurs where:
   (a) pollution is eliminated
   (b) the marginal benefit from pollution control equals zero
   (c) the marginal benefit from pollution control is maximized
   (d) the marginal benefit from pollution control equals the marginal cost of the controls

16. If the government places a $40 tax on each unit of pollution produced by a firm, all of the following hold with the exception of:
   (a) the firm saves $40 for each unit of pollution it eliminates
   (b) the tax creates an incentive to reduce the amount of pollution produced
   (c) the firm will eliminate pollution completely if the cost of eliminating the last unit is less than $40
   (d) the profits of the firm will decrease

17. The result of government legislation requiring newsprint producers to use a more costly production technique to reduce pollution will be:
   (a) an increase in production and the price of newsprint
   (b) a reduction in production and the price of newsprint
   (c) increased employment in the industries supplying inputs for newsprint
   (d) a reduction in production and an increase in the price of newsprint

18. Which of the following would tend to increase the demand for recycled glass?
   (a) an increase in the price of new glass
   (b) an increase in taxes on glass production

(c) a decrease in interest in protecting the environment

(d) a decrease in the price of raw materials used in the production of new glass

19. In order to encourage recycling instead of the use of landfill sites, government could do all of the following except:

(a) place specific taxes on the inputs substitutable for the recycled input

(b) legislate the use of recycled inputs in the production process

(c) subsidize garbage pickup

(d) shift its purchases toward goods produced with recycled inputs

20. In insurance, the moral hazard problem arises because:

(a) people tend to be untruthful when asked about their medical history

(b) large insurance payouts may prompt some people to act in an immoral manner

(c) people who have insurance coverage tend to alter their behaviour in a way that is costly to the seller of insurance

(d) of the random nature of accidents

21. The inclusion of a deductible clause (for example, the insured must pay for the first $250 of an accident claim) will:

(a) decrease the problems arising out of adverse selection

(b) decrease the moral hazard problem

(c) increase insurance premiums

(d) none of the above

22. If the government mandates that deposit insurance on deposits at financial institutions be increased to $240,000 for each depositor, this action would create a moral hazard problem because it may:

(a) lead to careful screening of depositors and the source of their funds

(b) reduce the amount of deposits made by customers

(c) encourage the making of riskier loans

(d) reduce bank investments in real estate

23. Franchising is at least a partial solution to the problem of:

(a) asymmetric information problems faced by consumers

(b) asymmetric information problems faced by producers

(c) free rider problems

(d) the tragedy of the commons

■ DISCUSSION QUESTIONS

1. What is "market failure" and what are the three major kinds of such failures?

2. What basic method does government employ in Canada to reallocate resources away from the production of private goods and toward the production of public goods?

3. Describe cost-benefit analysis and state the rules used to make a decision from a marginal and total perspective.

4. What rules can society use to determine the optimal level of pollution abatement? What are the problems with this approach?

5. Explain the "tragedy of the commons" and how this problem relates to property rights. How does the depletion of the stock of Pacific salmon or Atlantic cod relate to property rights?

6. Suppose the Canadian government decided to issue pollution rights and asked your advice on the following. What would be your advice?

(a) What volume of pollution rights should be created? Why shouldn't all pollution be eliminated?

(b) How should the pollution rights be distributed among firms and/or individuals?

(c) Should rights, once created, be purchased and sold on a "pollution rights market"?

7. The government can control pollution directly by setting pollution standards or indirectly by taxing pollution. List the advantages and problems with both methods.

8. From an economic perspective, what do the problems of global warming and your roommate's annoying music when you are studying have in common? What similarities and differences are there in the types of solutions that might work?

9. Explain what is meant by the "moral hazard problem" and describe how it affects sellers. Should an insurance company be allowed to refuse insurance to a driver with numerous accident claims on his/her record? Before you answer, remember there is an externality involved (insurance not only protects the insured but also other members of the travelling public).

10. How does workplace safety become an informational problem? How might this problem be resolved by government or business?

11. From a social perspective, why is the Lojack car retrieval system better than most car alarm systems (e.g., those with blinking red lights)?

■ ANSWERS

FILL-IN QUESTIONS

1. indivisible, exclusion, free rider, will not, understated

2. prices, utilities, vertical

3. benefits, costs

4. third, externalities

5. underallocated, overallocated

6. property rights, small, negligible, is not, bargain

7. property, liability

8. externality rights

9. may not, marginal benefit, marginal cost

10. conservation, waste, recycle (absorb)

11. left, price, decrease

12. opportunity, negative, recycling, demand, supply

13. subsidizing, taxing

14. expensive, standards, licensing

15. moral hazard, adverse selection, after, at the time

16. adverse selection, insurance, universal

17. safety, information, standards

PROBLEMS AND PROJECTS

1. (a) $33, 27, 20, 15, 12, 9; (b) no, MB > MC for every individual; (c) 3, where total MB = MC; (d) (33+27+20)-(16+18+20) = 26.

2. (a) MC: $12, 3, 2, 3; MB: $20, 6, 3, 2; (b) Yes; (c) (1) 5000, (2) $17 million, (3) $29 million, (4) $12 million.

3. (a) 4,000, 2,500; (b) 5,000; (c) 7,500,000; (d) 1,000, 1,500,000

4. (a) $3; (b) $3; (c) $11; (d) $6; (e) $17; (f) $4, (g) $10; (h) $14; will not; (i) 2; (j) 3; (k) will not; least, is.

5. (a) 3, 2, $7; $7, increase (b) 3, 4, $4; $4, increase (c) $4, $7 (d) For the next pollution right Smoky would have to charge at least $5 to cover the opportunity cost, whereas Acrid would only be willing to pay $3, so the trade is not mutually beneficial.

6. (a) bargaining between the individuals; if property rights are specified, then yes, since numbers are few and transactions costs seem to be low; (b) the increased numbers raise transactions costs

7. (a) 250, 3; (b) overallocation, 200; (c) the S curve will shift upwards by 2, parallel to its initial position

8. (a) beneficial spillover: (b) underallocate; (c) give a subsidy to producers or consumers of the activity, or have government provide the good directly

TRUE-FALSE

1. T
2. T
3. T
4. T
5. F   underallocated
6. F   a subsidy for producers or consumers
7. F   there are two other conditions: small number of parties affected, and negligible bargaining costs
8. F   where marginal benefit of further abatement equals marginal cost
9. T   this firm will incur extra costs, and lower profits, in an attempt to deal with pollution
10. F   increase marginal cost and reduce supply
11. T   people selfishly exploit the resource and have no incentive to conserve or maintain it
12. T   the pollution rights are valuable, transferable assets
13. F   perfectly inelastic
14. F   efficient level is where MB = MC for abatement; this is probably not where pollution is zero
15. F   demand for recycled newsprint would be increased

16. T   if newspaper producers are forced to produce papers in a different way from normal, it will raise their costs

17. T   consumers are less well informed about meat quality than suppliers are

18. T   the existence of the insurance causes them to behave in a way that places greater risk on the insurer

MULTIPLE-CHOICE

1.   (a)
2.   (b)
3.   (b) the output should be reduced; not to zero, but to the point where society's MC = MB
4.   (d)
5.   (a) to the extent that abatement is cheaper than paying the emission fee
6.   (c) the total amount that can be discharged is fixed
7.   (a) less cars would use these expressways
8.   (d) therefore, they can be consumed by everybody once they are produced
9.   (a) 4+3
10. (b) MB for the 4th unit = 2+3 = 5; this is also price at which Qs = 4
11. (a)
12. (a)
13. (a)
14. (b) production and consumption activities inevitably lead to waste products
15. (d)
16. (a) the firm saves $40 less the MC of pollution abatement
17. (d) the firm's MC will shift upward
18. (a) new and recycled glass are substitutes
19. (c) subsidizing garbage pickup would increase the amount of waste going to landfill sites
20. (c) once insured against a loss the person may take chances that raise the risk of that loss occurring
21. (b) with a deductible there is still some incentive for the insured party to take care to prevent a loss
22. (c) banks would be able to risk lending money to riskier borrowers knowing that depositors now have more insurance protection in case the bank can't meet its obligations
23. (a) franchises provide consumers with a predictable, standardized product, even in unfamiliar cities

CHAPTER 19

Public Choice Theory and the Economics of Taxation

Chapter 18 discussed problems of market failure and made the case for government intervention to correct the misallocation of resources resulting from market failure. Chapter 19 takes the opposite perspective, examining instances of government failure or inefficiency. The explanation is based on public choice theory, which is the economic analysis of public decision-making. The second half of the chapter is on public finance, which deals with the principles of taxation and the effects of particular kinds of taxes. The chapter ends with a look at recent Canadian tax reforms, and a comparison of conservative and liberal views on government and economic freedoms.

Government decision-making in Canada depends on a democratic process that relies heavily on a majority-voting rule. While democracy is probably the best system, a majority-voting rule can produce inefficient or inconsistent results. Sometimes the benefits from public goods are greater than the costs, but the majority vote against them; alternately, sometimes the costs are greater than the benefits, yet the majority vote in favour of providing the good. The reason is that majority voting does not reflect the intensity of individual preferences. Action by interest groups and political logrolling can overcome the inefficiencies of majority voting, but these tactics themselves often create inefficient outcomes.

The paradox of voting shows that, depending upon how the election is structured, majority voting can produce results inconsistent with the ranking of preferences by society. The median voter model predicts that in a system of majority voting the person holding the middle position strongly determines the result of a vote because this person holds the "swing vote" that will decide the majority.

There are several reasons for the failure of the public sector: (1) the special-interest effect and rent-seeking behaviour result in decisions and programs that are not in the interest of society as a whole; (2) politicians opt for programs that provide clear-cut benefits and hidden costs; (3) public choices are limited and inflexible because they tend to entail voting on "bundles" of programs; and (4) bureaucratic inefficiencies in the public sector arise from a lack of the economic incentives and competitive pressures found in most private sector industries.

A basic issue in public finance is how the burden of taxes is apportioned among members of society. Taxes can be levied based on the benefits-received principle or the ability-to-pay principle. The relationship between tax burden and taxpayer incomes is also important, and we see that some taxes are progressive, whereas others are regressive.

Using the supply and demand model, we can see that those on whom taxes are levied do not necessarily pay the tax, or at least not all of it. The incidence of an excise tax for buyers and sellers depends on the elasticity of demand and supply. The model also demonstrates how a tax creates an efficiency loss for society by reducing the production of a good that is taxed.

Canada's tax system has periodically undergone significant reforms. In 1987 the income tax structure was simplified and marginal tax rates reduced. Taxes were lowered again in 2000, and the income tax system was fully indexed to inflation. The replacement of the federal sales tax on manufactured goods with the GST was another significant change in recent years. These tax changes (as well as some by provincial governments) are motivated by the desire to improve the efficiency of the Canadian economy and keep it competitive with other jurisdictions.

No discussion of taxes and government in the economy would be complete without some consideration of the effect of government on the freedoms of individuals. Conservatives argue that expanded governmental activity reduces personal freedom, whereas liberals argue that government expands our choices and makes our freedoms more effective.

■ CHAPTER LEARNING OBJECTIVES

In this chapter you will learn:
□ That majority voting can produce inefficient voting outcomes.
□ Why public sector failure occurs.
□ The connection between elasticity and tax incidence.
□ About the efficiency cost of taxes.
□ About the Canadian tax system.

■ CHAPTER OUTLINE

1. Market failure often calls for government intervention to correct inefficiency in the allocation of resources in the private sector. However, there are also problems with efficiency and effectiveness of resource allocation decisions made in the public sector. In other words, government itself is subject to failure. This chapter begins by analyzing government decision making from a public choice perspective.

2. Majority voting can result in inefficient decisions.
   (a) Following the majority can result in accepting projects for which total costs outweigh the benefits, or rejecting projects for which benefits outweigh the costs. The problem is the voting mechanism – in contrast to a market mechanism – does not incorporate the strength of individual preferences.
   (b) Interest groups and political logrolling can offset some inefficiencies of majority voting, but there is no certainty of such an outcome.
   (c) The paradox of voting shows that situations can arise in which the public may not be able to rank its preferences consistently through pairwise choices put to a majority vote.
   (d) The median voter (or person holds the middle position on an issue) can determine the out-

come of the election. Public decisions reflect the median view.

3. The theory of public choice suggests that government failure stems from flawed incentives and decision-making processes. A government that makes decisions to maximize its chances of remaining in office will often make decisions that lead to an inefficient allocation of resources.
   (a) Public sector decision makers are subject to pressure from special-interest groups. The power of the government to create and allocate property rights encourages rent-seeking behaviour. Since benefits are often concentrated and costs are widely diffused and not easily identified, politicians tend to support programs demanded by special-interest groups, even though the programs' costs may exceed their benefits to society.
   (b) Politicians tend to favour programs with clear and immediate benefits and vague costs that can be deferred.
   (c) The political process forces voters to choose among limited and bundled choices. When the voters support one party they are accepting a whole set of programs, perhaps including some that have low priority for the voters.
   (d) Public sector employees do not usually face the same competitive pressures to perform that prevail in the market sector. The criteria used to measure success are not easily identified for the public sector.
   (e) The relevant comparison is not between a perfect market and a flawed government sector, or flawed market and perfect government. The realistic comparison is between inevitably imperfect market and government institutions.

4. The need to finance public programs raises questions about how to distribute the tax burden.
   (a) Taxes can be apportioned based on two alternative principles, both of which are subject to difficulties of measurement:
      (1) the benefits-received principle, which holds that beneficiaries of a public program should bear the cost;
      (2) the ability-to-pay principle, which holds that public programs should be financed in direct relation to one's income and wealth.
   (b) Taxes are classified as progressive, proportional, or regressive according to whether the average tax rate increases, stays the same, or decreases as income increases.

(c)   Canada's personal income tax is reasonably progressive, sales taxes and property taxes are regressive, and the corporate tax nominally proportional (with this tax becoming regressive if the tax is passed onto consumers).

5. The incidence of a tax refers to who ultimately pays the tax. A tax could be levied on one party, but then shifted onto someone else. Price elasticities of demand and supply determine the incidence of a sales or an excise tax. An excise tax shifts the supply curve upward by the amount of the tax and increases the price of the product. The price increase is generally less than the tax and indicates the portion of the tax paid by the buyer; the seller pays the rest.

(a) Given supply, the more elastic the demand for the commodity, the greater the portion of the tax borne by the seller.

(b) Given demand, the more inelastic the supply, the greater the portion of the tax borne by the seller.

6. A sales or excise tax causes an efficiency loss because the tax pushes output and consumption below the optimal level reached in a competitive market. The greater the elasticities of demand and supply, the greater is the efficiency loss. Thus society's total tax burden may differ, even though two different taxes bring in the same amount of revenue. Against the efficiency loss we should weigh other benefits of taxes (e.g. improved income redistribution, reduction of negative externalities).

7. The incidence of taxes in Canada depends on the type of tax:

(a) Personal income taxes are borne almost exclusively by the individuals being taxed.

(b) Corporate income taxes are borne mostly by the shareholders in the form of lower dividend payments, but firms with sufficient market power may be able to pass some of the tax on (in higher prices to consumers, or lower prices to resource suppliers).

(c) A sales tax such as the GST (levied on a wide range of consumer goods) will be borne mostly by consumers in higher product prices.

(d) An excise tax, levied on a particular product, is more likely to be borne only partly by the consumer because the consumer can shift spending to other goods instead.

(e) Property taxes are generally borne by the property owner, except in the case of rented and business property where some of the burden can be shifted to tenants or business customers.

8. Since 1987, Canada has undergone some major tax reforms.

(a) In 1987 the income tax system was revamped to reduce the number of different marginal tax rates, to reduce the highest marginal tax rate, and to change the tax treatment of some transfer payments.

(b) In 1991 the Goods and Services Tax (GST) replaced the federal sales tax (which applied mostly to manufactured goods). The GST is levied on the difference between the value of a firm's sales and the value of its purchases from other firms (making it a type of value-added tax).

(c) In 2000 income taxes were cut significantly through a combination of measures including: full indexation to inflation, low marginal tax rate on the middle income bracket, lower tax rate on small business profits, and reduction of the capital gains tax.

(d) Tax reforms are driven by the government's goals and constraints. Recent elimination of the budget deficit has made tax cuts possible. It is hoped that tax cuts will improve the business and investment climate and improve our productivity. This would help our incomes to keep pace with incomes in the U.S., and possibly to stem the brain drain.

9. Many people believe that the nature and amount of government activity and the extent of individual freedom are related.

(a)   Many conservative economists warn of the concentration of power that comes with large government, as well as losses of economic freedom and choice for individuals.

(b)   Liberal economists counter that the conservative position is subject to the fallacy of limited decisions. That is, appropriate government activity does not narrow the range of choices; instead, it expands the amount of effective freedom and choice for society by solving other market failure problems.

■ TERMS AND CONCEPTS

public choice theory	**progressive tax**
logrolling	**regressive tax**
paradox of voting	**proportional tax**

median-voter model
government failure
special-interest effect
rent-seeking behaviour
benefits-received prin-
  ciple
ability-to-pay principle

tax incidence
efficiency loss of a tax
Goods and Services
  Tax (GST)
value-added tax (VAT)
fallacy of limited deci-
  sions

■ HINTS AND TIPS

1. See if you can apply the ideas from the first part of the chapter, dealing with political decision making, to political behaviour in Canada. The median-voter model, logrolling, the influence of special-interest groups, rent-seeking behaviour, and limited and bundled choices are important concepts. Real world examples abound.

2. The technical part of the chapter is the portion dealing with tax incidence. If elasticity is not fresh in your mind, review Chapter 6.

■ FILL-IN QUESTIONS

1. Many public decisions are made on the basis of majority voting, but

(a) this procedure can produce outcomes that are _____, because projects can be accepted when public benefits are (greater than, less than) _____ total cost, or projects defeated where total benefits are _____ than total costs.

(1) The inefficiencies of majority voting may be offset by political pressure exerted by _____ groups or by political _____.

(2) Majority voting can lead to inefficient outcomes because it fails to incorporate the strength of _____ of the individual voters.

(b) Another difficulty that can result from majority voting is an _____ ranking of preferences and is called the _____ of _____.

(c) Under a majority voting rule the _____ voter is likely to determine the outcome of a vote.

2. Several possible reasons for public sector failure are that:

(a) political considerations may lead to the support of projects that maximize the probability of getting _____.

(b) government, instead of promoting the general interests (or welfare) of its citizens, may promote the _____ interests of small groups in the economy;

(c) the benefits from a program or project are often (clear, hidden) _____ while its costs are frequently _____;

(d) individual voters are unable to _____ the particular quantities of each public good and service they wish the public sector to provide;

(e) there are weak _____ to be efficient in the public sector and no way to _____ the efficiency of the public sector.

3. The two basic philosophies on apportioning the tax burden are: the _____ principle and the _____ principle.

4. With a progressive tax, the tax rate _____ as income increases; the tax rate decreases with increasing income for a _____ tax; and with a proportional tax the _____ stays the same as income increases.

5. In Canada the personal income tax is (regressive, progressive) _____, while property tax and corporate income tax are _____.

6. When a sales tax is levied on a commodity, the amount of the tax borne by the buyers of the commodity is equal to the amount the _____ of the commodity rises as a result of the tax. The incidence of the tax depends upon the price _____ of _____ and _____.

(a) The buyer's portion of the tax is larger the (more, less) _____ elastic the demand and the _____ elastic the supply.

(b) The seller's portion of the tax is larger, the _____ elastic the demand and the _____ elastic the supply.

7. When a tax reduces consumption and production below that achieved in a free market there exists an _____ loss. Other things being equal, the greater the _____ of supply and demand the greater this loss.

8. The Goods and Services Tax (GST) is a type of _____-added tax. The tax rate is applied to the _____ between the value of a firm's sales and the value of its _____ from other firms.

■ PROBLEMS AND PROJECTS

1. Preferences are consistent if when Project A is preferred to Project B and Project B is preferred to Project C, then Project A is preferred to Project C. The tables below illustrate two cases where the preferences of the individual voters are consistent, but majority voting on pairs of alternatives yields consistent choices in one case and inconsistent choices in the other.

Case 1	Preference Rankings		
Public Project	Voter A	Voter B	Voter C
Park	1	3	3
School	2	2	1
Dam	3	1	2

In an election determined by majority vote, which project would win each of the following contests?
School vs. Dam _____
Dam vs. Park _____
School vs. Park _____

Case 2	Preference Rankings		
Public Project	Voter A	Voter B	Voter C
Park	1	2	3
School	2	3	1
Dam	3	1	2

In an election determined by majority vote, which project would win each of the following contests?
School vs. Dam _____
Dam vs. Park _____
School vs. Park _____

Majority voting has led to inconsistent public preferences in Case _____.

2. In the table below are five levels of income and the amount of tax to be paid under two different tax systems: A and B.
   (a) Compute for each tax system the average rate of taxation at each income level.
   (b) Tax A is (regressive, progressive, proportional) _____ up to income level $_____ and then becomes _____. Tax B is consistently _____.

Income	Tax A		Tax B	
	Tax Paid	Average Tax Rate	Tax Paid	Average Tax Rate
$1500	$150	_____%	$300	_____%
3000	300	_____	390	_____
5000	500	_____	600	_____
7500	750	_____	825	_____
10,000	2,000	_____	1,000	_____

3. Three small towns stand to benefit from the construction of a shared regional airport in a central location. The costs of the airport would be $60 million per year, shared equally by the three towns. Whether or not the airport is built depends on the votes cast at the regional district meeting. Each town has one vote, which it will cast simply based on whether the airport produces enough benefit for their town to cover the cost.

	Benefits (million $ per year)		
Case	Ellis	Nevin	Selby
1	17	22	27
2	8	22	27
3	17	19	27

(a) In which case(s) would the majority voting rule lead to an outcome that is efficient for the region?
(b) In which case(s) would the majority voting rule lead to an inefficient outcome, and why?

4. The graph below shows the wine market before and after the imposition of a new production tax.
   (a) Which of the two supply curves is the "before tax" supply curve? _____
   (b) Before the tax, the price of wine was $_____ per bottle and the quantity produced was _____ bottles per week.
   (c) The amount of the tax is $_____ per bottle.
   (d) After the tax, the price of wine becomes $_____ per bottle and the quantity produced becomes _____ bottles per week.
   (e) The government's tax revenue is $_____ per bottle times _____ bottles per week, for a total of $_____ per week.
   (f) On the graph, shade in the area of tax revenue.
   (g) Of the total tax per bottle, the consumers' burden is $_____, and the producers' burden is $_____. The consumers bear a (larger, smaller) _____ share relative to the producers because the demand curve is relatively

_____ and the supply curve is relatively _____.

(h) On the graph shade in the area of efficiency loss due to the tax.

Price ($/bottle)

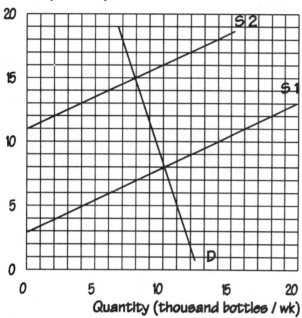

Quantity (thousand bottles / wk)

■ TRUE-FALSE

Circle T if the statement is true, F if it is false.

1. Certain characteristics of the public sector hinder the government's efforts to achieve an efficient allocation of resources.   **T F**

2. Since majority voting reveals the demand of the electorate, choices based on majority voting consistently lead to efficient use of society's resources.   **T F**

3. Logrolling and pressure by interest groups always diminish economic efficiency in government.   **T F**

4. The paradox of voting refers to the idea that, in a majority rule election, the median voter will likely determine the outcome.   **T F**

5. Even though the market economy may not always result in an efficient allocation, it does not follow that the political process will necessarily yield superior results.   **T F**

6. According to the median-voter model, people will have an incentive to move to political jurisdictions where the median voter's preferences are similar to their own.   **T F**

7. Rent-seeking behaviour occurs when one group seeks the transfer of wealth from others with the assistance of the government.   **T F**

8. When the costs of a program are hidden and the benefits are clear, vote-seeking politicians tend to reject an economically justifiable program.   **T F**

9. The limited-choice, bundled-goods problem refers to the inability of individual voters to select the precise bundle of public goods and services that best satisfies the citizen's wants.   **T F**

10. The benefits-received principle states that governments should spend tax receipts so that the benefits for society are maximized.   **T F**

11. According to the ability-to-pay principle, people should be taxed according to their income or wealth.   **T F**

12. A tax is progressive if the marginal tax rate increases as income increases.   **T F**

13. For a tax to be regressive, the amount paid in taxes represents a smaller percentage of income as income increases.   **T F**

14. One problem with applying the benefits-received principle is that it is difficult to determine the benefits that households receive.   **T F**

15. If the supply of a good is completely inelastic, a sales tax will be borne entirely by consumers. **T F**

16. An excise tax causes an efficiency loss because the equilibrium quantity is reduced from the competitive market equilibrium quantity.   **T F**

17. A firm with monopoly power can shift the burden of its corporate income tax to its consumers and resource suppliers.   **T F**

18. An excise tax is a general sales tax applied to a wide range of consumer goods and services. **T F**

19. Conservative economists agree that an expansion of government's role in the economy would reduce personal freedoms.　　　　**T　F**

20. The purpose of indexation of the income tax system is to protect the government from loss of tax revenue if interest rates fall.　　　　**T　F**

21. A flat tax system has a single marginal rate of tax.　　　　**T　F**

■ **MULTIPLE-CHOICE**

Circle the letter that corresponds to the best answer.

1. Deficiencies in the processes used to make collective decisions and economic inefficiencies caused by government are the primary focus of:
- **(a)** public finance
- **(b)** public choice theory
- **(c)** the study of tax incidence
- **(d)** the study of tax shifting

2. Majority voting may produce inefficient economic outcomes because:
- **(a)** of poor voter turnout
- **(b)** different voters have different preferences about the proposals they are voting on
- **(c)** majority voting fails to incorporate the intensity of preferences of individuals
- **(d)** politicians do not keep election promises

3. Suppose that MPs from British Columbia agree to vote for a bill providing crop insurance for Prairie farmers in exchange for Saskatchewan MPs voting for a bill subsidizing ferries to Vancouver Island. This is an example of:
- **(a)** rent-seeking behaviour
- **(b)** special-interest effect
- **(c)** due process
- **(d)** logrolling

Questions 4 through 7 are based on the following table, which shows the ranking of three public goods by three voters A, B, and C.

Public Good	Voter A	Voter B	Voter C
Pool	2	3	1
Road	3	1	2
Daycare	1	2	3

4. In a choice between a pool and a road:
- **(a)** a majority of voters favour the pool
- **(b)** a majority of voters favour the road
- **(c)** a majority of voters favour both the pool and the road
- **(d)** there is not a majority of voters for either good

5. In a choice between a road and daycare:
- **(a)** a majority of voters favour the road
- **(b)** a majority of voters favour daycare
- **(c)** a majority of voters favour both the road and daycare
- **(d)** there is not a majority of voters for either good

6. In a choice between daycare and a pool:
- **(a)** a majority of voters favour the pool
- **(b)** a majority of voters favour daycare
- **(c)** a majority of voters favour both daycare and the pool
- **(d)** there is not a majority of voters for either good

7. What do the rankings in the table indicate about choices made under majority rule? Majority voting:
- **(a)** reflects irrational preferences
- **(b)** can produce inconsistent choices
- **(c)** can produce consistent choices in spite of irrational preferences
- **(d)** results in economically efficient outcomes since everyone had a vote to indicate their preferences

8. The suggestion that the middle position will be chosen under majority voting is called:
- **(a)** the paradox of voting
- **(b)** the special-interest effect
- **(c)** logrolling
- **(d)** the median voter model

9. All of the following can be considered rent-seeking behaviour except:
- **(a)** political pressure by farm groups to set an effective floor price for an agricultural good
- **(b)** actions aimed at continuing the restrictions on the interprovincial movement of beer
- **(c)** actions aimed at eliminating tariffs on foreign automobiles
- **(d)** all are examples of rent-seeking

10. Which of the following is **not** among the reasons given in the textbook for the alleged greater efficiency of the private sector?
- **(a)** the least efficient workers in the economy gravitate to the public sector

(b) strong incentives to be efficient are largely absent in the public sector
(c) there is no simple way to measure or test efficiency in the public sector
(d) public sector agencies tend to be rewarded with larger budgets if they perform inefficiently

11. Which of the following would **not** be observed if society established taxes strictly on the benefits-received principle?
(a) the beneficiaries of public programs would pay for them
(b) families with more children would pay higher school taxes
(c) income would be redistributed from the wealthy to the poor
(d) there would be user charges for services provided by governments

12. Taxing people according to the ability-to-pay principle would be most characteristic of:
(a) a sales or excise tax
(b) a progressive income tax
(c) the GST
(d) property taxes

13. A tax that collects a greater amount of revenue the higher the taxpayer's income is called:
(a) progressive
(b) proportional
(c) regressive
(d) may be any of the above

14. In a competitive market the portion of a sales tax borne by the buyer is:
(a) equal to the amount of the tax
(b) equal to 50% of the amount of the tax
(c) equal to the rise in the price of the product
(d) any of the above is equally possible

15. The final resting place of an excise tax is the:
(a) incidence of the tax
(b) burden of the tax
(c) destination of the tax
(d) efficiency of the tax

Answer questions 16 through 20 based on this graph showing the imposition of a per unit tax.

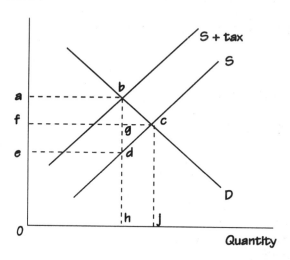

16. Before the tax is levied, the equilibrium price is:
(a) 0e
(b) 0a
(c) 0f
(d) 0b

17. The tax per unit of output is:
(a) 0a
(b) af
(c) ef
(d) ae

18. The consumer's burden of the tax, per unit, is:
(a) 0a
(b) af
(c) ef
(d) ae

19. The tax revenue for the government is:
(a) abgf
(b) abde
(c) fged
(d) bcd

20. The efficiency loss of the tax is the area:
(a) bgc
(b) bdc
(c) bcjh
(d) abfc

21. A value-added tax would tax a firm's:
(a) revenues from the sale of a product
(b) revenue from sales less input costs
(c) purchases of inputs

(d) revenues from sales less purchases from other firms

22. The GST was introduced as a replacement for:
- **(a)** the federal sales tax
- **(b)** import duties
- **(c)** excise taxes on tobacco and alcohol
- **(d)** royalties on oil and gas production

23. The GST most closely resembles:
- **(a)** a personal income tax
- **(b)** a corporate profits tax
- **(c)** a consumption tax
- **(d)** a property tax

24. Which of the following was included among the income tax changes in the February 2000 federal budget?
- **(a)** a reduction in the GST
- **(b)** the introduction of a flat tax
- **(c)** a new surtax on high-income earners
- **(d)** a reduction in the middle-income tax rate

■ DISCUSSION QUESTIONS

1. How do special-interest groups or the use of logrolling influence the efficiency of outcomes in the public sector? Construct an example to show that logrolling could result in an improvement in the efficiency of resource allocation.

2. What are consistent preferences? Why can there be a paradox with majority voting?

3. Describe how the median voter influences the results of majority rule elections on public issues.

4. The theory of public choice suggests that there are a number of possible causes of public sector failures. What are these causes? Explain how each would tend to result in the inefficient allocation of the economy's resources.

5. It is generally agreed that the government best provides a judicial system while beer is best provided by the private sector. Why is there disagreement on which sector should provide so many other goods and services?

6. Explain the two basic philosophies for apportioning the tax burden. What difficulties can be encountered when these two philosophies are put into practice?

7. Explain the difference between progressive, proportional, and regressive taxes. Which Canadian taxes fall into each category?

8. Define the *incidence* of a tax. Explain how the incidence of a sales or excise tax depends upon the elasticities of supply and demand.

9. Explain why a firm does not simply pass an excise tax on to the consumer by increasing the price of the taxed commodity by the full amount of the tax.

10. If government wishes to raise revenue from an excise tax, should they tax a commodity that has elastic supply and demand or a commodity that has inelastic supply and demand?

11. How does an excise or sales tax produce an efficiency loss for society? How is this efficiency loss affected by the elasticity of supply or demand?

12. Do you think that government limits or expands personal freedom? Do you think that the government's role in the economy should be increased or decreased?

13. What is the brain drain, and what policies do you think the government could introduce to address the problem? Would these policies increase or decrease the relative size of the public sector in our economy? Are there any tradeoffs between solving the brain drain problem and other goals of our society?

■ ANSWERS

FILL-IN QUESTIONS

1. (a) inefficient, less than, greater than; (1) special-interest, logrolling; (2) preferences; (b) inconsistent, paradox, voting; (c) median

2. (a) re-elected; (b) special; (c) clear, hidden; (d) select; (e) incentives, test (measure)

3. benefits-received, ability-to-pay

4. increases, regressive, tax rate

5. progressive, regressive

6. price, elasticity, demand, supply; (a) less, more; (b) more, less

7. efficiency, elasticities

8. value, difference, purchases

PROBLEMS AND PROJECTS

1. CASE 1; Winner: School; Dam; School; CASE 2; Winner: School; Dam; Park; CASE 2 (because for consistency the School should be preferred to the Park)

2. (a) Tax A: 10, 10, 10, 10, 20; Tax B: 20, 13, 12, 11, 10; (b) proportional, 7500, progressive; regressive.

3. (a) Case 1: benefits exceed costs (66 > 60) and airport approved as Nevin and Selby vote in favour; (b) Case 2: benefits are less than costs (57 < 60) but airport is approved as Nevin and Selby vote in favour; Also Case 3: benefits exceed costs (63 > 60), but Ellis and Nevin vote against.

4. (a) S1; (b) 8, 10,000; (c) 8; (d) 15, 8,000; (e) 8, 8,000, 64,000; (g) 7, 1, larger, inelastic, elastic; (h) the triangle from P=15, Q=8,000 to P=7, Q=8,000 to P=8, Q=10,000.

TRUE-FALSE

1. T these characteristics are the subject of public choice theory
2. F for example, such voting fails to reflect the relative intensity of different individuals' preferences
3. F sometimes, definitely not always
4. F paradox of voting refers to potential inconsistency problem
5. T public sector is also subject to failure
6. T since the median voter determines voting outcome, there is incentive to live where median voter has similar preferences to one's own
7. T
8. F under these conditions such politicians are unlikely to reject the program
9. T
10. F it states that those who benefit from a program or services should pay for it
11. T
12. T in this case the percentage of income paid in tax is higher at higher income levels
13. T
14. T
15. F since supply is not affected by the tax, the price is unchanged, and consumers face no burden
16. T
17. T through higher prices to consumers and lower prices to resource suppliers
18. F a sales tax is general excise tax applied to many goods and services
19. T
20. F the purpose is to protect taxpayers from inflation

21. T

MULTIPLE-CHOICE

1. (b)
2. (c) the vote of a person with strong feelings about a proposal counts the same as the vote of person who is indifferent to the proposal
3. (d)
4. (a) A and C vote for the pool
5. (a) B and C vote for the road
6. (b) A and B vote for daycare
7. (b)
8. (d)
9. (d) a certain group or industry is lobbying government for a targeted benefit
10. (a) it's not the quality of the workers; it's the incentives and structures under which they work
11. (c)
12. (b) the others are known to be regressive, which generally suggests higher taxes on those with lower ability to pay
13. (d) the key is the percentage that the tax represents of income
14. (d) depending on the elasticities of supply and demand
15. (a)
16. (c) at the intersection of S and D
17. (d) the vertical shift from S to S + tax
18. (b) the increase in price to the consumer
19. (b) tax per unit x number of units sold
20. (b)
21. (d) a tax on the value that the firm adds to resources it buys from other firms
22. (a)
23. (c)
24. (d) this rate is to come down from 26% to 23% over five years

CHAPTER 20

Canadian Agriculture: Economics and Policy

Agriculture is an important industry in Canada, and one with a long history of government intervention. This chapter assesses the problems that agriculture has faced, and some of the more important policies and programs designed to solve these problems. These policies have significant effects on farmers, consumers, and taxpayers.

Fundamentally, Canadian farmers' main problems can be analyzed as a short-run problem and a long-run problem: each with its own causes. In the short run, farm prices and incomes have fluctuated sharply from year to year. In the long run, farm incomes have been falling because farming is a declining industry. The concepts of elasticity, supply, demand, and competitive markets are very useful for analyzing these problems.

The price and income instability that farmers experience on a regular basis is the result of: (1) fluctuations in output (supply) due to weather and other factors, (2) an inelastic demand for agricultural products, and (3) shifts in demand for agricultural products. For example, an increase in supply will paradoxically lead to a drop in total income for producers because there will price will drop percentage-wise more than quantity rises. Similarly, even a small drop in demand leads to a significant drop in price, and in farm incomes.

In the long run, agriculture is a declining industry – at least in terms of income and employment – because rapid technological advancements have increased the supply of agricultural goods, while the demand for these goods has grown very slowly. In short, the amount of food that is needed can be produced with many less agricultural workers than were once required. Furthermore, agricultural operations need to be larger than the traditional family farm in order to capitalize on the cost savings available with new technologies.

Canadian agriculture has received government assistance fairly consistently since the 1930s. There are several reasons why governments have continued to help farmers: many farmers have relatively low incomes; the family farm is a valued Canadian institution; the industry is vulnerable to major natural hazards; and farmers are victims of market power in input markets, yet must sell their goods in purely competitive markets. Assistance for farmers has taken various forms, ranging from crop insurance to subsidized credit to price supports. The chapter emphasizes how marketing boards support farm prices above equilibrium levels through three types of plans: (1) offers to purchase whatever output farms cannot sell at the minimum price; (2) deficiency payments that make up the difference between the market price and the minimum price; and (3) reduction of surpluses by restricting supply or bolstering demand.

Such farm assistance programs have raised prices for consumers, cost large amounts of tax dollars, caused inefficient allocations of resources and environmental costs, yet have not solved the long-run problem. The problem also spills across international borders as the problems of Canadian agriculture are exacerbated by the subsidies that European and American governments give to their farmers, and vice versa.

After decades of price-support programs it is clear that subsidies do not solve the underlying problem that agriculture is a declining industry. In fact, subsidies keep some people in the industry, slowing down the movement of labour and other resources from agriculture and into other sectors. Furthermore, subsidies are not effectively targeted to those most in need of help. Another contradiction is that subsidies tend to encourage production, when overproduction is among the problems. Some of these policy choices are explained by concepts of public choice theory: rent-seeking behaviour and special interest effects. Farmers have traditionally been very powerful in Canadian politics, but the shrinking share of Canada's population that earns its living in agriculture is slowly reducing that power. Canada's opposition to trade barriers in agriculture, especially by EU countries, also puts some pressure on Canada to reduce protection and subsidies for her own farmers.

■ CHAPTER LEARNING OBJECTIVES

In this chapter you will learn:
□ That in the short run there is significant price and income instability in the agricultural sector.
□ The effects of subsidies and price supports and ceilings in agriculture.
□ About recent agricultural policy reforms in Canada.

■ CHAPTER OUTLINE

1. There are five reasons for devoting some time to the analysis of Canadian agriculture: it is one of the nation's largest industries; without government intervention it would be a real-world example of the purely competitive model; it illustrates the effects of government intervention in markets; it provides illustrations of rent-seeking and the special-interest effect of public choice theory; and domestic agricultural policy reflects the increasing globalization of markets.

2. The farm problem is both a short-run and a long-run problem. The short-run problem is the frequent sharp ups and downs in product prices and incomes of farmers from one year to the next; the long-run problem is the decline of the agricultural sector as a source of employment and incomes.

3. The causes of the short-run problem of unstable incomes are:
    (a) the inelastic demand for farm products,
    (b) fluctuations in the output of agricultural products, and
    (c) fluctuations in demand (both domestic and foreign).
Frequent fluctuations in the demand and supply curves cause huge, unpredictable price changes because demand is so price inelastic.

4. The long-run problem that agriculture is a declining industry is due to two basic causes:
    (a)   Rapid and sustained technological progress has markedly raised productivity and increased agricultural supply;
    (b)   Demand for agricultural products has grown slowly because, even though incomes have increased, the demand for food is income inelastic. Population growth also has also been slow.
Given rapid supply growth and slow demand growth, efficiency in the allocation of resources requires that labour resources move out of agriculture and into other industries. Because this has been very slow to happen, the average incomes of those remaining in agriculture are persistently low.

5. Farm interests present several arguments to justify special assistance:
    (a)   the low incomes of farmers
    (b)   the family farm is a fundamental part of our heritage and culture
    (c)   farmers are subject to extraordinary natural hazards, and
    (d)   farmers lack market power in their output markets, but buy inputs from suppliers with market power

6. Since the 1930s, government has attempted to increase farm prices and income mainly through marketing boards and price supports. Marketing boards have had a mandate to control product supply and attempt to stabilize prices at high levels.

7. Two types of price supports are common: offers to purchase (where a marketing board buys any surplus as a floor price) and deficiency payments (where a marketing board pays the difference between the market price and a floor price).
(a) Both strategies create production surpluses, and raise farm incomes and consumer prices. Which one costs more for consumers and taxpayers depends on the elasticities of demand and supply.
(b) Both strategies create an efficiency loss because too many resources are used for farming.
(c) Environmental costs arise from greater use of fertilizers and pesticides, reduction of wildlife habitat land, etc.
(d) International consequences arise because price supports in Canada make our market attractive to foreign producers. To avoid imports further increasing our surpluses, the government has an incentive to impose tariffs or quotas on imports. This

imposes further costs on our own efficiency, and on other nations.

8. Supply restriction solves some of the problems with simple price support programs. Payments to farmers who agree to restrict the number of hectares in production can help to reduce surplus production and excess resource usage. However, the intent of supply restriction is undermined because the high prices are a powerful incentive for farmers to maximize their production on the restricted amount of land.

9. Government has attempted to bolster demand for agricultural products by finding new uses (e.g., gasohol) and new domestic and foreign markets, the latter efforts including attempts to convince other nations to eliminate trade barriers.

10. Farm policies aimed at increasing producer incomes have not worked well and are subject to three criticisms.
(a) Policies have attacked symptoms rather than causes of the problem and failed to move resources out of agriculture.
(b) The major benefits of the program have not been directed toward the low-income farmers.
(c) The various farm programs of the federal government have often operated to offset (or contradict) each other.

11. The persistence of farm support programs can be explained by public choice concepts: rent-seeking by farmers, the special-interest effect that impairs public decision making, and the clear benefits to farmers and hidden costs to other Canadians. Nevertheless, falling farm populations spell shrinking political power for farmers. Given international pressures towards freer trade in agricultural products, Canada is under pressure to reduce subsidies to our farmers. These factors are likely to lead to declining farm subsidies over time.

■ TERMS AND CONCEPTS

short-run farm prob-
   lem
long-run farm problem
agribusiness

Canadian Wheat Mar-
   keting Board
support prices
deficiency payments
crop restriction

■ HINTS AND TIPS

1. Several earlier chapters cover topics used in this chapter to analyse agriculture: Chapter 3 (on supply and demand), Chapter 6 (on elasticities), and Chapter 19 (on public choice).

2. To understand whether a particular policy will be effective in the agricultural sector, it is crucial to understand the distinction between the short-run farm problem and the long-run farm problem. In principle, it would be perfectly possible to have either one of these problems exist without the other existing, so try to think of them separately, and to evaluate which particular problem a policy truly addresses.

■ FILL-IN QUESTIONS

1. The short-run problem for agriculture is the instability of farm _____ and _____.

2. Inelasticity of demand contributes to unstable farm prices and incomes in two ways. Relatively (large, small) _____ changes in the output of farm products result in relatively _____ changes in farm prices and incomes; and relatively _____ changes in demand result in relatively _____ changes in prices and incomes.

3. Demand for the products of Canadian farmers is volatile due to our dependence on _____ markets. Supply of agricultural products is volatile due mainly to variations in the _____.

4. The long-run problem for agriculture is that it is a _____ industry. Prices and incomes have (risen, fallen) _____ relative to other industries because: (a) the (demand, supply) _____ has increased rapidly because of technological change, and (b) the _____ has increased slowly over time because food demand is income _____. In addition, population growth has _____ in recent decades.

5. As the Canadian economy has grown and improved its agricultural technology, it has failed to reallocate enough _____ from _____ to _____ sectors of the economy.

6. Three of the reasons advanced to support the farmers' claim to assistance from the federal gov-

ernment are: (a) the low _____ of farmers; (b) uninsurable _____, such as drought, to which the industry is exposed; and (c) farmers sell in _____ markets but purchase inputs from industries in which market _____ is exercised.

7. If government supports prices at a level above equilibrium, the result will be (shortages, surpluses) _____ that government must _____ in order to maintain prices at their support level.
   (a)   Farmers benefit from this price-support program because it increases their _____.
   (b)   But the program hurts consumers who must pay   higher   _____   and   consume _____.
   (c)   Society (gains, loses) _____ because taxpayers will pay (higher, lower) _____ taxes to finance the purchase of the surplus by government, and because there is an economic _____ due to the (overallocation, underallocation) _____ of resources to agriculture.
   (d)   There are also _____ costs from distortion in worldwide supply and demand for agricultural products, the increased potential for _____ barriers, and a (positive, negative) _____ effect on less-developed countries.

8. As consumers, the public will prefer (an offers-to-purchase, a deficiency payments) _____ price support program because such a program will enable them to consume more of the product. As taxpayers and consumers, the public (will, will not) _____ prefer one program to another because total payments by the public to farmers are (identical, more, less) _____ with offers to purchase compared to deficiency payments.

9. Agricultural policies to stabilize farm income and prices (have, have not) _____ worked well for at least three reasons:
   (a)   they   have   confused   the   (symptoms, causes) _____ of the farm problem (low prices and incomes) with the _____ of the problem (misallocation of resources);
   (b)   most agricultural support goes to (high, low) _____-income farmers rather than _____-income farmers;
   (c)   the objectives of different farm programs have often offset or _____ each other.

10. Farm policies have received strong support from both the federal and provincial governments. This result can be explained by insights from _____ theory. Farm representatives are displaying _____ behaviour when they lobby for programs that transfer income to themselves. There is also a _____ effect because the cost to each   individual   taxpayer   is   (large,   small) _____ but the benefit for each individual farmer is _____.

■   PROBLEMS AND PROJECTS

1. This table shows a demand schedule for some farm product.

Price ($/kg)	Quantity demanded (kg/yr)	Total Producer Income ($/yr)
3.00	9,000	_____
2.50	10,000	_____
2.00	11,000	_____
1.50	12,000	_____
1.00	13,000	_____

   (a)   Fill in the column for producer income.
   (b)   Given that revenues (rise, fall) _____ when price rises, the demand for this product is (inelastic, elastic) _____, which (is, is not) _____ typical of agricultural products.
   (c)   To confirm your conclusion, calculate the price elasticity between P = 2.50 and P = 2.00. (Reminder: E = % change in Qd / % change in P.)

2. The following graph shows the market for a hypothetical agricultural product, X.
   (a)   In the absence of any government intervention, the equilibrium price of X is $_____ per bushel, and producers will sell _____ bushels per year, for an annual income of $ _____.
   Suppose that the government agrees to support the price of X at $4.80 per bushel.
   (b)   If this price support is implemented by an offers to purchase program, consumers will buy _____ bushels per year, farmers will produce _____ bushels per year, and the government will be required to purchase the (shortage, surplus) _____ of _____ bushels per year, at a total cost of $_____ per year.
   (c)   If the government becomes committed to this price support, using an offers to purchase program, what pressure is there to also implement supply management?

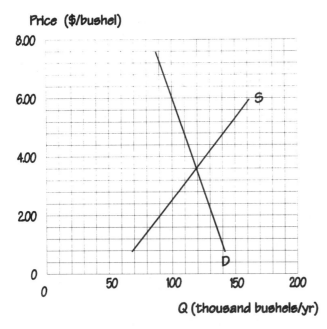

Price ($/bushel)

Q (thousand bushels/yr)

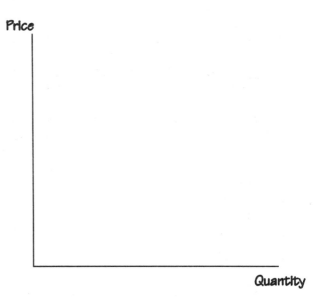

Price

Quantity

(d) If the same level of price support is done by a deficiency payments program, farmers will produce _____ bushels per year, consumers will buy _____ bushels per year, at a price of $_____ per bushel, and the government will be required to pay $_____ per bushel for _____ bushels per year, at a total cost of $_____ per year.

(e) Which of the two price support programs is the government (and taxpayers) likely to favour in this instance? _____

(f) Which of the two price support programs are consumers likely to favour? _____

(g) Farmers are indifferent between the two alternatives because their total annual income becomes $_____ under both schemes.

3. Consider the market for cabbages. Suppose the following:
i.   cabbages are inferior, and incomes are increasing
ii. population is growing slowly
iii. cabbages are price inelastic
iv. technology for producing cabbages is improving
Draw and explain a supply and demand diagram for cabbages to predict what will happen to prices and incomes for cabbage farmers in the near future.

■ **TRUE-FALSE**

Circle T if the statement is true, F if it is false.

1. Agriculture employs about 30% of the Canadian labour force. **T F**

2. The short-run farm problem is the sharp year-to-year fluctuations in farm incomes and prices. **T F**

3. The short-run problem in agriculture arises because some countries are dumping subsidized farm products in the Canadian market. **T F**

4. The demand for most farm products is price inelastic. **T F**

5. Because of the inelasticity of demand for farm products, a relatively large change in output will cause a relatively small change in price. **T F**

6. The supply of agricultural products tends to be subject to random variations due to weather and other unexpected factors. **T F**

7. Changes in crop production in other countries affects the demand and hence the income of Canadian farmers. **T F**

8. Changes in the farm subsidy programs of foreign countries have led to the loss of foreign markets for Canadian agricultural products. **T F**

9. The long-run farm problem could be solved by a substantial exodus of labour from the farm sector.
T F

10. Since World War II productivity in agriculture has increased at about half the rate of the nonfarm economy.
T F

11. Increases in Canadian consumer incomes lead to less-than-proportionate increases in expenditures on farm products.
T F

12. The supply of agricultural products has tended to increase more rapidly than the demand for these products in Canada.
T F

13. The Canadian Wheat Board attempts to benefit producers by stabilizing the price at a high level.
T F

14. When government supports farm prices at above-equilibrium levels, it can reduce the annual surpluses of agricultural commodities either by increasing the supply or by decreasing the demand.
T F

15. As consumers, the public prefers the offers-to-purchase method of price support to deficiency payments.
T F

16. Placing an agricultural product under a supply management scheme is an example of rent-seeking behaviour.
T F

17. One contradiction in farm policies is that policies to solve the short-run problem will tend to delay the adjustments needed to solve the long-run problem.
T F

■ **MULTIPLE-CHOICE**

Circle the letter that corresponds to the best answer.

1. In the absence of government intervention, most agricultural goods markets in Canada would correspond to our market structure model known as:
  (a) pure competition
  (b) monopoly
  (c) monopolistic competition
  (d) oligopoly

2. Which of the following is *not* characteristic of Canadian agriculture?
  (a) farmers sell their products in highly competitive markets
  (b) farmers buy resources in markets that are largely noncompetitive
  (c) the demand for agricultural products tends to be inelastic
  (d) agricultural resources tend to be highly mobile

3. The short-run farm problem is the result of all the following except:
  (a) an inelastic demand for agricultural products
  (b) fluctuations in farm output
  (c) rent-seeking behaviour by farm groups
  (d) shifts in the demand curve for farm products

4. If both the demand for and the supply of wheat increase:
  (a) the quantity of wheat bought and sold will increase
  (b) the quantity of wheat bought and sold will decrease
  (c) the price of wheat will increase
  (d) the price of wheat will decrease

5. Which one of the following is not a reason that increases in the demand for agricultural commodities have been relatively small?
  (a) the population of Canada has not increased as rapidly as the productivity of agriculture
  (b) the demand for farm products has risen more slowly than consumer incomes in Canada
  (c) the demand for agricultural products is inelastic with regard to price
  (d) the standard of living in Canada is well above the level of bare subsistence

6. The market system has failed to solve the problem of low farm incomes because:
  (a) the demand for agricultural products is relatively inelastic
  (b) the supply of agricultural products is relatively elastic
  (c) agricultural products have relatively few good substitutes
  (d) agricultural resources are relatively immobile

7. If the demand for agricultural products is inelastic, a relatively small increase in supply will result in:

(a) a relatively small increase in farm prices and incomes

(b) a relatively small decrease in farm prices and a relatively large increase in farm incomes

(c) a relatively large decrease in farm prices and incomes

(d) a relatively large increase in farm prices and a relatively small decrease in farm incomes

8. All of the following have contributed to the long-run farm problem except:

(a) increased supply of agricultural products due to technological change

(b) declining farm population

(c) income inelastic demand

(d) declining population growth

9. Which of the following is *not* one of the ways that governments have supported Canadian farmers?

(a) minimum wage laws

(b) crop insurance programs

(c) low interest loans

(d) price supports

10. A consequence of the government's offers-to-purchase program at a price above the equilibrium is:

(a) reduced farm incomes

(b) reduced consumer prices

(c) increased consumption of the farm product

(d) a surplus of the farm product

11. Deficiency payments mean that:

(a) the real income of the farmer remains constant

(b) through subsidies, the farmer enjoys a form of price support

(c) the purchasing power of the farmer's money income remains constant

(d) the money income of the farmer will buy a constant amount of goods and services

12. Which statement is correct?

(a) deficiency payments can lead to surpluses, which the government must then buy

(b) crop restriction is not appropriate if supply is elastic

(c) the offers-to-purchase method of price supports will cost more with an elastic demand

(d) consumers prefer the offers-to-purchase method of price supports

Use the diagram below to answer questions 13 to 15.

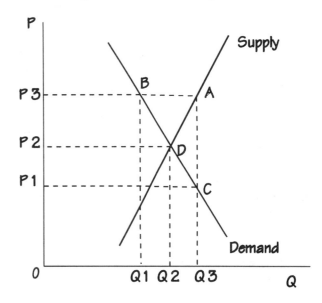

13. If the government supported the price of this product at P_3 through offers-to-purchase, the total amount it would have to spend to purchase the surplus of the product would be:

(a) $0Q_3AP_3$

(b) Q_1Q3AB

(c) P_1CAP_3

(d) $0Q_1BP_3$

14. If the government supported the price of this product at P_3, the total deficiency payments made by the government to producers of the product would be:

(a) $0QAP_3$

(b) Q_1Q_3AB

(c) P_1CAP_3

(d) $0Q_1BP_3$

15. Regardless of whether the government supports the price of the product at P_3 through offers-to-purchase or deficiency payments, the total income of producers of the product will be:

(a) $0Q_3AP_3$

(b) $0Q_1BP_3$

(c) $0Q_3CP_1$

(d) $0Q_2DP_2$

16. Which of the following will reduce the foreign demand for Canadian farm products?

(a) a reduction in foreign tariffs on farm products

(b) an elimination of foreign quotas on farm products

(c) an appreciation of the Canadian dollar

(d) crop failures in foreign countries

Answer Questions 17 and 18 on the basis of the demand and supply schedules for agricultural product Z as shown below.

Kilograms of Z Demanded	Price of Z per Kilogram	Kilograms of Z Supplied
850	$1.30	1,150
900	1.20	1,100
950	1.10	1,050
1,000	1.00	1,000
1,050	0.90	950
1,100	0.80	850
1,150	0.70	800

17. If the federal government supports the price of Z at $1.30 a kilogram, then at this price, there is:

(a) a surplus of 200 kilograms of Z

(b) a surplus of 300 kilograms of Z

(c) a surplus of 400 kilograms of Z

(d) a shortage of 400 kilograms of Z

18. With a federal price support based on an offer to purchase at $1.30 a kilogram, consumers spend:

(a) $1,040 — the federal government spends $410, and farmers receive income from product Z of $1,450

(b) $1,105 — the federal government spends $390, and farmers receive income from product Z of $1,495

(c) $1,296 — the federal government spends $240, and farmers receive income from product Z of $1,320

(d) $1,045 — the federal government spends $110, and farmers receive income from product Z of $1,155

19. How do price support programs create environmental costs?

(a) farmers use more fertilizers and pesticides to increase their productivity

(b) farmers are less likely to practice crop rotation

(c) farmers are more likely to farm environmentally sensitive land

(d) all of the above

20. One consequence of crop restriction programs is that farmers:

(a) retire their least productive land

(b) cultivate their best land more intensively

(c) reduce their output proportionately less than they reduce the amount of land that they cultivate

(d) all of the above

21. Criticisms of farm subsidy programs include all of the following except:

(a) these programs entail huge budgetary costs

(b) these program subsidies do not benefit the most needy farmers

(c) these programs promote the reallocation of resources out of agriculture

(d) these programs complicate international economic policies

22. We can expect that political support for farm subsidy program will diminish because:

(a) the population working in agriculture is declining

(b) farmers are becoming more efficient and less dependent on government assistance

(c) the amount of resources allocated to farming has reached the appropriate level

(d) globalization is resulting in higher world market prices for most agricultural products

■ **DISCUSSION QUESTIONS**

1. Why is the economics of agriculture an important topic for study?

2. What is the short-run farm problem, and what are its causes?

3. Why does the demand for agricultural products tend to be inelastic? What effect does the elasticity of demand have on price and income instability in agriculture?

4. What have been the specific causes of the large increases in the supply of agricultural products since World War I?

5. Why has the demand for agricultural products failed to increase at the same rate as the supply of these products?

6. Explain why the farm population tends to be relatively immobile. If farmers were more mobile, how would the price system reallocate their labour away from agriculture and into more prosperous occupations?

7. Why do agricultural interests claim that farmers have a special right to aid from government?

8. What devices does the government employ to support above-equilibrium agricultural prices? Why is the result of government-supported prices through offers-to-purchase invariably a surplus of farm commodities?

9. Why has the farm program not been successful in preventing falling farm prices and incomes, surpluses, and an unequal distribution of farm income?

10. Explain how the farm policies of other nations affect the export demand for Canadian farm products, as well as Canada's own policy choices.

11. What insights does public choice theory provide about the persistence of government support for the agricultural sector?

■ **ANSWERS**

FILL-IN QUESTIONS

1. price, incomes

2. small, large, small, large

3. export (foreign), weather

4. declining, fallen, supply, demand, inelastic, slowed

5. resources, the agricultural, nonagricultural

6. (a) income; (b) natural hazards; (c) competitive, power

7. surpluses, purchase; (a) incomes; (b) prices, less; (c) loses, higher, efficiency loss, overallocation; (d) international, trade, negative

8. deficiency payments, will not, identical

9. have not; (a) symptoms, causes; (b) high, low; (c) contradicted

10. public choice, rent-seeking, special-interest, small, large

PROBLEMS AND PROJECTS

1. (a) 27,000, 25,000, 22,000, 18,000, 13,000; (b) rise, inelastic, is; (c) (11,000/10,500)/(.50/3.25) = 0.68, this is below 1, so confirmed.

2. (a) 3.60, 120,000, 432,000; (b) 110,000, 140,000 surplus, 30,000 144,000: (c) there will be an ongoing surplus which government must buy; (d) 140,000, 140,000, 0.80, 4.00, 140,000, 560,000: (e) offers-to-purchase; (f) deficiency payments; (g) 4.80 x 140,000 = 672,000.

3. D is steep (inelastic), and shifting slightly to right; S is shifting significantly to right. Equilibrium price is falling, and though quantity is rising somewhat, total income falls.

TRUE-FALSE

1. F   in the 1930s the percentage was high; now it is only a few percent.
2. T
3. F   this factor contributes to the long-run decline in sociology
4. T
5. F   such an event would lead to a huge change in price
6. T
7. T   most of our producers sell in world markets
8. T
9. T
10. F   more like twice as fast
11. T   income elasticity is low
12. T
13. T
14. T   in principle, though bolstering demand is challenging
15. F   greater quantity to consume to under deficiency payments
16. T   because existing producers benefit from the protection, they are likely to lobby for it
17. T   raising incomes in the short run allows some farmers to stay in the industry longer

MULTIPLE-CHOICE

1. (a) many buyers and sellers, none with price-making power
2. (d) both land and labour employed in agriculture is difficult to move to other industries
3. (c)
4. (a) quantity increases, and price can either rise or fall, depending on relative shift in demand and supply
5. (c) price elasticity has to do with the steepness of demand, not how much demand shifts
6. (d) otherwise the relatively low incomes would have driven resources out of the industry
7. (c) since P falls by larger % than Q rises, total income falls
8. (b) declining population is helping, but happening too slowly

9. (a) when applied to workers hired by farmers, this raises farm costs
10. (d) and the government must deal with this surplus
11. (b)
12. (c) as price rises, and consumers have to pay whole price, Qd drops drastically
13. (b) the floor price x the surplus quantity
14. (c) the rectangle above the price on the demand curve and up to the floor price
15. (a) the floor price x the quantity produced
16. (c) if Cdn$ becomes more expensive, Canadian products are more expensive to foreigners
17. (b)
18. (b)
19. (d) these all happen
20. (d)
21. (c) the programs impede the reallocation of resources
22. (a)

Answers to Key Questions

■ CHAPTER 1

1-1 This behaviour can be explained in terms of marginal costs and marginal benefits. At a standard restaurant, items are priced individually — they have a positive marginal cost. If you order more, it will cost you more. You order until the marginal benefit from the extra food no longer exceeds the marginal cost. At a buffet you pay a flat fee no matter how much you eat. Once the fee is paid, additional food items have a zero marginal cost. You therefore continue to eat until your marginal benefit becomes zero.

1-5 Economic theory consists of factually supported generalizations about economic behaviour that can be used to formulate economic policies. Economic theory enables policymakers to formulate economic policies that are relevant to real-world goals and problems that are based upon carefully observed facts.

1-7 (a), (d), and (f) are macro; (b), (c), and (e) are micro.

1-8 (a) and (c) are positive; (b) and (d) are normative.

1-9 (a) The fallacy of composition is the mistake of believing that something true for an individual part is necessarily true for the whole. Example: A single auto producer can increase its profits by lowering its price and taking business away from its competitors. But matched price cuts by all auto manufacturers will not necessarily yield higher industry profits.

(b) The "after this, therefore because of this" fallacy is incorrectly reasoning that when one event precedes another, the first event *necessarily* caused the second. Example: Interest rates rise, followed by an increase in the rate of inflation, leading to the erroneous conclusion that the rise in interest rates caused the inflation. Actually, higher interest rates slow inflation.

Cause-and-effect relationships are difficult to isolate because "other things" are continually changing.

Appendix 1-2 (a) More tickets are bought at each price; the line shifts to the right. (b) and (c) Fewer tickets are bought at each price; the line shifts to the left.

Appendix 1-3 Income column: $0; $5,000; $10,000, $15,000; $20,000. Saving column: $–500; 0; $500; $1,000; $1,500. Slope = 0.1 (= $1,000 – $500)/$15,000 – $10,000). Vertical intercept = $–500. The slope shows the amount saving will increase for every $1 increase in income; the intercept shows the amount of saving (dissaving) occurring when income is zero. Equation: $S = \${-}500 + 0.1Y$ (where S is saving and Y is income). Saving will be $750 at the $12,500 income level.

Appendix 1-6 Slopes: at $A = +4$; at $B = 0$; at $C = –4$.

■ CHAPTER 2

2-5 Economics deals with the "limited resources — unlimited wants" problem. Unemployment represents valuable resources that could have been used to produce more goods and services — to meet more wants and ease the economizing problem.

Allocative efficiency means that resources are being used to produce the goods and services most wanted by society. The economy is then located at the optimal point on its production possibilities curve where marginal benefit equals marginal cost for each good. *Productive efficiency* means the least costly production techniques are being used to produce wanted goods and services. Example: manual typewriters produced using the least-cost techniques but for which there is no demand.

2-6 (a) See curve *EDCBA* below. The assumptions are full employment and productive efficiency, fixed supplies of resources, and fixed technology.

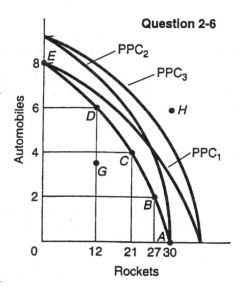

Question 2-6

(b) 4.5 rockets; .33 automobiles, as determined from the table. Increasing opportunity costs are reflected in the concave-from-the-origin shape of the curve. This means the economy must give up larger and larger amounts of rockets to get constant added amounts of automobiles — and vice versa.

(c) It must obtain full employment and productive efficiency.

2-9 The marginal benefit curve is downsloping; MB falls as more of a product is consumed because additional units of a good yield less satisfaction than previous units. The marginal cost curve is upsloping; MC increases as more of a product is produced because additional units require the use of increasingly unsuitable resources. The optimal amount of a particular product occurs where MB equals MC. If MC exceeds MB, fewer resources should be allocated to this use. The resources are more valuable in some alternative use (as reflected in the higher MC) than in this use (as reflected in the lower MB).

2-10 See the answer for Question 2-6. *G* indicates unemployment, productive inefficiency, or both. *H* is at present unattainable. Economic growth — through more inputs, better inputs, improved technology — must be achieved to attain *H*.

2-11 See the answer for Question 2-6. PPC₁ shows improved rocket technology. PPC₂ shows improved auto technology. PPC₃ shows improved technology in producing both products.

■ **CHAPTER 3**

3-2 Demand increases in (a), (c), (e), and (f); decreases in (b) and (d).

3-5 Supply increases in (a), (d), (e), and (g); decreases in (b), (c), and (f).

3-7 Data, from top to bottom: −13; −7; 0; +7; +14; and +21.
(a) P_e = $4.00; Q_e = 75,000. Equilibrium occurs where there is neither a shortage nor surplus of wheat. At the immediately lower price of $3.70, there is a shortage of 7,000 bushels. At the immediately higher price of $4.30, there is a surplus of 7,000 bushels.

(b)

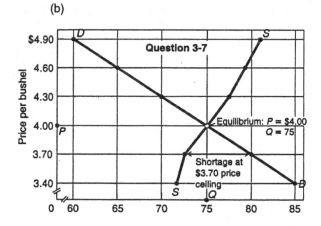

Quantity (thousands of bushels)

(c) Because at $3.40 there will be a 13,000 bushel shortage that will drive the price up. Because at $4.90 there will be a 21,000 bushel surplus that will drive the price down. Quotation is incorrect; just the opposite is true.

(d) A $3.70 ceiling causes a persistent shortage. Government might want to suppress inflation.

3-8 (a) Price up: quantity down; (b) Price down; quantity down; (c) Price down; quantity up; (d) Price indeterminate; quantity up; (e) Price up; quantity up; (f) Price down; quantity indeterminate; (g) Price up; quantity indeterminate; (h) Price indeterminate and quantity down.

■ **CHAPTER 4**

4-8   The quest for profit-led firms to produce these goods. Producers looked for and found the least-cost combination of resources in producing their output. Resource suppliers, seeking income, made these resources available. Consumers, through their dollar votes, ultimately decide on what will continue to be produced.

4-11   Public goods are indivisible (they are produced in such large units that they cannot be sold to individuals) and the exclusion principle does not apply to them (once the goods are produced nobody — including free riders — can be excluded from the goods' benefits). The free-rider problem explains the significance of the exclusion principle. The exclusion principle separates goods and services that private firms will supply (because those who do not pay for them can be excluded from their benefits) and goods and services that government must supply (because people can obtain the benefits without paying). Government must levy taxes to get revenues to pay for public goods.

4-12   On the curve, the only way to obtain more public goods is to reduce the production of private goods (from *C* to *B*.).

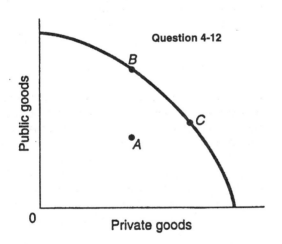

Question 4-12

An economy operating inside the curve can expand the production of public goods without sacrificing private goods (say, from *A* to *B*) by making use of unemployed resources.

■ **CHAPTER 5**

5-4   Greater exporting increases domestic output and thus increases revenues to domestic exporting firms. Because these firms would employ more resources, household income would rise. Households would then use part of their greater income to buy more imported goods (imports would rise).

Canadian exports in 1997 were $301.1 billion (flow 13) and imports were $276.8 billion (flow 16).

Flow 14 must equal flow 13. Flow 15 must equal flow 16.

5-5   (a)   Yes, because the opportunity cost of radios is less (1R = 1C) in South Korea than in Canada (1R = 2C). South Korea should produce radios and Canada should produce chemicals.

(b)   If they specialize, Canada can produce 20 tonnes of chemicals and South Korea can produce 30,000 radios. Before specialization South Korea produced alternative B and Canada alternative D for a total of 28,000 radios (24,000 + 4,000) and 18 tonnes of chemicals (6 tonnes + 12 tonnes). The gain is 2,000 radios and 2 tonnes of chemicals.

(c)   The limits of the terms of trade are determined by the comparative cost conditions in each country before trade: 1R = 1C in South Korea and 1R = 2C in Canada. The terms of trade must be somewhere between these two ratios for trade to occur.

If the terms of trade are 1R = 1 1/2 C, South Korea would end up with 26,000 radios (= 30,000 − 4,000) and 6 tonnes of chemicals. Canada would have 4,000 radios and 14 tonnes of chemicals (= 20 − 6). South Korea has gained 2,000 radios. Canada has gained 2 tonnes of chemicals.

(d)   Yes, the world is obtaining more output from its fixed resources.

5-7   The first part of this statement is incorrect. Canadian exports create a domestic *supply* of foreign currencies, not a domestic demand for them. The second part of the statement is accurate. The foreign demand for dollars (from Canadian exports) generates a supply of foreign currencies to Canadians.

A decline in Canadian incomes or a weakening of Canadian preferences for foreign goods would reduce our imports, reducing our demand for foreign currencies. These currencies would depreciate (the dollar would appreciate). Dollar appreciation means Canadian exports will decline and Canadian imports will rise.

5-11 The Uruguay Round Agreement established the World Trade Organization (WTO), as GATT's successor. Some 135 nations belong to the WTO, with China the last entrant. The WTO oversees trade agreements reached by member nations and rules on trade disputes among them. The WTO encourages members nations to lower trade barriers. The EU and NAFTA are free-trade blocs. The euro is the shared common currency among twelve out of fifteen EU members. The euro begins circulation January 1, 2002.

■ CHAPTER 6

6-2 See the graph accompanying the answer to 6-4. Elasticities, top to bottom: 3; 1.4; .714; .333. Slope does not measure elasticity. This demand curve has a constant slope of − 1 (= −1/1), but elasticity declines as we move down the curve. When the initial price is high and initial quantity is low, a unit change in price is a *low* percentage change while a unit change in quantity is a *high* percentage change. The percentage change in quantity exceeds the percentage change in price, making demand elastic. When the initial price is low and initial quantity is high, a unit change in price is a *high* percentage change while a unit change in quantity is a *low* percentage change. The percentage change in quantity is less than the percentage change in price, making demand inelastic.

6-4 See the graph below. Total revenue data, top to bottom: $5; $8; $9; $8; $5. When demand is elastic, price and total revenue move in the opposite direction. When demand is inelastic, price and total revenue move in the same direction.

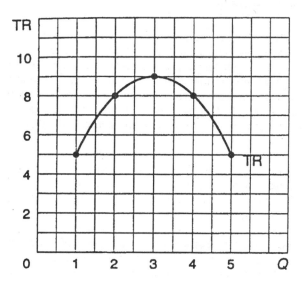

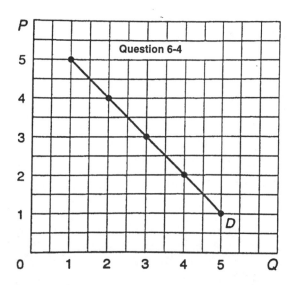

Question 6-4

6-5 Total revenue would increase in (c), (d), (e), and (f); decrease in (a) and (b); and remain the same in (g).

6-6 Substitutability, proportion of income, luxury versus necessity, and time. Elastic: (a), (c), (e), (g), (h), and (i). Inelastic: (b), (d), (f), and (j).

6-10 Supply was perfectly inelastic — vertical — at a quantity of 1 unit. The $71.5 million price was determined where the demand curve intersected this supply curve. Even if a painting can be forged well enough to fool some experts, the original is so valuable because only one exists.

6-12 A and B are substitutes; C and D are complements.

6-13 All are normal goods — income and quantity demanded move in the same direction. These coefficients reveal that a 1 percent increase in income will increase the quantity of movies demanded by 3.4 percent, of dental services by 1.0 percent, and of clothing by 0.5 percent. A negative coefficient indicates an inferior good — income and quantity demanded move in the opposite direction.

6-14 When demand is highly inelastic, virtually the whole tax is borne by consumers. When demand is highly elastic, virtually the whole tax is borne by producers. With a specific demand, the more inelastic the supply, the larger the portion of the tax borne by producers.

■ CHAPTER 7

7-2 Missing total utility data, top to bottom: 18; 33. Missing marginal utility data, top to bottom: 7; 5; 1.

(a) A decreasing rate; because marginal utility is declining. (b) Disagree. The marginal utility of a unit beyond the first may be sufficiently great (relative to product price) to make it a worthwhile purchase. (c) Agree. This product's price could be so high relative to the first unit's marginal utility that the consumer would buy none of it.

7-4 (a) 4 units of A; 3 units of B; 3 units of C, and 0 units of D. (b) Save $4. (c) 36/$18 = 12/$6 = 8/$4 = 2/$1. The marginal utility per dollar of the last unit of each product purchased is 2.

7-5 Buy 2 units of X and 5 units of Y. Marginal utility of last dollar spent will be equal at 4 (= 8/$2 for X and 4/$1 for Y) and the $9 income will be spent. Total utility = 48 (= 10 + 8 for X plus 8 + 7 + 6 + 5 + 4 for Y). When the price of X falls to $1, the quantity of X demanded increases from 2 to 4. Total utility is now 58 (= 10 + 8 + 6 + 4 for X plus 8 + 7 + 6 + 5 + 4 for Y).

Demand schedule: $P = \$2$; $Q = 2$. $P = \$1$; $Q = 4$.

Appendix 7-3 The tangency point places the consumer on the highest attainable indifference curve; it identifies the combination of goods yielding the highest total utility. All intersection points place the consumer on a lower indifference curve. MRS is the slope of the indifference curve; P_B/P_A is the slope of the budget line. Only at the tangency point are these two slopes equal. if $MRS > P_B/P_A$ or $MRS < P_B/P_A$, adjustments in the combination of products can be made to increase total utility (get to a higher indifference curve).

■ CHAPTER 8

8-2 Sole proprietorship, partnership, and corporation.

Proprietorship advantages: easy to start and provides maximum freedom for the proprietor to do what she or he thinks best. Proprietorship disadvantages: limited financial resources; the owner must be a Jack-or-Jill-of-all-trades; and unlimited liability.

Partnership advantages: easy to organize; greater specialization of management; and greater financial resources. Disadvantages: financial resources are still limited; unlimited liability; possibility of disagreement among the partners; and precarious continuity.

Corporation advantages: can raise large amounts of money by issuing stocks and bonds; limited liability; continuity.

Corporation disadvantages: red tape and expense in incorporating; potential for abuse of stockholder and bondholder funds; double taxation of profits; separation of ownership and control.

The dominant role of corporations stems from the advantages cited, particularly unlimited liability and ability to raise money.

8-4 Explicit costs: $37,000 (= $12,000 for the helper + $5,000 of rent + $20,000 of materials). Implicit costs: $22,000 (= $4,000 of forgone interest + $15,000 of forgone salary + $3,000 of entrepreneurship).

Accounting profit = $35,000 (= $72,000 of revenue − $37,000 of explicit costs); Economic profit = $13,000 (= $72,000 − $37,000 of explicit cost − $22,000 of implicit costs).

8-6 Marginal product data, top to bottom: 15; 19; 17; 14; 9; 6; 3; −1. Average product data, top to bottom: 15; 17; 17; 16.25; 14.8; 13.33; 11.86; 10.25. Your diagram should have the same general characteristics as text Figure 9-7.

MP is the slope — the rate of change — of the TP curve. When TP is rising at an increasing rate, MP is positive and rising. When TP is rising at a diminishing rate, MP is positive but falling. When TP is falling, MP is negative and falling. AP rises when MP is above it; AP falls when MP is below it.

MP first rises because the fixed capital gets used more productively as added workers are employed. Each added worker contributes more to output than the previous worker because the firm is better able to use its fixed plant and equipment. As still more labour is added, the law of diminishing returns takes hold. Labour becomes so abundant relative to the fixed capital that congestion occurs and marginal product falls. At the extreme, the addition of labour so overcrowds the plant that the marginal product of still more labour is negative — total output falls.

Because labour is the only variable input and its price (its wage rate) is constant, MC is found by dividing the wage rate by MP. When MP is rising, MC is falling; when MP reaches its maximum, MC is at its minimum; when MP is falling, MC is rising.

8-9 The total fixed costs are all $60. The total costs are all $60 more than the total variable cost. The other columns are shown in Question 4 in Chapter 10.

(a) See the graph. Over the 0 to 4 range of output, the TVC and TC curves slope upward at a decreasing rate because of increasing marginal returns. The slopes of the curves then increase at an increasing rate as diminishing marginal returns occur.

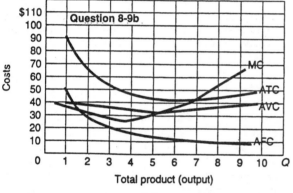

(b)   See the graph. AFC (= TFC/Q) falls continuously since a fixed amount of capital cost is spread over more units of output. The MC (= change in TC/change in Q), AVC (= TVC/Q), and ATC (= TC/Q) curves are U-shaped, reflecting the influence of first increasing and then diminishing returns. The ATC curve sums AFC and AVC vertically. The ATC curve falls when the MC curve is below it;

the ATC curve rises when the MC curve is above it. This means the MC curve must intersect the ATC curve at its lowest point. The same logic holds for the minimum point of the AVC curve.

(c1) If TFC had been $100 instead of $60, the AFC and ATC curves would be higher — by an amount equal to $40 divided by the specific output. Example: at 4 units, AVC = $25.00 [= ($60 + $40)/4]; and ATC = $62.50 [= ($210 + $40)/4)]. The AVC and MC curves are not affected by changes in fixed costs.

(c2) If TVC had been $10 less at each output, MC would be $10 lower for the first unit of output but remain the same for the remaining output. The AVC and ATC curves would also be lower — by an amount equal to $10 divided by the specific output. Example: at 4 units of output, AVC = $35.00 [= $150 − $10)/4], ATC = $50 [= ($210 − $10)/4.] The AFC curve would not be affected by the change in variable cost.

8-12   The long-run ATC curve is U-shaped. At first, long-run ATC falls as the firm expands and realizes economies of scale from labour and managerial specialization and the use of more efficient capital. The long-run ATC curve later turns upward when the enlarged firm experiences diseconomies of scale, usually resulting from managerial inefficiencies.

The MES (minimum efficient scale) is the smallest level of output needed to attain all economies of scale and minimum long-run ATC.

If long-run ATC drops quickly to its minimum cost which then extends over a long range of output, the industry will likely be composed of both large and small firms. If long-run ATC descends slowly to its minimum cost over a long range of output, the industry will likely be composed of a few large firms. If long-run ATC curve drops quickly to its minimum point and then rises abruptly, the industry will likely be composed of many small firms.

■   CHAPTER 9

9-3   Total revenue, top to bottom: 0; $2; $4; $6; $8; $10. Marginal revenue, top to bottom: $2, throughout.

(a)   The industry is purely competitive — this firm is a "price taker." The firm is so small relative to the size of the market that it can change its level of output without affecting the market price.

(b)   See the graph.

(c)   The firm's demand curve is perfectly elastic; MR is constant and equal to P.

(d)   Yes. Table: When output (quantity demanded) increases by 1 unit, total revenue increases by $2. This $2 increase is the marginal revenue. Figure: The change in TR is measured by the slope of the TR line, 2 (= $2/1 unit).

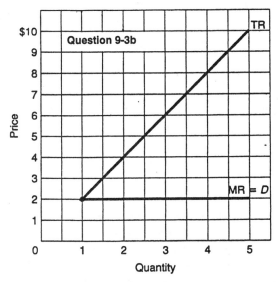

Question 9-3b

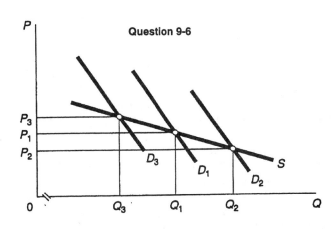

Question 9-6

9-4 (a) No, because $32 is always less than AVC. If it did produce, its output would be 4 — found by expanding output until MR no longer exceeds MC. By producing 4 units, it would lose $82 [= 4)$32 − $52.50)]. By not producing, it would lose only its total fixed cost of $60.
(b) Yes, $41 exceeds AVC at the loss-minimizing output. Using the MR = MC rule it will produce 6 units. Loss per unit of output is $6.50 (= $41 − $47.50). Total loss = $39 (= 6 × $6.50), which is less than its total fixed cost of $60.
(c) Yes, $56 exceeds AVC (and ATC) at the loss-minimizing output. Using the MR = MC rule it will produce 8 units. Profit per unit = $7.87 (= $56 − $48.13); total profit = $62.96.
(d) Column (2) data, top to bottom: 0; 0; 5; 6; 7; 8; 9. Column (3) data, top to bottom, in dollars: −60; −60; −55; −39; −8; +63; +144.
(e) The firm will not produce if P<AVC. When P>AVC, the firm will produce in the short run at the quantity where P (= MR) is equal to its increasing MC. Therefore, the MC curve above the AVC curve is the firm's short-run supply curve, it shows the quantity of output the firm will supply at each price level. See Figure 10-6 for a graphical illustration.
(f) Column (4) data, top to bottom: 0; 0; 7,500; 9,000; 10,500; 12,000; 13,500.
(g) Equilibrium price = $46; equilibrium output = 10,500. Each firm will produce 7 units. Loss per unit = $ 1.14, or $8 per firm. The industry will contract in the long run.

9-6 See Figures 9-8 and 9-9 and their legends. See Figure 9-10 for the supply curve for a constant cost industry, and Figure 9-11 for the supply curve for an increasing cost industry. The supply curve for a decreasing cost industry is below.

9-7 The equality of P and minimum ATC means the firm is achieving *productive efficiency*; it is using the most efficient technology and employing the least costly combination of resources. The equality of P and MC means the firm is achieving *allocative efficiency*; the industry is producing the right product in the right amount based on society's valuation of that product and other products.

■ **CHAPTER 10**

10-4 Total revenue, in order from Q = 0: $6.50; $12.00; $16.50; $20.00; $22.50; $24.00; $24.50; $24.00; $22.50. Marginal revenue in order from Q = 1: $6.50; $5.50; $4.50; $3.50; $2.50; $1.50; $.50; −$.50; −$1.50. See the accompanying graph. Because TR is increasing at a diminishing rate, MR is declining. When TR turns downward, MR becomes negative. Marginal revenue is below D because demand is not perfectly elastic. Four units sell for $5.00 each, but three of these four could have been sold for $5.50 had the monopolist been satisfied to sell only three. Having decided to sell four, the monopolist had to lower the price of the first three from $5.50 to $5.00, sacrificing $.50 on each for a total of $1.50. This "loss" of $1.50 explains the difference between the $5.00 price obtained on the fourth unit of output and its marginal revenue of $3.50. Demand is elastic from P = $6.50 to P = $3.50, a range where TR is rising. The curve is of unitary elasticity at P = $3.50, where TR is at its maximum. The curve is inelastic from then on as the price continues to decrease and TR is falling. When MR is positive, demand is elastic. When MR is zero, demand is of unitary elasticity. When MR is negative, demand is inelastic. If MC is zero, the monopolist should produce 7 units where MR is also zero. It would never produce where demand is inelastic because MR is negative there while MC is positive.

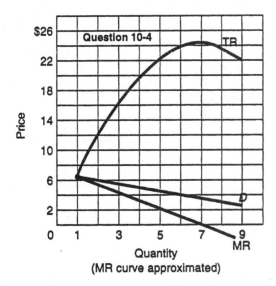

Question 10-4

(MR curve approximated)

10-5 Total revenue data, top to bottom, in dollars: 0; 100; 166; 213; 252; 275; 288; 294; 296; 297; 290. Marginal revenue data, top to bottom, in dollars: 100; 66; 47; 39; 23; 13; 6; 2; 1; –7.

Price = $63; output = 4; profit = $42 [= 4($63 – 52.50)]. Your graph should have the same general appearance as Figure 11-4. At Q = 4, TR = $252 and TC = $210 [= 4($52.50)].

10-6 Perfect price discrimination: Output = 6. TR would be $420 (= $100 + $83 + $71 + $63 + $55 + $48). TC would be $285 [= 6($47.50)]. Profit would be $135 (= $420 – $285).

Your single diagram should combine Figures 11-8a and 11-8b in the chapter. The discriminating monopolist faces a demand curve which is also its MR curve. It will sell the first unit at f in Figure 11-8b and then sell each successive unit at lower prices (as shown on the demand curve) as it moves to Q_2 units, where D (= MR) = MC. Discriminating monopolist: Greater output; total revenue, and profits. Some consumers will pay a higher price under discriminating monopoly than with nondiscriminating monopoly; others, a lower price. Good features: greater output and improved allocative efficiency. Bad feature: more income is transferred from consumers to the monopolist.

10-11 No, the proposal does not consider that the output of the natural monopolist would still be at the suboptimal level where P>MC. Too little would be produced and there would be an underallocation of resources. Theoretically, it would be more desirable to force the natural monopolist to charge a price equal to marginal cost and subsidize any losses. Even setting price equal to ATC would be an improvement over this proposal. This fair-return pricing would allow for a normal profit and ensure a greater production than the proposal would.

■ CHAPTER 11

11-2 Less elastic than a pure competitor and more elastic than a pure monopolist. Your graphs should look like Figures 10-12 and 12-1 in the chapters. Price is higher and output lower for the monopolistic competitor. Pure competition: P = MC (allocative efficiency); P = minimum ATC (productive efficiency). Monopolistic competition: P> MC (allocative inefficiency) and P> minimum ATC (productive inefficiency). Monopolistic competitors have excess capacity, meaning that fewer firms operating at capacity (where P = minimum ATC) could supply the industry output.

11-7 A four-firm concentration ratio of 60 percent means the largest four firms in the industry account for 60 percent of sales; a four-firm concentration ratio of 90 percent means the largest four firms account for 90 percent of sales. Shortcomings: (1) they pertain to the nation as a whole, although relevant markets may be localized; (2) they do not account for interindustry competition; (3) the data are for U.S. products — imports are excluded; and (4) they don't reveal the dispersion of size among the top four firms.

Herfindahl index for A: 2400 (=900 + 900 + 400 + 100 + 100). For B: 4300 (= 3600 + 625 + 25 + 25 + 25). We would expect Industry A to be more competitive than Industry B, where one firm dominates and two firms control 85 percent of the market.

11-8 The matrix shows the four possible profit outcomes for each of two firms, depending on which of two price strategies each follows. Example: If C sets price at $35 and D at $40, C's profits will be $59,000, and D's $55,000.

    (a)   C and D are interdependent because their profits depend not just on their own price, but also on the other firm's price.

    (b)   Likely outcome: Both firms will set price at $35. If either charged $40, it would be concerned the other would undercut the price and its profit by charging $35. At $35 for both, C's profit is $55,000; D's, $58,000.

    (c) Through price collusion — agreeing to charge $40 — each firm would achieve higher profit (C = $57,000; D = $60,000). But once both firms agree on $40, each sees it can increase its profit even more by secretly charging $35 while its rival charges $40.

11-9 Assumptions: (1) Rivals will match price cuts; (2) Rivals will ignore price increases. The gap in the MR curve results from the abrupt change in the slope of the demand curve at the going price. Firms will not change their price because they fear that if they do their total revenue and profits will fall. Shortcomings of the model: (1) It does not explain how the going price evolved in the first place; (2) it does not allow for price leadership and other forms of collusion.

11-11 There is much advertising in monopolistic competition and oligopoly because advertising campaigns are less easily duplicated than price cuts, which can lead to price wars. Advertising helps consumers by informing them about product characteristics and prices. By providing information about competing goods that are available, advertising diminishes monopoly power and stimulates competition, thereby promoting efficiency. Advertising may be excessive at times as firms attempt to establish brand loyalty.

■ CHAPTER 12

12-4 (a) 5 percent; (b) no, because the 5 percent rate of return is less than the 6 percent interest rate; (c) yes, because the 5 percent rate of return is now greater than the 4 percent interest rate.

12-5 (a) 50 million, where the interest-rate cost of funds i equals the expected rate of return r; (b) At $20 million of R&D, r of 14 percent exceeds i of 8 percent; (c) at $60 million, r of 6 percent is less than i of 8 percent.

12-6 (a) The person would now buy 5 units of product C and 0 units of A and B; (b) the MU/price ratio is what counts; a new product can be successful by having a high MU, a low price, or both relative to existing products.

12-8 (a) Total cost = $4,000; average total cost = $.80 (= $4,000/5,000 units). (b) Total cost = $4,000, average total cost = $.667 (= $4,000/6,000 units); (c) Process innovation can lower the average total cost of producing a particular output, meaning that society uses fewer resources in producing that output. Resources are freed from this production to produce more of other desirable goods. Society realizes extra output through a gain in efficiency.

■ CHAPTER 13

13-2 Strict enforcement of the anticombines laws could mean that a merger of two large firms would be prohibited or a dominant manufacturer in an industry might be broken up. (a) The targeted **firms** could be weakened, which might reduce their ability to compete successfully with strong foreign firms in sales abroad. This in turn conflicts with the goal of expanding Canadian exports. (b) Major mergers involving companies in banking, telecommunications, computer manufacturers, and software producers have led to questions of how strict anticombines enforcement should be in these industries, where emerging technology may benefit from industry restructuring. Hastening the development of the "information superhighway" could also benefit Canadian exports of these services, which would strengthen our trade balance.

Selective enforcement of anticombines laws is a type of government industrial policy that interferes with the market process to the extent that it favours some industries by easing the way for concentration in some industries and strictly limiting consolidation in others. Such a selective policy can be dangerous when one considers the opportunities for public sector failure discussed in Chapter 19. Selective enforcement encourages rent seeking and self-interest lobbying efforts, which may dictate policy more than the technological merits warrant.

13-3 (a) They would block this horizontal merger.
(b) They would charge these firms with price fixing.
(c) They would allow this vertical merger, unless both firms had very large market share.
(d) They would allow this conglomerate merger.

13-8 Natural monopolies should be subject to industrial regulations. Industrial regulations can lead to higher operating costs and inefficiency, they can perpetuate monopoly, and some industries seek regulation so that they may form a legal cartel.

13-10 Industrial regulation is concerned with prices and service in specific industries whereas social regulation deals with the broader impact of business on consumers, workers, and third parties. Benefits: increased worker and product safety, less environmental damage, reduced economic discrimination. Two types of costs: administrative costs, because regulations must be administered by costly government agencies; compliance costs, because firms must increase spending to comply with regulations.

■ CHAPTER 14

14-2 Marginal product data, top to bottom: 17; 14; 12; 10; 7; 5. Total revenue data, top to bottom: $0; $34; $62; $86; $106; $120; $130. Marginal revenue product data, top to bottom: $34; $28; $24; $20; $14; $10.
(a) Two workers at $27.95 because the MRP of the first worker is $34 and the MRP of the second worker is $28, both exceeding the $27.95 wage. Four workers at $19.95 because workers 1 through 4 have MRPs exceeding the $19.95 wage. The fifth worker's MRP is only $14, so he or she will not be hired.
(b) The demand schedule consists of the first and last columns of the table:

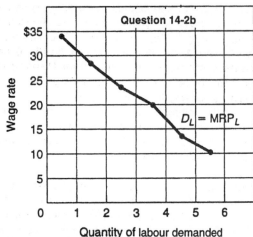

Question 14-2b

$D_L = MRP_L$

Quantity of labour demanded
(plotted at the halfway points along
the horizontal axis)

(c)   Reconstruct the table. New product price data, top to bottom: $2.20; $2.15; $2.10; $2.05; $2.00; $1.95. New total revenue data, top to bottom: $0; $37.40; $66.65; $90.30; $108.65; $120.00; $126.75. New marginal revenue product data, top to bottom: $37.40; $29.95; $23.65; $18.35; $11.35; $6.75. The new labour demand is less elastic. Here, MRP falls because of diminishing returns *and* because product price declines as output increases. A decrease in the wage rate will produce less of an increase in the quantity of labour demanded, because the output from the added labour will reduce product price and thus MRP.

14-3   Four factors: the rate at which the resource's MP declines; the ease of substituting other resources; elasticity of product demand; and the ratio of the resource cost to the total cost of production.
    (a)   Increases the demand for C. (b) The price increase for D will increase the demand for C through the *substitution effect*, but decrease the demand for all resources — including C — through the *output effect*. The net effect is uncertain; it depends on which effect outweighs the other. (c) Increases the elasticity of demand for C. (d) Increases the demand for C. (e) Increases the demand for C through the output effect. There is no substitution effect. (f) Reduces the elasticity of demand for C.

14-4   (a)   2 capital; 4 labour. $MP_L/P_L = 7/1$; $MP_c/P_c = 21/3 = 7/1$.
    (b)   7 capital and 7 labour. $MRP_L/P_L = 1 (= 1/1) = MRP_c/P_c = 1 (= 3/3)$. Output is 142 (= 96 from capital + 46 from labour). Economic profit is $114 (= $142 – $28). Yes, least-cost production is part of maximizing profits — the profit-maximizing rule includes the least-cost rule.

14-5   (a)   Use more of both; (b) use less labour and more capital; (c) use maximum profits obtained; (d) use less of both.

■   **CHAPTER 15**

15-3   See Figure 16-3 and its legend.

15-4   Total labour cost data, top to bottom: $0; $14; $28; $42; $56; $70; $84. Marginal resource cost data: $14, throughout.
    (a)   The labour supply curve and MRC curve coincide as a single horizontal line at the market wage rate of $14. The firm can employ as much labour as it wants, each unit costing $14; wage rate = MRC because the wage rate is constant to the firm.
    (b)   Graph: equilibrium is at the intersection of the MRP and MRC curves. Equilibrium wage rate = $14; equilibrium level of employment = 4 units of labour. Explanation: from the tables: MRP exceeds MRC for each of the first four units of labour, and MRP equals MRC for the fifth unit.

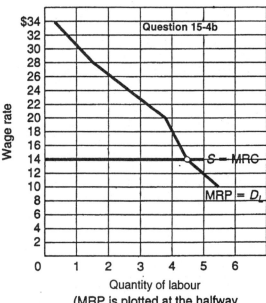

Question 15-4b

$S = MRC$

$MRP = D_L$

Quantity of labour
(MRP is plotted at the halfway
points on the horizontal axis)

15-6   The monopsonist faces the market labour supply curve S — it is the only firm hiring this labour. MRC lies above S and rises more rapidly than S because all workers get the higher wage rate that is needed to attract each added worker. Equilibrium wage rate = $12; equilibrium employment = 3 (where MRP = MRC). The monopsonist can pay a below-competitive wage rate by restricting its employment.

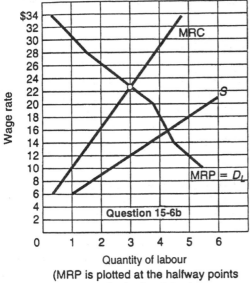

Quantity of labour
(MRP is plotted at the halfway points
on the horizontal axis)

15-7 The union wage rate W_c becomes the firm's MRC, which we would show as a horizontal line to the left of S. Each unit of labour now adds only its own wage rate to the firm's costs. The firm will employ Q_c workers, the quantity of labour where MRP = MRC (= W_c); Q_c is greater than the Q_m workers it would employ if there were no union.

15-12 (a)   See the graph.

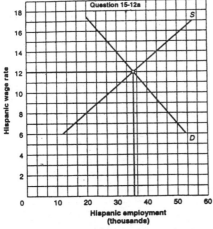

(b)   The equilibrium Hispanic wage rate is $12; the equilibrium quantity of Hispanic employment is 36,000 workers.
(c)   The Hispanic-to-white wage ratio is .75 (= $12/$16).
(d)   The employer will hire only white workers because the $5 discrimination coefficient exceeds the $4 difference between the wage rates of whites and Hispanics.

(e)   The new equilibrium Hispanic wage rate is $14 and the new equilibrium quantity of Hispanic employment is 44,000 workers. The Hispanic-white wage ratio rises to .875 (= $14/$16) because of the increased demand for Hispanic labour in relation to the unchanging supply of Hispanic labour.
(f)   The new equilibrium Hispanic wage rate is $10 and the new equilibrium quantity of Hispanic employment is 42,000. This Hispanic-white wage ratio falls to .625 (= $10/$16).

15-14 See Figure 15-12. Discrimination against women in two of the three occupations will crowd women into the third occupation. Labour supply in the "men's occupations" (X and Y) decreases, making them high-wage occupations. Labour supply in the "Women's occupation" (Z) increases, creating a low-wage occupation.

Eliminating occupational segregation would entice women into the high-wage occupations, increasing labour supply there and reducing it in the low-wage occupation. The wage rates in the three occupations would converge to B. Women would gain, men would lose. Society would gain because the increase in output in the expanding occupations would exceed the loss of output in the contracting occupation.

15-17 See Figure 15-13. Migration of labour from the low- to high-income country increases labor supply in the high-income country and decreases it in the low-income country. Wages are equalized at We. Output and business income increase in the receiving country; decline in the sending country. World output increases: the output gain in the **receiving** country exceeds the output loss in the sending country.

(a) The gains to the receiving country will not materialize if the **migrants** are unemployed after they arrive; there may be gains in the low-income country if the immigrant had been unemployed prior to moving. (b) Remittances to the home country will decrease the income gain in the receiving country and reduce the income loss in the sending country. (c) If migrants who return to their home country have enhanced their skills, their temporary departure might be to the long-run advantage of the home country. (d) Young, skilled migrants will increase output and likely be the net taxpayers in the receiving country, but the sending country will experience a "brain drain". Older or less skilled workers who are not so easily assimilated could be net recipients of government services.

In view of the sometimes large investments which sending countries have made in providing education and skills, there is a justification for levying a departure tax on such migrants. But if this tax were too high, it would infringe on a basic human right: the right to emigrate.

■ CHAPTER 16

16-2 Land is completely fixed in total supply. As population expands and the demand for land increases, rent first appears and then grows. From society's perspective this rent is a surplus payment unnecessary for ensuring that the land is available to the economy as a whole. If rent declined or disappeared, the same amount of land would be available. If it increases, no more land would be forthcoming. Thus, rent does not function as an incentive for adding land to the economy.

But land does have alternative uses. To get it to its most productive use, individuals and firms compete and the winners are those who pay the highest rent. To the high bidders, rent is a cost of production which must be covered by the revenue gained through the sale of the commodities produced on that land.

16-4 Supply is upsloping because households prefer present consumption to future consumption and must be enticed through higher interest rates to save more (consume less) now. The higher the interest rate, the greater the saving and the amount of money made available to the loanable funds market. Demand is downsloping because more business investment projects become profitable as the cost of borrowing (the interest rate) falls. The equilibrium interest rate is the rate at which the quantities of funds supplied and demanded in the loanable funds market are equal. Anything that changes the supply of loanable funds or the demand for loanable funds will change the equilibrium interest rate. Two examples: Higher taxes on interest income would reduce the supply of loanable funds and increase the equilibrium interest rate; a decrease in business optimism would reduce the expected return on investment, decrease the demand for loanable funds, and reduce the equilibrium interest rate.

16-6 The nominal interest rate is the interest rate stated in dollars of current value (unadjusted for inflation). The real interest rate is the nominal interest rate adjusted for inflation (or deflation). The real interest rate is more relevant for making investment decisions — it reflects the true cost of borrowing money. It is compared to the expected return on the investment in the decision process. Real interest rate = 4 percent (= 12 percent – 8 percent).

16-8 Accounting profit is what remains of a firm's total revenues after it has paid for all the factors of production employed by the firm (its explicit costs) but not for the use of the resources owned by the business itself. Economists also take into consideration implicit costs — the payment the owners could have received by using the resources they own in some other way. The economist adds these implicit costs to the accountant's explicit costs to arrive at total cost. Subtracting the total cost from total revenue results in a smaller profit (the economic profit) than the accountant's profit.

Sources of economic profit: (1) uninsurable risks; (2) innovations; and (3) monopoly.

(a) Profit from assuming uncertainties of innovation, as well as monopoly profit from the patent. (b) Monopoly profit arising from its locational advantage. (c) Profit from bearing the uninsurable risk of a change in demand (the change could have been unfavourable).

■ CHAPTER 17

17-2 See the figure. In this simple economy each person represents a complete income quintile — 20% of the total population. The richest quintile (A1) receives 50% of total income; the poorest quintile (Ed) receives 5%.

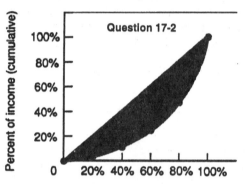

17-4 The reasons for income inequality may be grouped into three broad categories: unequal personal endowments; differences in individual character; and external social factors. The first is largely a matter of luck — some people possess high intelligence, particular talents, or physical dexterity that allow them to earn high incomes. Also, they may inherit property or be aided by the social status and financial resources of their parents. The second reason involves personal initiative — individuals may be willing to undergo costly training, accept risk, or tolerate unpleasant working conditions in the expectation of higher pay. They may also show high personal initiative on the job. The third factor relates to society as a whole. Market power and discrimination are two important social determinants of income inequality.

A high IQ normally does not lead to high income unless it is combined with personal initiative and favourable social circumstances. Inherited property — as long as it is competently managed — provides income irrespective of one's character and personal attributes. Both factors are largely a matter of luck to the recipient.

17-9 (a) Plan 1: Minimum income = $4,000; benefit-reduction rate = 50%; break-even income = $8,000 (= $4,000/.5). Plan 2: Minimum income =

$4,000; benefit-reduction rate = 25%; break-even income = $16,000 (= $4,000/.25). Plan 3: Minimum income = $8,000; benefit-reduction rate = 50%; break-even income = $16,000 (=$8,000/.5).

(b)   Plan 3 is the most costly. Plan 1 is the least costly. Plan 3 is most effective in reducing poverty (although it has a higher benefit-reduction rate than Plan 2, its minimum income is higher). Plan 1 is least effective in reducing poverty. Plan 3 has the strongest disincentive to work (although it has the same benefit-reduction rate as Plan 1, its higher minimum income discourages more work). Plan 2 has the weakest disincentives to work (its minimum income level and benefit-reduction rate are low).

(c)   The only way to eliminate poverty is to provide a minimum income high enough to lift everyone from poverty, including people who cannot work or choose not to work. But this large minimum income reduces the incentive to work, expands the number of people receiving transfer payments, and substantially boosts overall program costs.

■ CHAPTER 18

18-1   (a) Private good, top to bottom: $P = $8, Q = 1; P = $7, Q = 2; P = $6, Q = 4; P = $5, Q = 7; P = $4, Q = 10; P = $3, Q = 13; P = $2, Q = 16; P = $1, Q = 19. (b) Public good, top to bottom: $P = $19, Q = 1, P = $16, Q = 2; P = $13, Q = 3; P = $10, Q = 4; P = $7, Q = 5, P = $4, Q = 6; P = $2, Q = 7; P = $1, Q = 8. The first schedule represents a horizontal summation of the individual demand curves; the second schedule represents a vertical summation of these curves. The market demand curve for the private good will determine — in combination with market supply — an actual price-quantity outcome in the marketplace. Because potential buyers of public goods do not reveal their individual preferences in the market, the collective demand curve for the public good is hypothetical or needs to be determined through "willingness to pay" studies.

18-2   Optimal quantity = 4. It is optimal because at 4 units the collective willingness to pay for the final unit of the good (= $10) matches the marginal cost of production (=$10).

18-3   Program B since the marginal benefit no longer exceeds marginal cost for programs which are larger in scope. Plan B is where net benefits — the excess of total benefits over total costs — are maximized.

18-4   Spillover costs are called negative externalities because they are *external* to the participants in the transaction and *reduce* the utility of affected third parties (thus "negative"). Spillover benefits are called positive externalities because they are *external* to the participants

in the transaction and *increase* the utility of affected third parties (thus "positive"). See Figures 18-3 and 18-4. Compare (b) and (c) in Figure 18-4.

18-7   Reducing water flow from storm drains has a low marginal benefit, meaning the MB curve would be located far to the left of where it is in the text diagram. It will intersect the MC curve at a low amount of pollution abatement, indicating the optimal amount of pollution abatement (where MB = MC) is low. Any cyanide in public water sources could be deadly. Therefore, the marginal benefit of reducing cyanide is extremely high and the MB curve in the figure would be located to the extreme right where it would intersect the MC curve at or near 100 percent.

18-13   Moral hazard problem: (b) and (d). Adverse selection problem: (a), (c), and (e).

■ CHAPTER 19

19-2   The paradox is that majority voting does not always provide a clear and consistent picture of the public's preferences. Here the courthouse is preferred to the school and the park is preferred to the courthouse, so we would surmise that the park is preferred to the school. But paired-choice voting would show that the school is preferred to the park.

19-3   Project B (small reservoir wins) using a paired-choice vote. There is no "paradox of voting" problem here and B is the preference to the median voter. The two voters favouring No reservoir and Levees, respectively, will prefer Small reservoir — project B — to Medium or Large reservoir. The two voters preferring Large reservoir or Medium reservoir will prefer Small reservoir to Levees or No reservoir. The median voter's preference for B will prevail. However, the optimal size of the project from an economic perspective is C — it would provide a greater net benefit to society than B.

19-4   The electorate is faced with a small number of candidates, each of whom offers a broad range or "bundle" of proposed policies. Voters are then forced to choose the individual candidate whose bundle of policies most resembles their own. The chances of a perfect identity between a particular candidate's preferences and those of any voter are quite slim. As a result, the voter must purchase some unwanted public goods and services. This represents an inefficient allocation of resources.

   Government bureaucracies do not function on the basis of profit, so the incentive for holding down costs is less than in the private sector. Also, because there is no profit-and-loss test of efficiency, it is difficult to determine whether public agencies are operating efficiently. Nor is there entry of competing entities to stimulate efficiency and develop improved public goods and services. Furthermore, wasteful expenditures can be maintained through the self-seeking lobbying of bureaucrats themselves, and the public budgetary process can reward rather than penalize inefficiency.

19-7 Average tax rates: 20; 15; and 13.3 percent. Regressive.

19-9 The incidence of an excise tax is likely to be primarily on consumers when demand is highly inelastic and primarily on producers when demand is elastic. The more elastic the supply, the greater the incidence of an excise tax on consumers and the less on producers.

The efficiency loss of a sales or excise tax is the net benefit society sacrifices because consumption and production of the taxed product are reduced below the level of allocative efficiency which would occur without the tax. Other things equal, the greater the elasticities of demand and supply, the greater the efficiency loss of a particular tax.

■ CHAPTER 20

20-1 First sentence: Shifts in the supply curve of agricultural goods (*changes in supply*) relative to fixed inelastic demand curves produce large changes in equilibrium prices. Second sentence: But these drastic changes in prices produce only small changes in equilibrium outputs (where *quantities demanded* equal *quantities supplied*) because demands are inelastic.

Because exports are volatile from one year to the next, they increase the instability of demand for farm products.

20-3 (a) Because the demand for most farm products is inelastic, the frequent fluctuations in supply brought about by weather and other factors have relatively small effects on quantity demanded, but large effects on equilibrium prices of farm products. Farmers' sales revenues and incomes therefore are unstable. (b) Technological innovations have decreased production costs, increased long-run supply for most agricultural goods, and reduced the prices of farm output. These declines in prices have put a downward pressure on farm income. (c) The modest long-run growth in the demand for farm products has not been sufficient to offset the expansion of supply, resulting in stagnant farm income. (d) Because the number of producers in most agricultural markets is high, it is difficult if not impossible for producers to collude as a way to limit supply and lessen fluctuations in prices and incomes or halt their long-run declines.

20-7 Price supports benefit farmers, harm consumers, impose costs on society, and contribute to problems in world agriculture. Farmers benefit because the prices they receive and the output they produce both increase, expanding their gross incomes. Consumers lose because

the prices they pay for farm products rise and quantities purchased decline. Society as a whole bears several costs. Surpluses of farm products have to be bought and stored, leading to a greater burden on taxpayers. Domestic economic efficiency is lessened as the artificially high prices of farm products lead to an overallocation of resources to agriculture. The environment suffers: the greater use of pesticides and fertilizers contributes to water pollution; farm policies discourage crop rotation; and price supports encourage farming of environmentally sensitive land. The efficient use of world resources is also distorted because of the import tariffs or quotas which such programs often require. Finally, domestic overproduction leads to supply increases in international markets, decreasing prices and causing a decline in the gross incomes of foreign producers.